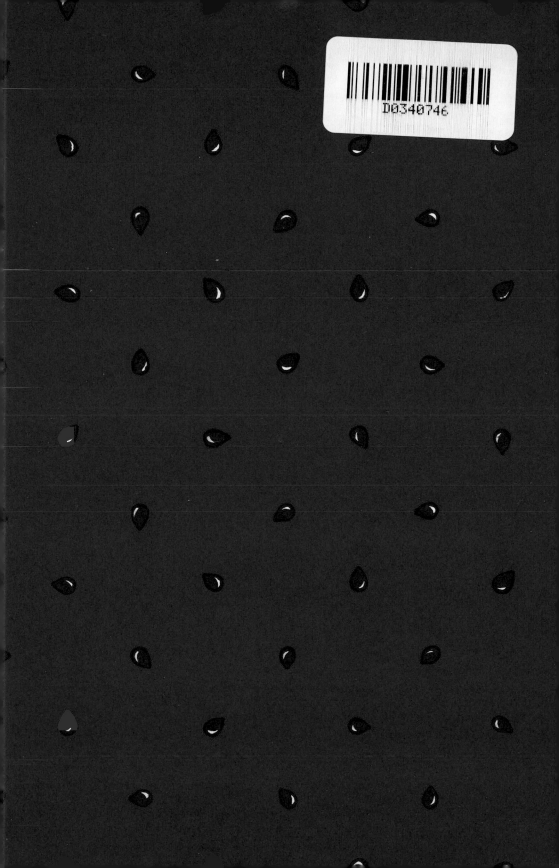

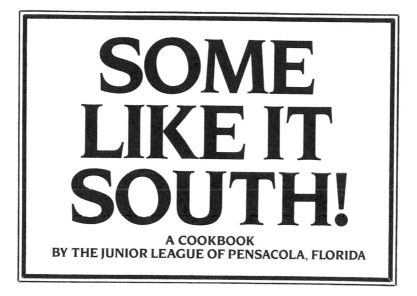

# SOME LIKE IT SOUTH!

**A COOKBOOK
BY THE JUNIOR LEAGUE OF PENSACOLA, FLORIDA**

The Purpose of the Junior League is exclusively educational and charitable and is to promote voluntarism; to develop the potential of its members for voluntary participation in community affairs; and to demonstrate the effectiveness of trained volunteers.

Additional copies of SOME LIKE IT SOUTH! may be obtained by sending $12.95 per book plus $1.50 per book for postage. (Florida residents add $.65 each for sales tax.)

JULEP Publications
P.O. Box 87
Pensacola, Florida 32591

1st Printing          August 1984          10,000 copies

Library of Congress Catalogue Card No. 84-081030
ISBN: 0-9613622-0-0

Printed in USA by
Hart Graphics, Inc.
8000 Shoal Creek Blvd.
Austin, Texas 78758

# SOME LIKE IT SOUTH!

Betsy Kinney Daniels, Cookbook Chairman
Helen Cleaveland Simmons, Cookbook Secretary-Treasurer

*Recipe Committee*
Carolyn Palmer Appleyard, Chairman
Kristin Shows Ball
Jeanne Agnew Bell
Joyce Allen Callahan
Tina Fleming Campbell
Susan Provost Endry
Ann Johnson Freeman
Judy Ruggerio Pace
Betty Gail Cooper Peters
Pat Shull Rawson
Judy Reynolds Richardson
Sandra Lowery Robinson
Catherine Dean Stackhouse
Kathryn A. Stuart, M.D.
Eleanor Williams Zieman

*Marketing Committee*
Barbara Hubbert Wiggins, Chairman
Carol Salter Armstrong
Gay McLeod Bell
Linda Wink Barrett
Lititia Drew Galloway
Claudia Elebash Hahn
Jeanie Glenn Hufford
Ellen O'Quinn Lea
Judy Ruggerio Pace
Claudia Mountcastle Post
Stephanie Hudson Sharpe
Deborah Weller Turner

*Format Committee*
Robin Jennings Carr, Chairman
Nancy Vaughn Brown
Marilyn McKinney Bullington
Joan Chapman Bullock
Sally Craig Chamberlin
Linnea Blomquist Daniel
Janet Servies Davis
Martha Cavender Dupuis
Isabel Wilson Fitzgerald
Suzanne Jones Galloway

Lynn Boege Hayes
Elizabeth Bird Holland
Lois Ann Barrineau Hudson
Patricia Mahan Marshall
Ann Adams Mazenko
Kay Kennedy Mitchell
Cherry Gorham Partington
Pat Shull Rawson
Ellen Watson Vinson
Frances McCarron Viviano
Elizabeth Rainwater Woolf

Cookbook Committee 1984-85
Pat Shull Rawson, Chairman
Elizabeth Bird Holland, Vice-chairman

**Some Like It South!** is a collection of 550 recipes selected from over 1,800 submitted. There is a special emphasis on the use of fresh ingredients. Each recipe has been thoroughly tested and enthusiastically approved by the food editors. We are most grateful to all the League members and friends who shared their recipes and gave unselfishly of their time. A special thank you to our families who have been so patient and supportive during the past two years.

# TABLE OF CONTENTS

Some Like It South! Entertains ....................9

Appetizers and Beverages ...........................29

Soups and Salads ...................................73

Entrées ...........................................125
    Seafood .......................................127
    Beef ..........................................160
    Chicken .......................................173
    Pork, Lamb, Veal, Game and Savory Sauces .......187

Vegetables and Fruits .............................207

Eggs, Grains and Pasta ............................239

Breads ............................................255

Desserts ..........................................285
    Cookies .......................................287
    Cakes .........................................300
    Pies ..........................................312
    Desserts ......................................322
    Ice Creams and Dessert Sauces .................337

Food Exchange List ................................339

Equivalents .......................................351

Index .............................................354

Order Form ........................................367

# SOME LIKE IT SOUTH! ENTERTAINS

# SOME LIKE IT SOUTH! ENTERTAINS

**Introduction** . . . . . . . . . . . . . . . . . . . . . . . . . . . . .11

**Spring**
A Post Performance Champagne Reception . . . . . . . . . . .12
A Traditional Easter Dinner . . . . . . . . . . . . . . . . . . . . .13
A Pasta Supper . . . . . . . . . . . . . . . . . . . . . . . . . . . . .14
A Raft-Up Picnic . . . . . . . . . . . . . . . . . . . . . . . . . . . .15

**Summer**
A Mexican Feast . . . . . . . . . . . . . . . . . . . . . . . . . . . .16
A Wedding Rehearsal Dinner . . . . . . . . . . . . . . . . . . . .17
Seville Square Supper . . . . . . . . . . . . . . . . . . . . . . . . .18
Bayfront Buffet . . . . . . . . . . . . . . . . . . . . . . . . . . . . .19
Tailgate Picnic . . . . . . . . . . . . . . . . . . . . . . . . . . . . . .20

**Fall**
Seafood Buffet . . . . . . . . . . . . . . . . . . . . . . . . . . . . . .21
Jazz Brunch . . . . . . . . . . . . . . . . . . . . . . . . . . . . . . . .22
Artist Awards Party . . . . . . . . . . . . . . . . . . . . . . . . . . .23
Hunt Breakfast . . . . . . . . . . . . . . . . . . . . . . . . . . . . . .24

**Winter**
A Holiday Dinner . . . . . . . . . . . . . . . . . . . . . . . . . . . .25
New Years Day Celebration . . . . . . . . . . . . . . . . . . . . .26
Mardi Gras Magic . . . . . . . . . . . . . . . . . . . . . . . . . . . .27
A Hearty Party . . . . . . . . . . . . . . . . . . . . . . . . . . . . . .28

# INTRODUCTION

**SOME LIKE IT SOUTH!** exemplifies Gulf Coast living and entertaining at its very best. This mouth-watering collection of delicious recipes and menus shows that there are many ways of entertaining and that each depends a great deal on thought, effort and caring. We hope you will begin this book with some enthusiasm for good food, good cooking and good friends. We have found that the real joy of entertaining is in sharing it. **SOME LIKE IT SOUTH!** is a *must* for any collector...a *treasure* for those who like to cook...a *treat* for those who love to eat!

The Junior League of Pensacola would like to extend special thanks to freelance graphic artist Lynn Evans for the cover design, The Appleyard Agency and the Gulf Coast Computer Shoppe for helping to make **SOME LIKE IT SOUTH!** a reality.

# SAENGER THEATRE

The elegantly restored Saenger Theatre sets the stage for year round musical and theatrical productions. A gala reception after the ballet, drama or concert provides an opportunity for patrons to socialize and to meet the performing artists or cast. Toast the black tie evening in grand style with champagne and an extravaganza of glorious desserts.

## A POST PERFORMANCE CHAMPAGNE RECEPTION

**Almond Tarts          Black-Eyed Susans**

**Lemon-Cream Cheese Cookies**

**Marzipan Cupcakes     Ladyfingers     Bishop's Bread**

**Southern Pound Cake          Spiced Pecans**

**Snow-Capped Pâté and Party Melba Toast**

**Champagne**

# EASTER DINNER

Easter broadcasts the arrival of spring! Dogwoods and azaleas in full bloom, baskets brimming with colored eggs, and the appearance of the Easter bunny symbolize this season of hope and rejuvenation. Welcome spring with this picture perfect dinner.

## A TRADITIONAL EASTER DINNER

**Cream of Celery Soup**

**Roast Leg of Lamb**          **Mint Jelly**

**Mandarin Lettuce Salad**

**Asparagus Caesar**          **Almond-Rice Casserole**

**Sour Cream Biscuits**

**Pecan Cream Cheese Pie**

# FIESTA OF FIVE FLAGS

In celebration of the colonization of Northwest Florida, the Fiesta of Five Flags pays tribute to Pensacola's heritage. Twice under the rule of Spain and dominated at different periods by France and England, West Florida became a territory of the United States in 1821. During the Civil War, Pensacola once again changed hands and was under the control of the Confederate government. In all, flags of five different nations have flown over Pensacola's historic forts. Cultural exchanges, parades, costume balls, antique shows, a treasure hunt, sport events, a juried art show and a Jazzfest crowd the calendar in May. Participants in the Fiesta Race will relish this hearty meal on the eve before the 10 kilometer run.

## A PASTA SUPPER

**Antipasto Spread      Italian Stuffed Mushrooms**

**Italian Spaghetti with Meatballs and Sausage**

**Basic Spinach Salad    Supreme Spinach Salad Dressing**

**Special Treat Italian Bread**

**Ice Cream Crunch**

# AROUND THE BAY REGATTA

After a sailing regatta or a day of boating, a favorite scene is boats anchored and tied up together on the waters of Escambia Bay or Santa Rosa Sound. Refreshing foods prepared in advance and packed in coolers of ice whet the appetites of sailors and crews. Good food and good friends combine to make the floating picnic the place we would most like to be.

### A RAFT-UP PICNIC

Vichyssoise          Bayley's West Indies Salad

Marinated Roast Beef          Deli Rolls

Rice Salad          Summer Fruit Salad          Green Bean Salad

Bread and Butter Pickles

Cream Cheese Brownies

Rum Swizzles

# A WEEK AT THE BEACH

The sugary white sands of Pensacola Beach create a vacation mecca not limited to tourists. We natives capitalize on our short drive to Santa Rosa Island's sun and fun. Reserving a beach cottage or condominium on the Gulf of Mexico for a week is popular for family retreats. In celebration of graduation, groups of high school seniors flock to the beach. The dress code is casual and the most simple foods satisfy our tastes. This festive Mexican feast travels well to a beach houseparty and can be easily adapted to a progressive dinner.

### A MEXICAN FEAST

**Tex-Mex Appetizer**        **Green Chili Bites**

**Tomatoes and Onions au Naturel**    **Three-Bean Salad**

**Enchiladas Suisse**

**Sopaipillas**            **Honey**

# JUNE BRIDE

The gazebo in the historic Seville Square District and the white sands of Pensacola Beach are unique and picturesque scenarios for marriage ceremonies. Many engaged couples continue to choose a traditional church setting or their home or garden for the exchange of vows. A romantic prenuptial dinner honors members of the wedding party. The bride and groom invite their families and attendants to share their excitement, anticipation and joy with this memorable dinner following the wedding rehearsal.

## A WEDDING REHEARSAL DINNER

**Shrimp Remoulade I or Bayley's West Indies Salad**

**Creamy Cucumber Soup**

**Heavenly Tenderloin**

**Green Beans à la Niçoise**      **Bacon-Bleu Cheese Potatoes**

**Dinner Rolls**

**Chocolate Lovers' Pie or Apple Cream Crumble Pie**

# AN EVENING IN OLD SEVILLE SQUARE

The harmonious mixture of the old and the new has made Seville Square one of the most attractive features of Pensacola. Fine specialty shops, galleries, museums and restaurants have been housed within restored cottages. On July 4th, the Pensacola Heritage Foundation presents An Evening in Old Seville Square. The historic district nostalgically reminisces to the turn-of-the-century for parades, music, entertainment, contests and even a crab race. In the midst of preserved dwellings, the crowd savors the famed fried mullet with trimmings and exclaims to the gigantic display of patriotic fireworks.

### SEVILLE SQUARE SUPPER

**Fried Mullet**

**Gaspachee Salad**          **Nassau Grits**

**Jalapeño Hushpuppies**

**Watermelon**

**Fudge/Mocha Frosted Brownies**          **Camille's Carrot Cake**

**Buttermilk Ice Cream**

**Beer**

# PENSACOLA INTERNATIONAL BILLFISH TOURNAMENT

The Pensacola Big Game Fishing Club is host to the annual Pensacola International Billfish Tournament. Presented as the "largest billfishing tournament in the world," the tournament attracts anglers from all over the country. Crowds gather at the Municipal Pier to watch the weigh-ins of prizewinning blue and white marlin, sailfish, swordfish, wahoo and dolphin. Seafood enthusiasts agree that there is nothing more delicious than an informal dinner that includes the catch of the day.

### BAYFRONT BUFFET

**Spinach Balls**      **Marinated Vegetable Appetizer**

**Grilled King Mackeral Steaks**      **Char-broiled Shrimp**

**Ann's Potato Salad**      **Creole Salad**

**Hopkins Boarding House Squash Casserole**

**Hushpuppies**

**Hummingbird Cake**      **Mississippi Mud Cake**

# BLUE ANGELS AIR SHOW

Pensacola, the Cradle of Naval Aviation, is home base to the Navy's Flight Demonstration Squadron, the Blue Angels. Twice a year, the famed Blue Angels perform precision aerial maneuvers before the hometown crowd at Pensacola's Naval Air Station. Other points of interest at the navy base include the Naval Aviation Museum and the USS Lexington. Families pack a picnic lunch and enjoy a full day of exciting activities at the Naval Air Station.

## TAILGATE PICNIC

**Marinated Mushrooms**          **Pig's Delight**

**Curry Rice Salad**          **Summer Fruit Salad**

**Chicken Fiesta**

**Whole Wheat Bread or Strawberry Bread**

**Oatmeal Cookies**          **Peanut Butter Brownies**

# SEAFOOD FESTIVAL

An annual event, the Seafood Festival is a celebration of Pensacola's important seafood industry. Shrimp boats and pleasure boats are gaily decorated with party flags as they participate in the boat parade and Blessing of the Fleet. Land and water activities offer entertainment both in town and at the beach. Events include a water ski show, a sandcastle contest, and an arts and crafts show as well as booths of seafood specialties everywhere. The annual Seafood Cooking Contest is also held during this festival. Prizewinning recipes help make this Seafood Buffet a meal to remember.

**SEAFOOD BUFFET**

**Crab Stuffed Mushrooms**

**Combo Gumbo Josephs**

**Trout Amandine**

**Herb-Seasoned Broccoli**      **Feta Spinach Salad**

**Spoon Rolls**

**Cream Cheese Pound Cake**

# PENSACOLA OPEN

Golfing is a popular pastime for many Pensacolians. The two major golf events held in Pensacola are the Pensacola Open and the American Amateur Golf Classic. Well-known professional golfers and celebrities participate in the Pensacola Open, one of the oldest PGA tour events. Held in the fall, when the weather is almost always perfect, the Open provides an excellent opportunity to extend southern hospitality to friends and visitors with a Jazz Brunch.

## JAZZ BRUNCH

**Bloody Mary Pitcher**          **Milk Punch**

**Old English Cheese Squares**

**Baked Chicken Salad**          **Spinach Soufflé Roll**

**Layered Salad**

**Blueberry-Orange Muffins**          **Blueberry Jam**

**Bananas Foster**

# GULF COAST ARTS FESTIVAL

The Greater Gulf Coast Arts Festival is a celebration of the arts. Held annually in Pensacola, the first weekend in November, it is one of the finest juried art shows in the southeast. The Youth Orchestra, Children's Festival, Crafts of the Past and the visual and performing arts are among the highlights of the festival. Award winning artists are honored and entertained by area collectors at the Artist Awards Party.

## ARTIST AWARDS PARTY

**Oysters Lydia with Party Melba Toast**

**New Potatoes with Caviar**

**Crunchy Fried Mushrooms**

**Microwave Crab Dip**          **Cold Spinach Dip**

**Sandwich for a Crowd**

**Sangria**

# HUNTING SEASON

When there is the first hint of crispness in the air, fall and hunting season begin. Hunters spend long weekends traveling to North Florida, Alabama and Louisiana to hunt quail, dove, turkey, deer and duck. Hunters gather at the lodge, after the hunt, for a superb breakfast that is sure to bring the glow of warmth and cheer to any fall weekend.

### HUNT BREAKFAST

**Milk Punch**            **Hot Spiced Punch**

**Broccoli Soup**

**Quail and Wild Rice**

**Sweet Potato Soufflé**          **Scalloped Oysters**

**Curried Fruit**

**English Muffin Bread**            **Cinnamon Bread or Rolls**

**Strawberry Fig Jam**

**Poached Pears in Grand Marnier Sauce**

# CHRISTMAS

Christmas in most of our homes is an energetic domestic endeavor. Families create visible expressions of the joyous celebration — decorating the house, trimming the tree, wrapping the gifts and baking holiday treats. When these projects are completed, there is a welcomed time of pleasurable relaxation. The wonderful smells of Christmas fill the house as loved ones gather for the singing of carols, toasting a glass of Christmas Cheer and savoring this lovely holiday dinner.

## A HOLIDAY DINNER

**Wassail**

**Cocktail Crabmeat Spread**          **Hot Mushroom Spread**

**Artichoke and Oyster Soup**

**Crown Roast of Pork Valencia**

**Lemon Pilaf**          **Julienne Zucchini and Carrots**

**Red Apple Spinach Salad**

**Applesauce Muffins**          **Spoon Rolls**

**Walnut Torte**          **Chocolate Mousse**

# NEW YEARS DAY

Friends and family gather together on January 1st, not only to celebrate the beginning of a new year but to also cheer for their favorite college football team in the super sports spectacular — bowl games. Pensacolians young and old follow their teams throughout the season in anticipation of who will be crowned #1 on this final day of college football. This menu will satisfy even the most enthusiastic fan for a long day of arm chair coaching.

### NEW YEARS DAY CELEBRATION

**Bloody Mary Pitcher**

**Southern Caviar**          **Hot Crab Dip**

**Zucchini Soup**

**Bacon and Cheese Stuffed Mushrooms**

**Chutney Almond Ball**          **Roasted Salted Pecans**

**Marinated Smoked Sausage**

**Fresh Vegetables with Fruit and Vegetable Dip**

**Chocolate Caramel Squares**

**Poppy Seed Cake with Lemon Icing**

# MARDI GRAS

Mardi Gras in Pensacola generates merrymaking and frivolity to rival the New Orleans celebration. Masquerade balls, costume parades and festive parties crowd our calendars prior to Lent. Carnival dance groups execute clever party themes where members are revealed in surprise court presentations. Revelers delight in a lavish cocktail buffet before an evening of music and dancing.

### A COCKTAIL BUFFET

**Cocktail Puffs**          **Spinach Squares**

**Sesame Chicken Bits**

**Marinated Roast Beef**

**Creole Marinated Shrimp**    **Oysters Pierre**    **Party Melba Toast**

**Chicken Liver Pâté**    **Marinated Vegetable Appetizer**

**Refrigerator Rolls**

**Horseradish Sauce**          **Hot Mustard**

# VALENTINE'S DAY

Lacey cards, homemade hearts, and delicious treats are all a very important part of Valentine's Day. Mothers and teachers will find this party a delightful way to help children celebrate this occasion for the young and young at heart.

## A HEARTY PARTY

**Apiece - Old Fashioned Rolled Cookies**

**Gingerbread Cookies**          **Oatmeal Cookies**

**Vanilla Custard Ice Cream**

**Hot Caramel Sauce**          **Hot Fudge Sauce**

**Strawberry Topping**

**Fruit Punch**

# APPETIZERS
# AND
# BEVERAGES

# APPETIZERS AND BEVERAGES

**Beverages**
Afternoon Delight, 68
Bloody Mary Pitcher, 72
Boiled Custard, 69
Champagne Punch, 68
Cranberry Tea, 71
Eggnog Richardson, 64
Frozen Daiquiris, 65
Fruit Punch, 70
Golden Sunset, 66
Hawaiian Julep, 65
Hot Buttered Rum, 72
Hot Spiced Cider, 70
Hot Spiced Punch, 70
McGuire's Irish Coffee, 67
Milk Punch, 71
Orange Julius, 71
Peach Daiquiris, 65
Peppermint Patti, 67
Rich and Creamy Eggnog, 64
Rum Swizzles, 66
Sangria, 69
Velvet Coffee Refresher, 67
Vodka Slush, 66
Wassail, 68

**Cold Hors d'oeuvres**
Caponata, 42
Creole Marinated Shrimp, 34
Marinated Mushrooms, 53
Marinated Mushrooms and Onions, 51
Marinated Shrimp, 36
Marinated Smoked Sausage, 39
Marinated Vegetable Appetizer, 49
New Potatoes with Caviar, 43
Roasted Salted Pecans, 56
Sandwich for a Crowd, 62
Southern Caviar, 31
Spiced Pecans, 56
Sugar Frosted Peanuts, 57
Tex-Mex Appetizer, 41

**Dips**
Clam Dip, 32
Cold Spinach Dip, 45
Creamy Crab Dip, 36
Fruit and Vegetable Dip, 55
Hot Crab Dip, 33
Microwave Crab Dip, 37
Pig's Delight, 55

Polynesian Ginger Dip, 63
River Club Cheese Dip, 54
Shrimp Dip, 37

**Hot Hors d'oeuvres**
Bacon and Cheese Stuffed Mushrooms, 50
Cheese Balls, 49
Cheese Squares, 47
Cocktail Puffs, 35
Crab Puffs, 33
Crab Stuffed Mushrooms, 51
Crunchy Fried Mushrooms, 50
Favorite Potato Skins, 43
Glazed Sausage Bites, 38
Green Chili Bites, 47
Italian Stuffed Mushrooms, 52
Marinated Ginger Chicken Wings, 39
Mushroom-Sausage Appetizer, 53
Old English Cheese Squares, 48
Oyster and Artichoke au Gratin, 54
Oysters Lydia, 31
Oysters Pierre, 32
Seafood-Stuffed Artichokes, 60
Sesame Chicken Bits, 38
Spinach Balls, 44
Spinach Squares, 44
Stuffed Grape Leaves, 58

**Molds**
Creamy Aspic, 63
Green Goddess Crab Mold, 34
Shrimp Mold, 57

**Spreads**
Antipasto Spread, 45
Bleu Cheese Ball, 40
Caviar and Artichoke Spread, 46
Chicken Liver Pâté, 59
Chili Cheese Ball, 41
Christmas Pepper Jelly, 61
Chutney Almond Ball, 48
Cocktail Crabmeat Spread, 59
Corned Beef Cheese Ball, 52
Hot Dried Beef Spread, 60
Hot Mushroom Spread, 46
Jezebel Sauce, 61
Oyster-Olive Spread, 35
Pineapple Cream Cheese Log, 42
Pineapple-Nut Sandwich Spread, 55
Snow-Capped Pâté, 40

# SOUTHERN CAVIAR

3 16-ounce cans black-
eyed peas, drained
8 small white onions,
thinly sliced and
separated into rings

1 tablespoon coarsely
ground pepper
1/4 teaspoon Tabasco sauce
1 small jar capers, drained
1 teaspoon garlic powder
1 16-ounce bottle Italian
dressing

Mix above ingredients. Cover and refrigerate at least 24 hours, stir-ring occasionally.

Drain and place in serving bowl. Serve with Triscuits.

This may be made up to 5 days ahead.

Yield: 15-20 servings for cocktails

# OYSTERS LYDIA

1 bunch parsley, chopped
8 green onions, finely
chopped
2 large cloves garlic,
minced
3/4 stick butter
2 tablespoons olive oil
4 tablespoons
Worcestershire sauce

1 lemon
1/4 teaspoon salt
1 teaspoon Tabasco sauce
2 pints raw oysters,
drained
1/4 cup Italian seasoned
bread crumbs
2 small loaves French
bread, sliced

Preheat oven to 450°.

Sauté parsley, onions and garlic in butter and olive oil until tender. Pour into 2-quart baking dish. Add Worcestershire, juice of lemon and remaining lemon rind, salt, Tabasco and drained oysters. Sprinkle with bread crumbs.

Bake on upper oven rack for 10-15 minutes, until bread crumbs are lightly browned.

Serve at once with French bread.

Yield: 6-8 servings

# OYSTERS PIERRE

8 ounces mushrooms,
   fresh, sliced
1 stick butter, divided
3 tablespoons flour
2 small cloves garlic,
   minced
3 tablespoons chopped
   onion
3 tablespoons chopped
   parsley

⅛ teaspoon cayenne
   pepper
1 teaspoon salt
⅓ cup dry sherry
4 dozen raw oysters,
   drained, chopped
   (about 2 pints)
⅓-½ cup Italian seasoned
   bread crumbs

Preheat overn to 350°. Sauté mushrooms until tender in 2 table-spoons butter. Set aside.

In skillet, melt 4 tablespoons butter; add flour and cook on low heat, stirring constantly, until light brown. Add garlic, onion and parsley. Cook 5 minutes. Add pepper and salt; then blend in sherry. Add oysters and mushrooms. Stir and cook 3 minutes. Blend in bread crumbs and remove from heat.

Spoon mixture into individual baking shells and dot with butter. Place shells on baking sheet and bake 15-20 minutes.

Yield: 6 servings

# CLAM DIP

1 can minced clams plus 2
   teaspoons clam juice
1 3-ounce package cream
   cheese, softened
2 tablespoons mayonnaise

2 teaspoons chopped onion
1 teaspoon Worcestershire
   sauce
Dash Tabasco sauce

Drain clams, reserving 2 teaspoons liquid. Blend softened cream cheese with clam juice; add mayonnaise and mix well.

Add onion, clams, Worcestershire sauce and Tabasco sauce. Mix well. Cover and refrigerate overnight. Serve with chips.

Yield: 6-8 servings

# CRAB PUFFS

6-8 ounces frozen Alaskan
  King Crab, thawed
2 tablespoons butter
¼ cup chopped green
  onion
1 cup chopped mushrooms
1 cup grated monterey jack
  cheese

1 3-ounce package cream
  cheese, softened
⅓ cup mayonnaise
2 tablespoons finely
  chopped parsley
¼ pound phyllo pastry
  sheets
½ cup butter, melted

Drain and chop crabmeat.

In a skillet, sauté onion for 1 minute in 2 tablespoons of butter. Add mushrooms; sauté 1 minute longer. Remove from heat. Add crab, cheeses, mayonnaise and parsley. Blend.

Cutting 2 phyllo sheets at a time, make strips 2 inches by 10 inches. Brush each strip with melted butter. Spoon a tablespoon of crab mixture onto end of each strip. Fold pastry over filling to form a triangle. Continue folding strip over as you would a flag. Seal seam with melted butter and place seam side down on lightly greased baking sheet. Bake in 350° oven for 30 minutes or until crisp and golden brown.

Yield: 3 dozen puffs

# HOT CRAB DIP

1 8-ounce package cream
  cheese
1 teaspoon lemon juice
1 teaspoon Worcestershire
  sauce

2 drops Tabasco sauce
½ teaspoon pressed garlic
½ cup mayonnaise
1 pound crabmeat, picked
  and cleaned

Melt cream cheese in top of double boiler. Stir in remaining ingredients. Heat thoroughly and serve with crackers of your choice.

Yield: 4 cups

# GREEN GODDESS CRAB MOLD

2 10½-ounce cans cream of
    asparagus soup
1 8-ounce package cream
    cheese
2 envelopes unflavored
    gelatin
½ cup cold water
¼ cup chopped green
    stuffed olives
¼ cup chopped black
    olives
½ cup chopped pimento
1 small onion, minced
½ cup finely chopped
    celery
¾ teaspoon garlic powder
3 cups flaked crabmeat
½ cup creamy Green
    Goddess dressing
1-2 teaspoons Tabasco
    sauce
Salt and pepper to taste

In a 1½-quart saucepan heat soup to a simmer. Add cream cheese and stir until melted. Remove from heat; set aside. Soften gelatin in cold water. Add to soup mixture.

Mix olives, pimento, onion, celery, garlic powder, crabmeat, dressing, Tabasco sauce, salt and pepper. Blend into soup mixture.

Pour mixture into a buttered 5-cup mold. Chill overnight. Serve with crackers. This is especially good with stone-ground wheat crackers.

Yield: Appetizer for 12 people

# CREOLE MARINATED SHRIMP

1 cup cider vinegar
1 cup vegetable oil
1 tablespoon creole
    mustard
½ cup finely chopped
    onion
1 clove garlic, crushed
½ cup chili sauce
⅛ teaspoon salt
2 tablespoons paprika
2 pounds shrimp, cooked,
    peeled and deveined

In a glass or plastic container, blend vinegar, oil, mustard, onion, garlic, chili sauce, salt and paprika. Add shrimp. Marinate, covered, in the refrigerator for at least 4 hours.

Yield: 4 servings

# COCKTAIL PUFFS

*Cream Puffs:*

1 stick butter
1 cup water
1 cup sifted flour

½ teaspoon salt
4 eggs

Place water and butter in a saucepan. Bring to a boil over medium heat. Add flour and salt; reduce heat and stir until mixture leaves sides of pan. Remove from heat. Stir in eggs one at a time, beating well after each addition. Drop ½ teaspoons of mixture onto very lightly greased baking sheet. Bake in a preheated 400° oven for 20-30 minutes until lightly browned. These can be frozen and filled later.

*Filling:*

½ cup finely chopped
 celery
1½ cups fresh crabmeat or
 cooked, chopped,
 shrimp or cooked,
 chopped, chicken
2 cups grated sharp
 cheddar cheese

1½-2 cups mayonnaise
2 tablespoons
 Worcestershire sauce
2 tablespoons Tabasco
 sauce
½ tablespoon minced
 onion

Combine all filling ingredients and chill.

Cut top off each puff, fill with mixture and replace top. Place on baking sheet and warm in 350° oven until cheese begins to melt.

Yield: 45-50 puffs

# OYSTER-OLIVE SPREAD

1 3¾-ounce can smoked
 oysters

1 4¼-ounce can chopped
 black olives
Mayonnaise

Finely chop oysters. Combine with olives and just enough mayonnaise to bind them together. Chill before serving. Serve with crackers.

Yield: 1 cup

# CREAMY CRAB DIP

8 tablespoons butter
8 tablespoons flour
3 cups milk
1 5-ounce jar Old English
    Cheese Spread
4 tablespoons butter
¼ cup minced onion
¼ cup minced green bell
    pepper
½ cup minced celery
2 tablespoons
    Worcestershire sauce
¼ teaspoon Tabasco sauce
1 pound fresh or frozen
    crabmeat
8 ounces mushrooms,
    sliced
¼ cup dry sherry

To make a cream sauce, melt butter; then add flour, stirring until mixture bubbles. Slowly add milk, whisking constantly, until thick and smooth.

Melt 4 tablespoons butter in small saucepan. Sauté onion, green bell pepper and celery until soft. Add to cream sauce along with Worcestershire, salt, pepper and Tabasco. When ready to serve, add crab, mushrooms and sherry. Adjust seasonings to taste.

Serve from chafing dish with toast points or small tart shells.

Yield: Serves 25 for cocktails

# MARINATED SHRIMP

1 package Good Seasons
    Italian dressing mix
1 cup cider vinegar
½ cup vegetable oil
2 tablespoons water
2 pounds shrimp, cooked,
    peeled and deveined
1 pound mushrooms
1 large onion, sliced and
    separated into rings

Combine dressing mix, vinegar, oil and water. Add shrimp, mushrooms and onions. Cover and marinate in refrigerator for 4 hours.

Yield: 8 servings

# SHRIMP DIP

1 3-ounce package cream
   cheese, softened
1 cup sour cream
2 teaspoons lemon juice

1⅝-ounce package Italian
   dressing mix
1-1½ cups shrimp, cooked,
   peeled, deveined and
   chopped

Blend well cream cheese, sour cream, lemon juice and dressing mix. Fold in shrimp. Chill at least 1 hour before serving. Serve with crackers or chips.

Yield: 4 servings

# MICROWAVE CRAB DIP

6 tablespoons butter
¼ cup finely chopped
   onion
1 clove garlic, minced
1 tablespoon chopped
   fresh parsley
1 8-ounce package cream
   cheese, cubed

1-2 teaspoons
   Worcestershire sauce
¼ teaspoon Tabasco sauce
⅛ teaspoon salt
12 ounces crabmeat,
   picked and cleaned

Place butter in 2-quart casserole. Microwave on HIGH 45 seconds or until butter melts. Add onion, garlic and parsley. Cover and microwave on HIGH 2½-3½ minutes, until onions are tender. Add cream cheese; cover. Microwave on HIGH 30 seconds to 1 minute, stirring once.

Stir in Worcestershire, Tabasco and salt. Mix well. Gently stir in crabmeat. Microwave on HIGH 1½-2½ minutes until thoroughly heated. Serve with crackers.

Dip can be served hot or cold.

Yield: 8 servings

# GLAZED SAUSAGE BITES

1 egg, slightly beaten
1 pound mild pork sausage
1/3 cup milk
1/2 teaspoon sage

1/2 cup finely crushed
Saltines (about 14
crackers)

In a large mixing bowl, combine egg, sausage, milk, sage and cracker crumbs. Mix well and shape sausage mixture into 3/4-inch balls. Brown in skillet over medium-high heat for about 10 minutes. Drain.

*Glaze:*

1/2 cup water
1/4 cup ketchup
2 tablespoons dark brown
  sugar

1 tablespoon cider vinegar
1 tablespoon soy sauce

Combine glaze ingredients in a 2-quart pan. Add meatballs and simmer for 15 minutes.

Place in chafing dish to serve.

Yield: 50 meatballs

# SESAME CHICKEN BITS

4 chicken breasts, skinned
  and boned

1 can sesame seeds
2 cups oil for deep frying

Cut chicken into 1x2-inch pieces.

*Marinade:*

1 egg white
1/2 tablespoon white wine

1 teaspoon salt
2 tablespoons cornstarch

Blend marinade ingredients; add chicken. Marinate 15 minutes.

Heat oil to frying temperature, about 350°.

Dredge marinated bits in sesame seeds and deep fry. Serve with sweet and sour sauce or hot mustard.

Yield: 6 servings

# MARINATED GINGER CHICKEN WINGS

5 pounds chicken wings
1 jar apricot junior baby
  food
1 cup soy sauce

1 tablespoon ground ginger
2 cloves garlic, crushed
2 tablespoons apricot jam
  or preserves

Disjoint chicken wings and discard tips. Place in large bowl. Combine baby food, soy sauce, ginger, garlic and preserves. Pour over wings and marinate overnight in refrigerator.

Preheat oven to 350°. Line baking sheet with foil; grease with vegetable oil. Arrange wings in single layer on sheet and bake 1 hour, turning once after 30 minutes.

Yield: 3 dozen

# MARINATED SMOKED SAUSAGE

*Marinade:*
⅓ cup vegetable oil
¼ cup white wine vinegar
1 tablespoon chopped
  parsley
½ teaspoon salt
½ teaspoon basil

½ teaspoon cracked black
  pepper
¼ teaspoon sugar
3-4 green onions, thinly
  sliced with tops

Mix marinade ingredients in blender.

1 pound pre-cooked
  smoked sausage
3 medium tomatoes, thinly
  sliced

2 small round loaves
  Italian or French bread

Slice sausage into ¼-inch slices. Layer sausage and tomato slices; add marinade. Cover and refrigerate 4 hours to several days. Toss occasionally.

Serve with sliced bread.

Yield: Hearty appetizer for 12 people

# SNOW-CAPPED PÂTÉ

½ cup chopped green
   onion
1 clove garlic, crushed
¼ cup butter
1 pound chicken livers,
   drained
2 teaspoons flour
¼ teaspoon crushed thyme
⅛ teaspoon black pepper

2-4 tablespoons dry sherry
2 3-ounce packages cream
   cheese, softened
3 tablespoons half and half
½ cup freshly chopped
   parsley
½ cup coarsely chopped
   pecans

In a large skillet, sauté onion and garlic in butter until tender. Add livers and cook, covered, over low heat until no longer pink, about 7-8 minutes. Stir in flour, thyme, pepper and sherry. Cook, stirring constantly, for 1 minute.

Transfer to food processor or blender; process until smooth.

Mold mixture in a small, deep bowl that has been well greased. Chill at least 6 hours, preferably overnight. Unmold.

Blend cream cheese and half and half until smooth. Spread over mold. Chill until serving time.

Chop parsley and pecans in blender or food processor. Sprinkle on pâté just before serving.

Serve with crackers or toasted French bread rounds.

Yield: 3 cups

# BLEU CHEESE BALL

1 8-ounce package cream
   cheese, softened
1 8-ounce package bleu
   cheese, crumbled
¼ cup butter, softened

1 4½-ounce can chopped
   black olives, drained
1 tablespoon chives
½ cup chopped pecans

Blend cheeses and butter. Add olives and chives. Mix well. Chill. Shape in a ball and sprinkle with nuts. Serve with snack crackers.

Yield: 3 cups

# TEX-MEX APPETIZER

3 medium avocados
2 tablespoons lemon juice
½ teaspoon salt
¼ teaspoon pepper
1 cup sour cream
½ cup mayonnaise
1 package taco seasoning
   mix
2 10½-ounce cans plain or
   jalapeño bean dip
8 green onions, chopped
3 medium tomatoes, fresh,
   seeded, chopped
2 3½-ounce cans black
   olives, chopped
1 8-ounce package sharp
   cheddar cheese, grated
Tortilla chips or rounds

Peel, pit and mash avocados with lemon juice, salt and pepper.

Combine sour cream, mayonnaise and taco seasoning mix.

To assemble: spread bean dip on a large shallow serving platter; spread seasoned avocado mixture over bean dip; spread sour cream mixture over avocado mixture. Sprinkle chopped onion, tomatoes and olives over all. Cover with grated cheese. Serve chilled or at room temperature with tortilla chips.

Yield: 20-30 servings

# CHILI CHEESE BALL

2 8-ounce packages cream
   cheese, softened
4 ounces bleu cheese,
   softened
1 clove garlic, crushed
¼ cup mayonnaise
6 drops Tabasco sauce
1 teaspoon chili powder
1 small onion, grated
1 cup pecans, ground
2 tablespoons chili powder

Blend cheeses. Add garlic, mayonnaise, Tabasco, 1 teaspoon chili powder and onion. Mix well and chill. Shape into a ball; roll in a mixture of pecans and 2 tablespoons chili powder. Serve with snack crackers.

Yield: 1 cheese ball

# CAPONATA

2 pounds eggplant (about 8
   cups), peeled and cut
   into ½-inch cubes
Salt
½ cup olive oil
2 cups chopped celery
¾ cup chopped onion
4 cloves garlic, minced
⅓ cup red wine vinegar
4 teaspoons sugar

3 cups chopped tomato,
   fresh or canned
2 tablespoons tomato
   paste
6 large green olives, pitted
   and slivered
¾ cup sliced black olives
2 teaspoons anchovy paste
Salt and pepper to taste
2 tablespoons pine nuts
Pita bread

Salt eggplant cubes and let sit 30 minutes; then squeeze out excess liquid. Heat ¼ cup olive oil. Add celery and cook over medium heat for 10 minutes, stirring frequently. Add onion and cook 8-10 minutes. Remove celery and onion from pan. Add remaining olive oil to pan. Sauté eggplant about 8 minutes, or until lightly browned. Return celery and onion to skillet and add remaining ingredients except pine nuts. Bring to a boil, reduce heat and simmer uncovered about 1 hour, stirring occasionally. Add pine nuts about 15 minutes before done.

Cut pita bread into triangles; then toast. Serve caponata at room temperature with pita toast.

Yield: 8 cups

# PINEAPPLE CREAM CHEESE LOG

2 8-ounce packages cream
   cheese, softened
¼ cup finely chopped green
   onion
¼ cup finely chopped green
   bell pepper
1 8-ounce can crushed
   pineapple, drained

1 teaspoon seasoned salt
½ cup chopped pecans
⅛ teaspoon garlic salt
⅛ teaspoon celery seed
1 teaspoon chopped
   parsley
1 cup finely ground pecans

Blend all ingredients except pecan meal. Mix well. Shape into 2 8-inch logs and roll in pecans. Wrap first in wax paper, then foil; chill overnight. Serve with Triscuits or Wheat Thins.

Yield: 2 8-inch logs

# NEW POTATOES WITH CAVIAR

**30 tiny new potatoes**
**1 4-ounce jar black caviar,**
  **chilled**

**½ cup sour cream**
**Finely chopped chives**

Select the smallest, most uniform new potatoes available. Scrub and peel, if desired. Boil in salted water until tender, about 10 to 15 minutes. Drain in colander and rinse immediately with cold water.

When potatoes are cool enough to handle, trim a small slice off the bottom of each so that they will stand upright. Then scoop out a small hollow on top with tip of spoon.

Just before serving, fill hollow with small spoonful of sour cream and top with ½ teaspoon of chilled black caviar. Sprinkle with chives. Serve at room temperature.

Yield: 30 appetizers

# FAVORITE POTATO SKINS

**2 baking potatoes,**
  **preferably Idaho**
**1½ tablespoons butter,**
  **melted**

**½ cup finely shredded**
  **cheddar or Parmesan**
  **cheese**
**4 strips of bacon, cooked**
  **and crumbled**

Preheat oven to 400°. Scrub, dry and pierce with fork each potato. Bake for 1 hour 10 minutes, or until very tender. When cool enough to handle, cut in half lengthwise and scoop out potatoes, leaving ¼ inch shell.

Brush inside of skins generously with melted butter. Sprinkle with cheese and bacon. Bake at 375° for 30 minutes, or until the tops are golden and the skins are crisp. Cut into strips.

Yield: 4 servings

# SPINACH BALLS

2 10-ounce packages
    frozen chopped
    spinach
3 cups herb-seasoned
    stuffing mix
1 large onion, finely
    chopped

6 eggs, well beaten
¾ cup butter, melted
½ cup grated Parmesan
    cheese
½ tablespoon black pepper
1½ teaspoons garlic salt
½ teaspoon thyme

Cook spinach according to package direction. Drain well; squeeze spinach to remove excess moisture. Add remaining ingredients, blending well.

Shape mixture into ¾-inch balls and place on lightly greased baking sheets. Bake in preheated 325° oven for 15-20 minutes. Balls may be frozen and cooked without thawing.

Yield: 10 dozen

# SPINACH SQUARES

1½ 10-ounce packages
    frozen chopped
    spinach
1 pound cheddar cheese,
    grated
½ cup chopped onion

1 cup flour
1 teaspoon salt
1 teaspoon baking powder
2 eggs, beaten
1 cup milk
¼ cup butter, melted

Cook spinach according to package directions. Drain well. Combine with cheese and onion. Set aside.

Preheat oven to 350°. Combine flour, salt and baking powder in bowl. Add eggs, milk and butter. Mix well. Add spinach mixture. Pour into lightly greased 13x9x2-inch pan.

Bake in 350° oven for 35 minutes. Let cool slightly; then cut into 1-inch squares. These can be frozen at this point and then reheated (without thawing) at 300° for 15 minutes.

Yield: 12 squares

# COLD SPINACH DIP

1 10-ounce package frozen chopped spinach
1 8-ounce carton sour cream
1 cup mayonnaise
1 small onion, chopped
1 8½-ounce can water chestnuts, chopped
1 package Knorr vegetable soup

Defrost, drain and squeeze water from spinach. Add sour cream, mayonnaise, onion, chestnuts and soup mix. Blend well and refrigerate overnight.

Serve with crackers, raw vegetables or party pumpernickel bread.

Yield: 6 servings

# ANTIPASTO SPREAD

1 8-ounce can mushrooms
1 14-ounce can artichoke hearts
1 9-ounce jar green olives
1 4½-ounce can chopped black olives
1 small green bell pepper, chopped
4 celery ribs, chopped
¾ cup white vinegar
¾ cup olive oil
¼ cup minced dry onion
2 teaspoons Italian seasoning
1 teaspoon salt
1 teaspoon seasoned salt
1 teaspoon sugar
1 teaspoon black pepper
½ teaspoon garlic powder

Drain and finely chop mushrooms, artichoke hearts, olives, pepper and celery. Food processor may be used. Place ingredients in a 1½-quart container with a tight lid.

Combine and bring to a boil in a saucepan the remaining ingredients. Pour over chopped vegetables. Refrigerate overnight or several days. Stir ingredients several times a day.

Serve as an appetizer with crackers, as a relish for meat sandwiches or as a salad dressing.

Yield: 1 quart

## CAVIAR AND ARTICHOKE SPREAD

1 8-ounce package cream
   cheese, softened
2 tablespoons sour cream
2 tablespoons mayonnaise
1½ tablespoons minced
   onion

1 8-ounce can artichoke
   hearts, drained and
   chopped
1 1-ounce jar caviar

Cream until smooth cream cheese, sour cream, mayonnaise and onion. Food processor may be used.

Place well-drained, chopped artichoke hearts into a mound on serving plate. Cover with cream cheese mixture. Shape mound until smooth. Ice with caviar.

Store in refrigerator but serve at room temperature. Serve with crackers, toast points or as a filling for tomatoes or avocados.

Yield: 2 cups

## HOT MUSHROOM SPREAD

2 cups canned chopped
   mushrooms
2 green onions, chopped
¼ cup butter
¼ cup flour

½ teaspoon salt
White wine
⅓ cup sour cream
Toast squares

Drain mushrooms, reserving liquid.

In skillet over low heat, sauté mushrooms and onion in butter; add flour and salt and cook 2-3 minutes longer.

Combine reserved liquid from mushrooms with enough white wine to make 1 cup liquid. Add to skillet and cook 3 minutes. Cool.

Stir in sour cream. Spread mixture on toast squares and broil until bubbly.

Yield: 4-6 servings

# CHEESE SQUARES

9 slices day-old bread
Margarine, softened
1 3-ounce package cream
cheese

4 ounces cheddar cheese,
grated
1 stick margarine
2 egg whites

Trim crusts from bread; spread margarine on each slice. Stack 3 slices at a time and cut into thirds.

In double boiler melt cream cheese, cheddar cheese and margarine. Beat egg whites until stiff. Fold into melted cheese mixture.

Dip or spread bread slices with warm cheese mixture. Keeping cheese mixture over hot water will make it easy to spread. Place slices on baking sheet and refrigerate to cook same day or freeze and store in plastic bag for later use. Bake in preheated 350° oven until lightly browned, about 10 minutes.

Yield: 27 squares

# GREEN CHILI BITES

2 4-ounce cans whole
green chilies
2 cups grated monterey
jack cheese

2 cups grated cheddar
cheese
6 eggs, beaten
Salt and pepper to taste

Preheat oven to 325°.

Butter an 8 or 9-inch square baking dish. Slice and open chilies and arrange on bottom of baking dish. Mix grated cheeses together and sprinkle over chilies. Add salt and pepper to beaten eggs and pour over cheese and chilies.

Bake 30-40 minutes or until firm when dish is shaken. Cut into squares and serve hot.

Yield: 20 squares

# OLD ENGLISH CHEESE SQUARES

2-3 loaves Pepperidge
Farm thin-sliced white
bread
2 teaspoons dill weed
1 teaspoon Tabasco sauce
4 5-ounce jars Old English
Cheese Spread

1½ teaspoons
Worcestershire sauce
1½ teaspoons Beau Monde
seasoning
1 pound butter, softened
⅛ teaspoon cayenne
pepper

Stack 3 slices of bread at a time, trim crusts and cut into quarters. Mix dill weed, Tabasco, cheese spread, Worcestershire, butter and seasonings; blend well. Spread mixture on both sides of middle slice of bread; restack and spread mixture on top and sides of each square (like a cake). Freeze on cookie sheet; then place in plastic bags to store.

Bake in 350° oven for 20 minutes if cooking frozen squares. If squares are not frozen, bake 10-15 minutes.

Yield: 5 dozen squares

# CHUTNEY ALMOND BALL

2 8-ounce packages cream
cheese, softened
1 cup chopped chutney

2 teaspoons curry powder
½ teaspoon dry mustard
¾ cup chopped almonds

Combine cream cheese, chutney, curry powder and dry mustard. Blend well. Place in small bowl lined with plastic wrap. Cover and refrigerate at least two hours.

Remove from bowl and roll in almonds. Serve on platter with crackers.

Ball can be rolled in shredded coconut or chopped green onion, if desired.

Yield: 1 cheese ball

# MARINATED VEGETABLE APPETIZER

4 ounces wine vinegar
½ cup olive oil
2 tablespoons sugar
1 tablespoon salt
½ teaspoon oregano
¼ cup water
¼ teaspoon pepper
2 carrots, peeled and
    sliced
2 celery stalks, sliced

1 small head cauliflower,
    separated into
    flowerets
1 green bell pepper,
    seeded and cut into
    chunks
1 small jar button
    mushrooms
1 4-ounce jar green olives
1 can ripe olives
1 4-ounce jar pickled
    onions

In large skillet combine first 7 ingredients. Add carrots. Cover and simmer 2 minutes. Add celery and cauliflower. Cover and simmer 2 more minutes. Add bell pepper, mushrooms, olives and onions. Cover and simmer 1 more minute.

Refrigerate in marinade for 24 hours.

Drain and serve with toothpicks.

Yield: 10-12 servings

*For softer vegetables, increase simmering time.*

# CHEESE BALLS

1 pound sharp cheese,
    grated
1 pound butter, softened
1 teaspoon salt

1 teaspoon cayenne
1 teaspoon paprika
4-4½ cups flour

Put butter in a large mixing bowl. Add cheese and seasonings. Add flour 1 cup at a time until dough is stiff enough to hold its shape. Make into small balls and place 1 inch apart on ungreased baking sheet. Bake at 375-400° for 18-20 minutes or until golden brown.

Yield: 3 dozen

# BACON AND CHEESE STUFFED MUSHROOMS

1 pound fresh mushrooms
10 slices bacon, cooked
   and crumbled
1 8-ounce package cream
   cheese, softened

1 small onion, finely
   chopped
Salt and pepper to taste

Wash mushrooms; trim and remove stems. Reserve half of stems and chop.

Mix bacon, cream cheese, onion, salt, pepper and chopped stems. Spoon into mushroom caps.

Broil 3-5 minutes or until browned.

Mushrooms can be stuffed a day ahead and then broiled as needed.

Yield: 6-8 servings

# CRUNCHY FRIED MUSHROOMS

1 pound fresh, medium
   mushrooms
2 eggs
1 cup milk
1 cup flour
2 teaspoons salt

1 teaspoon pepper
½-1 teaspoon dill weed
¼ cup Parmesan cheese
1 cup seasoned bread
   crumbs

Wash and remove stems from mushrooms. Combine eggs and milk in a bowl. In another bowl, mix remaining ingredients.

Dip mushrooms in milk mixture, then dry mixture. Let mushrooms sit for 5 minutes.

Deep fry until golden brown.

Serve immediately with Ranch dressing, tartar sauce or cocktail sauce.

Yield: 4-6 servings

# CRAB STUFFED MUSHROOMS

12 large or 24 medium
    mushrooms
2 tablespoons minced
    green onion
2 tablespoons butter
1 teaspoon lemon juice
1 cup flaked crabmeat
½ cup soft bread crumbs
1 egg, slightly beaten

½ teaspoon salt
¼ teaspoon pepper
½ teaspoon dill weed
¼ cup grated monterey
    jack cheese
3 tablespoons butter
½ cup grated monterey
    jack cheese
¼ cup dry white wine

Preheat oven to 400°. Wash mushrooms; trim and remove stems. Finely chop stems and sauté them with onion in 2 tablespoons butter until onion is tender. Remove from heat and stir in lemon juice, crabmeat, bread crumbs, egg, salt, pepper, dill weed and ¼ cup cheese.

In a 13x9x2-inch baking pan melt 3 tablespoons butter. Turn mushroom caps in butter to coat. Fill caps with stuffing. Arrange stuffed side up in pan. Sprinkle with ½ cup cheese. Pour wine over mushrooms.

Bake for 15-20 minutes. Serve with lemon wedges.

Yield: 12 servings

# MARINATED MUSHROOMS AND ONIONS

2 6-ounce cans mushroom
    caps
1 onion, thinly sliced
½ cup mushroom broth
½ cup wine vinegar
¼ cup tarragon vinegar
½ cup dark brown sugar

¼ teaspoon salt
¼ teaspoon black pepper
¼ teaspoon whole black
    peppercorns
1 bay leaf
1 clove garlic, crushed

Layer onion slices and mushrooms in a 1-quart jar. Combine all other ingredients in a saucepan and boil 3 minutes. Cool.

Pour over mushrooms and onions. Cover and refrigerate 24 hours.

Yield: 6-8 servings

# ITALIAN STUFFED MUSHROOMS

| | |
|---|---|
| 15 fresh, medium mushrooms | ¼ cup grated Parmesan cheese |
| 3 teaspoons olive oil | 1 tablespoon ketchup |
| 1 tablespoon minced onion | 1 teaspoon butter |
| ¼ cup finely chopped salami | 2 tablespoons fine soft bread crumbs |

Wash and dry mushrooms. Trim and remove stems; chop enough stems to make ⅓ cup. Brush mushroom caps lightly with 2 teaspoons of the olive oil.

Preheat oven to 425°.

In an 8-inch skillet, heat remaining 1 teaspoon of olive oil. Add chopped stems and onion; cook over low heat until golden. Stir in salami, cheese and ketchup. Spoon mixture into mushroom caps.

In the skillet, melt the butter and mix in bread crumbs. Sprinkle over the tops of stuffed mushrooms. Arrange mushrooms in a shallow baking pan.

Bake at 425° until hot, about 6-8 minutes. Serve immediately.

Yield: 5-6 servings

# CORNED BEEF CHEESE BALL

| | |
|---|---|
| 4 2½-ounce packages pressed, chopped corned beef | 1 tablespoon Accent |
| | ½ teaspoon garlic powder |
| 4 green onions, chopped | 1 cup finely chopped pecans or Ritz cracker crumbs |
| 4 8-ounce packages cream cheese, softened | |

Mix onion and chopped beef. Blend with cream cheese, Accent and garlic powder. Roll into a ball.

Refrigerate until slightly firm; roll ball in nuts or cracker crumbs.

Serve with snack crackers.

Yield: 2 large cheese balls

# MARINATED MUSHROOMS

1½ pounds fresh
   mushrooms
¾ cup olive oil
⅓ cup wine vinegar
3 tablespoons lemon juice
4 teaspoons chopped
   chives
¼ cup chopped parsley

1½ teaspoons tarragon
1½ teaspoons salt
½ teaspoon finely ground
   black pepper
2 teaspoons honey
Lemon slices and parsley
   sprigs

Wash and trim mushrooms.

Mix remaining ingredients and pour over mushrooms. Cover and chill several hours. Turn occasionally.

Drain to serve. Garnish with lemon slices and parsley sprigs.

Yield: 6-8 servings

# MUSHROOM-SAUSAGE APPETIZER

1 pound small mushrooms
1 1-pound package bulk,
   medium-hot sausage

Garlic salt to taste
Worcestershire sauce
Parsley flakes

Wash and dry mushrooms. Remove stems. Place caps in baking pan.

Shape sausage into small balls; place in mushroom caps. Preheat oven to 350°.

Punch a small hole in sausage ball with a toothpick. Drop in several drops of Worcestershire sauce. Sprinkle a few more drops Worcestershire over all.

Sprinkle with garlic salt and parsley flakes to taste.

Bake for 30-35 minutes.

Yield: 8-12 servings

# OYSTER AND ARTICHOKE AU GRATIN

1¼ quarts oysters
2 9-ounce packages frozen
   artichoke hearts, cut
   in half
2 cups sliced green onions
1 cup unsalted butter
⅔ cup flour
2 tablespoons minced
   parsley
1 tablespoon minced garlic

2 tablespoons fresh lemon
   juice
3 tablespoons
   Worcestershire sauce
¼ teaspoon Tabasco sauce
2 tablespoons freshly
   grated Parmesan
   cheese
½ cup fresh bread crumbs
Paprika to taste
Salt and Pepper

In a heavy saucepan, bring oysters and their liquor to a simmer. Cook oysters for 1 minute, or until the edges begin to curl. Drain the oysters, reserving the liquor. In a saucepan, cook the artichoke hearts in 1 cup boiling water with salt to taste for 5 minutes. Drain artichoke hearts, reserving ½ cup of the cooking liquid.

In a large stainless steel or enamel saucepan, cook the green onion in butter, stirring over moderate heat for 2 minutes. Stir in flour and cook over low heat for 3 minutes. Add parsley and garlic and cook mixture for 2 minutes. Add reserved liquids and bring to boil, stirring until very thick. Stir in oysters, artichoke hearts, lemon juice, Worcestershire, Tabasco and salt and pepper to taste. Cook mixture over low heat for 10 minutes and divide among individual gratin dishes. Combine Parmesan cheese and bread crumbs and sprinkle over each dish. Sprinkle with paprika.

Bake in preheated 375° oven for 20 minutes or until hot and bubbly.

Yield: 6 servings

# RIVER CLUB CHEESE DIP

1 pound cream cheese at
   room temperature
½ cup sour cream
1 tablespoon chopped
   green onion
1 teaspoon dry mustard

1 tablespoon prepared
   mustard
2-3 drops Worcestershire
   sauce
2-3 drops Tabasco sauce
Salt and pepper to taste

Combine all ingredients and blend well. Refrigerate several hours before serving. Serve with crackers or sliced vegetables.

Yield: 12 servings

# FRUIT AND VEGETABLE DIP

½ cup sour cream
½ cup mayonnaise
2 tablespoons chopped
  parsley
2 tablespoons sesame
  seeds

2 tablespoons poppy seeds
1 tablespoon minced onion
1 tablespoon sugar
1 teaspoon lemon juice
½ teaspoon black pepper
⅛ teaspoon nutmeg

Blend all ingredients together. Cover and chill. Serve with fresh fruit or sliced vegetables such as carrots, celery, zucchini, squash, green pepper, cucumber and cauliflower. This dip is good with snack crackers.

Yield: 10-15 servings

# PIG'S DELIGHT

1 cup sour cream
1 cup Hellmann's
  mayonnaise
2 teaspoons dill weed
1 teaspoon garlic salt

1 teaspoon grated onion or
  2 teaspoons chopped
  chives
1 round loaf pumpernickel
  bread

Scoop out center of bread to form a bowl. Serve chunks of bread for dipping. Combine other ingredients and mix well. Put dip inside bread "bowl" with chunks on the side. You may also eat the bowl!

Yield: 6 servings

# PINEAPPLE-NUT SANDWICH SPREAD

1 cup crushed pineapple,
  drained
1 cup sugar
½ cup chopped pecans

2-3 tablespoons
  mayonnaise
Thin-sliced white bread

Cook pineapple and sugar over medium heat until thick. Add nuts and cool. Thin with mayonnaise until mixture is of spreading consistency. Trim crust from bread. Spread on bread for party sandwiches.

Yield: 2 cups

# ROASTED SALTED PECANS

**1 pound pecan halves**          **Salt to taste**
**¾ cup butter, melted**

Preheat oven to 300°.

Spread pecans on a large baking sheet. Pour melted butter over pecans. Sprinkle with salt to taste.

Bake 20-30 minutes or until crisp.

Roasted pecans can be cooled and stored in an airtight container.

Yield: 4-6 servings

# SPICED PECANS

**1 stick butter**              **1 tablespoon ground cloves**
**4 cups pecan halves**         **1 tablespoon cinnamon**
**1½ cups confectioners'**      **1 tablespoon nutmeg**
**    sugar**

Melt butter in a large, heavy skillet. Add pecan halves. Cook 20 minutes over low heat, stirring. Drain on paper towels.

Mix sugar, cloves, cinnamon and nutmeg in a paper bag. Add warm pecans and shake to coat. Spread on paper towels to dry.

Store in an airtight container.

Yield: 4 cups

*Spiced pecans make an excellent gift.*

# SUGAR FROSTED PEANUTS

**2 cups shelled raw peanuts**　**1 cup sugar**
**½ cup water**　**1 teaspoon vanilla**

Preheat oven to 300°.

Mix all ingredients in a heavy saucepan. Cook over medium heat, stirring constantly, until all the liquid is gone.

Place sugared peanuts on foil-lined baking sheet; separate with fork. Bake for 15 minutes; stir; then bake 15 minutes longer. Cool and store in airtight container.

Yield: 2 cups

# SHRIMP MOLD

**1 10¾-ounce can tomato soup**
**1 8-ounce package cream cheese**
**2 envelopes unflavored gelatin**
**¼ cup lukewarm water**

**2 pounds shrimp, cooked, peeled and finely chopped**
**1 cup finely chopped celery**
**1 cup finely chopped onion**
**Salt and pepper**
**⅛ teaspoon Tabasco sauce**
**1 cup mayonnaise**
**2 tablespoons horseradish**

Heat soup and add cream cheese. Stir with a whisk until cheese is melted and mixture is smooth. Dissolve gelatin in water and add to soup. Stir in remaining ingredients. Pour into a well-greased mold. This recipe will fill a 4-cup mold with a small amount left over. Refrigerate until mold is set. Unmold by running a sharp knife around the edge of the mold and inverting on a serving dish. Serve with Escort crackers.

Yield: 16 servings

# STUFFED GRAPE LEAVES

| | |
|---|---|
| 1 16-ounce jar grape leaves | 1 teaspoon parsley |
| 1 tablespoon oil | ½ teaspoon salt |
| ½ pound ground beef | ⅛ teaspoon cinnamon |
| 1 onion, finely chopped | ½ cup raisins |
| 1 clove garlic, pressed | ¼ cup port |
| 1 cup water | ¼ cup pine nuts or walnuts |
| ¼ cup tomato sauce | 2 cups water |
| ½ cup rice, uncooked | Juice of lemon |
| 1 teaspoon spearmint | Lemon slices |

Wash grape leaves 3 times in cold water to remove brine.

Brown meat in a heavy skillet; drain and set aside. Heat oil and sauté onion and garlic for 5 minutes. Add beef, 1 cup water and the next 9 ingredients. Cover and bring to a boil. Reduce heat and simmer until water is absorbed. Set aside until cool enough to handle.

Reserve 8 leaves for lining casserole. Using 1 teaspoon per leaf, place the filling at the end of the leaf, fold the sides of the leaf in over the filling and roll up tightly. The shiny surface of the leaf should be on the outside.

Line the bottom of a large flame-proof casserole with 4 empty leaves. Put stuffed leaves in layers. Cover with remaining empty leaves; then place a heavy plate over them inside the casserole. Add 2 cups water and lemon juice. Bring to boil. Reduce heat to simmer and cook 30-45 minutes until all water is absorbed.

Garnish with lemon slices and serve cold with toothpicks. Stuffed grape leaves can be made ahead and kept refrigerated up to a week.

Yield: 50 servings

# CHICKEN LIVER PÂTÉ

1 pound chicken livers
1 cup sliced mushrooms
12 tablespoons butter
¼ cup chopped green
   onion
¼ cup cognac
1 teaspoon salt

¼ teaspoon freshly ground
   black pepper
⅛ teaspoon cayenne
   pepper
¼ teaspoon allspice
⅛ teaspoon thyme
Parsley sprigs

Wash, dry and chop livers. Sauté mushrooms and onion in butter for 5 minutes. Add livers to pan and cook until barely pink on the inside, about 5 minutes. In a food processor fitted with a steel blade, process liver mixture, cognac and seasonings until smooth. If mixture is too thick, add more melted butter (1 or 2 tablespoons). Pack in crocks or a mold and chill.

Serve in crock or unmold and decorate with parsley and mushroom slices. Serve with homemade melba toast or Triscuits.

Yield: 3 cups

# COCKTAIL CRABMEAT SPREAD

1 pound fresh crabmeat,
   undrained
1 pint Hellmann's
   mayonnaise
1 teaspoon minced onion
1 tablespoon capers

2 dashes Tabasco sauce
¼ teaspoon Worcestershire
   sauce
¼ cup sherry
Salt to taste

Combine all ingredients and chill at least 4 hours before serving. Serve cold with an assortment of crackers or homemade melba toast.

Yield: 20-30 servings

*This is a great recipe for a crowd because 1 pound of crabmeat goes a long way!*

# SEAFOOD-STUFFED ARTICHOKES

½ pound crabmeat or 1
    lobster tail, chopped
4 tablespoons vegetable oil
3 tablespoons cider vinegar
4 tablespoons ice water
2 tablespoons tartar sauce

¼ teaspoon Tabasco sauce
2 teaspoons chopped
    anchovies
2 teaspoons ketchup
2 artichoke bottoms

*Garnish:*
    **Chopped, hard-boiled egg**
    **Sliced stuffed olive**

    **Caviar**

Marinate crab or lobster in oil, vinegar and ice water for 2 hours. Mix together tartar sauce, Tabasco, anchovies and ketchup. Drain seafood and add to sauce. Mix well. Stuff artichoke bottoms with mixture and decorate with chopped egg, a slice of stuffed olive and ¼ teaspoon caviar.

Yield: 2 servings

*Stuffed artichokes are wonderful for luncheon guests. Serve with melba toast and a glass of chablis.*

# HOT DRIED BEEF SPREAD

1 2½-ounce jar dried beef
1 8-ounce package cream
    cheese, softened
¼ cup finely chopped green
    bell pepper

¼ cup finely chopped green
    onion
1 8-ounce carton sour
    cream
½ cup chopped pecans

Combine dried beef, cream cheese, bell pepper, green onion and sour cream in food processor, using steel blade. Process with 4 or 5 on/off turns. Pour mixture into 1-quart casserole. Sprinkle pecans on top. Heat at 350° for 25 minutes. Serve with crackers.

Yield: 2 cups

# JEZEBEL SAUCE

1 1.2-ounce can dry
   mustard
1 4-ounce jar horseradish
1 16-ounce jar pineapple
   preserves

1 16-ounce jar apple jelly
2 tablespoons coarsely
   ground black pepper

Make a paste of dry mustard and horseradish. Add pineapple preserves, apple jelly and pepper; stir by hand until thoroughly mixed. Sauce will keep several months in the refrigerator.

Serve over cream cheese with Waverly Wafers for an appetizer or as a sauce for ham.

Yield: 1 quart

# CHRISTMAS PEPPER JELLY

1 cup seeded and chopped
   green bell pepper
½ cup rinsed and seeded
   canned jalapeño
   pepper
1¼ cups apple cider
   vinegar

6 cups sugar
1 cup seeded and diced red
   bell pepper
1 bottle liquid fruit pectin
8-9 drops green food
   coloring

Place green pepper and jalapeños in a blender or processor with ½ cup of vinegar; blend until smooth. Pour mixture into a 4-quart saucepan. Rinse blender with remaining vinegar and add it to the green pepper mixture. Stir in the sugar and diced red pepper. Bring mixture to a hard boil that cannot be stirred down. Remove from heat and let stand 5 minutes. Skim foam carefully off top, leaving as many red peppers as possible. Add pectin and food coloring. Stir until blended. Pour into sterilized jars and seal. Serve over cream cheese with crackers.

Yield: 7 half-pint jars

*Pepper jelly makes an excellent gift.*

# SANDWICH FOR A CROWD

*Filling:*

1 36-inch loaf of French bread
Mustard
Mayonnaise
½ pound American cheese, sliced
½ pound smoked salami, sliced
½ pound caraway cheese, sliced
½ pound Kosher bologna, sliced
½ pound Muenster cheese, sliced
1 quart marinated cabbage slaw
½ pound Kosher salami, sliced
½ pound baby swiss cheese, sliced
1 8-ounce jar Kosher dill pickles, sliced
1 8-ounce jar dill pickles, sliced

Have delicatessen bake a 36-inch loaf of French bread. Slice the loaf in half, lengthwise. Spread a thin layer of mustard and mayonnaise on sides of bread. Layer the next 5 ingredients on the bread. Cover with marinated cabbage slaw. Layer the next 4 ingredients on top of slaw. Sandwich should be served on a 6x36-inch bread board. Slice and serve. Other meats and cheeses can be substituted.

*Marinated Cabbage Slaw:*

1 large green bell pepper
2 onions
1 red bell pepper or 1 2-ounce jar pimento, drained
1 large head cabbage, shredded
2 cups vinegar
2½ cups sugar
2½ teaspoons celery seed
1 teaspoon mustard seed
½ teaspoon turmeric
1 teaspoon salt

Finely chop green pepper, onion and red pepper. Add to shredded cabbage. In a saucepan, combine vinegar, sugar, celery seed, mustard seed, turmeric and salt. Bring to a boil. Pour over cabbage and vegetables and let stand at room temperature until cooled. Marinate in refrigerator at least 12 hours. Slaw can be made ahead of time and will keep up to a month. This recipe will make enough slaw for 3 or 4 36-inch sandwiches.

Yield: 25 servings

*This sandwich is great for a large crowd. Guests can serve themselves.*

# CREAMY ASPIC

2 envelopes unflavored
    gelatin
½ cup cold water
1 10¾-ounce can tomato
    soup
1 cup water
1 8-ounce package cream
    cheese, softened
1 14-ounce can artichoke
    hearts, rinsed and
    drained

1 cup sliced pimento-
    stuffed green olives
1 cup diced celery
2 tablespoons grated onion
½ teaspoon salt
⅛ teaspoon Tabasco sauce
1 cup mayonnaise
Additional mayonnaise and
    horseradish

Soak gelatin in cold water to soften. Heat tomato soup with 1 cup water until very hot. Add to gelatin and stir until gelatin is completely dissolved. Chill mixture until the consistency of egg white. Whip cream cheese. Coarsely chop artichoke hearts and mix with cream cheese, olives, celery, onion, salt, Tabasco and mayonnaise. Fold into thickened gelatin mixture. Pour into an 11x8x2-inch pan or an oiled 6-cup mold. Chill at least 2-3 hours or until set. Aspic can be prepared ahead. If desired, serve with a topping of additional mayonnaise seasoned with horseradish. Serve with homemade melba toast or crackers.

Yield: 24 servings

*Shrimp or crabmeat can be substituted for the artichoke hearts.*


# POLYNESIAN GINGER DIP

1 cup mayonnaise
1 cup sour cream
¼ cup finely chopped
    onion
¼ cup minced parsley
¼ cup chopped water
    chestnuts

2 tablespoons finely
    chopped crystallized
    ginger
2 cloves garlic, minced
1 tablespoon soy sauce
Salt to taste

Combine all ingredients and blend well. Chill. Serve with raw vegetables.

Yield: 2 cups

# RICH AND CREAMY EGGNOG

| | |
|---|---|
| 12 eggs, separated | 18 ounces whiskey |
| 12 rounded tablespoons | 1 quart whipping cream |
|    sugar | Nutmeg |

Beat egg yolks slowly. Add 6 tablespoons of sugar and continue beating until light and fluffy. Add whiskey slowly. Let stand overnight in refrigerator.

Beat egg whites with remaining 6 tablespoons of sugar until they form soft peaks. Whip cream. Fold whites into whiskey; then fold in cream. Sprinkle freshly grated nutmeg on top. This recipe may be doubled or halved.

Yield: 14 servings

# EGGNOG RICHARDSON

| | |
|---|---|
| 1 dozen eggs, separated | 1 fifth white rum |
| 1½-2 cups sugar | 2 quarts half and half |
| 1 quart cognac | 1½ quarts whipping cream |
| 1 pint Myers' rum | 1 cup confectioners' sugar |
| 1 quart bourbon | |

Beat egg yolks until light. Add sugar and continue beating until sugar is dissolved. Slowly add cognac. Myers' rum, bourbon and white rum.

Divide egg whites into 2 bowls. Beat egg whites in 1 bowl until stiff. Fold 2 quarts half and half into the egg whites. In another bowl, beat remaining egg whites until stiff.

In a separate bowl, beat whipping cream until thick. Gradually add confectioners' sugar and continue beating until stiff. Fold whipped cream mixture into remaining bowl of egg white mixture.

Add both bowls of egg white mixture to spirits mixture. Fold together gently. Chill at least 6 hours before serving.

Yield: 2½ gallons

# FROZEN DAIQUIRIS

2 6-ounce cans frozen
    lemonade, thawed
2 6-ounce cans frozen
    limeade, thawed
2 46-ounce cans pineapple
    juice

1 fifth light rum
1-1½ cups diluted orange
    juice
Mint, cherries or lemons

This recipe is better when prepared 2 days ahead. Combine all ingredients and stir well. Place in a large plastic container and cover tightly; put in freezer. Stir occasionally until all liquid is frozen. Garnish with mint, cherries or lemons before serving.

Yield: 20 servings

# PEACH DAIQUIRIS

3 ripe peaches, peeled,
    seeded and chopped
1 6-ounce can frozen pink
    lemonade or limeade

1 teaspoon sugar
½ cup white rum
1 tray ice cubes (14)

Combine ingredients in a blender and blend for 10 seconds.

Yield: 4 servings

# HAWAIIAN JULEP

1 46-ounce can Hawaiian
    Punch

1 12-ounce can frozen
    lemonade
1 cup or more bourbon

Mix all ingredients and freeze overnight. Stir before serving.

Yield: 6-8 servings

# RUM SWIZZLES

**2 18-ounce cans
unsweetened
pineapple juice
2 6-ounce cans frozen
orange juice, thawed
¼ cup fresh lime juice**

**12 drops Angostura Bitters
1 8-ounce jar maraschino
cherries
2 cups white rum
Pineapple chunks and mint
for garnish**

Combine pineapple juice and orange juice and mix well. Add lime juice, bitters and 3 tablespoons cherry juice; mix well. Refrigerate several hours until well chilled.

Before serving, add rum and mix well. Serve in tall glasses and garnish with cherries, pineapple and mint.

Yield: 8 servings

# VODKA SLUSH

**1 6-ounce can frozen
orange juice
2 6-ounce cans frozen
lemonade
2 6-ounce cans frozen
limeade**

**3½ cups water
2 cups vodka
1 cup sugar
Sprite**

Thaw frozen juices and mix together. Add water, vodka and sugar. Place in freezer for 48 hours, stirring occasionally.

Put ⅔ cup slush in an 8-ounce glass and fill with Sprite.

Yield: 12 servings

# GOLDEN SUNSET

**1 cup vanilla ice cream
2 tablespoons Galliano**

**½ cup orange juice
Grated orange rind**

Combine first 3 ingredients in a blender and blend until smooth. Garnish with orange rind.

Yield: 1½ cups

## VELVET COFFEE REFRESHER

1 quart coffee ice cream     ¼ cup crème de cacao
¼ cup brandy

Combine all ingredients in a blender. Blend until smooth.

Yield: 4 servings

*This is a wonderful after-dinner drink.*

## MCGUIRE'S IRISH COFFEE

Sugar                        ¼ teaspoon Schnapps or
1½ ounces Irish whiskey          Kahlúa
Strong hot black coffee      Irish green cherry
Chilled whipped cream

Into a stemmed glass or cup rimmed with sugar, pour 1½ ounces Irish whiskey. Fill to within ½ inch of the top with coffee. Add choice of mint (Schnapps) or chocolate (Kahlua). Cover surface to the brim with whipped cream. Top with green cherry.

Yield: 1 serving

## PEPPERMINT PATTI

1 cup hot chocolate          1 tablespoon crème de
1 tablespoon peppermint          menthe
    Schnapps                 Whipped cream
2 tablespoons crème de
    cacao

Mix first 4 ingredients in a large mug. Top with whipped cream.

Yield: 1 serving

# WASSAIL

1 gallon apple cider
10 cinnamon sticks
½ of a 6-ounce can frozen
   orange juice
1 teaspoon aromatic
   bitters
½ cup honey

¾ cup lemon juice
6 whole oranges
Whole cloves
1 teaspoon nutmeg
1 teaspoon allspice
1 pint fruit-flavored brandy
Cheesecloth bag

Stud oranges with cloves ½ inch apart. Place in a shallow pan with ½ inch water and bake at 325° for 30 minutes.

Place nutmeg and allspice in a cheesecloth bag.

Place oranges and other ingredients, except brandy, in a large covered pot and simmer for 30 minutes. Add brandy just before serving. Stir frequently and serve warm.

Yield: 20 cups

# CHAMPAGNE PUNCH

1 25.4-ounce bottle Cold
   Duck, chilled
1 25.4-ounce bottle pink
   champagne, chilled

4 cups cranberry juice
   cocktail, chilled
1 33.8-ounce bottle ginger
   ale, chilled

Combine all ingredients and keep cold with decorative ice ring in a punch bowl.

Yield: 3½ quarts

# AFTERNOON DELIGHT

1 fifth pale dry sherry or
   Dubonnet
3 6-ounce cans frozen
   lemonade, thawed

Crushed ice
Lemons, limes, cherries,
   mint for garnish

Mix wine and lemonade well in a pitcher. Pour over crushed ice in old-fashioned glasses. Garnish with lemon, lime, cherries or mint.

Yield: 8-10 servings

# SANGRÍA

1 large orange, sliced
1 lemon, sliced
1 lime, sliced
½ cup sugar
½ cup brandy

1 6-ounce can frozen pink
  lemonade, thawed
1 quart red wine
1 quart rosé wine
2 cups soda

Place orange, lemon, lime, sugar and brandy in a 3-quart pitcher and let sit 1-2 hours. Add remaining ingredients, except soda, and chill several hours.

Before serving, add soda. Serve with or without ice.

Yield: 3 quarts

# BOILED CUSTARD

1 tablespoon flour
¾ cup sugar
⅛ teaspoon salt
4-6 eggs, beaten

1 quart whole milk
1 teaspoon vanilla
Nutmeg

Mix dry ingredients; add beaten eggs and mix well. Heat milk slowly in a double boiler until hot, but not boiling. Add egg mixture to milk gradually, stirring constantly until it thickens sightly. Cool and add vanilla.

Serve hot or cold. Custard can be strained if there are any lumps. Top with freshly grated nutmeg.

Yield: 6-8 servings

*Boiled custard is a very old southern alternative to eggnog.*

# FRUIT PUNCH

1 6-ounce can frozen
  orange juice
2 6-ounce cans frozen
  limeade
1 6-ounce can frozen
  lemonade
1 46-ounce can pineapple
  juice

1 pint cranberry juice
  cocktail
2-4 cups cold water
2 quarts ginger ale, chilled
Fruit and fresh mint for
  garnish

Combine juices and add water. Stir well. Pour mixture into punch bowl. Add ice. Just before serving, slowly add ginger ale. Top with fruit ice ring and sprigs of mint or other fruit garnishes.

Yield: 30 servings

# HOT SPICED CIDER

2 quarts apple cider
4 cinnamon sticks
16 whole cloves
16 whole allspice

2 tablespoons packed
  brown sugar
1 lemon, sliced
1 orange, sliced

Combine all ingredients. Microwave for 14-15 minutes on HIGH or heat on stove until hot and bubbly (about 160°). Stir, remove spices and serve.

Yield: 8 cups

# HOT SPICED PUNCH

3 cups unsweetened
  pineapple juice
3 cups cranberry juice
  cocktail
2 cups water

1/3 cup brown sugar
1 1/2 teaspoons whole cloves
1 cinnamon stick
1/8 teaspoon salt

Combine juices, water and sugar. Pour into a percolator. Fill basket with cloves, cinnamon and salt. Perk.

Yield: 8 cups

*This punch is delicious and aromatic for Christmas.*

# CRANBERRY TEA

5 tea bags
2½ cups boiling water
¼ teaspoon cinnamon
¼ teaspoon nutmeg
⅔ cup sugar
1 pint cranberry juice
     cocktail

1½ cups water
½ cup orange juice
5 teaspoons lemon juice
Lemon or lime slices for
     garnish

Pour boiling water over tea bags and spices. Cover and let steep 5 minutes. Strain; stir in sugar. Cool and add remaining ingredients.

Serve hot or cold. Garnish with lemon or lime slices, if desired. Store in refrigerator.

Yield: 6-8 servings

# ORANGE JULIUS

½ of a 6-ounce can frozen
     orange juice
½ cup milk
½ cup water

2 tablespoons sugar
½ teaspoon vanilla
5-6 ice cubes

Combine all ingredients in a blender. Cover; blend until smooth.

Yield: 4 servings

*Orange Julius is a festive and nutritious way to begin the day.*

# MILK PUNCH

1¼ ounces bourbon
3 ounces half and half
1 teaspoon confectioners'
     sugar

⅛ teaspoon vanilla
Grated nutmeg

Combine ingredients in a cocktail shaker. Shake and strain into old-fashioned glass. Top with grated nutmeg.

Yield: 1 serving

# BLOODY MARY PITCHER

1 46-ounce can tomato
   juice
1½ cups vodka
4 tablespoons
   Worcestershire sauce
1 teaspoon salt

¾ teaspoon freshly ground
   pepper
2 teaspoons Louisiana hot
   sauce
2 teaspoons celery salt
2 teaspoons horseradish
Juice of 3 large limes

Combine all ingredients and chill several hours. Stir well and serve over ice. Garnish with lime slices.

Yield: 10 servings

# HOT BUTTERED RUM

1 pound butter, softened
1 16-ounce package light
   brown sugar
1 16-ounce package
   confectioners' sugar
2 teaspoons ground
   cinnamon

2 teaspoons ground
   nutmeg
1 quart vanilla ice cream,
   softened
Light rum
Whipped cream
Cinnamon sticks

Combine butter, sugar and spices; beat until light and fluffy. Add ice cream and stir until well blended. Spoon mixture into a 2-quart freezer container; freeze.

To serve, thaw slightly. Place 3 tablespoons of butter mixture and 1 jigger of rum in a large mug; fill with boiling water, stirring well. (Butter mixture can be refrozen.) Top with whipped cream and serve with a cinnamon stick.

Yield: 25 cups

# SOUPS
# AND
# SALADS

# SOUPS AND SALADS

**Chicken**
Chicken and Pasta Salad, 93
Chicken Salad Sensational, 91
Chinese Chicken Salad, 92
Curried Chicken Salad, 92
Marinated Chicken-Artichoke Salad, 91

**Congealed**
Apricot Molded Salad, 95
Apricot-Pineapple Salad, 95
Blueberry Mold, 96
Congealed Beet Salad, 96
Congealed Cucumber Mold, 97
Cranberry Chicken Mold, 90
Cranberry-Pineapple Salad, 98
Cranberry Salad, 99
Horseradish Salad, 97
Pineapple Pimento Mold, 98
Shamrock Salad, 99
V-8 Aspic, 101

**Dressings**
Greek Salad Dressing, 118
Hoolihan's Spinach Salad Dressing, 109
Italian Dressing, 119
Mayonnaise, 120
Poppy Seed Dressing, 119
Roquefort Dressing, 119
Russian Dressing, 120
Supreme Spinach Salad Dressing, 109
Sweet-Sour Dressing for Spinach Salad, 109
Tomato French Dressing, 120

**Fruit**
Frozen Fruit Salad, 100
Summer Fruit Salad, 100

**Relishes**
Brandied Cranberries, 121
Bread and Butter Pickles, 123
Cranberry Relish, 121
Dilled Cucumbers, 121
Pickled Squash, 124
Refrigerator Pickles, 123
Sauerkraut Relish, 122
Vidalia Sweet Onion Relish, 122

**Seafood**
Bayley's West Indies Salad, 107
Curried Shrimp Salad, 106
Shrimp Remoulade I, 106
Shrimp Remoulade II, 107

**Soups**
Artichoke and Oyster Soup, 75
Blythe Island Shrimp Mull, 88
Bouillabaisse, 89
Broccoli Soup, 75

Cauliflower Soup, 76
Combo Gumbo Josephs, 82
Country Chowder, 85
Cream of Celery Soup, 77
Creamy Cucumber Soup, 76
Creamy Potato Soup, 88
Diane's Crab Bisque, 79
Duck Gumbo, 83
Gazpacho Madrileño, 81
Ham and Cheese Chowder, 84
Jamie's Cream of Crab Soup, 80
Low Cal Borsch, 78
Microwave Seafood Gumbo, 84
Mushroom Soup, 80
Old-Fashioned Vegetable Soup, 87
Oriental Cucumber Soup, 78
Oyster Stew, 81
Seafood Gumbo, 85
Swedish Summer Soup Josephs, 79
Tomato Bisque, 86
Vichyssoise, 86
Zucchini Soup, 89

**Vegetable**
Ann's Potato Salad, 103
Apple Bacon Salad, 102
Basic Spinach Salad, 108
Broccoli Salad, 114
Brussels Sprouts Salad, 114
Cabbage-Pepper Slaw, 104
Caesar Salad, 101
Cracker Salad, 105
Creole Salad, 111
Cucumber Sunomono, 115
Curry Rice Salad, 103
Dorothea's Cole Slaw, 108
Easy Salad Niçoise, 115
Feta Spinach Salad, 110
Fresh Vegetables in Poppy Seed
    Marinade, 118
Gaspachee Salad, 90
Green Bean Salad, 113
Layered Salad, 116
Mandarin Lettuce Salad, 102
Marinated Green Beans, 113
Onion-Lima Salad, 116
Oriental Salad, 111
Pasta Salad, 94
Red Apple Spinach Salad, 110
Rice Salad, 104
Three-Bean Salad, 112
Tomatoes and Onions au Naturel, 112
Tomatoes Gervais, 117
Venetian Risotto Salad, 105

# ARTICHOKE AND OYSTER SOUP

6 green onions, finely
    chopped
4 cloves garlic, minced
3 tablespoons butter
3 tablespoons flour
3 cups chicken broth

1 15-ounce can artichoke
    hearts
2 tablespoons minced
    parsley
2 bay leaves
¼ teaspoon thyme
1 pint oysters, drained

In a 2-quart saucepan place butter, onion and garlic. Cook until onion is barely wilted. Stir in flour and cook until roux is golden. Pour in stock and stir until smooth. Add artichokes which have been rinsed, drained and chopped. Add parsley and seasoning. Cover and simmer for 30 minutes. Add well drained oysters and poach until oysters are plump.

Yield: 6 servings

# BROCCOLI SOUP

¼ cup vegetable oil
1 medium onion, diced
1 large potato, peeled and
    diced
⅔ cup diced celery (3-4
    stalks)

1 garlic clove, minced
¼ teaspoon cayenne
1 bunch broccoli, chopped
5 cups chicken broth
1 tablespoon dried basil
Salt to taste

Heat oil; add onion and sauté until tender. Add potato, celery, garlic and pepper. Cook for 10 minutes, stirring occasionally. Stir in broccoli, broth and basil. Cover and simmer 20 minutes. Place in blender or processor and purée. Return to saucepan and heat.

Yield: 12-14 servings

*Two cups cream or half and half can be added to make a creamed soup.*

# CAULIFLOWER SOUP

¼ cup butter
1 large white onion,
  minced
1 clove garlic, pressed
1 large head cauliflower,
  chopped

4½ cups chicken stock
Salt and pepper to taste
4 tablespoons half and half
Fresh parsley, minced
Croutons

Heat butter in large heavy saucepan. Add onion and garlic and sauté slowly until soft. Add cauliflower and chicken stock and simmer, covered, for 40 minutes.

Sieve the soup or purée in a blender. Return soup to the pan and season to taste.

Reheat soup prior to serving. Add half and half during last few minutes. Do not boil. Garnish with fresh parsley and croutons, if desired.

Yield: 4-6 servings

# CREAMY CUCUMBER SOUP

1 10¾-ounce can cream of
  celery soup
1 cup milk
1 small cucumber,
  chopped
1 small green bell pepper,
  chopped
¼ cup sliced pimento-
  stuffed olives

⅛ teaspoon Louisiana hot
  sauce
1 cup sour cream
1 tablespoon fresh lemon
  juice
Cucumber and paprika for
  garnish

Combine soup, milk, cucumber, green pepper, olives and hot sauce in blender or processor. Blend 2 minutes. Add sour cream and lemon juice; mix well. Chill at least 4 hours. Garnish with sliced cucumber and paprika.

Yield: 6-8 servings

# CREAM OF CELERY SOUP

1 large or 2 small bunches celery
2 medium carrots, peeled and diced
4 tablespoons butter
2 cups diced onion or leeks

3 tablespoons flour
6 cups hot chicken stock
Salt
White pepper
1 cup whipping cream

Dice enough of the celery stalks into ¼-inch pieces to make 1 cup; set remainder aside. Put the 1 cup diced celery and the diced carrots into a saucepan with 1 cup stock. Bring to boil and cook until barely tender, about 5 minutes. Drain and set aside. Chop remainder of celery.

Melt butter in a 4-quart saucepan over moderate heat. Add onion and sauté gently for 3-4 minutes; add flour and cook 1-2 minutes stirring constantly; do not brown. Add 5 cups chicken stock and whisk constantly until mixture boils, being sure to reach bottom of pan. Season with salt and pepper. Add chopped celery; reduce heat and simmer, partially covered, for 30 minutes.

When celery and onion are very tender, strain vegetables from the stock and purée them in blender until smooth. Add 1½ cups of the liquid stock and blend with the vegetables. Stir the mixture back into the stock.

Stir in the cream and the previously cooked carrots and celery.

Adjust seasoning to taste. Heat thoroughly.

Yield: 10 servings

# LOW CAL BORSCH

1 can Campbell's chicken
    broth
1 20-ounce can beets, with
    juice

1 medium cucumber,
    peeled and seeded
4 teaspoons cider vinegar
Sour cream

In food processor, using steel blade, combine first 4 ingredients. Process until smooth. Chill and serve with a spoonful of sour cream on top.

Yield: 4 servings

*This is a fast and easy soup.*

# ORIENTAL CUCUMBER SOUP

1 tablespoon dry sherry
2 tablespoons soy sauce
1 tablespoon cornstarch
½ pound lean pork, finely
    shredded
2 tablespoons vegetable oil
6 cups chicken broth

2 green onions, including
    tops, finely chopped
1 medium cucumber,
    peeled and finely
    chopped
Salt to taste
¼ teaspoon pepper
1 egg

Combine sherry, soy sauce and cornstarch. Mix and add pork, stirring to coat meat evenly. In a 6-8 quart Dutch oven, heat the oil over moderate heat and quickly brown the meat about 5-7 minutes. Add chicken broth, reduce heat, and simmer 10-12 minutes. Add remaining ingredients except the egg. Adjust seasoning to taste. Simmer 5 minutes longer; then bring to a boil.

In a small bowl, beat the egg well and set aside. Remove soup from the heat and add egg, stirring constantly. The egg white will turn into cooked shreds. Serve immediately.

Yield: 6-8 servings

*This makes an excellent first course for a Chinese dinner.*

# SWEDISH SUMMER SOUP JOSEPHS

1 tablespoon butter
1 tablespoon flour
4 carrots, thinly sliced
2 cups cauliflower, thinly
   sliced

½ pound snowpeas, tips
   and strings removed
1½ quarts chicken broth
2 egg yolks
¼ cup whipping cream
Parsley, chopped

In a large pot or Dutch oven, melt butter over low heat. Add flour; cook 5 minutes. Prepare vegetables. Add chicken broth to pot and bring to a gentle boil. Add carrots; simmer 5 minutes. Add cauliflower and snowpeas; simmer 5 minutes. Mix yolks and cream. Beat in a little hot broth; then add to the soup. Heat just to boiling point.

Serve immediately. Sprinkle each bowl with parsley.

Yield: 6-8 servings

*This is a great low-calorie soup at 63 calories per serving.*

# DIANE'S CRAB BISQUE

½ cup butter
½ cup chopped green bell
   pepper
½ cup chopped onion
2 green onions, chopped
¼ cup chopped parsley
3 cups sliced fresh
   mushrooms

¼ cup flour
2 cups milk
2 teaspoons salt
¼ teaspoon white pepper
Tabasco sauce
3 cups half and half
3 cups crabmeat
6 tablespoons dry sherry or
   4 tablespoons cognac

Sauté vegetables in butter for 5 minutes. Add flour and cook 1-2 minutes. Add remaining ingredients. Cook over low heat. Add sherry or cognac right before serving.

Yield: 8 servings

# JAMIE'S CREAM OF CRAB SOUP

| | |
|---|---|
| ¼ cup butter | 2 egg whites, beaten |
| 2 slices fresh ginger | ¼ cup half and half |
| 1 green onion, chopped | 2 tablespoons chicken |
| ½ cup crabmeat | stock |
| 1 tablespoon sherry | 1½ teaspoons cornstarch |
| ¼ teaspoon salt | Salt |
| 4 cups chicken stock | White pepper |

Melt butter; sauté green onion and ginger. Add crabmeat, sherry, salt and 4 cups chicken stock. Bring to a boil; then reduce to simmer.

Combine egg whites, half and half, 2 tablespoons chicken stock and cornstarch and gradually add to above mixture. Season to taste with salt and white pepper.

Yield: 4-6 servings

# MUSHROOM SOUP

| | |
|---|---|
| 1 pound mushrooms | 1 teaspoon salt |
| Juice of ½ lemon | ½ teaspoon freshly ground |
| 1 tablespoon butter | pepper |
| 2 tablespoons minced | 1 teaspoon cornstarch, |
| green onion | dissolved in 1 |
| ½ bay leaf | tablespoon water |
| ¼ teaspoon dried thyme | 1 tablespoon chopped |
| 2 cups whipping cream | fresh parsley for |
| 1½ cups chicken stock | garnish |

Thinly slice mushrooms and toss with lemon juice. Melt butter in large skillet over medium heat. Add green onion and sauté lightly. Add mushrooms, bay leaf and thyme; cook, stirring frequently, until liquid is completely evaporated, about 10 minutes.

Blend in cream, chicken stock, salt and pepper and bring to a boil. Reduce heat and simmer 20 minutes. Add dissolved cornstarch and simmer 10 minutes longer. Adjust seasoning to taste. Garnish with parsley.

Yield: 4-6 servings

# GAZPACHO MADRILEÑO

| | |
|---|---|
| 6 thin slices bread | 2 teaspoons salt |
| 3 very ripe tomatoes, medium to large, homegrown are best | 2 cloves garlic, pressed |
| | ½ teaspoon ground cumin |
| | 1 large tomato |
| 1 cucumber | 1 small cucumber |
| 4 tablespoons olive oil | 2 slices of bread |
| 2½ cups water | 1 green bell pepper |
| 2 tablespoons wine vinegar | |

Mix in a large bowl 6 slices bread, 3 tomatoes and 1 cucumber, all coarsely chopped. Add olive oil, water, vinegar, salt, cumin and garlic. Let soak 1 hour, then purée in blender until smooth. Refrigerate purée at least 1 hour. Serve in well-chilled bowls.

For garnishes, dice 1 large tomato, cucumber, green pepper and bread (crust trimmed), and put in small separate bowls. Place these on the table when the soup is served and invite each person to sprinkle some of each in his gazpacho.

Yield: 8-10 servings

*Each province of Spain has its own version of Gazpacho—the renowned Spanish Summer Soup—and this recipe is the one most favored by the people of Madrid.*

# OYSTER STEW

| | |
|---|---|
| 1 pint fresh oysters | ⅛ teaspoon Tabasco sauce |
| 4 tablespoons butter | 1 pint milk |
| ¾ teaspoon salt | 1 pint half and half |
| Pepper to taste | Paprika |

Drain oysters and reserve liquid. Melt all but 2 teaspoons butter and add salt, pepper and Tabasco sauce. Add oyster liquid to butter and seasonings; stir to blend. Add oysters and cook until edges begin to curl. Stir in milk and half and half and bring almost to a boil.

Serve in hot bowls. Top with remaining butter and sprinkle with paprika.

Yield: 4 servings

# COMBO GUMBO JOSEPHS

1 3-pound broiler-fryer
2 quarts water
½ cup bacon drippings
½ cup flour
4 stalks celery, chopped
2 medium onions, chopped
1 large green bell pepper, chopped
2 cloves garlic, minced
½ cup chopped fresh parsley
2 pounds shrimp, shelled
1 pound okra, sliced
2 tablespoons bacon drippings
4 medium tomatoes, peeled, seeded and coarsely chopped

2 tablespoons Worcestershire sauce
¼ teaspoon Tabasco sauce
1 bay leaf
2 teaspoons thyme
½ teaspoon rosemary
1 teaspoon salt
½ teaspoon pepper
1 teaspoon paprika
1 ham hock
1½ cups cubed cooked ham
4 crabs
2 teaspoons molasses
Juice of 1 large lemon
Hot cooked rice
Gumbo filé

Combine chicken and water in a Dutch oven. Bring to a boil; cover and simmer 1½ hours or until chicken is tender. Remove chicken from broth; cut into 1-inch cubes. Strain broth, reserving 6 cups.

Heat ½ cup bacon drippings in an 8-quart Dutch oven; stir in flour. Cook over medium heat, stirring occasionally, until roux is the color of a copper penny (20-30 minutes). Add celery, onion, green pepper, garlic and parsley; cook over low heat for 45 minutes. Mixture will be dry.

Peel shrimp, reserving shells. Refrigerate shrimp until needed. Combine shells and enough water to cover in a saucepan. Bring to a boil and boil 20 minutes. Strain shell stock, reserving 2 cups.

Cook okra in 2 tablespoons bacon drippings until tender, stirring occasionally. Add okra, chicken stock, shell stock and next 9 ingredients to roux mixture. Bring to a boil; reduce heat and simmer 2½ hours, stirring occasionally.

Add chicken, ham hock and cubed ham, crabs and molasses; simmer 30 minutes. Add shrimp and simmer 10 minutes longer. Stir in lemon juice.

Serve over rice. Add a small amount of filé to each serving, if desired.

Yield: 3½ quarts

*This is Julie Josephs' prize winning recipe.*

# DUCK GUMBO

6 wild ducks, skinned,
    with meat cut off
    bones in chunks
¼ cup vegetable oil
1½ pounds good rolled
    pork sausage, sliced
2 sticks butter
1 cup flour
3 quarts water
2 bay leaves
1 teaspoon crushed thyme

1 tablespoon
    Worcestershire sauce
1 clove garlic, minced
2 tablespoons parsley
Salt and pepper to taste
1 tablespoon gumbo filé
1 cup chopped celery
6 thinly sliced carrots
1 green bell pepper,
    chopped
1 cup chopped green onion

Cook duck in oil in a skillet; remove from heat, drain and set aside. Cook sausage; remove from heat and drain. In a 6-quart stockpot, melt butter and add flour to make the roux. Stir constantly over medium heat until the roux becomes a rich brown; be careful not to burn!

Add water and seasonings and mix well. Add vegetables; cover and reduce heat to simmer for 1-1½ hours, or until vegetables are tender and liquid has thickened slightly. Stir occasionally. Add the duck and sausage and simmer 30-45 minutes. Serve in bowls over rice.

This tastes better if made a day or two in advance.

Yield: 12 servings

# MICROWAVE SEAFOOD GUMBO

| | |
|---|---|
| ⅓ cup butter | ¼ teaspoon sugar |
| ⅔ cup chopped green onion | ¼ teaspoon thyme |
| | 1 bay leaf |
| ½ cup chopped celery | 6 drops Tabasco sauce |
| 2 cloves garlic, finely chopped | 2 1-pound cans tomatoes |
| | 1 teaspoon filé |
| 2 cups sliced okra or 1 10-ounce package frozen okra | 1½ cups cooked rice |
| | ½ pound raw, cleaned shrimp |
| 1½ teaspoons salt | ½ pound fresh crabmeat |
| ½ teaspoon pepper | |

Combine butter, onion, celery, garlic, okra and seasonings in a 3-quart bowl. Cover. Cook 12 minutes in microwave on HIGH, stirring occasionally to separate okra. Add tomatoes, shrimp and crabmeat. Recover and cook 16 minutes on MEDIUM HIGH, stirring occasionally. Remove bay leaf. Place ¼ cup rice in each of six soup bowls. Fill with gumbo. You may continue to simmer on 50% power or MEDIUM for a longer time to achieve more blending of flavors.

Yield: 6 servings

# HAM AND CHEESE CHOWDER

| | |
|---|---|
| 1 cup water | 3 tablespoons flour |
| Salt and pepper | 3 cups milk |
| 2 cups peeled and cubed potatoes | 1½ cups diced cooked ham |
| | 1½ cups (6 ounces) grated cheddar cheese |
| 3 tablespoons butter | |
| 1 cup chopped onion | Croutons |

Place water and salt in a small saucepan and bring to a boil. Add potatoes, reduce heat and cook 15 minutes or until potatoes are tender. Drain and reserve liquid. Set potatoes aside. Add enough water to potato liquid to make 1 cup and set aside.

Melt butter in a 3-quart Dutch oven; add onion and sauté until tender. Blend in flour and pepper. Stir in milk and potato liquid; cook over medium heat until mixture thickens and is bubbly. Add cooked potatoes and ham; heat gently. Remove from heat and stir in cheese. Garnish with croutons.

Yield: 6-8 servings

# SEAFOOD GUMBO

6 tablespoons flour
5 tablespoons bacon
   drippings
2 onions, finely chopped
1½ cups finely chopped
   celery
1 clove garlic, minced
1 16-ounce can tomatoes
1 8-ounce can tomato
   sauce
5-6 cups chicken stock

3 teaspoons salt
1 teaspoon pepper
3 pounds raw shrimp,
   peeled
2 pounds fresh crabmeat
2 cups fresh or 1 package
   frozen chopped okra
1 pint oysters
3 tablespoons
   Worcestershire sauce

Brown flour in bacon drippings to make roux using a large heavy skillet. Add onion, celery and garlic and brown 5 minutes. Roux should be a rich brown and must be stirred constantly to prevent burning.

Add tomatoes, tomato sauce, chicken stock, salt and pepper and simmer 1 hour over medium heat, stirring occasionally to prevent sticking. Add shrimp, crabmeat, oysters and okra and simmer 20 minutes. Add Worcestershire sauce and stir well. Serve over rice.

Yield: 2 quarts

# COUNTRY CHOWDER

1 meaty ham bone
6 cups water
4 cups diced potatoes
1 medium onion, chopped
1 1-pound can cream-style
   corn

2 cups milk
¼ cup minced fresh parsley
Salt and pepper
4 slices rye or whole wheat
   bread, diced
3 tablespoons butter

Break bone at joints and put into a kettle with 6 cups water. Bring to a boil; cover and simmer 1½ hours. Remove bone and trim off ham bits. Skim broth to remove fat. Add ham bits to broth with potatoes and onion. Bring again to a boil and cook until potatoes are tender. Add next 3 ingredients and salt and pepper to taste; heat.

Sauté bread cubes in butter until crisp and brown. Serve as garnish with soup.

Yield: 6 servings

# VICHYSSOISE

3 tablespoons butter
3 cups sliced leeks
3 tablespoons flour
6 cups hot water
1 tablespoon salt
White pepper to taste

4 cups peeled and sliced
   red potatoes
½ cup whipping cream
2-3 tablespoons minced
   fresh parsley and/or
   chives for garnish

Melt butter over moderate heat; stir in leeks. Cover and cook slowly for 5 minutes without browning. Blend in flour and stir over moderate heat for 2 minutes. Remove from heat, let cool a moment, then gradually beat in a cup of hot water. Blend thoroughly with flour and leeks; then stir in the rest of the water. Stir in salt, pepper and potatoes. Bring to a boil and simmer, partially covered, for 40 minutes or until vegetables are tender. Let cool slightly. Purée in blender until very smooth. Stir in cream and season with salt and white pepper to taste.

Cover and chill at least one full day. Garnish with chopped parsley and/or chives.

Yield: 8-10 servings

# TOMATO BISQUE

2 pounds ripe tomatoes or
   2 15-ounce cans
   tomatoes, chopped
1 medium onion, chopped
1 tablespoon butter
1 bay leaf
1 heaping tablespoon
   brown sugar

2 teaspoons finely chopped
   fresh basil or 1
   teaspoon dried basil
2 whole cloves
1 teaspoon salt
½ teaspoon pepper
2 cups half and half
1 cup milk
Chopped fresh chives for
   garnish

Peel and seed tomatoes. Sauté onion in butter and add chopped tomatoes, bay leaf, sugar, basil, cloves, salt and pepper. Simmer, stirring occasionally, until tomatoes are throughly cooked, about 25 minutes. Remove bay leaf and cloves and transfer mixture to blender or food processor. Purée and strain. Add cream and milk and heat thoroughly. Sprinkle with chives.

Yield: 6 servings

# OLD-FASHIONED VEGETABLE SOUP

*Stock:*

1 pound lean beef, cubed
2 tablespoons butter
2 pounds marrow bones
3 quarts water
1 bay leaf

1 cup celery leaves
2 teaspoons salt
2 carrots, pared and sliced
2 onions, sliced

Brown meat in 2 tablespoons butter in a large heavy pot. Add marrow bones and water and bring to a boil. Cook a few minutes; skim surface of water. Add bay leaf, celery leaves, 2 teaspoons salt, sliced carrots and onion. Simmer 1½-2 hours. Skim fat from surface. Strain and reserve meat. (Stock may be prepared ahead and kept in refrigerator or freezer.)

*Soup:*

¼ cup butter
2 cups diced carrots
2 cups diced onion
2 cups diced celery
2 1-pound cans tomatoes
2 cups cubed potatoes

1 10-ounce package frozen
  peas or lima beans
1 teaspoon salt
2 tablespoons chopped
  parsley

Heat ¼ cup butter in a large heavy pot over low heat. Add diced carrots, onion and celery. Cook 5 minutes, stirring occasionally. Add stock, tomatoes, potatoes, peas or beans, meat and 1 teaspoon salt. Bring to a boil; simmer 30 minutes or until vegetables are tender. Add parsley. Adjust seasoning to taste. For added appeal to children you can add ½-1 cup broken, thin spaghetti or alphabet noodles.

Yield: 8-10 servings

## BLYTHE ISLAND SHRIMP MULL

2 quarts water
2 16-ounce cans whole
   tomatoes
1 10½-ounce can tomato
   soup
1 cup chopped onion
2 cloves garlic, sliced
1 whole lemon, sliced
1 cup diced salt pork
1 cup chopped onion
½ cup butter
1 cup chopped celery

1 teaspoon celery seed
15 drops Tabasco sauce
1 12-ounce bottle ketchup
2 tablespoons
   Worcestershire sauce
¼ teaspoon allspice
¼ teaspoon curry powder
½ cup sliced mushrooms
5 pounds peeled raw
   shrimp
1 cup sherry
½ cup butter

Into a heavy Dutch oven put water, tomatoes, tomato soup, 1 cup chopped onion, garlic and lemon. Brown salt pork and additional cup of chopped onion in ½ cup butter in a skillet; then add to mixture in Dutch oven. Add celery, celery seed, Tabasco, ketchup, Worcestershire, allspice, curry powder and mushrooms and simmer for 2 hours. Add shrimp and cook gently 1 hour. Add sherry and ½ cup butter just before serving. Serve over rice.

Yield: 20 servings

## CREAMY POTATO SOUP

4 cups peeled, cubed
   potatoes
1 cup celery, ¾-inch slices
1 cup chopped onion
2 cups water
2 teaspoons salt
1 cup milk
1 cup whipping cream

3 tablespoons butter,
   melted
2 tablespoons fresh parsley
½ teaspoon caraway seeds
⅛ teaspoon pepper
Fresh chopped parsley for
   garnish

Combine potatoes, celery, onion, water and salt in a large Dutch oven. Simmer, covered, about 20 minutes or until potatoes are tender.

Mash mixture once or twice with a potato masher or fork, leaving some vegetable pieces whole. Stir in remaining ingredients; return to heat and cook, stirring constantly until soup is thoroughly heated. Garnish with parsley.

Yield: about 7 cups

# BOUILLABAISSE

4 cups sliced onion
1 tablespoon minced garlic
2 cups olive oil
1 cup chopped celery
4 potatoes, cubed
6 carrots, cut into 1-inch
pieces
3 16-ounce cans whole
tomatoes, chopped
3 8-ounce cans tomato
sauce
4 cups sherry
9 cups water
2 tablespoons salt

2 3-inch strips orange peel
2 teaspoons dried thyme
2 bay leaves
2 tablespoons paprika
2 pounds crabmeat
2 pounds scallops
4-6 pounds raw shrimp,
peeled and deveined
3 scamp or snapper fillets,
cut into 1-inch pieces
6 lobster tails, cleaned and
cut into 1-inch pieces
Hot cooked rice

In a 16-quart stock pot, sauté onion and garlic in olive oil. Stir in celery, potatoes, carrots, chopped tomatoes, tomato sauce, sherry and water. Bring to a boil, then reduce heat to simmer. Season with salt, orange peel, thyme, bay leaves and paprika. Simmer, covered, for 2-3 hours. One hour before serving, add crabmeat, scallops, shrimp, fish and lobster. Adjust seasonings. Serve over rice.

Yield: 25 servings

# ZUCCHINI SOUP

4-5 medium zucchini,
thinly sliced
3-4 medium white onions,
thinly sliced
1 quart milk

1 pound Velveeta cheese,
grated
2 teaspoons salt
15 drops Tabasco sauce
Pepper to taste

Steam sliced vegetables until tender. Purée vegetables until smooth.

Pour milk into saucepan and heat slowly. Add grated cheese to milk. Simmer until cheese melts. Add vegetables. Add Tabasco sauce, salt and pepper to taste. Simmer 30 minutes.

Yield: 8 servings

*This soup freezes beautifully.*

# GASPACHEE SALAD

6 hardtack (rock hard sea
    biscuits)
4 medium tomatoes
3 white onions
4 medium cucumbers,
    peeled

2 large green bell pepper
1 quart mayonnaise
    (Hellmann's or
    homemade)
Salt
Paprika

Soak hardtack in water until they are very soft. This takes about 2 hours. Press water out of hardtack and put bread into colander. Slice tomatoes and cucumbers. Chop onion and bell pepper.

Use a large, deep container and spread a layer of hardtack over the bottom. Cover with plenty of mayonnaise and salt generously. Next, layer overlapping slices of tomato. Sprinkle with salt and cover with a thin layer of mayonnaise. Then layer onion, bell pepper and cucumber. Cover with plenty of mayonnaise and salt. Repeat entire process. Top with a layer of hardtack and mayonnaise. Garnish with paprika and bell pepper rings. Refrigerate at least 6 hours. Serve cold.

Yield: 14 servings

# CRANBERRY CHICKEN MOLD

1 envelope unflavored
    gelatin
1/4 cup cold water
2 16-ounce cans whole
    cranberry sauce
1 8-ounce can crushed
    pineapple, drained
1/2 cup chopped walnuts

1 envelope unflavored
    gelatin
1/4 cup cold water
1 cup mayonnaise
1/2 cup evaporated milk
2 1/2-3 cups diced chicken
1 cup diced celery
Salt and pepper

Soften 1 envelope of gelatin in cold water; dissolve over hot water. Break up cranberry sauce with fork. Add cranberry sauce, pineapple and walnuts to gelatin. Pour into mold and chill until congealed.

Dissolve remaining gelatin as before. Combine mayonnaise and milk in a large bowl. Blend in gelatin. Add remaining ingredients and salt and pepper to taste. Spoon over cranberry layer. Chill until congealed. Top with mayonnaise.

Yield: 8 servings

# MARINATED CHICKEN-ARTICHOKE SALAD

1 chicken, cooked, boned and cubed
1 cup drained salad olives
1 14-ounce can artichoke hearts, drained and sliced
1 medium red onion, sliced
½ large green bell pepper, sliced
½ cup coarsely chopped celery
½ pound fresh mushrooms, sliced
½ cup sliced ripe olives

In a medium mixing bowl, combine chicken, salad olives, artichoke hearts, onion, bell pepper, celery, mushrooms and ripe olives.

*Dressing:*
¼ cup Wesson oil
¼ cup olive oil
¼ cup wine vinegar
Salt and pepper

Whisk 2 oils and vinegar together. Season to taste with salt and pepper. Toss with chicken mixture and marinate in refrigerator for several hours.

Yield: 8 servings

# CHICKEN SALAD SENSATIONAL

3 cups diced, cooked chicken
1½ cups diced celery
3 tablespoons lemon juice
1½ cups seedless green grapes
¾ cup slivered almonds, toasted

*Dressing:*
1 cup mayonnaise
¼ cup half and half
1½ teaspoons salt
⅛ teaspoon pepper
1 teaspoon dry mustard
1 hard-boiled egg, sliced
Chopped fresh parsley

Combine chicken, celery and lemon juice and chill at least 1 hour. Add grapes and almonds. Mix ingredients for the dressing and combine with chicken mixture. Garnish with egg and parsley, if desired.

Yield: 6-8 servings

# CHINESE CHICKEN SALAD

6 chicken breasts
1 head lettuce, shredded
3 green onions, thinly
   sliced
1 3-ounce can chow mein
   noodles
¼ cup slivered almonds,
   toasted
2 tablespoons sesame
   seeds, toasted

Cover chicken with boiling salted water and cook until tender, about 25 minutes. Drain and cool. Skin and bone chicken and cut into strips.

Combine chicken, lettuce, onion, noodles, almonds and sesame seeds in a large bowl. Set aside.

*Dressing:*
2 tablespoons sugar
2 teaspoons salt
¼ teaspoon pepper
¼ cup vegetable oil
¼ cup cider vinegar

Combine sugar, salt, pepper, oil and vinegar. Mix well and pour over chicken mixture. Toss lightly. Serve immediately.

Yield: 8-10 servings

# CURRIED CHICKEN SALAD

2 cups diced cooked
   chicken
½ cup diced celery
3 hard-boiled eggs,
   chopped
1 9-ounce jar chutney
1 cup shelled peanuts
½ cup raisins
½ cup mayonnaise
2 teaspoons curry powder
Salt

Toss all ingredients together. Chill several hours and serve on crisp lettuce.

Yield: 4-5 servings

# CHICKEN AND PASTA SALAD

*Chicken:*

1 small hen or fryer (about 3 pounds)
1 small onion, chopped
5 stalks celery, chopped

1 small green bell pepper, chopped
Salt and pepper
½ teaspoon lemon juice
½ cup mayonnaise

Cook hen with onion, ½ cup celery, bell pepper, salt and pepper. Cool, bone and skin chicken; dice for salad. Stir in 1 cup celery, mayonnaise and lemon juice.

*Dressing:*

¼ cup plus 2 tablespoons cider vinegar
⅔ cup plus 3 tablespoons olive oil
1 teaspoon salt

1 teaspoon sugar
1 teaspoon paprika
⅛ teaspoon Tabasco sauce
¼ teaspoon garlic powder

Shake ingredients together in covered jar or mix in processor.

*Pasta:*

1 7-ounce package vermicelli or other pasta

Lawry's Seasoned Salt
Tabasco sauce

Cook, as directed, in boiling salted water; drain; mix with dressing. Add Lawry's salt and Tabasco to taste. Marinate overnight.

Mix chicken with marinated pasta and refrigerate overnight again.

Yield: 8-10 servings

*Chicken and Pasta Salad travels well, making it a good dish for a picnic or boating trip.*

# PASTA SALAD

8 ounces fettuccini
5 fresh asparagus spears
1 2½-pound chicken,
   cooked, boned and
   chopped
2 zucchini, thinly sliced
¼ pound fresh mushrooms,
   sliced
1 2-ounce jar pimento,
   drained and chopped
½ cup finely chopped green
   onion

½ cup mayonnaise
1 clove of garlic, crushed
2 tablespoons tarragon
   vinegar
1 teaspoon curry powder
¼ cup finely chopped
   parsley
¼ cup chopped fresh basil
Lettuce
Cherry tomatoes
Freshly grated Parmesan
   cheese

Cook fettuccini according to package directions. Drain and cool. Blanch asparagus spears for 2 minutes. Drain and cut into bite-sized pieces. In a large bowl, combine chopped chicken, fettuccini, asparagus, zucchini, mushrooms, pimento and green onion.

In a small bowl, mix together mayonnaise, garlic, vinegar, curry powder, parsley and basil. Pour over salad and toss well. Chill thoroughly. To serve, allow salad to come to room temperature. Serve in a shallow bowl lined with lettuce leaves and garnish with cherry tomatoes and freshly grated Parmesan cheese.

Yield: 8-10 servings

*For a delicious variation, cooked shrimp may be substituted for the chicken.*

# APRICOT MOLDED SALAD

1 28½-ounce jar spiced
    peaches (not pickled
    peaches)
1 3-ounce package apricot-
    flavored gelatin

1 10-ounce jar maraschino
    cherries, drained and
    chopped
1 cup chopped pecans
3 oranges, peeled, seeded
    and sectioned

Drain peaches and reserve juice. Mash peaches. Measure juice and if necessary add water to obtain 1½ cups liquid. Heat to boiling and dissolve gelatin. Add the rest of the ingredients to the dissolved gelatin. Pour into a 2-quart rectangular baking dish and chill overnight. Slice into squares and serve on lettuce with a dab of mayonnaise on top.

Yield: 8-10 servings

# APRICOT-PINEAPPLE SALAD

1 6-ounce package orange-
    flavored gelatin
2 cups boiling water
1 20-ounce can crushed
    pineapple, drained,
    juice reserved

1 17-ounce can apricots,
    drained and chopped,
    juice reserved
100 miniature
    marshmallows

Drain pineapple and apricots and reserve 1 cup juice from each can of fruit. Mix gelatin with boiling water and ½ cup of each juice, reserving remaining juice for topping. Add fruit and marshmallows. Pour into a 2-quart dish and chill until set.

*Topping:*
2 eggs
½ cup sugar
2 tablespoons flour
2 tablespoons butter
½ cup pineapple juice

½ cup apricot juice
1 cup frozen whipped
    topping, thawed
1 cup grated cheddar
    cheese

Cook, eggs, sugar, flour, butter and juices until thick. Cool and add whipped topping. Spread over top of congealed fruit mixture. Top with grated cheese. Keep chilled until served.

Yield: 16 servings

*This topping is unusual and good on any congealed fruit salad.*

# BLUEBERRY MOLD

2 3-ounce packages
    raspberry-flavored
    gelatin
2 cups boiling water
⅛ teaspoon salt
1 cup sour cream

Juice of ½ lemon
1 8-ounce can crushed
    pineapple, drained,
    juice reserved
1 17-ounce can
    blueberries, drained,
    juice reserved

Dissolve gelatin in boiling water. Measure strained pineapple juice and add enough blueberry juice to make 1 cup. To dissolved gelatin add juices and salt. Let mixture stand about 5 minutes, or until consistency of syrup; then whip with a whisk or egg beater. Add sour cream and whip again. Add lemon juice and fold in pineapple and blueberries. Pour into a greased 1-quart mold and chill until set.

Yield: 8-10 servings

# CONGEALED BEET SALAD

1 16-ounce can diced or
    shredded beets
1 8-ounce can crushed
    pineapple
1 3-ounce package lemon-
    flavored gelatin
1 tablespoon horseradish

½ teaspoon salt
2 teaspoons grated onion
1 tablespoon vinegar
1 teaspoon sugar
1 cup diced celery
Sour cream
Sliced stuffed olives

Drain beets and pineapple, reserving juices. Add water to make 1¾ cups liquid. Bring to a boil and add gelatin. When gelatin is dissolved, add horseradish, salt, onion, vinegar and sugar. Chill until mixture begins to thicken. Fold in beets and pineapple; stir in celery, if desired. Pour into a 13x9x2-inch pan. Chill several hours or overnight.

Top with a thin layer of sour cream and slices of stuffed olives.

Yield: 10-12 squares

*The horseradish and pineapple really spice up the beets! For a different flavor, serve salad topped with whipped cream mixed with mayonnaise instead of sour cream and olives.*

# CONGEALED CUCUMBER MOLD

1 3-ounce package lime-
   flavored gelatin
1 cup hot water
½ teaspoon salt
½ teaspoon grated onion

1 tablespoon vinegar
1 cup shredded cucumber
   with seeds removed
Mayonnaise
Sour cream

Dissolve gelatin in hot water and add seasonings. Chill until it begins to set. Fold in cucumber and pour into mold. Serve with a mixture of mayonnaise and sour cream.

Yield: 4 servings

# HORSERADISH SALAD

1 3-ounce package lime-
   flavored gelatin
1 3-ounce package lemon-
   flavored gelatin
2 cups boiling water
1 20-ounce can chilled
   crushed pineapple,
   drained
1 12-ounce carton cottage
   cheese

1 cup mayonnaise
1 cup finely chopped
   pecans
4 tablespoons horseradish
3 tablespoons lemon juice
¼ teaspoon salt
1 14-ounce can sweetened
   condensed milk

*Topping:*
  ½ cup mayonnaise
  ½ cup sour cream
  1 teaspoon horseradish

Dissolve gelatin in boiling water and cool. Add pineapple. In separate bowl combine cottage cheese with mayonnaise until smooth and add to gelatin mixture. Add all other ingredients and stir until mixture begins to congeal. Pour into mold or 13x9x2-inch pan and refrigerate overnight. For topping, combine mayonnaise, sour cream and horseradish. Place individual servings on lettuce and top with a spoonful of topping mixture.

Yield: 12 or more servings

# PINEAPPLE PIMENTO MOLD

1 6-ounce package lemon-
   flavored gelatin
¾ cup sugar
1 8-ounce can crushed
   pineapple
1 8-ounce jar pimento
   cheese

1 cup chopped pecans
1 cup chopped ripe olives
1 8-ounce carton whipping
   cream
Sour cream and pimento
   for garnish

Dissolve gelatin in boiling water according to package directions. Add sugar, pineapple and pimento cheese and stir over low heat until dissolved. Remove from heat; add pecans and olives. Cool slightly. Whip cream and fold into gelatin mixture. Pour into a 13x9x2-inch glass dish which has been sprayed with vegetable spray, or use other mold of your choice. Decorate each serving with sour cream and pimento, if desired.

Yield: 15 servings

# CRANBERRY-PINEAPPLE SALAD

2 3-ounce packages lemon-
   flavored gelatin
3 cups boiling water
1 16-ounce can cranberry
   sauce

1 cup crushed pineapple,
   drained
½ cup chopped pecans

Dissolve gelatin in boiling water. Beat cranberry sauce with mixer on low speed. Add cranberry sauce, pineapple and pecans to gelatin. Pour into an 12x8x2-inch pan and chill until firm.

Yield: 12 servings

# CRANBERRY SALAD

2 3-ounce packages cherry-
    flavored gelatin
3 cups boiling water
1 cup sugar
½ pound fresh cranberries,
    rinsed

1 navel orange
1 8-ounce can crushed
    pineapple
½ cup chopped nuts

Dissolve sugar and gelatin in boiling water. Finely chop cranberries and whole orange in food processor or blender. Fold into gelatin mixture along with pineapple and nuts. Pour into 6-cup mold and chill overnight.

Yield: 12 servings

# SHAMROCK SALAD

1 3-ounce package lime-
    flavored gelatin
¼ teaspoon salt
1 cup boiling water
1 16-ounce can pears,
    drained and cut into
    chunks, syrup reserved

Ginger ale or water
1 tablespoon lemon juice
2 3-ounce packages cream
    cheese, softened
½ teaspoon grated candied
    ginger

Dissolve gelatin and salt in boiling water. Measure pear syrup and add water or ginger ale to make ¾ cup liquid. Add to gelatin with lemon juice. Measure 1¼ cups into a 1-quart mold which has been sprayed with vegetable spray. Chill until set, but not firm.

Beat cream cheese until creamy. Add remaining gelatin mixture gradually, beating until smooth. Add ginger and chill until very thick. Fold in pears and spoon into mold on top of the clear gelatin layer. Chill overnight or until firm.

Yield: 4 cups or 8 servings

# FROZEN FRUIT SALAD

*Dressing:*

| | |
|---|---|
| ¼ **cup sugar** | **1 egg** |
| ½ **teaspoon salt** | **2 tablespoons vinegar** |
| 1½ **tablespoons flour** | ¾ **cup pineapple juice** |

Combine dressing ingredients in a saucepan. Cook over low heat until thick and smooth, stirring constantly. Cool before adding to fruit.

*Salad:*

| | |
|---|---|
| **3 ripe bananas, mashed** | **1 10-ounce package frozen** |
| **1 cup diced canned** | **strawberries, sliced** |
| **pineapple** | **1 cup whipping cream,** |
| **1 cup diced canned pears** | **whipped** |

Combine fruit and dressing and fold in whipped cream. Pour into a 12x8x2-inch pan or paper-lined muffin tins and freeze until firm. Thaw for 20 minutes before serving. Garnish each serving with mint, a strawberry or a cherry.

Yield: 12 servings

# SUMMER FRUIT SALAD

| | |
|---|---|
| **1 cantaloupe, peeled and** | **2 bananas, peeled and cut** |
| **cubed or made into** | **into** ¼**-inch slices** |
| **melon balls** | **1 cup strawberries, halved** |
| **1 20-ounce can pineapple** | **1 6-ounce can frozen** |
| **chunks and juice** | **orange concentrate,** |
| **1 unpeeled apple, cubed** | **thawed** |
| **2 peaches, peeled and cut** | **Any other good fruits in** |
| **into wedges** | **season** |

Layer fruits in a large glass bowl in order given. Spoon orange juice concentrate on top. Cover and chill 6-8 hours or overnight.

Yield: 8-10 servings

# CAESAR SALAD

1-2 cloves garlic
6 tablespoons olive or
    vegetable oil
1 cup croutons
6 cups mixed salad greens
4 tablespoons lime juice
1½ teaspoons
    Worcestershire sauce
1 teaspoon freshly ground
    pepper
½ teaspoon salt
1 1-minute coddled egg
4 tablespoons grated
    Parmesan cheese or
    crumbled bleu cheese
    or a combination of
    both
8 anchovy fillets

Quarter garlic into oil in a small bowl and let stand several hours at room temperature. Wash greens and dry thoroughly. Tear into bite-sized pieces; place in large bowl and refrigerate.

At serving time remove garlic from the oil. In another small bowl beat 3 tablespoons of the oil, lime juice, Worcestershire, pepper, salt and egg. To coddle egg: place in boiling water; remove pan from heat; remove egg from water after 1 minute.

Add cheese to the greens. Pour dressing over greens and toss lightly. Add croutons to remaining oil, toss to coat well and immediately remove from the oil. Add croutons to the greens and toss lightly. Decorate with anchovies, if desired. Serve immediately.

Yield: 4-6 servings

# V-8 ASPIC

1½ cups V-8 juice
1 3-ounce package lemon-
    flavored gelatin
Juice of one lemon
1 teaspoon Worcestershire
    sauce
½ teaspoon salt
¼ cup sliced pimento-
    stuffed green olives
1-2 tablespoons grated
    onion
⅓ cup chopped celery
⅓ cup chopped green bell
    pepper
⅓ cup chopped cucumber

Heat V-8 juice, add gelatin and stir until dissolved. Add lemon juice, Worcestershire and salt. Chill until mixture begins to thicken. Fold vegetables into thickened gelatin mixture. Pour into 6 ½-cup individual molds or an 8x8x2-inch pan.

Yield: 6 servings

# APPLE BACON SALAD

2-3 cloves garlic, minced
⅔ cup vegetable oil
½ pound sliced bacon
1 head red leaf or romaine
    lettuce, or fresh
    spinach
3 red apples
2 teaspoons lemon juice

½ cup grated Parmesan
    cheese
1 bunch green onions,
    sliced
1 cup croutons
½ teaspoon pepper
¼ teaspoon salt
1 raw egg

Prepare ahead: Add minced garlic to oil. Let stand several hours.

Cook bacon until crisp; drain and crumble. Tear lettuce into bite-sized pieces. Dice unpeeled apples into oil and add lemon juice. Add remaining ingredients and toss with lettuce.

Yield: 6-8 servings

# MANDARIN LETTUCE SALAD

½ head red leaf lettuce
½ head iceberg lettuce
1 11-ounce can mandarin
    oranges, drained and
    chilled
1 medium red onion, thinly
    sliced and separated
    into rings

1 green bell pepper, sliced
    into rings
½-1 cup walnut halves
Fresh mushrooms, sliced
Avocado, sliced

Mix lettuces, oranges, onion and pepper rings. Sliced fresh mushrooms and/or sliced avocado are also nice additions. Toss with dressing just before serving. Top with walnuts.

*Dressing:*
    ⅓ cup vegetable oil
    ⅓ cup cider vinegar
    2 tablespoons sugar
    ½ teaspoon basil
    Garlic salt to taste

Mix all ingredients in a jar and shake.

Yield: 6 servings

# ANN'S POTATO SALAD

6-8 medium potatoes,
  peeled
4-6 eggs, hard-boiled
6-8 small sweet pickles

1 small carrot, peeled
1 medium onion, peeled
1 stalk celery

Boil potatoes until soft but not mushy; grate on a medium grater. Grate eggs, pickles and carrot on fine grater. Finely chop onion and celery. Toss all vegetables lightly with a spoon until well mixed.

*Dressing:*
1 cup mayonnaise
3 tablespoons vinegar
3 tablespoons sweet pickle
  juice

½ teaspoon salt
½ teaspoon sugar
2-3 grinds black pepper
⅛ teaspoon paprika

Place all ingredients for dressing in a covered jar and shake well. Combine dressing with vegetables and stir well.

Yield: about 10 servings

# CURRY RICE SALAD

2 7-ounce packages curry
  rice
2 chicken bouillon cubes
¾ cup chopped green bell
  pepper

8 green onions, chopped
16 stuffed olives, sliced
1 cup mayonnaise
1 cup marinated artichoke
  hearts, quartered
1 tablespoon curry powder

Cook rice according to directions, adding bouillon cubes to water. Drain.

In a large bowl, combine rice, bell pepper, onion and 10 olives. Add mayonnaise and stir well. Add artichoke hearts, then curry to taste. This should be chilled overnight to blend flavors. When ready to serve, garnish with remaining olives.

Yield: 12-15 servings

*Shrimp can be added for a main dish.*

# RICE SALAD

1 cup chicken stock
1 cup water
1 teaspoon salt
1 cup uncooked rice
1 cup thinly sliced
    zucchini
¾ cup chopped green bell
    pepper
½ cup thinly sliced green
    onion
½ cup thinly sliced
    radishes

½ cup thinly sliced black
    olives
1 14-ounce can artichoke
    hearts, drained and cut
    into eighths
½ cup of any of the
    following: fresh broccoli,
    fresh green beans, green
    peas, yellow squash

*Dressing:*
¾ cup olive oil
3 tablespoons wine vinegar
2 cloves garlic, minced
½ teaspoon dry mustard

1 teaspoon salt
½ teaspoon pepper

Cook rice in chicken stock, water and salt. Rinse with cold water and set aside to drain well. Beat dressing ingredients together until well combined. To the rice, add zucchini, pepper, onion, radishes, olives and artichoke hearts. Combine well. Add dressing and adjust seasonings to taste. Chill well before serving. Rice Salad can also be molded.

Yield: 6-8 servings

# CABBAGE-PEPPER SLAW

4 cups coarsely shredded
    cabbage
1 cup chopped green bell
    pepper
1 teaspoon salt
¼ teaspoon pepper
2 tablespoons sugar

1 teaspoon celery seed
2 tablespoons tarragon
    vinegar
1 teaspoon dry mustard
½ cup mayonnaise,
    preferably homemade

Combine first 6 ingredients in a large bowl. Mix vinegar, dry mustard and mayonnaise; add to cabbage mixture. Chill overnight.

Yield: 6-8 servings

# VENETIAN RISOTTO SALAD

1 10-ounce package frozen
   peas
1 cup converted rice
1 tablespoon olive oil or
   vegetable oil
2½ cups water
1 teaspoon salt
¾ cup Italian dressing

¼ cup grated Parmesan
   cheese
½ pound mushrooms,
   sliced
4 green onions with tops,
   sliced
1 2-ounce jar pimentos,
   drained and diced

Cook peas according to package directions and drain well. Cook rice in oil in a large saucepan over low heat, stirring constantly, about 5 minutes or until golden. Add water and salt. Stir and bring to a boil. Cover tightly and cook over very low heat for 20 minutes. Remove from heat and let stand until all water is absorbed, about 5 minutes. Pour into a large bowl.

Stir dressing and cheese into hot rice. Cover and chill thoroughly.

Add remaining ingredients and toss. Chill at least 1 hour before serving.

Yield: 8-10 servings or about 8 cups

# CRACKER SALAD

1 16-ounce box Saltines
   crackers
6 hard-boiled eggs,
   chopped
4 small to medium sweet
   pickles, finely chopped
20 pimento-stuffed green
   olives, finely chopped

1 heart of celery, chopped
1 20-ounce can whole
   tomatoes, drained and
   chopped
1 green bell pepper, finely
   chopped
2 cups mayonnaise

Crumble crackers in a bowl. Add eggs, pickles, olives, celery, tomatoes and bell pepper. Mix together. Add mayonnaise and stir well. Chill before serving.

Yield: about 15 servings

*Cracker salad comes from the Louisiana Bayou country and is a good alternative to potato salad.*

# CURRIED SHRIMP SALAD

1⅓ cups Minute Rice
1⅔ cups water
½ teaspoon salt
½ cup French dressing
¾ cup mayonnaise
1 tablespoon minced onion
¾ teaspoon curry powder

⅛ teaspoon pepper
½ teaspoon salt
½ teaspoon dry mustard
1 cup diced celery
1⅓ cups cooked frozen
  peas, chilled
1 pound shrimp, cooked,
  peeled and deveined

In a saucepan cook rice with water and salt according to package directions. Toss cooked rice in French dressing and cool. About 1 hour before serving, mix in a large bowl mayonnaise; onion, curry powder, pepper, salt and dry mustard. Add celery, peas and rice. Toss. Add shrimp, toss and chill. Serve on a bed of lettuce.

Yield: 4 servings

# SHRIMP REMOULADE I

¼ cup tarragon vinegar
2 tablespoons horseradish
  mustard
½ teaspoon salt
¼ teaspoon cayenne
  pepper
1½ teaspoons paprika
1 tablespoon ketchup

1 clove garlic, minced
½ cup vegetable oil
¼ cup finely chopped green
  onion
¼ cup finely chopped
  celery
2 pounds shrimp, cooked,
  peeled and deveined

Combine all ingredients except shrimp and blend thoroughly.

Pour over shrimp and marinate several hours or overnight.

Serve on a bed of lettuce.

Yield: 8 servings

# SHRIMP REMOULADE II

1½ cups mayonnaise,
    preferably homemade
½ cup prepared mustard
¼ teaspoon garlic salt
½ cup minced onion
¼ teaspoon sugar
Salt and pepper
1 teaspoon horseradish
½ teaspoon celery seed
2 teaspoons Worcestershire
    sauce
2 tablespoons lemon juice
2 pounds shrimp, cooked,
    peeled and deveined
Lettuce
2 tablespoons capers

Combine all ingredients except shrimp, lettuce and capers. Salt and pepper to taste. Chill at least 1 hour, preferably overnight.

Serve over shrimp on a bed of lettuce. Garnish with capers.

Yield: 4 servings

# BAYLEY'S WEST INDIES SALAD

1 pound fresh white lump
    crabmeat
1 medium white onion,
    finely chopped
Salt and pepper
4 ounces vegetable oil
3 ounces cider vinegar
4 ounces ice water

Place a layer of onion in the bottom of a 1-quart glass or ceramic bowl, then add a layer of crabmeat. Salt and pepper to taste. Continue layering until crabmeat is completely used. Pour oil over crabmeat, then vinegar, then water. Cover and refrigerate several hours. Toss before serving.

Yield: 4-6 servings

*Drain and serve on lettuce leaves as a salad, or with crackers as an appetizer.*

# DOROTHEA'S COLE SLAW

1 large head green cabbage
3 medium onions
1 tablespoon sugar
1 teaspoon prepared
    mustard
1 cup vinegar

1 cup vegetable oil
1 teaspoon celery seed
⅔ cup sugar
1½ teaspoons salt
Pepper

Shred cabbage and onions together.

Mix in saucepan 1 tablespoon sugar, mustard and vinegar. Bring to a boil; remove from heat and add oil. Bring to a second boil.

To cabbage-onion mixture add celery seed, ⅔ cup sugar, salt and pepper to taste. Pour hot dressing over cabbage and mix thoroughly. Chill well, preferably overnight. Drain before serving.

Yield: 10-12 servings

# BASIC SPINACH SALAD

10 ounces-1 pound fresh
    spinach
4 green onions and tops,
    sliced
8-10 fresh mushrooms,
    sliced

2 hard-boiled eggs,
    chopped, sliced or
    quartered
4 slices bacon, fried crisp
    and crumbled

*Interesting additions:*
    1 8-ounce can sliced water
        chestnuts, drained
    1 cup fresh sprouts

Combine prepared spinach and onion (and sprouts, if desired) in a large salad bowl. Sprinkle sliced mushrooms (water chestnuts, if desired), egg and bacon on top. Just before serving, add dressing of your choice and toss.

Yield: 6-8 servings

# SWEET-SOUR DRESSING
# FOR SPINACH SALAD

½ cup vegetable oil
¼ cup vinegar
1 tablespoon
    Worcestershire sauce

½ cup brown sugar
⅓ cup ketchup

Mix all ingredients well and chill. Just before serving, shake dressing and toss with salad ingredients.

Yield: dressing for 1 spinach salad

# SUPREME SPINACH SALAD DRESSING

1 cup vegetable oil
5 tablespoons red wine
    vinegar
4 tablespoons sour cream
1½ teaspoons salt
½ teaspoon dry mustard
2 tablespoons sugar

Coarsely ground black
    pepper
2 teaspoons chopped
    parsley
2 cloves garlic, pressed or
    minced

Mix all ingredients at least 6 hours before using.

Yield: dressing for 6-12 servings of salad

# HOOLIHAN'S SPINACH SALAD DRESSING

1 tablespoon sugar
1½ tablespoons minced
    onion
4 tablespoons Dijon
    mustard
1½ tablespoons salt

⅔ cup vinegar
⅔ cup warm water
1 teaspoon Worcestershire
    sauce
Tabasco sauce
2 cups vegetable oil

Mix sugar, onion, mustard, salt, vinegar and water. Add remaining ingredients and mix well. Serve with basic spinach salad or any other green salad.

Yield: dressing for 12-15 servings of salad

# RED APPLE SPINACH SALAD

10 ounces-1 pound fresh
  spinach
1 red apple, unpeeled
4 slices bacon, fried crisp
  and crumbled

½ cup frozen orange juice
  concentrate, thawed
¾ cup mayonnaise

Dice apple. Mix orange juice concentrate and mayonnaise. Just before serving, mix spinach and apple; pour dressing over salad and top with bacon.

Yield: 4-6 servings

*This is a delicious and unusual dressing which would also be good with fruit. Recipe makes about twice as much dressing as is needed for this salad.*

# FETA SPINACH SALAD

4 cups fresh spinach
½ cup cooked white rice
2 tablespoons pimento, cut
  into ¼-inch pieces
1 small cucumber, thinly
  sliced
2 ounces feta cheese,
  crumbled

3 green onions and tops,
  sliced
4 Greek olives (or black
  olives)
2 hard-boiled eggs,
  quartered

Mix spinach with rice, pimento, cucumber, cheese, onion and olives. Either mix in eggs or save them for a garnish.

*Dressing:*
½ teaspoon dry mustard
¼ cup wine vinegar
1½ tablespoons water (or
  oil, if desired)

½ teaspoon chopped
  capers
½ teaspoon minced parsley
½ teaspoon seasoned salt
⅛ teaspoon pepper

Dissolve mustard in a little vinegar by rubbing with the back of a spoon. Put all ingredients into a small covered jar and shake. Add about ¼ cup dressing to salad, toss and serve at once. Refrigerated dressing keeps well.

Yield: 2 servings

# ORIENTAL SALAD

1 cup bean sprouts
1 16-ounce can Chinese
  vegetables, drained
1 pound fresh spinach
6 slices bacon

1 cup thinly sliced water
  chestnuts
3 tablespoons sesame
  seeds

Soak bean sprouts and Chinese vegetables in cold water several hours until crisp. Drain thoroughly. Wash spinach, remove tough stems and dry thoroughly. Chill. Fry bacon until crisp.

*Dressing:*

1 cup sesame or peanut oil
½ cup soy sauce
4 tablespoons lemon juice
3 tablespoons grated onion
1½ teaspoons sugar
1 teaspoon pepper

1 tablespoon
  Worcestershire sauce
1 tablespoon vinegar
2 tablespoons ketchup
1 tablespoon bacon
  drippings

Combine oil, soy sauce, lemon juice, onion, sugar, pepper, Worcestershire, vinegar, ketchup and bacon drippings in a jar; shake well and let stand at least an hour. Lightly toast sesame seeds in a 350° oven for 15 minutes.

To assemble salad, arrange spinach in a salad bowl; add bean sprouts and Chinese vegetables; then add water chestnuts. Top with sesame seeds and crumbled bacon. Pour dressing over salad and toss thoroughly.

Yield: 12 servings

# CREOLE SALAD

8 small unpeeled zucchini,
  thinly sliced
4 tomatoes, chopped
1 green bell pepper, finely
  chopped
1 avocado, peeled and
  cubed

1 small onion, grated, or 3
  green onions, chopped
1 teaspoon sugar
1 teaspoon salt
½ teaspoon ground pepper

Toss all ingredients together. Leave at room temperature for 1 hour to blend flavors. Serve at room temperature.

Yield: 8 servings

# THREE-BEAN SALAD

1 16-ounce can wax beans, drained
1 16-ounce can green beans, drained
1 16-ounce can kidney beans, rinsed and drained
½ cup sugar
½ cup olive oil
½ cup chopped green bell pepper
½ onion, cut in rings
½ teaspoon tarragon
½ teaspoon basil leaves
2 tablespoons dried parsley
½ teaspoon dry mustard
½ cup vinegar

Mix all ingredients thoroughly and refrigerate in covered bowl several hours or overnight. Stir several times while marinating. Serve chilled.

Yield: 12-16 servings

# TOMATOES AND ONIONS AU NATUREL

4 large tomatoes
1 small Bermuda onion (about ½ pound)
½ cup vegetable oil
2 tablespoons lemon juice
½ teaspoon dried oregano leaves
½ teaspoon salt
⅛ teaspoon pepper
1 tablespoon chopped parsley
Cucumbers

Peel and slice tomatoes and onion. In a serving dish, alternate rows of tomato and onion slices.

Combine oil, lemon juice, oregano, salt and pepper. Pour over tomato and onion slices. Refrigerate, covered, at least 1 hour. Sprinkle with parsley before serving. Cucumbers can also be added, if desired.

Yield: 4-6 servings

# GREEN BEAN SALAD

3 16-ounce cans French-
    style green beans
1 small red onion, chopped
Salt and pepper
3 tablespoons vegetable oil
3 tablespoons lemon juice
1 cup sour cream

½ cup mayonnaise
1 teaspoon lemon juice
1 teaspoon horseradish
Bacon, fried crisp and
    crumbled
Parsley
Paprika

Drain green beans and add chopped onion. Season with salt and pepper. Marinate in oil and 3 tablespoons lemon juice for 2 hours. Drain.

Add sour cream, mayonnaise, 1 teaspoon lemon juice and horseradish. Chill at least 4 hours (preferably 24 hours). Garnish with bacon, parsley and/or paprika.

Yield: 12 servings

*Salad can be served as a stuffing for tomatoes.*


# MARINATED GREEN BEANS

1 pound fresh green beans
2 tablespoons vegetable oil
2 tablespoons olive oil
2 tablespoons vinegar
1 clove garlic, pressed

1 tablespoon prepared
    mustard
½ teaspoon savory or
    rosemary
½ teaspoon salt

Cook green beans for 10 minutes. Drain. Combine other ingredients and pour over beans. Marinate several hours or overnight. Serve cold.

Yield: 3-4 servings

# BROCCOLI SALAD

1 bunch broccoli
⅔ cup black olives,
    chopped
1 small onion, grated
5 hard-boiled eggs,
    chopped

1 cup mayonnaise
1 tablespoon lemon juice
½ teaspoon sugar
Salt and pepper
10 fresh mushrooms

Wash broccoli and cut into small pieces, discarding toughest stems. Add olives, onion and eggs. Mix together mayonnaise, lemon juice and sugar and pour over broccoli mixture. Season to taste with salt and pepper. Chill at least 1 hour. Just before serving, chop mushrooms and use for garnish.

Yield: 6-8 servings

# BRUSSELS SPROUTS SALAD

1 pint Brussels sprouts
2 medium unpared yellow
    squash or zucchini,
    sliced

¼ cup sliced green onion

Cook Brussels sprouts in boiling, salted water until tender but crisp (4-5 minutes). Plunge into cold water. Cut into wedges. Toss with green onion and squash.

*Dressing:*
1 cup vegetable oil
¼ cup fresh lemon juice
¼ cup cider vinegar
2 cloves garlic, crushed
2 teaspoons seasoned salt

1 teaspoon sugar
½ teaspoon dry mustard
½ teaspoon salt
¼ teaspoon crushed red
    pepper

Shake together all ingredients. Pour over sprouts and squash mixture. Refrigerate, covered, at least 4 hours but no longer than 24 hours, stirring occasionally.

Serve on plates lined with salad greens; garnish with tomato slices.

Yield: 8 servings

# CUCUMBER SUNOMONO

2 large cucumbers,
    unpeeled and thinly
    sliced
⅓ cup white or rice vinegar

4 teaspoons sugar
1 teaspoon salt
2 slices fresh ginger root

Mix all ingredients together and chill at least 1 hour in airtight container.

Yield: 4 servings

# EASY SALAD NIÇOISE

Garlic salad dressing,
    prepared from a dry
    mix
1 pound potatoes
1 pound fresh green beans
3 hard-boiled eggs
1 red onion

2-3 ripe tomatoes
1 green bell pepper
1 4-ounce can black olives
1 7-ounce can tuna
Boston or other mild leaf
    lettuce

Prepare dressing according to package directions using red wine vinegar and olive oil, if desired.

Cook potatoes in salted water until just tender, about 20 minutes. Drain and cool. Peel and slice about ¼ inch thick. Trim and wash beans. Cook whole in salted water until just tender, 5-10 minutes. Drain and cool 10 minutes. Put potatoes and beans into a shallow dish. Add ½ cup garlic dressing. Toss gently until coated. Refrigerate, covered, until well chilled.

Quarter eggs; slice onion thinly. Cut tomatoes into wedges and bell pepper into strips. Drain olives. Drain tuna and break into chunks.

To serve, arrange lettuce in a shallow dish. On lettuce arrange vegetables with tuna mounded in the center. Surround tuna with olives. Drizzle with additional dressing, according to taste. Serve well chilled.

Yield: 4 main dish servings

# LAYERED SALAD

4 stalks celery
3 small onions
4 large carrots
2 cucumbers

3 tomatoes
1 10-ounce package green
    peas, thawed

Slice all vegetables, except peas. Layer ingredients in a clear glass bowl (1½-quart with straight sides). Pour dressing over salad and refrigerate several hours or overnight.

*Sweet Basil Dressing:*
1 clove garlic
⅓ cup red wine vinegar
¼ cup tomato sauce
1½ tablespoons sugar

1½ teaspoons salt
1 teaspoon basil
¼ teaspoon dry mustard
1 cup vegetable oil

Mix all ingredients except oil in blender or food processor. With blender or processor on, slowly drizzle in oil.

Yield: 6-8 servings

# ONION-LIMA SALAD

2 10-ounce packages
    frozen baby lima beans
2 medium sweet Spanish
    onions, very thinly
    sliced (approximately
    4 cups)
1 cup sour cream

2 tablespoons cider vinegar
1 tablespoon sugar
1 teaspoon salt
¼ teaspoon white pepper
1 teaspoon horseradish
¼ cup chopped parsley

Cook limas according to package directions and drain well. Separate onion slices into rings and place in bowl with limas. Mix sour cream, vinegar, sugar, salt, pepper and horseradish. Fold gently into onions and limas. Marinate in refrigerator several hours. Serve very cold, sprinkled with parsley.

Yield: 6-8 servings

# TOMATOES GERVAIS

| | |
|---|---|
| 4 large or 8 medium tomatoes | 3-4 tablespoons half and half |
| Salt and pepper | 2 tablespoons chopped chives |
| 2 3-ounce packages cream cheese, softened | ½ cup vinaigrette dressing |
| | Watercress for garnish |

Peel tomatoes by placing them in a bowl and covering with boiling water for 10 seconds. Drain and cover with cold water. Remove skins. Cut a slice from the bottom of each tomato, reserving slices. Scoop out seeds with a spoon, removing the core. Drain tomatoes; then lightly season insides with salt.

Soften cheese by beating with electric mixer. Add enough half and half to make a smooth, light cream. Season well with salt, pepper and half the chives. Fill tomatoes with cream cheese mixture, piling high; then replace slices on a slant. Arrange on serving plate. Spoon a little of the vinaigrette dressing over tomatoes, reserving some to be added at the table. Cover and chill up to 2 hours. Just before serving, sprinkle with remaining chives and garnish with watercress, if desired.

*Vinaigrette Dressing:*

| | |
|---|---|
| ¼ teaspoon salt | 2 tablespoons vinegar or lemon juice, divided |
| ¼ teaspoon pepper | ¼ teaspoon dry mustard |
| 6 tablespoons olive oil, divided | 1 clove garlic |

Combine salt, pepper, 1 tablespoon oil, 1 tablespoon vinegar and mustard in a small bowl; beat with a wire whisk until smooth. Add 2 more tablespoons oil; beat well. Add remaining ingredients (3 tablespoons oil, 1 tablespoon vinegar and garlic). Store dressing in a covered jar. Shake well before using.

Yield: 4-8 servings

*Prepare in cherry tomatoes for an appetizer.*

# FRESH VEGETABLES
# IN POPPY SEED MARINADE

| | |
|---|---|
| 1 large bunch fresh broccoli | 1 green bell pepper, chopped |
| 1 small head cauliflower | 3 stalks celery, chopped |
| 8 large mushrooms, sliced | |

Cut broccoli and cauliflower into flowerets. Combine all vegetables and toss lightly.

*Marinade:*

| | |
|---|---|
| 1 cup sugar | 1½ cups vegetable oil |
| 1 teaspoon dry mustard | 1 small onion, grated |
| 1 teaspoon salt | 2 tablespoons poppy seeds |
| ½ cup cider vinegar | |

Combine ingredients, mix well and pour over vegetables. Chill at least 3 hours before serving.

Yield: 10-12 servings

*Poppy seed marinade is also good on fruit.*


# GREEK SALAD DRESSING

| | |
|---|---|
| ¾ cup Greek olive oil | 1 teaspoon oregano |
| ¼ cup red wine vinegar | 2 tablespoons fresh dill |
| ⅛ teaspoon dry mustard | weed or 1 teaspoon |
| 2 teaspoons Cavender's Greek Seasoning | dried dill weed |
| 1 teaspoon salt | Freshly ground black pepper |

Mix all ingredients in blender or food processor.

Yield: 1 cup

# ITALIAN DRESSING

1 package Good Seasons
   Italian dressing mix
¼ cup wine vinegar
⅔ cup vegetable oil

1 teaspoon soy sauce
1 egg white (whole egg
   may be used)
½ teaspoon dry mustard

Place all ingredients into a blender and blend until thickened. Use immediately or refrigerate. If necessary, thin with a small amount of water. Blend again before using, if needed.

Yield: 2 cups

# POPPY SEED DRESSING

1½ cups sugar
2 teaspoons dry mustard
2 teaspoons salt
⅔ cup cider vinegar

3 tablespoons grated onion
2 cups vegetable oil
3 tablespoons poppy seeds

In the food processor with steel blade, or in blender, place sugar, dry mustard, salt, vinegar and onion. Blend thoroughly. With machine running, gradually add oil. Continue processing until thick. Add poppy seeds and blend quickly. Dressing will keep for months in the refrigerator.

Yield: about 3 cups

# ROQUEFORT DRESSING

1 cup mayonnaise
2 cups sour cream
1 3-ounce package
   Roquefort or bleu
   cheese

1 tablespoon grated onion
Juice of ½ lemon

Mix all ingredients well and chill.

Yield: 3 cups

# RUSSIAN DRESSING

¾ cup sugar
2 cups ketchup
3 teaspoons vinegar
1 medium onion, finely
    grated

1½ cups vegetable oil
1 teaspoon salt
¼ teaspoon garlic salt
Celery salt
Seasoned salt

Combine all ingredients and season to taste. Mix well in a blender, processor or mixer. Refrigerate.

Yield: 1 quart

# TOMATO FRENCH DRESSING

1 cup condensed tomato
    soup
¾ cup vinegar
1 teaspoon salt
½ teaspoon paprika
1 tablespoon
    Worcestershire sauce

½ teaspoon pepper
⅓ cup sugar
1 teaspoon minced onion
1 teaspoon prepared
    mustard
1½ cups vegetable oil
1 clove garlic, minced

Combine all ingredients and blend well.

Yield: 1 quart

# MAYONNAISE

1 egg
1 teaspoon salt
1 tablespoon fresh lemon
    juice or vinegar

1 cup oil (combination of
    vegetable oil and olive
    oil)

Place egg, salt, lemon juice and ¼ cup oil in a blender. With blender on, slowly add remaining oil until mayonnaise is thick.

Yield: 1½ cups

# BRANDIED CRANBERRIES

4 cups fresh cranberries
2 cups sugar

⅓ cup fruit brandy (apricot, peach or pineapple)

Put 4 cups fresh cranberries into a 13x9x2-inch glass pan. Sprinkle evenly with sugar. Cover and bake at 350° for 1 hour. Stir carefully; then add ⅓ cup fruit brandy; stir again. Store in a covered container in the refrigerator.

Yield: 3 cups

# CRANBERRY RELISH

1 pound raw cranberries, rinsed
1½ cups water
1 navel orange, quartered and unpeeled

½ cup raisins
1 8-ounce can crushed pineapple
½ cup chopped pecans
2 cups sugar

Boil cranberries in water for 7-8 minutes. In a food processor, using the steel blade, process orange until very finely chopped. Add orange, raisins, pineapple, pecans and sugar to cranberries and cook together for 20 minutes. Store in refrigerator.

Yield: 2 pints

# DILLED CUCUMBERS

¾ cup sour cream
2 tablespoons minced onion
2 tablespoons vinegar
½ teaspoon salt
½ teaspoon dill weed

⅛ teaspoon pepper
2 medium cucumbers, peeled and very thinly sliced
Paprika

Mix sour cream, onion, vinegar, salt, dill weed and pepper. Fold in cucumbers. Chill 24 hours. Sprinkle with paprika before serving. Serve as a relish or salad.

Yield: 4-6 servings

# SAUERKRAUT RELISH

1 1-pound can sauerkraut,
    drained
1 large onion, chopped
½ cup chopped green bell
    pepper

1 12-ounce jar pimentos,
    drained and chopped
½ cup sugar
½ cup cider vinegar

Combine all ingredients and mix until well blended. Store in a tightly covered container in the refrigerator for 24 hours before serving. Drain well before serving.

Yield: 8-10 servings

*Sauerkraut Relish is also good as a salad.*

# VIDALIA SWEET ONION RELISH

1 gallon water
1 cup pickling salt
4 quarts sweet Vidalia
    onions, chopped
4 green bell peppers,
    chopped
1 large cabbage, chopped
    or shredded

4 tablespoons dry mustard
2 tablespoons turmeric
1 cup flour
4 cups sugar
2 teaspoons celery seed
1 quart Twelve Oaks red
    vinegar

Make a brine of one gallon cold water and one cup pickling salt. Pour over onion, pepper and cabbage and let stand overnight.

The next morning, scald vegetables in same brine water. Drain well. Mix dry mustard, turmeric, flour, sugar and celery seed. Add one quart vinegar and mix well. Pour vegetables into a large kettle. On low heat, cook until thick, stirring often. Seal in hot jars. Process in boiling water for 20 minutes.

Yield: 8-10 pints

# BREAD AND BUTTER PICKLES

7 pounds medium
    cucumbers, thinly
    sliced
8 small white onions,
    thinly sliced
1 large green bell pepper,
    cut into thin strips
1/2 cup salt
Cracked ice

4 cups vinegar
1 cup water
5 cups sugar
1 1/2 teaspoons turmeric
1/2 teaspoon ground cloves
2 tablespoons mustard
    seed
2 teaspoons celery seed

Combine cucumbers, onion and pepper in a large bowl; add salt; cover with ice. Mix thoroughly and let stand 3 hours. Drain. Combine remaining ingredients and bring to a boil. Add cucumber mixture and bring to a boil. Put into scalded jars and seal.

Yield: approximately 10 pints

# REFRIGERATOR PICKLES

12-15 cucumbers, thinly
    sliced
1 cup onion, thinly sliced
4 cups cider vinegar
4 cups sugar

1/2 cup salt
1 1/2 teaspoons turmeric
1 1/2 teaspoons celery salt
1 1/2 teaspoons dry mustard
    or mustard seed

Divide cucumbers and onion evenly among 4 quart jars. Heat remaining ingredients until sugar is dissolved. Pour over cucumbers and onion to cover. Store in refrigerator.

Yield: 4 quarts

*Here is the version of homemade pickles for cooks of all ages and skills!*

# PICKLED SQUASH

4 one pint jars with lids
   and seals, sterilzed
8 cups yellow squash,
   thinly sliced
2 cups yellow onion, thinly
   sliced
1½ tablespoons salt
2 cups white vinegar

3 cups sugar
2 teaspoons celery seed
2 teaspoons mustard seed
2 cups sweet green pepper,
   chopped
2 cups sweet red pepper,
   chopped

Combine squash and onion in large bowl; sprinkle with salt and set aside for one hour. Drain off liquid. Combine vinegar, sugar, celery seed, mustard seed and green and red peppers in a large saucepan. Bring to a boil. Pack jars with squash and onion to just below bottom of mouth. Pour boiling liquid over squash and onion. Seal and place in water bath for 5 minutes or seal and let stand undisturbed for 24 hours. Serve at room temperature or chilled.

Yield: 4 pints

# ENTRÉES

# ENTRÉES

**Beef**
A Very Special Lasagna, 166
Beouf Bourguignon, 160
Carpetbag Steak Josephs, 163
Chili, 171
Chinese Beef and Snow Peas, 170
Chuckwagon Stew, 171
Cincinnati Chili, 172
Country Brisket, 169
Grilled Steak Logs, 162
Heavenly Tenderloin, 161
Italian Spaghetti (Meatballs/Sausage), 168
Lasagna Florentine, 165
Manicotti, 167
Marinated Roast Beef, 163
Moussaka, 164
Peppered Steaks, 162
Reuben Casserole, 170
Sicilian Meat Roll, 169

**Chicken**
Baked Chicken Salad, 178
Cashew Chicken, 174
Cashew-Ginger Chicken, 175
Chicken-Crab Rolls, 173
Chicken Cumberland, 174
Chicken Fiesta, 186
Chicken Marengo, 182
Chicken Piccata, 183
Chicken/Sour Cream Sauce, 180
Chicken Teriyaki, 182
Chicken and Wild Rice, 179
Creamed Chicken/Corn Bread Ring, 176
Easy Chicken Kiev, 178
Enchiladas Suisse, 177
Garlic Sour Cream Chicken, 177
Italian Chicken, 181
Lemon Chicken, 184
Mozzarella Chicken, 180
Sherried Mushroom Chicken, 184
Spaghetti Caruso, 185
Tennessee Club Chicken, 179

**Game**
Doves in Red Wine, 197
Ducks in White Wine, 198
Quail and Wild Rice, 200
Smoked Herb-Seasoned Quail, 199

**Lamb**
Leg of Lamb de Luna, 193
Roast Leg of Lamb, 192

**Pork**
Crown Roast of Pork Valencia, 187
Fiesta Casserole, 188
Gingered Ham Steak, 189
Gulf Winds Pork Chops, 190
Herbed Pork Roast, 192
Orange Pork Chops, 189
Pork Chops Peasant Style, 188
Sausage and Wild Rice Supreme, 190
Sweet and Sour Pork, 191

**Savory Sauces**
Barbecue Sauce for Chicken, 202
Comeback Sauce, 202
Easy Hollandaise Sauce, 203
Flank Steak Marinade, 205
Horseradish Sauce, 202
Hot Mustard, 201
Marchand de Vin Sauce, 205
Mock Bernaise, 204
Mushroom Sauce, 204
Raisin Sauce, 205
Shish Kabob Wine Sauce, 205
Super Uncooked Barbecue Sauce, 201

Sweet-Hot Mustard, 201
Teriyaki Marinade, 206
Teriyaki-Pineapple Marinade, 206
Texas Meat Sauce, 200
Venison Marinade, 206

**Seafood**
Baked Crabs, 127
Baked Oysters, 143
Broiled Fish, 150
Char-Broiled Shrimp, 135
Coe's Crabs, 127
Company Crab Casserole, 129
Coquilles St. Jacques, 154
Crab and Artichoke Casserole, 128
Crab Florentine, 129
Crab Imperial, 131
Crab Supreme, 132
Crabmeat Pie, 128
Deviled Crabs, 130
Easy and Delicious Fish, 150
Fish Fillets India, 151
Flounder Florentine, 152
Fried Fish Pieces, 149
Fried Mullet, 149
Grilled King Mackeral Steaks, 151
Judson's Oysters, 148
Lemon-Wine Shrimp, 138
Mandarin Shrimp, 139
Oysters Bienville, 144
Oysters Bon Secour, 145
Oyster Fritters, 145
Oysters Rockefeller I, 146
Oysters Rockefeller II, 147
Parmesan Scampi, 139
Perfect Fried Oysters, 148
Polynesian Fish Dish, 153
Redfish, 153
Red Snapper/Sour Cream Dressing, 154
Red Snapper, Veracruz Style, 155
Scalloped Oysters, 146
Shrimp-Artichoke Casserole, 132
Shrimp in Beer Creole, 134
Shrimp Creole, 133
Shrimp Creole made with a Roux, 133
Shrimp de Jonghe, 138
Shrimp Destin, 136
Shrimp Florentine, 135
Shrimp Jambalaya, 137
Shrimp Jambalaya/Sausage and Bacon, 136
Shrimp Loaf, 137
Shrimp and Lobster Newburg, 157
Shrimp and Rice Casserole (Microwave), 140
Shrimp Rockefeller, 142
Shrimp Scampi, 140
Shrimp and Wild Rice Casserole, 141
Shrimp ans Zucchini Sauté, 143
Snapper in Velouté Sauce, 156
Spanish Paella, 158
Steamed Shrimp, 131
Stuffed Crab, 130
Sweet and Sour Shrimp, 141
Trout Amandine, 157

**Seafood Batters**
Perfect Shrimp Batter, 159
Tempura Batter, 159
Tempura Batter for Seafood, 159
World's Simplest Tempura Batter, 159

**Veal**
Veal Cordon Bleu, 194
Veal Marchello, 195
Veal Romano, 196
Veal Scallops Amandine, 194

# COE'S CRABS

2 dozen fresh blue crabs
1 pound raw shrimp,
  headed
6-8 ounces water
⅓ cup lemon juice or juice
  of 1 lemon
Worcestershire sauce
Cavender's Greek
  seasoning

1 head of garlic, each pod
  cut in half
½ cup butter or margarine
⅓-½ fresh jalapeño pepper,
  sliced
1 lemon or lime, sliced
Salt and pepper
5 fresh ears of corn
12 new potatoes

Clean crabs, remove claws and lightly crack. Layer whole crabs face down in a large pot; top with claws, then shrimp. Over this pour water and lemon juice. Liberally add Worcestershire, Cavender's and garlic. Slice butter and place on top; then complete layering with jalapeño pepper, lemon slices, salt and pepper. Cover pot and cook on high heat, steaming 20 minutes. Turn stove off and let set until ready to serve.

For complete meal, add 5 fresh ears of corn and 12 new potatoes. Place potatoes first in the bottom of the pot; then add corn, broken in half, standing upright. Then follow the original recipe.

Yield: 6 servings

*This is best when crabs are fresh out of the trap, cleaned and straight into the pot. Proper attire also adds flavor—bare feet and wet swim suit, towel optional. This is Gulf Coast at its finest!*

# BAKED CRABS

Fresh crabs, cleaned
Butter

Garlic salt
Worcestershire sauce

Preheat oven to 350°. Clean crabs by removing outer shell and insides but leaving legs. Place crabs, cavity-side up on a baking sheet with a dab of butter in each one. Sprinkle each with garlic salt and a dash of Worcestershire. Bake for 20-30 minutes.

Yield: 3-4 crabs per person

# CRAB AND ARTICHOKE CASSEROLE

1 16-ounce can artichoke
   hearts, drained
4 hard-boiled eggs,
   quartered
1½ cups fresh lump
   crabmeat
4 tablespoons butter
3 tablespoons flour
1 cup milk

¼ cup sauterne or dry
   sherry
½ cup grated Swiss cheese
2 teaspoons Worcestershire
   sauce
Salt and pepper
½ teaspoon curry powder
Parmesan cheese

Preheat oven to 350°. Cut artichokes in half. Put into a buttered casserole dish with eggs and crabmeat. Blend butter, flour and milk over low heat. Add wine, cheese, Worcestershire, salt, pepper and curry powder. Cook until slightly thickened. Pour over mixture in casserole. Sprinkle with Parmesan cheese. Bake for 30 minutes.

Yield: 5-6 servings

# CRABMEAT PIE

½ cup mayonnaise
3 tablespoons flour
3 eggs, beaten
⅔ cup milk
1 pound fresh lump
   crabmeat
8 ounces Swiss cheese,
   grated
⅓ cup chopped green
   onion

¼ cup chopped green bell
   pepper
4 slices bacon, cooked and
   crumbled
2 8-or 9-inch pastry shells,
   unbaked
½ cup grated Parmesan
   cheese

Preheat oven to 350°. Mix together mayonnaise, flour, eggs and milk. Add crabmeat, Swiss cheese, onion, bell pepper and bacon.

Pour into pastry shells. Sprinkle Parmesan cheese on top. Bake for 40-45 minutes.

Yield: 2 pies or 12 servings

# COMPANY CRAB CASSEROLE

4 tablespoons butter
3 tablespoons flour
1 tablespoon minced
    parsley
1 medium onion, minced
2 tablespoons minced
    green bell pepper
1 teaspoon dry mustard
1 teaspoon salt
1/4 teaspoon pepper
1 tablespoon sugar

2 tablespoons Madeira
    wine or dry sherry
1 cup half and half
1/8 teaspoon Tabasco sauce
2 hard-boiled eggs,
    chopped
1/2 cup sliced fresh
    mushrooms
1 pound fresh lump
    crabmeat
1/2 cup bread crumbs
Grated Parmesan cheese

Preheat oven to 425°. Melt butter, add flour and stir until smooth. Add parsley, onion, bell pepper, mustard, salt, pepper, sugar (if desired), wine, half and half and Tabasco. Stir until smooth. Cook until it thickens, stirring constantly, to prevent burning or lumping. Add eggs, mushrooms and crabmeat. Fold together gently to prevent breaking up crab lumps. Place into a 2-2½-quart buttered casserole or 8 individual crab shells or ramekins. Sprinkle with bread crumbs and Parmesan cheese. Bake for 25 minutes, until brown and bubbly.

Yield: 8 servings

# CRAB FLORENTINE

1 10-ounce package frozen
    chopped spinach
1 cup fresh claw crabmeat
1 8-ounce can tomato
    sauce
1 cup sour cream
1 cup grated mild cheddar
    cheese

1 tablespoon grated onion
1/2 teaspoon salt
1/8 teaspoon freshly grated
    nutmeg
Bread crumbs, buttered

Preheat oven to 350°. Cook spinach according to package directions. Drain well. Place in a greased baking dish or individual shells. Combine all other ingredients except bread crumbs and spoon over spinach. Top wtih buttered bread crumbs. Bake for 25 minutes.

Yield: 4-6 servings

# DEVILED CRABS

2 tablespoons chopped
onion
3 tablespoons butter
2 tablespoons flour
¾ cup milk
1 tablespoon lemon juice
1½ teaspoons dry mustard
1 tablespoon
Worcestershire sauce
½ teaspoon salt
⅛ teaspoon pepper
3 drops Tabasco sauce
1 egg, beaten
1 pound fresh crabmeat,
cartilage removed
Bread crumbs, buttered

Preheat oven to 400°. Sauté onion in butter. Add flour, stirring well.
Add milk gradually to make a smooth sauce. Add lemon juice, dry
mustard, Worcestershire, salt, pepper and Tabasco. Combine egg
with a small amount of hot mixture; then add back to the remaining
mixture. Fold in crabmeat. Put into shells and top with buttered
crumbs. Bake for 20-25 minutes.

Yield: 4-6 servings

# STUFFED CRAB

2 tablespoons butter
2 tablespoons flour
1 cup milk
1 pound crabmeat
1 green bell pepper,
chopped
4 sprigs parsley, chopped
½ onion, chopped
3 stalks celery, chopped
4 hard-boiled eggs,
chopped
1 tablespoon
Worcestershire sauce
Buttered bread crumbs
(approximately 8 thin
slices of bread)
1 cup mayonnaise

Preheat oven to 350°. Melt butter, add flour and stir in milk. Cook,
stirring constantly, until sauce is smooth and thick. Add crabmeat,
bell pepper, parsley, onion, celery, eggs, Worcestershire and half
of bread crumbs to the white sauce. Mix well. Add mayonnaise, mixing well. Fill crab shells with mixture and sprinkle tops with remaining bread crumbs. Bake for 20 minutes.

Yield: 6-8 servings

# CRAB IMPERIAL

4 tablespoons butter
4 tablespoons flour
2 cups milk
1 teaspoon salt
⅛ teaspoon pepper
½ teaspoon celery salt
⅛ teaspoon cayenne
⅛ teaspoon thyme
⅛ teaspoon garlic salt
1 egg yolk, beaten

1 cup soft white bread
   crumbs
2 tablespoons sherry
1 teaspoon minced onion
1 teaspoon minced parsley
1 pound fresh lump white
   crabmeat
¼ cup dry bread crumbs,
   buttered
Paprika

Preheat oven to 400°. Melt butter; add flour and blend. Gradually add milk, salt, pepper, celery salt, cayenne, thyme and garlic salt. Cook over low heat, stirring constantly until thickened. Add a little sauce to beaten egg yolk; then stir into remaining sauce. Cook and stir 2 minutes. Remove from heat.

Add soft bread crumbs, sherry, onion, parsley and crabmeat. Mix lightly. Pile into shells or a greased shallow baking dish. Top with buttered bread crumbs and dust with paprika. Bake for 10-15 minutes.

Yield: 4-6 servings

# STEAMED SHRIMP

Shrimp (½ pound per
   person)
Bay leaf

Salt
2-3 teaspoons liquid
   crab-boil

Rinse whole, head-on shrimp under a faucet. Place in a large pot, being careful not to shake off excess water. Add bay leaf, salt to taste and 2-3 teaspoons of liquid crab-boil, if desired.

Cover and cook over medium heat, stirring occasionally, until shrimp are very pink. Taste to see if done.

When cooked, drain liquid and run under cold water to stop cooking. Remove shrimp heads and shells. Serve hot or cold.

Yield: ½ pound per person.

*This is a great way to avoid overcooking your shrimp.*

# CRAB SUPREME

½ pound fresh mushrooms, sliced
1 medium onion, finely chopped
2 medium tomatoes, peeled and diced
4 tablespoons butter
½ cup half and half
2 tablespoons flour

¼ cup dry sherry
½-1 teaspoon salt
1 tablespoon Worcestershire sauce
¼ teaspoon pepper
2 pounds fresh lump crabmeat
½ cup bread crumbs, buttered

Preheat oven to 350°. Sauté mushrooms, onion and tomato in butter for 10 minutes. Mix half and half with flour to make a paste. Add to mushroom mixture. Cook until slightly thickened. Add sherry, salt, Worcestershire and pepper. Stir lightly into the crabmeat. Spoon into individual buttered ramekins or shells and top with crumbs. Bake for 15 minutes.

Yield: 8 servings

# SHRIMP-ARTICHOKE CASSEROLE

1 package frozen artichoke hearts, or 1 8½-ounce can, drained
1 pound shrimp, boiled and peeled
¾ pound fresh mushrooms
4 tablespoons butter, divided
2 tablespoons flour
1½ cups milk

1 tablespoon Worcestershire sauce
Salt
White pepper
3 tablespoons dry sherry
¼ cup grated Parmesan cheese
Paprika
Chopped parsley

Preheat oven to 375°. Arrange artichokes in a buttered 1-1½-quart baking dish with shrimp on top. Sauté mushrooms in 2 tablespoons of butter and put on top of artichokes and shrimp. Heat remaining 2 tablespoons butter, stir in flour and gradually add milk to make a smooth sauce. Add Worcestershire, salt, white pepper and sherry. Pour sauce over contents of baking dish and sprinkle with Parmesan cheese. Garnish with paprika and chopped parsley. Bake for 20 minutes.

Yield: 4 servings

# SHRIMP CREOLE

1 large onion, chopped
1½ tablespoons olive oil
1 16-ounce can tomatoes,
    chopped and
    undrained
1 15-ounce can tomato
    sauce
1 bay leaf

1 teaspoon parsley
½ teaspoon thyme
1 teaspoon salt
½ teaspoon black pepper
2 pounds raw shrimp,
    peeled
1½-2 green bell peppers,
    chopped

Sauté onion in olive oil until golden. Add tomatoes, tomato sauce, bay leaf, parsley, thyme, salt and pepper. Cook 20 minutes. Add shrimp and bell pepper and cook 10 minutes. Do not overcook shrimp. Serve over rice.

Yield: 6-8 servings

# SHRIMP CREOLE MADE WITH A ROUX

⅓ cup bacon drippings
¼ cup flour
½ cup chopped onion
½ cup chopped green bell
    pepper
½ cup chopped celery
1 cup water

1 8-ounce can tomato
    sauce
½ teaspoon thyme
1 bay leaf
⅛ teaspoon cayenne
1 lemon slice
1-1½ pounds raw shrimp,
    peeled

Heat bacon drippings and blend in flour. Cook over medium heat, stirring constantly, until brown. Add onion, bell pepper and celery. Cook, stirring constantly, for 2 minutes. Add water, tomato sauce, thyme, bay leaf, cayenne and lemon slice. Cover tightly and simmer for 20-30 minutes. Add shrimp and cook for approximately 10 minutes. Serve over rice.

Yield: 4 servings

# SHRIMP IN BEER CREOLE

½ cup sliced blanched
    almonds
1 tablespoon vegetable oil
7 tablespoons butter,
    divided
Salt and pepper
2 pounds raw shrimp,
    peeled
¼ cup chopped green
    onion

1 green bell pepper, cut
    into strips
½ pound mushrooms,
    sliced
1 tablespoon sweet
    Hungarian paprika
1 teaspoon tomato paste
1 cup light beer
¾ cup heavy cream
¼ cup sour cream

In a small skillet sauté almonds in oil and 1 tablespoon butter, tossing until they are golden. Drain the almonds on paper towels, sprinkle with salt and set aside.

In a saucepan cook 2 pounds shrimp in 4 tablespoons butter over medium heat; toss until they turn pink. Transfer shrimp and pan juices into a bowl and reserve; cover with buttered wax paper.

Add 2 tablespoons butter to the pan and sauté green onion and bell pepper until soft. Add mushrooms, paprika, salt and pepper; cook, tossing until mushrooms are tender. Stir in tomato paste, beer and reserved pan juices; cook over high heat until liquid measures ½ cup. Reduce heat to low and add cream, sour cream and shrimp. Arrange shrimp mixture on a heated platter and garnish with almonds. This can also be served over rice.

Yield: 6 servings

# CHAR-BROILED SHRIMP

3 pounds raw shrimp
1 cup olive oil
2 cloves garlic, crushed
1/3 cup chopped fresh
　　parsley

2 tablespoons fresh lemon
　　juice
1 teaspoon salt

Peel shrimp, leaving tails. Combine all other ingredients in a large bowl and add shrimp. Allow to marinate at least 8 hours.

When ready to cook, place shrimp on skewers and broil on a grill for 5 minutes, until shrimp turn white. Baste shrimp with marinade while cooking.

Yield: 4-6 servings

# SHRIMP FLORENTINE

1/4 cup finely chopped
　　onion
1/4 cup butter
1/4 cup flour
1 teaspoon salt
1/2 teaspoon dry mustard
2 cups milk
1/2 cup grated Swiss cheese
1 cup grated Parmesan
　　cheese

2 10-ounce packages
　　frozen chopped
　　spinach, cooked and
　　drained
1 8-ounce can water
　　chestnuts, drained and
　　sliced
1 1/2 pounds shrimp, boiled
　　and peeled
1 tablespoon lemon juice
Paprika

Preheat oven to 400°. Cook onion in butter until tender. Stir in flour, salt and dry mustard. Add milk. Cook, stirring constantly, until thickened. Remove from heat. Add Swiss cheese and stir until melted. Fold in half the Parmesan cheese.

Combine spinach and water chestnuts and spread in a greased, shallow 1 1/2-2-quart baking dish. Drizzle lemon juice over spinach. Add shrimp, then sauce; top with remaining Parmesan cheese. Garnish with paprika. Bake for 15-20 minutes or until hot.

Yield: 6 servings

# SHRIMP DESTIN

¼ cup chopped onion
2 teaspoons minced garlic
1 cup butter, melted
2 pounds large raw shrimp,
    peeled
1 teaspoon lemon juice
1 tablespoon white wine
½ teaspoon salt

Black pepper, coarsely
    ground
1 teaspoon dried whole dill
    weed
1 teaspoon chopped fresh
    parsley
3 French rolls, split
    lengthwise, or pita
    bread

Sauté onion and garlic in butter until tender. Add shrimp, lemon juice, wine, salt and pepper; cook over medium heat about 5 minutes, stirring occasionally. Stir in dill weed and parsley. Spoon mixture onto French rolls or into pita bread. Serve at once.

Yield: 4-6 servings

*Mixture can be served in individual ramekins for appetizers.*

# SHRIMP JAMBALAYA WITH SAUSAGE AND BACON

1 pound hot pork sausage
1 pound bacon
2 large onions, chopped
1 green bell pepper,
    chopped
3 tablespoons parsley
2 cloves garlic, chopped

2 teaspoons salt
½ teaspoon thyme
1 16-ounce can tomatoes,
    drained and chopped
2 pounds raw shrimp,
    peeled
1½ cups uncooked rice

Fry sausage and bacon. Remove and drain all but 2 tablespoons of fat. Add onion and bell pepper; cook until tender. Add parsley, bacon, sausage, garlic, salt, thyme and tomatoes (if desired); mix well.

Place shrimp over mixture; do not stir. Sprinkle rice over mixture and add water just to cover. Cover pan and bring to a boil; then lower heat. Cook for 30 minutes over very low heat. Remove from heat and stir; cover and cook 15 minutes. Stir well before serving.

Yield: 8 servings

# SHRIMP JAMBALAYA

1 green bell pepper,
   chopped
½ cup chopped onion
3 tablespoons olive oil
½ teaspoon salt
⅛ teaspoon sugar
¼ teaspoon cayenne
¼ teaspoon thyme

½ cup water
1 12-ounce can tomato
   juice
2 pounds raw shrimp
3 cups cooked rice
½ cup grated sharp
   cheddar cheese
Chopped parsley

Sauté bell pepper and onion in olive oil; add salt, sugar, cayenne, thyme, water and tomato juice. Cover and simmer for 2 hours.

Peel shrimp and add to sauce; cook 15 minutes. Combine shrimp sauce with the rice and place in a greased 11x7-inch bowl. Sprinkle with cheese and parsley. Serve immediately.

Yield: 4-6 servings

# SHRIMP LOAF

3 cups cooked rice
¼ cup chopped onion
½ cup chopped parsley
¼ cup chopped pimento
1 cup (about ¼ pound)
   grated sharp cheese

1½ teaspoons salt
1½ teaspoons pepper
2 eggs, beaten
2 cups milk
1 teaspoon Worcestershire
   sauce

Preheat oven 350°. Mix all loaf ingredients together. Pour into a greased 1½-quart square dish and bake for 45 minutes.

*Sauce:*

1 tablespoon butter
3 tablespoons flour
2 cups milk
1 teaspoon salt

1 teaspoon pepper
1 teaspoon lemon juice
2 cups shrimp, cooked,
   peeled and deveined

In a saucepan, melt butter and stir in flour. Slowly add milk, stirring constantly over low heat until quite thick. Add salt, pepper and lemon juice. Just before serving, add shrimp. Cut loaf into squares and pour sauce over each serving.

Yield: 8 servings

## SHRIMP DE JONGHE

2 pounds shrimp, cooked
    and peeled
½ cup butter, softened
½ cup seasoned bread
    crumbs
2 tablespoons sour cream
2 tablespoons chopped
    parsley

1 large garlic clove
1 teaspoon salt
½ teaspoon Worcestershire
    sauce
Coarsely ground pepper
2 teaspoons fresh lemon
    juice

Preheat oven to 450°. Layer shrimp in a buttered 1-quart casserole. In a food processor fitted with the steel blade, process butter, bread crumbs, sour cream, parsley, garlic, salt, Worcestershire, pepper and lemon juice until smooth. Crumble mixture evenly over shrimp and pat down with a spatula. Bake for 10 minutes or until bubbly and lightly browned.

Yield: 4 servings

## LEMON-WINE SHRIMP

2 pounds raw shrimp,
    peeled (leave tails on)
1 cup butter, melted
¼ cup fresh lemon juice

¼ cup Worcestershire
    sauce
1 cup white wine
Lemon-pepper marinade
Tony's Creole Seasoning

Arrange shrimp in a 13x9x2-inch pan. Pour melted butter over shrimp; turn shrimp to coat. Mix lemon juice, Worcestershire and white wine in a small mixing bowl; pour over shrimp. Season to taste with lemon-pepper marinade and Tony's Creole Seasoning. Allow shrimp to marinate at least 30 minutes.

Broil shrimp in oven until pink (5-10 minutes).

Yield: 4 servings

*Serve with French bread which can be dipped into the sauce. Shrimp are also good with corn-on-the-cob that has been cooked with crab-boil.*

# MANDARIN SHRIMP

2 tablespoons cornstarch
1 egg white
½ pound raw shrimp, peeled
⅓ cup sliced water chestnuts
1 cup Chinese pea pods
½ cup sliced fresh mushrooms
1 tablespoon dry sherry
1 tablespoon water
½ teaspoon sesame oil
¼ teaspoon salt
1 cup peanut oil
1 tablespoon minced green onion
Yellow rice

Combine 1 tablespoon cornstarch with egg white. Cut shrimp in half lengthwise and add to cornstarch mixture. Set aside.

Combine water chestnuts, pea pods and mushrooms and set aside.

Blend sherry, water, sesame oil, salt and 1 tablespoon cornstarch.

Have a bowl and strainer ready. Add 1 cup oil to wok and heat to 350°; then add shrimp, stir-frying about 2 minutes. Add vegetables and stir-fry 1 minute. Pour oil, shrimp and vegetables into the strainer to drain. Heat 1 tablespoon strained oil in wok. Add green onion and stir 10 seconds. Add shrimp mixture and sherry mixture, stirring about 30 seconds. Serve with rice.

Yield: 2 servings

# PARMESAN SCAMPI

24 large raw shrimp, peeled (leave tails on)
½ cup butter
3-4 cloves garlic, crushed
¼ cup ice water
¾ cup coarsely chopped fresh parsley
Salt and pepper
1 cup freshly grated Parmesan cheese

Butterfly the shrimp, leaving tail shells intact. Melt butter and stir in garlic, being careful not to burn. Add shrimp and cook, turning constantly, until pink. Add ice water and parsley; season to taste with salt and pepper. Simmer, covered, until parsley wilts. Sprinkle with cheese and heat until cheese melts.

Yield: 4 servings

# SHRIMP AND RICE CASSEROLE
## (MICROWAVE)

2 medium eggplants,
    peeled and diced
2 tablespoons water
½ teaspoon salt
½ cup butter, melted
2 cups chopped onion
½ cup chopped celery
½ cup chopped green
    onion
¼ cup chopped parsley

3 cloves garlic, minced
1 pound or more raw
    shrimp, peeled
2 cups cooked rice
2 teaspoons salt
2 teaspoons black pepper
¼ teaspoon cayenne, or
    less
Seasoned bread crumbs
Parmesan cheese

Place eggplant and salted water in a 2-quart dish. Cover with plastic wrap. Cook in microwave on HIGH for 7 minutes. Stir and drain; set aside.

Melt butter in a 3-quart casserole. Sauté onion and celery on HIGH for 5 minutes. Add green onion, parsley and garlic. Sauté on HIGH for 3 minutes. Stir in shrimp; mix well. Cover with wax paper and microwave on HIGH 10 minutes. Stir two times. Drain fat.

Add rice, eggplant, salt, pepper and cayenne. Stir to mix. Top with crumbs and Parmesan cheese. Cover. Microwave on MEDIUM for 5 minutes or until well heated.

Yield: 6-8 servings

# SHRIMP SCAMPI

1½ pounds raw shrimp,
    peeled
½ cup butter (no
    substitute)
3 cloves garlic, pressed

¼ cup fresh lemon juice
Salt and pepper
Tabasco sauce
Chopped parsley

Preheat oven broiler. Melt butter and sauté garlic; add lemon juice. Arrange shrimp in a single layer in a shallow pan and add several dashes of Tabasco, if desired. Pour garlic butter over shrimp and salt lightly; pepper to taste. Broil 2 minutes; turn shrimp and broil 2 more minutes. Using a slotted spoon, place shrimp on serving dish and sprinkle with parsley. Reserve garlic butter and serve separately.

Yield: 2-4 servings

# SHRIMP AND WILD RICE CASSEROLE

1½ pounds shrimp, boiled
   and peeled
1 can cream of mushroom
   soup
2 tablespoons chopped
   green bell pepper
2 tablespoons chopped
   onion
2 tablespoons butter,
   melted
1 tablespoon lemon juice

½ teaspoon Worcestershire
   sauce
½ teaspoon pepper
1½ cups cubed cheddar
   cheese
1 package Uncle Ben's
   Long Grain and Wild
   Rice, cooked
   according to directions

Preheat oven to 350°. Combine all ingredients and bake in a greased 1½-quart casserole. Bake for 30-35 minutes.

Yield: 6-8 servings

# SWEET AND SOUR SHRIMP

1¾ cups apple juice,
   divided
½ cup vinegar
¼ cup sugar
¼ cup ketchup
2 tablespoons vegetable oil
1 tablespoon soy sauce
¼ teapoon salt
½ cup diagonally sliced
   carrots

½ cup chopped green bell
   pepper
¼ cup chopped green
   onion tops
3 tablespoons cornstarch
¾ pound shrimp, boiled
   and peeled
2 cups cooked rice
½ cup toasted slivered
   almonds

Combine 1½ cups apple juice, vinegar, sugar, ketchup, oil, soy sauce and salt; bring to a boil. Add carrots and simmer 10 minutes. Add bell pepper and onion and cook 5 more minutes.

Dissolve cornstarch in remaining ¼ cup apple juice. Gradually add to hot mixture and stir constantly until thick. Add shrimp and heat. Add almonds to rice. Serve shrimp over rice.

Yield: 6 servings

# SHRIMP ROCKEFELLER

½ cup butter
1 tablespoon
    Worcestershire sauce
2 teaspoons anchovy paste
1½ teapoons salt
⅛ teaspoon Tabasco sauce
2 10-ounce packages
    frozen chopped
    spinach

1 clove garlic, minced
6 green onions, chopped
½ head lettuce, chopped
2 tablespoons chopped
    parsley
1½ stalks celery, chopped
½ cup soft bread crumbs
2 pounds shrimp, cooked
    and peeled

Heat together butter, Worcestershire, anchovy paste, salt and Tabasco. Add spinach, garlic, onion, lettuce, parsley and celery. Simmer 10 minutes. Add soft bread crumbs. Spoon over bottom of 1½-quart shallow baking dish. Cover with shrimp.

*Sauce:*

3 tablespoons butter
3 tablespoons flour
1½ cups milk
¼ teaspoon Worcestershire
    sauce

6-8 tablespoons Parmesan
    cheese
¾ teaspoon salt
½ teaspoon pepper
½ cup bread crumbs,
    buttered

Cook butter and flour until smooth; gradually add milk, stirring constantly to avoid lumps. Add Worcestershire, cheese, salt and pepper.

Pour sauce over shrimp and sprinkle with buttered crumbs. Bake for 20 minutes.

Yield: 6 servings

# SHRIMP AND ZUCCHINI SAUTÉ

¼ cup butter or olive oil
3 green onions, chopped
1 green bell pepper,
  chopped
2 cloves garlic, minced
3 zucchini, thinly sliced
1 pound raw shrimp,
  peeled

1 teaspoon basil
1 teaspoon Cavender's
  seasoning
Juice of one lemon or lime
Black pepper
½ cup sherry or white wine
⅓ cup grated Parmesan
  cheese

Melt butter in a large skillet. Sauté onion, bell pepper and garlic. Add zucchini and sauté 1 minute. Add shrimp, basil, Cavender's, lemon juice, black pepper and wine. Stir gently, cover and simmer until shrimp are pink (about 10 minutes). Stir in Parmesan cheese. Do not overcook vegetables, or they will be mushy. Serve over rice, if desired. One medium, peeled eggplant can be substituted for or used with the zucchini.

Yield: 2-4 servings

# BAKED OYSTERS

1⅔ cups dry bread crumbs
¾ cup freshly grated
  Parmesan cheese
2 teaspoons basil
1 tablespoon chopped
  fresh parsley
1½ teaspoon freshly ground
  pepper

¼ teaspoon garlic powder
1 pint fresh oysters,
  drained well
2 tablespoons olive oil
2 tablespoons dry white
  wine
1 tablespoon fresh lemon
  juice
Rock salt

Preheat oven to 400°. Combine bread crumbs, Parmesan cheese, basil, parsley, salt, oregano, pepper and garlic powder. Mix well. Sprinkle ⅓ of mixture in bottom of a greased shallow baking dish. Place oysters over this mixture in a single layer and top with remaining bread crumb mixture. Combine oil, wine and lemon juice and drizzle evenly over oysters. Bake uncovered for 30 minutes. Serve at once.

The oysters can also be baked on the half shell and topped with crumb mixture. Bake in a pan of rock salt for 15 minutes.

Yield: 8 servings

# OYSTERS BIENVILLE

Rock salt
3 tablespoons butter, divided
3 tablespoons flour
¾ cup milk
½ cup whipping cream
Salt and pepper
2 teaspoons finely chopped shallots or onion
1 clove garlic, finely minced
¼ pound fresh mushrooms, finely chopped

¼ pound raw shrimp, peeled, deveined and finely chopped
2 tablespoons dry sherry
1 egg yolk
¼ teaspoon nutmeg
⅛ teaspoon cayenne
1 tablespoon finely chopped fresh parsley
24-36 oysters on the half shell

Preheat oven to 500°. Pour rock salt into 4-6 rimmed, oven-proof dishes large enough to hold oysters in a single layer. Place in oven for at least 5 minutes to heat salt.

Melt 2 tablespoons butter in a small saucepan. Add flour, blending well with wire whisk. Add milk and cream; whisk rapidly. Add salt and pepper to taste.

Heat remaining tablespoon of butter in saucepan or skillet and add shallots. Cook 3 minutes on medium-high heat, stirring well. Add garlic and mushrooms. Continue cooking on high heat 2-3 minutes longer, until vegetables are limp, being careful not to burn. Reduce heat and stir in shrimp; cook for 1 minute. Add sherry, egg yolk, nutmeg, cayenne and parsley. Blend well. Stir mixture into cream sauce.

Top each oyster with 1 tablespoon sauce. Arrange oysters on rock salt and bake for 10 minutes.

Sauce doubles easily and freezes well. It can also be prepared a day ahead.

Yield: 4-6 servings

# OYSTERS BON SECOUR

¼ cup sliced almonds
2 strips bacon, cooked and crumbled, drippings reserved
½ pound fresh mushrooms, chopped and sautéed
1 whole green onion, finely chopped
½ cup grated mozzarella cheese

1 pint oysters, well drained
8 Saltine crackers, crumbled
Seasoned salt and pepper
2 tablespoons lemon juice
2 tablespoons pale dry sherry
Tabasco sauce

Combine almonds, bacon, mushrooms, green onion and cheese. Oil a broiler pan with bacon drippings. Roll oysters in cracker crumbs and place in 2 oblong mounds about 2 inches wide and 8 inches long. Sprinkle liberally with seasoned salt and pepper. Put 1 tablespoon each of lemon juice and sherry on each loaf; add Tabasco to taste. Divide almond mixture in half and place ½ on each oyster mound. Shape into 2 loaves, adding additional cracker crumbs if needed to soak up excess moisture.

Broil 6 inches from heat until cheese melts and oysters curl. Turn off broiler and let set 5 minutes in hot oven.

Yield: 3-4 servings

# OYSTER FRITTERS

1 pint oysters
1½ cups flour
2 tablespoons baking powder

¼ teaspoon salt
⅓ cup milk
⅓ cup oyster liquor
Oil for deep frying

Drain oysters, reserving liquor. Chop oysters. Mix flour, baking powder, salt, milk and oyster liquor to make a batter. Fold oysters into batter and drop by spoonfuls into deep, hot fat. Cook only until golden brown; drain on rack.

Yield: 4-6 servings

*Oyster fritters are great by themselves or as part of a seafood platter.*

# OYSTERS ROCKEFELLER I

4 stalks celery, finely
    chopped
1 pound green onions
    (4 bunches), chopped
3 large cloves garlic,
    mashed
1¼ cups butter, melted
½ teaspoon anise
4 tablespoons chopped
    parsley
2 cups slightly cooked
    chopped spinach, well
    drained

2 teaspoons salt
⅛ teaspoon cayenne
1 tablespoon lemon juice
3 tablespoons
    Worcestershire sauce
3 tablespoons ketchup
2 ounces anchovy fillets,
    mashed to paste
Bread crumbs
4 dozen oysters
Rock salt

Preheat oven to 350°. Sauté celery, onion and garlic in butter for 5 minutes. Remove from heat; add all ingredients, except bread crumbs and oysters, and mix well. Mix completely by hand or process ¼ at a time in food processor for a smooth sauce.

Drain oysters well. Put into oyster shells or ramekins. Cover tops of oysters with spinach mixture and top with bread crumbs. Place oyster shells in a flat, shallow pan lined with rock salt and bake for 10 minutes.

Yield: 4 dozen

# SCALLOPED OYSTERS

1 tablespoon grated onion
1 cup butter, melted
3-4 cups oyster crackers
2 teaspoons salt
½ teaspoon pepper
1 tablespoon lemon juice

⅛ teaspoon cayenne
⅛ teaspoon Worcestershire
    sauce
2 quarts oysters, drained
⅔ cups half and half

Preheat oven to 450°. Butter a 2-quart casserole or soufflé dish. Sauté grated onion in butter. Mix thoroughly crackers, salt, pepper, lemon juice, cayenne and Worcestershire. Put ⅓ cracker mixture in the bottom of the casserole; cover with half the oysters and half the cream. Repeat with remaining ingredients and top with remaining cracker mixture. Bake for 30 minutes.

Yield: 12 servings

# OYSTERS ROCKEFELLER II

36 oysters, in the shells
2 pounds fresh spinach
1 cup finely chopped green
  onion
½ cup finely chopped
  celery
½ cup finely chopped
  parsley
1 clove garlic, finely
  minced

1 2-ounce can anchovies,
  drained
8 tablespoons butter,
  divided
1 tablespoon flour
½ cup whipping cream
Tabasco sauce
1-2 tablespoons Pernod or
  anise-flavored liqueur
⅓ cup grated Parmesan
  cheese

Preheat oven to 450°. Open oysters, pour off liquid and reserve; leave oysters on the half shell.

Wash spinach; remove tough stems. Rinse well and place in saucepan with no water except what is remaining on spinach. Cover and cook, stirring occasionally, until spinach is wilted; then cook an additional 2-3 minutes. Drain well, squeezing to remove excess moisture. Chop in food processor. There should be approximately 2 cups chopped spinach. Set aside.

Blend green onion, celery and parsley in the processor or blender. Remove from processor and reserve. Process garlic and anchovies until smooth. Heat 4 tablespoons butter in skillet. Add green onion mixture. Cook and stir for about 1 minute. Add anchovy mixture, cooking and stirring for 1 minute more. Add spinach and blend well. Remove from heat.

Heat remaining 4 tablespoons butter in a small saucepan. Add flour and blend with a whisk. Add oyster liquid, whisking to blend. Add cream and whisk; then add Tabasco to taste. Stir in spinach mixture and blend. Add liqueur, if desired. Cool. Do not use any salt, as anchovies contain enough for seasoning.

Place equal portions of spinach mixture (about 1 tablespoon) on top of each oyster. Sprinkle with Parmesan cheese. Bake for approximately 25 minutes. Shells can be baked on rock salt to retain heat and balance shells. Sauce can be prepared a day ahead and freezes well for a short time.

Yield: 4-6 servings

# PERFECT FRIED OYSTERS

| | |
|---|---|
| 1 pint oysters | ⅛ teaspoon Tabasco sauce |
| 24 Saltine crackers | 1 tablespoon water |
| 1 egg | Oil for deep frying |

Drain oysters well. Make crumbs from Saltines and roll oysters gently in crumbs. Place them on a baking sheet in a single layer. Beat egg, Tabasco and water to make egg wash. Dip each oyster, one at a time, in egg wash. Roll oysters again in crumbs, pressing crumbs firmly onto each one. Return oysters to baking sheet, placing wax paper between layers if a second layer is needed. This can be done early in the day and refrigerated until ready to fry. Deep fry in small batches in oil preheated to 350°. Cook oysters a few minutes until brown. (Do not overcook.) Place on rack (not paper) to drain while frying remainder of oysters. Serve with tartar sauce or ketchup.

Yield: 2-4 servings

# JUDSON'S OYSTERS

| | |
|---|---|
| 1 quart oysters, drained, ½ cup liquor reserved | 1 tablespoon soy sauce |
| 1 medium onion, chopped | 1 tablespoon Heinz 57 sauce |
| 6 green onions, chopped | Juice of 1 lemon |
| 1 green bell pepper, chopped | 3 inches anchovy paste |
| 1 clove garlic, pressed | 3 slices bacon, cooked and crumbled |
| ½ cup butter | 2 tablespoons Parmesan cheese |
| 1 tablespoon Worcestershire sauce | |

Preheat oven to 350°. Sauté onion, green onion, bell pepper and garlic. Add Worcestershire, soy sauce, Heinz 57, lemon juice, oyster liquor, anchovy paste and bacon. Simmer gently for 1 hour, covered.

While sauce is simmering, bake oysters in ramekins for 15 minutes. Drain oysters, saving juice in case sauce needs to be thinned a little. Cover oysters with sauce. Bake 15 minutes. Remove from oven and sprinkle with Parmesan cheese. Return to oven and bake for 1-2 minutes.

Yield: 8 servings

# FRIED FISH PIECES

5 pounds fish fillets
1½ cups milk
½ cup Kellogg's corn flake
   crumbs
1 cup flour

1 teaspoon salt
½ teaspoon pepper
1 teaspoon Lawry's
   seasoned salt
Peanut oil

Skin and fillet fish. Cut into bite-sized pieces. Put fish into a small bowl and cover with milk; refrigerate for 1 hour.

In a bowl mix corn flake crumbs, flour, salt, pepper and Lawry's salt. Roll fish in flour mixture. Fry fish in deep fryer at 400° until brown, 3-5 minutes. Fry 8-10 pieces at a time, keeping oil very hot.

Yield: 10 servings

# FRIED MULLET

20 mullet
1½ cups white cornmeal
2 tablespoons salt

1 tablespoon pepper
Tabasco sauce
Vegetable or peanut oil

Scale and fillet mullet. Wash fillets and keep refrigerated until ready to use. In a paper grocery bag, put cornmeal, salt and pepper. Add fillets, a few at a time, and shake well. Season oil with Tabasco and heat to 400-425°. Fry mullet until golden. Drain on paper towels and serve at once.

Yield: 8 servings

# BROILED FISH

4 fish fillets (scamp,
    snapper, Spanish
    mackerel)
4 tablespoons butter
4 tablespoons lemon juice

4 teaspoons prepared
    mustard
Parmesan cheese
Paprika

Preheat oven to 350°. Line a shallow baking dish with aluminum foil. Place fish fillets, skin side down, in baking dish. In a saucepan, melt butter. Stir in lemon juice and mustard. Pour over fish fillets. Bake for 10-20 minutes, depending on thickness of fillets. Baste several times with sauce. Sprinkle with Parmesan cheese and paprika and broil until brown and bubbly.

Yield: 4 servings

# EASY AND DELICIOUS FISH

Fish fillets
Lemon juice
Salt and pepper

Mayonnaise
Parmesan cheese
Paprika

Preheat oven to 450°. Wash fish and pat dry. Line a baking dish with foil. Place fish skin side down in baking dish. Squeeze lemon juice over fish; sprinkle generously with salt and pepper. Spread mayonnaise evenly over fish, including the edges. Sprinkle lightly with Parmesan cheese and paprika. Bake for 15-20 minutes, or until done. Run under broiler for 1 minute or until lightly browned and puffed.

Yield: ½ pound fish per person

# FISH FILLETS INDIA

½ cup flour
1 teaspoon curry powder
¼ teaspoon salt

1 pound fresh or frozen
   fish fillets
½ cup butter
½ cup blanched almonds

Combine flour, curry powder and salt. Mix well. Cover fish completely with mixture.

Melt butter in a skillet. Brown fish over medium heat until it flakes easily—about 4 minutes on each side. Remove fish. Brown almonds in skillet; then pour over fish.

Yield: 4 servings

# GRILLED KING MACKEREL STEAKS

2 pounds fresh or frozen
   king mackerel steaks
¼ cup orange juice
¼ cup soy sauce
2 tablespoons ketchup
2 tablespoons oil

2 tablespoons chopped
   parsley
1 tablespoon lemon juice
1 clove garlic, crushed
½ teaspoon oregano
½ teaspoon pepper

Thaw frozen steaks. Cut into serving-size portions and place in single layer in shallow baking dish. Combine remaining ingredients to make sauce and pour over fish. Let stand for 30 minutes, turning once. Remove fish, reserving sauce for basting. Place fish in well-greased, hinged wire grills. Cook about 4 inches from moderately hot coals for 8 minutes. Baste with sauce. Turn and cook 7-10 minutes longer, or until fish flakes easily when tested with a fork.

Yield: 6 servings

# FLOUNDER FLORENTINE

2 10-ounce packages
  frozen chopped
  spinach
2 tablespoons butter
1/4 cup finely chopped
  onion
2 cloves garlic, pressed
1/2 teaspoon salt
1/4 teaspoon pepper
1/4 teaspoon freshly grated
  nutmeg
2 tablespoons butter
2 tablespoons flour

1/2 cup half and half
1/2 cup fish stock
10 flounder fillets, skinned
1/3 cup lemon juice
2 teaspoons Worcestershire
  sauce
1/2 cup butter
2 cups finely chopped
  mushrooms
2 tablespoons flour
1 cup sour cream
1/2 cup Parmesan cheese

Cook spinach according to package directions. Drain well. Set aside. In a heavy skillet, melt 2 tablespoons butter and sauté onion and garlic. Add drained spinach, salt, pepper and nutmeg. Simmer 4 minutes.

In a heavy saucepan, melt 2 tablespoons butter over medium-high heat. Add flour and cook, stirring constantly, until mixture is bubbling. Add half and half and fish stock. Continue stirring until sauce is thick and smooth. Add white sauce to spinach mixture and stir well. Remove from heat.

Preheat oven to 400°. Place a spoonful of spinach mixture on each flounder fillet. Roll up and place seam-side down in a buttered baking dish. In a small saucepan, melt 1/2 cup butter. Add Worcestershire sauce and lemon juice; pour over fillets. Cover baking dish with foil and bake for 20 minutes.

Pour liquid from fish into a skillet and sauté mushrooms until most of the liquid is reduced. Remove from heat. Combine flour and sour cream; gently stir into mushrooms. Pour over fish and sprinkle with cheese. Brown fish lightly under broiler.

Yield: 8 servings

# REDFISH

2 or 3 pounds redfish
Salt and pepper
1 pound butter
Lemon juice

1 tablespoon dry white
 wine
Parmesan cheese
Paprika

Preheat oven to 400°. Fillet fish and sprinkle with salt and pepper. Put butter into shallow baking pan in hot oven until it is browned. Place fillets flesh side down in sizzling hot butter and return pan to oven for 10 or 15 minutes. Turn fillets with spatula and baste with pan juices. Sprinkle each piece with lemon juice, wine, cheese and paprika. Return to oven until done, about 5 minutes. Then broil for 1 minute. Baste fish with sauce.

Yield: 4 servings

*This recipe works well for any fish fillet.*

# POLYNESIAN FISH DISH

3 pounds snapper, scamp,
 or any similar fish, cut
 into fillets
1/3 cup lime juice
1/4 cup butter, melted
1/2 teaspoon salt
1/4 teaspoon pepper

1/2 teaspoon marjoram
1/2 can cream of shrimp
 soup
1/2 cup sour cream
3 green onions and tops,
 thinly sliced
1/2 cup tiny boiled shrimp

Wash fish and pat dry. Place in oven-proof, shallow baking dish, pour lime juice over fish and marinate 15 minutes. Pour off lime juice and pour melted butter over fish. Sprinkle with salt, pepper and marjoram. Broil 10 minutes; baste with pan juices. Cool slightly. Mix soup and sour cream; spoon some over each piece of fish. Garnish with onion and shrimp. Bake in a preheated 350° oven until thoroughly heated.

Yield: 6 servings

# RED SNAPPER WITH SOUR CREAM DRESSING

½ cup chopped onion
1 cup chopped celery
½ cup butter, melted
½ cup dry bread crumbs
½ cup sour cream
¼ cup lemon, peeled and
   diced

3 pounds red snapper
   fillets
Lemon juice
Salt
Paprika
Chopped parsley

Preheat oven to 350°. Combine onion, celery, butter, bread crumbs, sour cream and lemon. Spread mixture in a greased baking dish. Place fillets on top and season with lemon juice, salt, paprika and parsley. Bake for 30-40 minutes, depending on thickness of fillets. Fish is done when it flakes, but is not dry.

Yield: 6 servings

# COQUILLES ST. JACQUES

1 pound scallops
1 onion, minced
5 sprigs parsley, chopped
1 bay leaf
2 sprigs thyme
1 cup white wine
1 teaspoon salt
⅛ teaspoon pepper

¼ cup butter
¼ cup flour
½ cup milk
1 egg yolk, beaten
⅔ cup grated Swiss cheese
Parmesan cheese, grated
Bread crumbs

Preheat oven to 300°. Combine scallops, onion, parsley, bay leaf, thyme, white wine, salt and pepper in a saucepan. Cover and simmer 10 minutes. Drain broth and reserve. Melt butter, blend in flour and add reserved broth. Stir until smooth. Add milk and egg yolk, stirring until smooth. Do not boil.

Dice or halve scallops. Add to sauce and cook gently for 5 minutes. Stir in grated Swiss cheese. Spoon into 4 shells or ramekins. Top with bread crumbs and Parmesan cheese. Bake for 10-12 minutes.

Yield: 4 servings

# RED SNAPPER, VERACRUZ STYLE

3 pounds fresh snapper
   fillets
2 tablespoons fresh lime
   juice
1 teaspoon salt

Flour
Salt and pepper
Vegetable oil for frying
3 tablespoons olive oil

Sprinkle fish with lime juice and salt; set aside for two hours. While fish marinates, prepare sauce.

*Sauce:*

¼ cup olive oil
1 medium onion, thinly
   sliced
2 large cloves garlic,
   peeled and sliced
2 pounds fresh tomatoes,
   peeled, seeded and
   chopped

1 large bay leaf
¼ teaspoon oregano
12 pitted green olives,
   halved
2 tablespoons capers
2 pickled jalapeños, cut
   into strips
Salt

Heat oil and cook onion and garlic until tender but not brown. Add remaining ingredients and simmer about 30 minutes.

Preheat oven to 325°. Dredge fish in flour, seasoned with salt and pepper, and fry in hot oil until golden brown. Place in a large baking dish or in individual baking dishes and top with sauce. Sprinkle top of sauce with olive oil and bake uncovered about 20 minutes or until just tender.

This can also be done with a whole 3-pound snapper. Cook 30 minutes.

Yield: 6-8 servings

# SNAPPER IN VELOUTÉ SAUCE

*Snapper:*

4 tablespoons butter, divided
4 tablespoons finely chopped green onion, divided
Salt
White pepper
4 pounds snapper fillets
⅓ pound sliced mushrooms
⅓ cup dry white wine
Fish stock to cover (about 1 cup)

Butter a large flame-proof baking dish with 2 tablespoons butter. Sprinkle 2 tablespoons green onion over bottom of pan. Sprinkle with salt and white pepper. Layer fillets over green onion, skin side down. Sprinkle fillets with salt and white pepper. Set aside.

Preheat oven to 400°. Sauté mushrooms and 2 tablespoons green onion in the remaining 2 tablespoons butter. Spread this mixture over fillets. Gently pour white wine and fish stock over fillets. Cover with 2 pieces of buttered wax paper, with buttered side down. Press close to fillets. On medium-high heat bring to a simmering boil on top of stove, then bake for 15 minutes. Remove wax paper. Pour liquid from fish into a saucepan, bring to a boil and reduce to 1 cup.

*Velouté:*

9 tablespoons butter, divided
4 tablespoons flour
1 cup reduced liquid from fish
⅓ cup whipping cream, divided
Salt and White pepper
1 tablespoon lemon juice
10 mushrooms, fluted

In a heavy saucepan, melt 4 tablespoons butter. Add flour and mix until bubbly. Whisk in reduced fish liquid, stirring constantly. Remove from heat and add ½ cup whipping cream and season with salt and white pepper. Return to heat, stir in 4 tablespoons butter, 1 tablespoon at a time. Stir in lemon juice. Remove from heat. Beat remaining ¼ cup whipping cream until thick. Gently fold into velouté sauce. Pour over fillets.

In a small skillet, sauté fluted mushrooms in 1 tablespoon butter. Garnish fillets with mushrooms. Place baking dish under broiler for 1 or 2 minutes or until velouté is very lightly browned.

Yield: 10 servings

*To make a fish stock, use snapper back bones and 3 cups water. Bring to a boil and add green onion tops, celery tops, 1 small carrot and a bay leaf. Boil 20 minutes. Strain stock and reserve.*

# SHRIMP AND LOBSTER NEWBURG

1 8-ounce can sliced
    mushrooms
2 cups diced cooked
    lobster or shrimp or 1
    cup of each
3 tablespoons butter,
    divided
1 teaspoon paprika
2 tablespoons flour

⅛ teaspoon salt
⅛ teaspoon pepper
⅛ teaspoon nutmeg
1 cup half and half
1 egg yolk, beaten
1 tablespoon sherry
4 Holland rusks or toast
    points
Chopped chives

Drain mushrooms and reserve broth. Cook lobster, shrimp and mushrooms in 2 tablespoons butter and paprika until mushrooms are brown. Melt remaining 1 tablespoon butter; add flour, salt, pepper and nutmeg; blend together. Remove from heat and stir in mushroom broth and half and half.

Return to heat and cook over medium heat, stirring constantly, until thickened. Stir a little hot broth into the egg yolk and then add egg to sauce. Add mushrooms, shrimp, lobster and sherry; heat but do not boil. Stir often until served.

Serve on Holland rusks or toast points. Garnish with fresh chopped chives, if desired.

Yield: 4 servings

# TROUT AMANDINE

1½ cups half and half
3 eggs
1 teaspoon salt
½ teaspoon white pepper
3 pounds fresh speckled
    trout, filleted and
    skinned

Flour
Vegetable oil for frying
2 cups sliced almonds
1 cup butter
Lemon wedges

Make a batter of half and half, eggs, salt and white pepper. Dredge fish in flour; dip into batter and then into flour again. Fry in hot oil until golden brown. Drain on paper towels.

Sauté almonds in butter until golden brown. Serve fish topped with almonds and garnished with a wedge of lemon.

Yield: 6 servings

# SPANISH PAELLA

½ cup olive oil
2 pounds chicken breasts,
    each breast cut into 3
    pieces
1 pound Spanish or Italian
    sausage, sliced
½ pound scallops or squid
    (cut into rings)
1½ pounds shrimp in
    shells, heads on or off
1 large green bell pepper,
    chopped
1 large onion, chopped
3 cloves garlic, minced
2 cups Uncle Ben's
    converted rice,
    uncooked

1 4-ounce jar whole
    pimento, half chopped
    and half cut into strips
3 fresh tomatoes, chopped
3 cups chicken broth
1 teaspoon saffron,
    dissolved in broth
1 bottle clam juice
1 can minced clams
2 teaspoons salt
1 teaspoon turmeric
1 10-ounce package frozen
    small green peas
Artichoke hearts
Lemon wedges
Parsley

Heat oil in paella pan or large cast iron skillet. Brown chicken and remove from pan. Fry sausage briefly; then remove. Sauté seafood until it changes color and remove at once. Add in order: bell pepper, onion, garlic, rice, chopped pimento and tomato, sautéing each briefly before adding the next ingredient. Add the broth, saffron, clam juice, clams, salt, turmeric and peas. Stir.

Simmer on top of stove over medium heat until the rice begins to absorb most of the liquid (20-30 minutes). Arrange the reserved meats, seafood and artichokes on top of rice mixture. Let simmer until liquid is gone and rice is tender. Cover if necessary, but do not stir. This will take about 30 minutes.

Garnish with pimento strips, lemon wedges and parsley.

Yield: 8 servings

# PERFECT SHRIMP BATTER

2 pounds raw shrimp,
    peeled
1 cup flour
½ teaspoon salt
½ teaspoon sugar

1 cup cold beer
1 egg, beaten
2 tablespoons oil
Vegetable oil for deep
    frying

Combine flour, salt and sugar. Slowly stir in beer. Add egg and oil; stir well. Dip shrimp in batter and deep fry in hot oil (425°) for 3-5 minutes.

Yield: 4-6 servings

# TEMPURA BATTER FOR SEAFOOD

Oil for deep frying
2 eggs
⅔ cup milk
1 cup sifted flour

1 teaspoon baking powder
½ teaspoon salt
2 tablespoons butter,
    melted

Preheat oil to 350°. Beat eggs and add milk. Sift dry ingredients and add to liquid mixture. Add butter and heat until blended. Dip seafood or vegetables into batter and fry until golden brown.

Yield: 4 servings

# WORLD'S SIMPLEST TEMPURA BATTER

1 part flat beer

1 part flour

Mix beer with flour and let stand at least 30 minutes. Dip vegetables or shrimp into batter and fry in hot oil.

# TEMPURA BATTER

¾ cup flour
1 cup cold water

2½ teaspoons baking
    powder

Sift flour. Gradually stir in cold water until smooth. Add baking powder and mix well. Use within 30 minutes.

Yield: batter for 1 pound of shrimp

# BEOUF BOURGUIGNON

8 ounces salt pork, cut into ¼-inch cubes
1 tablespoon butter
30 peeled white onions, about 1 inch in diameter
3 tablespoons pork fat
3 tablespoons butter
1 pound small mushrooms, whole or quartered
4 pounds boneless chuck, cut into 2-inch chunks
2½ cups red Burgundy
Bouquet garni (4 parsley sprigs, celery tops, bay leaf, garlic and fresh thyme)

2 tablespoons chopped green onion or shallots
¼ cup finely chopped carrots
3 tablespoons flour
1 cup hot beef stock
1 tablespoon tomato paste
1 teaspoon finely chopped garlic
1 teaspoon dried thyme
1 teaspoon salt
Freshly ground black pepper
2 tablespoons finely chopped parsley
Pork cracklings

*Onions:* Preheat oven to 350°. Blanch salt pork in 1 quart water for 5 minutes. Drain on paper towels and pat dry. In a heavy skillet, heat 1 tablespoon butter and fry salt pork until all fat is rendered and pork is crispy. Remove, drain and set aside. Brown onions in rendered pork fat; then braise onions in 3 tablespoons pork fat in a shallow baking dish in a 350° oven for 30 minutes or until barely tender. Remove and set aside.

*Mushrooms:* Sauté mushrooms in 3 tablespoons butter for 2-3 minutes, tossing frequently, until slightly soft. Set aside.

*Meat:* Preheat oven to 325°. Marinate meat in 2½ cups wine for several hours; then drain, reserving the wine. Dry meat and brown in a small amount of pork fat. Cook only a few chunks at a time, adding more fat as needed. Place browned meat in an oven-proof 4-6-quart casserole and add the bouquet garni.

In the same skillet, brown green onion and carrots. Stir in the flour, adding more fat if necessary. Cook on low heat until flour browns, being careful not to burn. Pour in hot beef stock, blending with a wire whisk. Add reserved wine and tomato paste, bring to a boil and whisk until sauce thickens. Add garlic, thyme, salt and pepper. Pour over meat. Sauce should almost cover meat. A bit more wine or stock can be added. Bake at 325° for 2 hours 30 minutes, or until meat is tender. Gently add onions and mushrooms and bake 15 more minutes.

Before serving, remove bouquet garni and skim fat. Garnish with parsley and pork cracklings.

Yield: 8-10 servings

# HEAVENLY TENDERLOIN

1 6-pound tenderloin
2 lobster tails (4 ounces
   each)
1 tablespoon butter,
   melted
1½ teaspoons lemon juice
6 slices bacon, partially
   cooked

½ cup green onion
½ cup butter
½ cup dry white wine
⅛ teaspoon crushed garlic
   (1 clove)
¼ pound whole mushrooms
Watercress

Cut tenderloin lengthwise to within ½ inch of bottom to butterfly. Place lobster tails in boiling salted water just to cover. Return to boiling; reduce heat and simmer 5 minutes. Carefully remove lobster tails from shells. Cut lobster tails in half lengthwise and place pieces end to end inside tenderloin. Combine 1 tablespoon melted butter and lemon juice and drizzle over lobster. Close meat around lobster; tie together securely with string at 1-inch intervals. Place on rack in shallow roasting pan. Cook 20 minutes at 425° for rare. Lay bacon slices on top and cook 5 minutes more.

Meanwhile, in saucepan, cook green onion in remaining butter over very low heat until tender. Add wine and garlic and heat, stirring frequently. Slice meat and serve with wine sauce. Garnish platter with whole sautéed mushrooms and watercress.

Yield: 8-10 servings

# PEPPERED STEAKS

1 2½-3-pound eye of the
  round roast
Meat tenderizer
1½-2 tablespoons
  peppercorns
2 tablespoons butter

2 tablespoons vegetable oil
½ cup chopped green
  onion
½ cup beef bouillon
⅓ cup brandy or red wine

Trim meat of excess fat; cut crosswise into six even steaks. Sprinkle steaks with meat tenderizer following container directions. Crush the peppercorns coarsely with a wooden mallet and press into both sides of meat. Cover and let stand at least 1 hour.

In a large heavy skillet heat butter and oil. Add 2 or 3 steaks at a time and sauté over high heat 3-4 minutes on each side for medium rare. Keep warm on a serving platter. You may choose to under-cook slightly and reheat in the microwave.

Add green onion to pan juices and sauté 1 minute. Add bouillon and wine. Bring to a boil, stirring to blend. Cook 2 minutes longer and pour over steaks.

Yield: 6 servings

# GRILLED STEAK LOGS

1½ pound sirloin or flank
  steak
6-8 slices bacon
¼ cup prepared mustard

¼ cup pineapple juice
1 tablespoon light brown
  sugar

Slice steak into 6-8 1-inch wide strips. If using flank steak, slice, diagonally. Wrap each strip in bacon, securing with a toothpick. Combine mustard, pineapple juice and brown sugar. Pour mixture over meat and marinate at least 1 hour; overnight or all day is better. Grill over hot coals until done. Baste with sauce while cooking.

Yield: 4 servings

# MARINATED ROAST BEEF

5-6 pound chuck roast
1 bottle Wishbone Italian
   dressing
3 cups sliced onion
Bay leaves
2 cups vegetable oil
1 cup white vinegar

4 tablespoons capers with
   juice
3 teaspoons celery seed
2 teaspoons salt
2-3 drops Tabasco sauce
2 ounces pimento

Pierce meat and cover with Italian dressing. Cook in Dutch oven, covered, at 350° for 3 hours. Let cool. Slice paper thin (butcher can do it best) and layer with onion slices and bay leaves (about 8 bay leaves per layer) in large glass bowl. Mix remaining ingredients and pour over layers. Marinate 1 hour at room temperature and at least 24 hours in refrigerator before serving. Serve cold.

Yield: 20-30 servings

*This makes a wonderful buffet item.*

# CARPETBAG STEAK JOSEPHS

2 pints oysters, well
   drained (reserve liquor)
½ cup dry croutons
2 tablespoons chopped
   parsley
2 cloves garlic, pressed
½ cup minced onion
3 tablespoons butter,
   softened

½ teaspoon freshly ground
   pepper
½ teaspoon salt
3 tablespoons lemon juice
1 2-pound flank steak
½ cup flour
¼ cup clarified butter
1 cup oyster liquor
1½ cups beef bouillon

Mix first nine ingredients for stuffing. Make a deep pocket in flank steak with a sharp knife, being careful not to cut through. Stuff pocket with stuffing mixture. Skewer opening tightly or sew, using unwaxed dental floss or strong thread and large needle. Dust with flour and brown in butter. Add oyster liquor and bouillon to pan and cover.

Bring to a boil; then put in 325° oven for 1 hour 30 minutes. Remove and let sit 15 minutes before carving. Serve pan drippings separately.

Yield: 4-6 servings

# MOUSSAKA

6 tablespoons olive oil, divided

3 cups finely chopped onion

3 cups concentrated beef broth

3 pounds lean ground chuck

Salt and freshly ground pepper

2 cups tomato sauce

1 tablespoon nutmeg

½ teaspoon cinnamon

2 tablespoons sugar

¾ cup red wine

3 large eggplants (about 4 pounds)

3 cups water

1 cup butter

¾ cup flour

½ cup cornstarch

7 cups milk

3 eggs, slightly beaten

¼ teaspoon nutmeg

2 eggs

4 cups freshly grated cheese (Parmesan and mozzarella)

¼ cup bread crumbs

*Meat:* Heat 4 tablespoons olive oil in a large kettle and add onion. Cook until wilted and add ½ cup beef broth. Cook until liquid has evaporated. Add beef and stir briefly. Add remaining broth, salt and pepper to taste, and simmer 1 hour 30 minutes.

*Tomato Sauce:* Combine tomato sauce, salt, pepper, nutmeg, cinnamon and sugar and cook 30 minutes, uncovered. When meat is cooked, strain off most of the liquid. Add tomato sauce and red wine to the meat and cook 1 hour until meat sauce is thick. Let cool.

*Eggplant:* Trim ends of the eggplant and cut lengthwise into ⅛-inch slices. Do not peel. Arrange slices in 17x11x2-inch baking pan, neatly overlapping. Add 3 cups water and cover tightly with foil. Bake 35 minutes at 400°. Drain most of liquid and let cool.

*Béchamel Sauce:* Heat butter in heavy 3-quart saucepan. Add flour, then cornstarch, constantly stirring with a whisk. Add ⅓ of milk, stirring rapidly; then add remaining milk slowly, constantly stirring. When thick and smooth, remove from heat. Beat 3 eggs and nutmeg and stir into sauce; cook briefly over low heat, stirring constantly.

*Cheese:* Beat 2 eggs with ¼ cup grated cheese and add to meat sauce. Bring to a boil and stir briefly.

*Assembly:* Grease 17x11x2-inch pan with 2 tablespoons olive oil. Sprinkle with bread crumbs and layer ½ eggplant in pan, overlapping slices. Sprinkle with ¾ cup cheese. Spoon meat sauce into pan evenly. Arrange a second layer of eggplant and sprinkle with ¾ cup cheese. Spoon béchamel sauce over top and sprinkle with remaining cheese. Bake 40-45 minutes at 350° or until barely set in the center. Let cool at least 30 minutes.

Yield: 12-20 servings

# LASAGNA FLORENTINE

**2-3 pounds lean ground beef**
**2 medium onions, chopped**
**2 16-ounce cans stewed tomatoes**
**18 ounces tomato paste**
**3 bay leaves**
**Salt and pepper to taste**
**3 cloves garlic, pressed**
**1 tablespoon basil**
**½ teaspoon crushed red pepper**
**½ teaspoon oregano**
**2 10-ounce packages frozen chopped spinach**
**4 cups grated mozzarella cheese, divided**
**1 cup grated Parmesan cheese, divided**
**8 ounces lasagna noodles**

*Sauce:* Brown beef and onion in a large heavy pan. Add tomatoes, tomato paste, bay leaves, salt, pepper, garlic, basil and crushed red pepper. Simmer 1 hour. Remove from heat and add oregano.

*Spinach Mixture:* Cook spinach according to package directions. Drain, add 3 cups mozzarella cheese and ½ cup Parmesan cheese. Mix well.

*Pasta:* Cook according to package directions; drain; place in pan of cool water. Pat dry before layering.

*Assembly:* Layer ingredients in two 11x7x2-inch baking pans or one deep-dish lasagna pan. First, spread a small amount of sauce in the pan. Then layer pasta, spinach mixture and meat sauce to fill the pan, ending with meat sauce. Sprinkle remaining 1 cup mozzarella and ½ cup Parmesan on top. Bake at 350° for 45 minutes.

Yield: 10-12 servings

# A VERY SPECIAL LASAGNA

1 pound lean ground beef
½ cup chopped onion
3 cloves garlic, minced
1 tablespoon olive oil
3 16-ounce cans whole
  tomatoes, drained
1½ teaspoons seasoned
  salt
2 tablespoons chopped
  parsley
1 teaspoon basil
½ teaspoon oregano
¼ teaspoon pepper
½ cup butter

4 tablespoons flour
1 cup milk
1 cup chicken stock
⅛ teaspoon salt
1 egg
8 ounces ricotta cheese
1¾ cups grated Parmesan
  cheese
⅛ teaspoon nutmeg
½ teaspoon salt
8 ounces mozzarella
  cheese, sliced
Butter
8 ounces lasagna noodles

*Meat Sauce:* Sauté beef, onion and garlic in olive oil. Add tomatoes, seasoned salt, parsley, basil, oregano and pepper; simmer 30-40 minutes or until very thick. Skim fat.

*Béchamel Sauce:* Melt butter, add flour and cook for 1 minute, stirring constantly with a whisk. Slowly add milk and chicken stock; stir until smooth. Bring to a boil, stirring constantly. Add salt.

*Ricotta Filling:* Beat egg and add ricotta, ¼ cup Parmesan cheese, nutmeg and salt. Mix well.

*Pasta:* Cook noodles in boiling, salted water until al dente. Drain and keep in cool water until ready to use.

*Assembly:* Layer in a 13x9x2-inch pan a little meat sauce, noodles, meat sauce, ½ cup béchamel, ½ cup Parmesan, ½ of mozzarella, ½ of ricotta filling. Repeat layers, ending with meat sauce. Top with remaining Parmesan and dot with butter. Bake at 400° for 30 minutes. This can also be frozen before baking.

Yield: 8 servings

# MANICOTTI

1 medium onion, chopped
2-4 cloves garlic, pressed
½ pound ground beef or
  Italian sausage
2 tablespoons olive oil
2 16-ounce cans whole
  tomatoes, chopped
2 tablespoons tomato
  paste
1 teaspoon oregano
1 teaspoon thyme
1 teaspoon salt
2 tablespoons chopped
  fresh parsley

2 bay leaves
½ teaspoon pepper
1 10-ounce package frozen
  chopped spinach
16 ounces ricotta cheese
8 ounces freshly grated
  Parmesan cheese
1 tablespoon fresh or 1
  teaspoon dried basil
1 8-ounce package
  manicotti shells
8 ounces mozzarella
  cheese, grated

*Sauce:* Sauté onion, garlic and meat in olive oil. Add tomatoes and spices; cook slowly until thick.

*Filling:* Cook spinach and drain well. Combine ricotta, Parmesan, spinach and basil. If you use processor, filling will be green; if you mix by hand or mixer, it will be white with green flecks.

*Pasta:* Cook according to package directions with one tablespoon olive oil in water; drain and return to pan of cool water.

*Assembly:* Place spoonful of sauce in casserole to line bottom. Fill shells and place in casserole in one layer. Cover with sauce and top with grated mozzarella. Bake 45 minutes at 350°.

Yield: 6 servings

# ITALIAN SPAGHETTI
# WITH MEATBALLS AND SAUSAGE

*Meatballs:*

1½ pounds ground beef
2 onions, minced
2 cloves garlic, minced
¼ cup chopped parsley
½ cup grated Parmesan
　　cheese
½ cup fine dry bread
　　crumbs
1 egg, beaten

2 teaspoons salt
½ teaspoon pepper
1 bay leaf
1 teaspoon Italian
　　seasoning
¼ teaspoon oregano
¼ teaspoon marjoram
¼ teaspoon rosemary
2 tablespoons olive oil

Mix ground beef, onion, garlic, parsley, Parmesan cheese, bread crumbs, egg, salt, pepper and herbs. You can add a little water, if too dry. Shape into meatballs and brown in olive oil before adding to the sauce. Meatballs can be frozen separately or added to the sauce and frozen.

*Sauce:*

2 onions, chopped
2 cloves garlic, minced
2 tablespoons olive oil
1 pound hot or mild Italian
　　sausage, cut into
　　2-inch pieces
3½ cups tomatoes
1 cup water
1 tablespoon fresh basil or
　　1 teaspoon dried basil
¼ cup chopped parsley
½ teaspoon crumbled
　　thyme
2½ teaspoons salt
¼ teaspoon pepper

¼ teaspoon crushed dried
　　red pepper
1 6-ounce can tomato
　　paste
2 8-ounce cans tomato
　　sauce
¼ teaspoon oregano
¼ teaspoon marjoram
¼ teaspoon rosemary
1 bay leaf
1 teaspoon Italian
　　seasoning
12 ounces spaghetti,
　　cooked

Brown Italian sausage and set aside. Sauté onion and garlic in olive oil in a large saucepan. Add tomatoes and water and bring to a boil. Simmer, uncovered, for 20 minutes, stirring occasionally. Add next 13 ingredients, the browned meatballs, the browned Italian sausage and simmer, uncovered, for 2 hours, stirring occasionally. Add more seasoning, if desired. Serve on hot spaghetti.

Yield: 8 servings

# SICILIAN MEAT ROLL

| | |
|---|---|
| 2 eggs, beaten | 1 clove garlic, minced |
| ¾ cup soft bread crumbs | 2 pounds lean ground |
| ½ cup tomato juice | chuck |
| 2 tablespoons chopped | 8 thin slices boiled ham |
| parsley | 1½ cups grated mozzarella |
| ½ teaspoon oregano | cheese |
| ¼ teaspoon salt | 3 slices mozzarella cheese, |
| ¼ teaspoon pepper | halved diagonally |

Preheat oven to 350°. Combine eggs, bread crumbs, tomato juice, parsley, oregano, salt and pepper. Stir in beef, mixing well. On foil or wax paper, pat meat into a 10x12-inch rectangle. Arrange ham on top of meat, leaving a small margin around edges. Sprinkle grated cheese over ham.

Starting from short end, carefully roll meat, using fork to lift; seal edges and ends. Place roll, seam-side down, in a 13x9x2-inch baking pan. Bake at 350° for 1 hour 15 minutes, or until done. Center of meat will be pink because of ham. Place cheese slices on top and bake 5 minutes more. Garnish with parsley.

Yield: 8-10 servings

# COUNTRY BRISKET

| | |
|---|---|
| 1 4-5 pound boneless beef | 1 teaspoon garlic powder |
| brisket | ¼ cup melted butter |
| 2 teaspoons salt | 1 cup hot water |
| ½ teaspoon coarse black | 2 tablespoons cornstarch |
| pepper | 1 cup cold water |
| 3 medium onions, thickly | |
| sliced | |

Trim brisket of excess fat. Place brisket, fat side up, in large roasting pan. Season with salt, pepper, butter and garlic powder. Top with onion slices. Bake 1 hour at 350°. Add 1 cup hot water, cover tightly with foil and cook 2 hours at 300°. Remove meat.

To thicken gravy, dissolve cornstarch in cold water, add to pan juices and cook until thick, stirring constantly.

Yield: 6 servings

## CHINESE BEEF AND SNOW PEAS

1½ pounds steak, cut in
   ½-inch strips
2 tablespoons soy sauce
1 tablespoon sherry
1 teaspoon sugar
¼ teaspoon pepper
2 teaspoons cornstarch
¼ teaspoon garlic powder
1 tablespoon oil

¼ pound sliced fresh
   mushrooms
6 ounces fresh or 1
   package frozen snow
   peas
2 green onions, chopped
1½ teaspoons sherry
1 cup fresh bean sprouts
1 teaspoon sugar

Combine soy sauce, 1 tablespoon sherry, sugar, pepper, cornstarch and garlic powder. Pour over meat; mix well and set aside. Combine mushrooms, snow peas, green onion and bean sprouts; set aside.

Heat oil in wok or skillet. Add steak, cooking and stirring over high heat about 2 minutes. Remove steak. Add vegetables and cook 1 minute, stirring constantly. Add remaining sherry, sugar and steak. Cook 2 minutes. Serve over rice.

Yield: 4 servings

## REUBEN CASSEROLE

1 12-ounce can corned
   beef
¼ cup thousand island
   dressing
1 16-ounce can sauerkraut

½ pound Swiss cheese,
   grated
½ cup butter, melted
6 slices Pepperidge Farm
   rye bread, cubed

Crumble beef and place in buttered 2-quart casserole. Spread on dressing. Drain sauerkraut and spread on top of beef. Add grated cheese. Top with bread cubes that have been tossed with butter. Bake, uncovered, 30 minutes at 350°, until hot and bubbly.

Yield: 6-8 servings

*Try this for a quick Sunday night supper.*

# CHILI

1 pound ground round or
lean ground chuck
1 tablespoon vegetable oil
1 cup chopped onion
1 cup chopped green bell
pepper
1 large clove garlic
1 28-ounce can whole
tomatoes, chopped
1 8-ounce can tomato
sauce
1 tablespoon chili powder

1 teaspoon oregano
2 teaspoons salt
1 teaspoon sugar
1/8 teaspoon cayenne
pepper
1/8 teaspoon paprika
1 teaspoon cumin
1 15 1/2-ounce can kidney
or pinto beans,
drained
Hot cooked rice
Grated cheese

In a 5-quart Dutch oven, brown beef; drain and discard fat. In a skillet, sauté onion, bell pepper and garlic in oil. Stir vegetables and remaining ingredients into beef. Cook on low heat 3 hours, covered, stirring occasionally. Adjust seasonings. Serve over rice and top with grated cheese, if desired.

Yield: 6 servings

# CHUCKWAGON STEW

2 pounds rump roast, cut
into 1-inch cubes
1/4 cup flour
2-3 tablespoons shortening
2 teaspoons salt
1/4 teaspoon pepper
1 teaspoon chili powder
1/4 teaspoon thyme
1 small bay leaf
1 16-ounce can whole
tomatoes
1 10 1/2-ounce can beef
broth

6 potatoes, peeled and
quartered
6 carrots, cut into 2-inch
pieces
6 white onions, peeled and
quartered
4 stalks celery, cut into
2-inch pieces
1 10-ounce package frozen
peas

Pat beef dry. Coat with flour and brown in hot shortening in a 5-quart Dutch oven. Pour off fat, leaving a small amount. Add seasonings, tomatoes, broth and vegetables to meat. Cover and simmer 2-2½ hours. Adjust seasoning to taste.

Yield: 6-8 servings

# CINCINNATI CHILI

1 quart water
2 pounds ground beef
2 medium onions, finely grated
2 8-ounce cans tomato sauce
1 tablespoon Worcestershire sauce
2 tablespoons vinegar
4 tablespoons chili powder
4 cloves garlic, minced
1 teaspoon cinnamon
1 teaspoon red pepper flakes

1 teaspoon allspice
½ ounce unsweetened chocolate, grated
1½ teaspoons salt
1 bay leaf
16 ounces spaghetti noodles, cooked and drained
2 cups grated cheddar cheese
1 cup chopped onion
1 16-ounce can chili beans

Add ground beef to water in 4-quart pot; stir until beef separates into a fine texture. Boil slowly for 30 minutes. Add next 12 ingredients. Bring to a boil, stirring to blend; reduce heat and simmer, uncovered, for 3 hours. Refrigerate overnight so fat can be skimmed from top before reheating.

Cincinnati chili may be served over hot noodles and topped with cheese, onion and chili beans.

Yield: 8 servings

# CHICKEN-CRAB ROLLS

4 large chicken breasts,
   skinned and boned
3 tablespoons butter
¼ cup flour
¾ cup milk
¾ cup chicken broth
⅓ cup dry white wine
¼ cup chopped onion
1 tablespoon butter
8 ounces fresh crabmeat,
   cartilage removed

½ cup chopped mushrooms
½ cup crumbled Saltine
   crackers
2 tablespoons snipped
   parsley
½ teaspoon salt
⅛ teaspoon pepper
4 ounces grated Swiss
   cheese
½ teaspoon paprika

Flatten chicken breasts between 2 sheets of wax paper until about ⅛ inch thick. Set aside. In a saucepan, melt 3 tablespoons butter; blend in flour. Add milk, chicken broth and wine all at once; cook, stirring constantly, until mixture thickens and bubbles. Set aside.

In a skillet sauté onion in butter until tender, but not brown. Stir in crabmeat, mushrooms, cracker crumbs, parsley, salt and pepper. Top each chicken breast with ¼ cup crab mixture. Fold in sides and roll up. Place seam-side down in a 12x8x2-inch baking dish. Pour sauce over chicken. Bake, covered, at 350° for 1 hour. Uncover; sprinkle with cheese and paprika. Bake 2 minutes or until cheese melts.

Yield: 4 servings

# CASHEW CHICKEN

6-8 chicken breasts,
   skinned, boned and
   cut into 1-inch pieces
1 egg
1 13-ounce can evaporated
   milk
Corn oil
Flour

2 tablespoons cornstarch
2 cups chicken broth
1 tablespoon soy sauce
Cooked rice
Shredded lettuce
Chopped green onion
Dry roasted cashews

Beat egg and milk together. Soak chicken in this mixture overnight. Dredge chicken pieces in flour and fry in hot oil until golden brown. Drain.

Mix cornstarch with ¼ cup cold broth. Blend cornstarch mixture, remainder of broth and soy sauce; bring to a boil; reduce heat and simmer 5 minutes. Layer over rice in this order: shredded lettuce, chopped green onion, chicken, sauce and cashews.

Yield: 4-6 servings

# CHICKEN CUMBERLAND

3 2-pound chickens,
   quartered
1 teaspoon salt
Freshly ground pepper
½ cup butter, melted
3 tablespoons lime juice
1 cup red currant jelly

1 6-ounce can frozen
   orange juice
4 tablespoons dry sherry
1 teaspoon dry mustard
⅛ teaspoon ground ginger
¼ teaspoon Tabasco sauce

Season chicken with salt and pepper. Line broiler pan with foil; place chicken on broiler rack. Broil chicken under medium heat for 1 hour, turning once and basting often with combined butter, lime juice and pan drippings.

Combine remaining ingredients in saucepan and simmer until smooth and hot, stirring constantly. Spoon some sauce over chicken as it is served. Remaining sauce can be served in a sauceboat. Serve with wild rice.

Yield: 8-12 servings

# CASHEW-GINGER CHICKEN

1 tablespoon cornstarch
1 cup chicken broth
3 tablespoons dry sherry
2 tablespoons soy sauce
1/4-1/2 teaspoon Tabasco
   sauce
1/4 cup peanut oil
3 chicken breasts, skinned,
   boned and cut into
   1-inch pieces
2 slices fresh ginger

3 cups broccoli flowerets
1 medium red or green bell
   pepper, cut into 1-inch
   squares
1/2 pound mushrooms,
   thickly sliced
1 bunch green onions,
   slivered
1 clove garlic, minced
1/3 cup dry roasted cashews

Assemble all ingredients ahead of time. Combine cornstarch, chicken broth, sherry, soy sauce and Tabasco in a small bowl and set aside. Ten minutes before serving, heat the oil in a wok or heavy skillet. When oil is very hot, add chicken and ginger. Cook, stirring constantly, until chicken is white. If using a skillet, remove chicken and discard the ginger. If using a wok, remove ginger slices and push chicken up the sides.

Place broccoli, bell pepper, mushrooms, green onions and garlic in wok. Cook 3 minutes, stirring constantly. Combine chicken and cornstarch mixture with the vegetables and continue cooking and stirring until the sauce thickens slightly. Sprinkle with cashews and serve immediately with steaming hot rice.

Yield: 4-6 servings

# CREAMED CHICKEN WITH CORN BREAD RING

*Corn Bread:*

| | |
|---|---|
| 1 teaspoon poultry seasoning | ½ teaspoon salt |
| 1 cup corn meal | 4 teaspoons baking powder |
| 1 cup flour | 1 egg |
| ¼ cup sugar | 1 cup milk |
| | ¼ cup vegetable oil |

Preheat oven to 400°. Sift dry ingredients. Add egg, milk and vegetable oil. Mix well. Pour batter into a buttered 8-inch ring mold. Bake at 400° for 15-20 minutes. Turn out onto a serving platter. Fill center with creamed chicken.

*Creamed chicken:*

| | |
|---|---|
| ⅓ cup butter | 2 cups chicken broth |
| ½ cup chopped onion | ¾ cup milk |
| ½ cup chopped celery | ¼ teaspoon Worcestershire sauce |
| ⅓ cup flour | 2 cups cooked and diced chicken |
| ½ teaspoon salt | |
| ¼ teaspoon thyme | |

In a 3-quart saucepan, melt butter over low heat. Sauté onion and celery until lightly browned. Add flour, salt and thyme. Stir well. Add chicken broth and milk; blend until smooth over medium heat. Season with Worcestershire and add diced chicken to sauce. Heat thoroughly. Pour into corn bread ring and serve immediately.

Yield: 8 servings

# ENCHILADAS SUISSE

1 onion, chopped
2 tablespoons vegetable oil
1 clove garlic, crushed
2 cups tomato purée
1 4-ounce can chopped green chilies, drained
2-3 cups chopped, cooked chicken

Salt to taste
3 cups whipping cream
6 chicken bouillon cubes
8-10 six-inch flour or corn tortillas
¾ pound Swiss cheese, grated

Sauté onion in oil until soft. Add garlic, tomato purée, chilies and chicken. Season with salt and simmer 10 minutes.

Heat 3 cups cream and dissolve bouillon cubes in cream.

Fry tortillas in a small amount of oil until soft; not crisp. Dip each tortilla in cream mixture; fill each with about ¼ cup chicken mixture. Roll up tortillas and place seam-side down in a 13x9x2-inch pan. Pour remaining cream mixture over tortillas and sprinkle with grated cheese. Bake at 350° for 30 minutes.

Yield: 8-10 servings

*This is an authentic Mexican recipe from the Yucatan. However, monterey jack cheese may be substituted for the Swiss cheese.*

# GARLIC SOUR CREAM CHICKEN

1 2½-3-pound chicken, cut up
¾ cup sour cream
2 cloves garlic, crushed
2 teaspoons Worcestershire sauce
1 teaspoon lemon juice

1 teaspoon celery salt
1 teaspoon salt
1 teaspoon paprika
Pepper to taste
½ cup butter, melted
¾ cup bread crumbs

After washing chicken, pat dry and coat with a mixture of sour cream, garlic, Worcestershire, lemon juice, celery salt, paprika and pepper. Arrange skin-side up in a shallow, greased pan. Top with butter mixed with bread crumbs.

Bake at 350° for 1 hour 15 minutes or until brown.

Yield: 4-6 servings

# EASY CHICKEN KIEV

4 tablespoons butter,
   softened
¼ clove garlic, minced
Juice of 1 lemon
2 tablespoons dried parsley
   flakes

4 chicken breast halves,
   skinned and boned
Milk
1 egg, beaten
About 12 Saltine crackers,
   crushed

Combine butter, garlic, lemon juice and parsley. Form into 4 long rolls and freeze until solid. Flatten chicken breasts between sheets of wax paper. Brush inside of each chicken piece with milk; place one butter roll in the center; then roll chicken around butter, securing with toothpicks.

Dip chicken rolls in beaten egg and roll in cracker crumbs. Refrigerate for 1 hour. Heat 1 inch of oil to 350°. Fry chicken about 7 minutes, until brown on all sides. Chicken can be prepared, then frozen until cooked. If cooking frozen chicken, increase cooking time to 15-20 minutes.

Yield: 4 servings

# BAKED CHICKEN SALAD

3 cups chopped, cooked
   chicken
1½ cups sliced celery
1 cup grated cheddar
   cheese
2 tablespoons chopped
   onion
1 tablespoon lemon juice

1½ teaspoons salt
⅛ teaspoon pepper
Mayonnaise
1 medium tomato, sliced
1½ cups crushed whole
   wheat crackers
1 cup grated cheddar
   cheese

Combine chicken, celery, 1 cup cheese, onion, lemon juice, seasonings and enough mayonnaise to moisten; mix. Spoon into a 1½-quart casserole. Top with tomato slices. Bake 35 minutes at 350°. Top with mixture of crackers and cheese and bake until cheese is melted.

This can be made in a pie shell, adding ½ cup grated cheese to the pastry. Bake the pie shell before filling with chicken salad.

Yield: 6 servings

# CHICKEN AND WILD RICE

⅔ cup wild rice
½ cup chopped onion
½ cup butter
¼ cup flour
6 ounces mushrooms,
  sliced
1½ cups chicken broth
1½ cups half and half

3-4 cups chopped, cooked
  chicken
¼ cup chopped pimento
2 tablespoons snipped
  parsley
1½ teaspoons salt
¼ teaspoon pepper
½ cup slivered almonds

Cook rice according to package directions.

Sauté onion in butter until tender but not brown. Remove from heat and stir in the flour. Gradually stir chicken broth into the flour mixture. Add half and half; cook until mixture thickens. Add the rice, mushrooms, chicken, pimento, parsley, salt and pepper. Place in a casserole and sprinkle with almonds. Bake at 350° for 30 minutes.

Yield: 10 servings

# TENNESSEE CLUB CHICKEN

6 boneless chicken breasts
6 tablespoons flour
6 tablespoons shortening
6 slices country ham
2 tablespoons butter
3 tablespoons flour
2 cups milk

½ cup sherry
Salt and pepper
6 slices bread, toasted, cut
  into 4-inch rounds
12 broiled, fresh
  mushroom caps

Dredge chicken breasts in flour and brown in melted shortening in a heavy skillet. In a separate pan, brown ham slices. Remove from pan and trim fat. Add 2 tablespoons butter to ham drippings. Blend in flour, add milk and cook, stirring constantly until smooth and thick. Add sherry, mix well and season lightly with salt and pepper. Place chicken pieces in sauce and cover tightly. Bake at 325° for 20 minutes.

On toast rounds, place a slice of country ham trimmed to fit; on the ham place a chicken breast. Decorate with 2 broiled mushroom caps. Pour sauce over each and heat in oven. Serve immediately.

Yield: 6 servings

# CHICKEN WITH SOUR CREAM SAUCE

6 boneless chicken breasts
½ cup butter
½ pound fresh mushrooms,
    sliced
1 medium onion, sliced

2 9-ounce packages frozen
    artichoke hearts,
    cooked and drained
½ teaspoon thyme
½ teaspoon basil
½ cup chicken broth
Salt and pepper to taste

In a heavy skillet, sauté chicken breasts in butter. Cook about 4 minutes on each side. Remove chicken and sauté mushrooms and onions until tender. Add artichoke hearts, thyme, basil, chicken broth and salt and pepper to skillet. Cook for 5 minutes, stirring well. Add chicken to vegetable mixture and heat through.

*Sauce:*

1 cup sour cream
2 tablespoons chopped
    parsley

1 tablespoon lemon juice
¼ teaspoon salt

In a small bowl, mix sour cream, parsley, lemon juice and salt. Serve at room temperature.

Serve chicken over rice and pour sour cream sauce over the top.

Yield: 6 servings

# MOZZARELLA CHICKEN

4 boneless chicken breasts
4 tablespoons butter
Salt and pepper
4 slices mozzarella cheese

½ cup flour
1 egg, slightly beaten
½ cup seasoned bread
    crumbs

Flatten chicken between sheets of wax paper. Spread butter over each piece and season with salt and pepper. Place one slice mozzarella over each piece; roll up and fasten with toothpicks. Roll each in flour, dip in egg and then roll in bread crumbs. Place in a medium-sized casserole; cover and bake at 350° for 30 minutes. Remove cover and bake 15 minutes longer.

Yield: 4 servings

# ITALIAN CHICKEN

½ pound mushrooms, sliced
2 tablespoons butter
1 tablespoon basil
2 tablespoons white wine
5 tablespoons olive oil
4 cloves garlic, minced
5 tablespoons tomato paste
¼ cup grated Parmesan cheese
¼ cup flour
Salt and pepper
6 boneless chicken breasts
2 tablespoons butter

Sauté mushrooms in butter; set aside.

Soak basil in wine for 10 minutes. Heat olive oil in a small saucepan and sauté garlic for 3 minutes. Add basil, wine and tomato paste. Cook and stir for about 15 minutes on low heat. Add cheese and sautéed mushrooms. Remove from heat.

Flatten chicken breasts between sheets of wax paper. Dredge chicken breasts in flour and salt and pepper to taste. Melt butter in a 12-inch skillet and sauté chicken until browned on both sides (about 3 minutes per side). Place chicken in casserole and top each breast with sauce. Bake at 350° about 20 minutes or until bubbly.

Yield: 6 servings

# CHICKEN MARENGO

8 chicken breasts
¼ cup butter
2 tablespoons sherry
½ pound mushrooms,
   sliced
2 tablespoons flour
1½ cups chicken broth
1 tablespoon tomato paste
1 bay leaf, crushed
2 tablespoons chopped
   chives
½ teaspoon salt
⅛ teaspoon pepper
1 cup lobster, shrimp or
   king crabmeat, cooked

Sauté chicken breasts in 2 tablespoons butter until golden brown. Spoon on sherry and transfer from skillet to shallow baking dish. Cover with foil and bake in a slow oven (300°) about 30 minutes.

In a skillet, sauté mushrooms in 2 tablespoons butter and blend in flour. Add chicken broth, tomato paste and seasonings and simmer until thickened (about 15 minutes).

Add cooked seafood and simmer until thoroughly heated. Serve sauce over cooked chicken breasts. It is also delicious over cooked rice.

Yield: 6-8 servings

# CHICKEN TERIYAKI

1 cup teriyaki sauce
1 cup sugar
1½ cups dry sherry
4 green onions, chopped
2 teaspoons chopped
   cilantro
2 cloves garlic, minced
½ teaspoon grated fresh
   ginger
2 tablespoons sesame oil
2 teaspoons dark corn
   syrup
¼ teaspoon salt
⅛ teaspoon pepper
12 chicken breasts

Combine all ingredients except chicken. Pour marinade over chicken and marinate in refrigerator 24 hours or longer, turning chicken several times. Cook on charcoal grill, basting with sauce frequently.

Yield: 8 servings

# CHICKEN PICCATA

| | |
|---|---|
| 2 pounds boneless chicken breasts | 1 large onion, chopped |
| 1 teaspoon salt | 1½ cups chicken broth |
| ½ teaspoon pepper | ¼ cup fresh lemon juice |
| 3 tablespoons flour | 8 slices lemon, cut paper thin |
| ¾ teaspoon oregano | 2 tablespoons capers |
| 3 tablespoons olive oil | ¼ cup finely chopped parsley |
| 3 cloves garlic, crushed | |

Cut each chicken breast into 9-10 small pieces. Flatten between sheets of wax paper. Combine salt, pepper, flour and oregano in a small bowl. Dredge chicken pieces in flour mixture.

Heat the oil over low heat in a 12-inch skillet. Add the garlic and onion and sauté 3-5 minutes or until soft but not browned. With a slotted spoon, remove the onion and garlic and set aside.

Raise heat to medium-high and brown the chicken pieces on both sides. Return the onion and garlic to the pan and add the broth. Bring to a boil. Cover and simmer for 10-15 minutes. Stir in the lemon juice and coat chicken pieces evenly with the juice.

Arrange on a heated serving platter and garnish with lemon slices, parsley and capers.

Yield: 4 servings

# SHERRIED MUSHROOM CHICKEN

1 cup sliced fresh
   mushrooms, or 1
   8-ounce can, drained
2 tablespoons butter
4 large chicken breasts
2 tablespoons butter
1 teaspoon salt
¼ teaspoon pepper

⅛ teaspoon garlic salt
½ teaspoon paprika
¼ teaspoon crushed
   rosemary
¾ cup dry sherry
¼ cup water
1 teaspoon cornstarch
¼ cup minced green onion

Lightly brown mushrooms in 2 tablespoons butter; remove from pan and set aside. Remove skin from chicken breasts and wipe dry with a paper towel. Brown chicken in 2 tablespoons butter. Sprinkle with salt, pepper, garlic salt, paprika and rosemary. Add sherry. Cover pan and simmer 30-40 minutes or until chicken is tender.

Blend water and cornstarch and stir into the pan liquids. Add mushrooms and green onion and cook 30 minutes.

Yield: 2-3 servings

# LEMON CHICKEN

1 tablespoon soy sauce
½ teaspoon salt
½ teaspoon pepper
¼ cup vegetable oil

½ cup fresh lemon juice
2 tablespoons grated
   lemon peel
1 clove garlic, crushed

Combine soy sauce, salt, pepper, oil, lemon juice, lemon peel and garlic; mix well. Refrigerate at least 1 hour before using.

2½-3-pound broiler-fryer,
   cut up, or 8 chicken
   breasts
½ cup unsifted flour

1 teaspoon salt
¼ teaspoon pepper
2 teaspoons paprika
½ cup butter, melted

Preheat oven to 400°. Combine flour, salt, pepper and paprika. Coat chicken with flour mixture. Arrange chicken, skin side down, in single layer in a shallow pan. Brush chicken well with butter. Bake, uncovered, 30 minutes. Turn chicken. Pour sauce over and bake 30 minutes longer or until golden brown.

Yield: 4 servings

# SPAGHETTI CARUSO

*Brown Sauce:*

½ cup butter
6 tablespoons flour

2 cups beef bouillon
Salt and pepper to taste

Melt butter in a heavy skillet; stir in flour, stirring until flour is browned but not burned. Gradually add 2 cups beef bouillon, stirring constantly until thickened. Add salt and pepper to taste. Set aside.

*Chicken Livers:*

½ cup olive oil
1 pound chicken livers,
    blanched
½ pound mushrooms,
    sliced
2 teaspoons finely chopped
    onion

¼ tablespoon basil
Salt and pepper
1 clove garlic, minced
1 cup Burgundy
2 medium tomatoes,
    peeled and diced

Heat olive oil in a heavy skillet. Add chicken livers, mushrooms, onion, basil and salt and pepper to taste. Sauté until chicken livers are golden brown. Add garlic and sauté 1 minute more. Add wine, tomatoes and brown sauce and bring to a boil. Reduce heat and simmer 20 minutes, uncovered.

*Spaghetti:*

1 pound spaghetti, cooked
    al dente
1½ cups tomato sauce,
    homemade or Ragú

1 cup freshly grated
    Parmesan cheese

Combine tomato sauce with cooked spaghetti in a large bowl. Top with chicken liver mixture. Serve with grated Parmesan cheese.

Yield: 6 servings

# CHICKEN FIESTA

2 chickens, cut up
1 small head of garlic,
  minced
2 tablespoons fresh
  oregano
1 teaspoon salt
½ teaspoon freshly ground
  pepper
¼ cup red wine vinegar
¼ cup olive oil
¼ cup pitted Spanish green
  olives

1 cup sliced fresh
  mushrooms
¼ cup capers with 1
  tablespoon juice
2-3 bay leaves
½ cup light brown sugar
½ cup dry vermouth or
  white wine
2 tablespoons minced fresh
  parsley

In a large bowl combine chicken pieces, garlic, oregano, salt, pepper, wine vinegar, olive oil, olives, mushrooms, capers, juice and bay leaves. Cover and let marinate in refrigerator overnight.

Preheat oven to 350°.

Arrange chicken in a single layer in a large, shallow baking pan and spoon marinade over it evenly. Sprinkle chicken pieces with brown sugar and pour vermouth around them. Bake at 350° for 50 minutes, basting frequently with pan juices.

With a slotted spoon, transfer chicken, olives, mushrooms and capers to a serving dish. Spoon pan juices over chicken and sprinkle with parsley. Serve remaining pan juices in a sauceboat.

Yield: 6 servings

*Chicken Fiesta is a spectacular party dish. It travels well and makes excellent picnic fare when served at room temperature. When prepared with small drumsticks, it makes a delicious hors d'oeuvre.*

# CROWN ROAST OF PORK VALENCIA

**1 6-7 pound crown roast of pork**    **Salt and pepper**

Preheat oven to 350°. Sprinkle roast with salt and pepper. Place on rack in shallow roasting pan with rib ends up. Fill center cavity with crumpled aluminum foil to keep crown shape; cover rib ends with foil. Roast in oven 35-40 minutes per pound or until meat thermometer reaches 185°.

*Stuffing:*

**1 pound bulk pork sausage**
**1 cup chopped onion**
**2 cups cooked rice**
**½ cup orange juice**
**1 tablespoon parsley**

**½ teaspoon poultry seasoning**
**4 oranges, sectioned**
**½ cup raisins**
**½ cup chopped pecans**

Meanwhile, break up sausage in large skillet and cook with onion until meat is done and onion is golden, but not brown. Drain fat. Add rice, orange juice, parsley, poultry seasoning, orange sections, raisins and pecans; mix lightly.

One hour before end of roasting time, remove pork roast from oven. Remove foil and fill cavity with stuffing mixture, piling high in center. Return to oven and roast 1 hour longer. Serve with Valencia sauce.

*Valencia Sauce:*

**3 tablespoons pork drippings from roasting pan**
**3 tablespoons flour**
**2 cups orange juice**

**¾ teaspoon salt**
**¼ teaspoon poultry seasoning**
**1 orange, sectioned**

Blend pan drippings and flour in roasting pan. Gradually stir in orange juice; add seasoning. Stir constantly over medium heat until mixture thickens and comes to a boil. Stir in brown particles from bottom of pan. Add orange slices and heat.

Yield: 8-10 servings

# FIESTA CASSEROLE

1½ cups wild rice
1 tablespoon shortening
1 pound lean veal, pork or
chicken, cut into
1-inch cubes
1 teaspoon salt
1 can mushroom soup
¼ cup chopped onion
½ cup chopped celery
1 green onion cut into long
thin slices

1 tablespoon
Worcestershire sauce
1 tablespoon soy sauce
½ cup dry sherry
½ cup crushed pineapple,
drained
¼ cup grated cheddar
cheese
¼ cup sliced, blanched
almonds

Prepare rice according to package directions. Brown meat in hot shortening. Add all ingredients except cheese and almonds and simmer 10 minutes. Pour into greased 2-quart casserole. Sprinkle cheese and almonds on top. Bake at 350° for about 40 minutes.

Yield: 4-6 servings

# PORK CHOPS PEASANT STYLE

4 loin or shoulder pork
chops
Flour
1 clove garlic, minced
Salt and pepper
Vegetable oil
4 Irish potatoes, peeled
and sliced

2 large onions, sliced
1½ cups sour cream
1 can cream of mushroom
soup
½ teaspoon dry mustard
1½ teaspoons salt

Trim excess fat from chops and roll in flour. Brown chops and garlic in a small amount of oil over medium heat. Season with salt and pepper. Place potatoes in a 13x9x2-inch casserole. Top with chops. Separate onion slices into rings and arrange over chops. Blend sour cream, soup, salt and mustard. Pour over potatoes, chops and onions. Cover with foil and bake 1 hour 30 minutes at 350°.

Yield: 4 servings

# GINGERED HAM STEAK

1 fully cooked center-cut
   ham slice, 1 inch thick
½ cup ginger ale
½ cup orange juice
¼ cup brown sugar
1 tablespoon vegetable oil

1½ teaspoons wine vinegar
1 teaspoon dry mustard
1 slice fresh ginger
⅛ teaspoon ground cloves

Slash fat edge of ham. Combine remaining ingredients and pour over ham in a shallow glass bowl. Refrigerate overnight, spooning marinade over ham several times. Grill ham over charcoal about 15 minutes per side.

Yield: 2-4 servings

# ORANGE PORK CHOPS

4 pork chops, thick enough
   for stuffing
2 tablespoons butter
⅓ cup chopped onion
½ cup chopped celery
1½ cups bread cubes

2 tablespoons chopped
   parsley
1 teaspoon salt
½ teaspoon grated orange
   peel
3 tablespoons orange juice

Preheat oven to 375°. Sauté onion and celery in butter until tender. Add bread cubes and brown slightly. Remove from heat. Add parsley, salt, orange peel and orange juice. Stir. Fill pockets in pork chops with stuffing. Put chops on a rack over a pan filled with ½ inch water. Cover pan and rack with foil. Bake at 375° for 1 hour 30 minutes.

*Glaze:*
½ cup orange juice
¼ cup light brown sugar

¼ cup orange marmalade
2 tablespoons vinegar

Combine orange juice, brown sugar, marmalade and vinegar; simmer 15 minutes.

Remove foil from chops. Pour off water. Brush chops with glaze. Bake 30 minutes more, basting every 5-10 minutes.

Yield: 4 servings

# GULF WINDS PORK CHOPS

8 pork chops
2 tablespoons vegetable oil
1 clove garlic, minced
¾ cup sherry
¼ cup soy sauce

¼ cup vegetable oil
1 slice fresh ginger,
   minced
¼ teaspoon oregano
1 tablespoon maple syrup

Preheat oven to 350°. Brown chops in 2 tablespoons oil in a skillet. Place chops in baking dish. Combine remaining ingredients and pour over chops. Bake, covered, 1 hour-1 hour 30 minutes, turning once.

Yield: 4-6 servings

# SAUSAGE AND WILD RICE SUPREME

1 pound sausage
1 pound mushrooms,
   sliced
1 cup chopped onion
2 cups wild or brown rice,
   washed
¼ cup plus 2 tablespoons
   flour
½ cup whipping cream

2½ cups chicken broth
⅛ teaspoon dried oregano
⅛ teaspoon dried thyme
⅛ teaspoon dried marjoram
1 teaspoon salt
⅛ teaspoon pepper
⅛ teaspoon Tabasco sauce
½ cup slivered almonds,
   toasted

Cook sausage, drain and reserve 3 tablespoons fat. Sauté mushrooms and onion in sausage fat. When slightly brown, add cooked sausage. Meanwhile, cook rice in boiling salted water according to package directions. Drain.

Mix flour and cream until smooth. Add chicken broth and cook until sauce thickens. Season with herbs, salt and pepper. Combine all ingredients and toss together. Adjust seasonings to taste.

Pour into greased 2½-quart casserole. Bake at 350° for 25-30 minutes or until hot. Sprinkle almonds around edge of casserole before serving.

Yield: 10-12 servings

# SWEET AND SOUR PORK

*Pork:*

1 pound pork tenderloin,
   cut into 1-inch cubes
½ cup flour
6 tablespoons cornstarch
⅔ cup cold water

1 teaspoon soy sauce or 1
   teaspoon salt
2 teaspoons baking powder
Vegetable or peanut oil

Combine flour, cornstarch, water and soy sauce. Stir until batter is smooth. Pour oil into a wok or heavy skillet, filling ⅓ full; heat oil. Stir 1 tablespoon hot oil and 2 teaspoons baking powder into batter. Dip meat into batter and fry in hot oil. Fry until lightly brown. Drain meat on paper towels. Place in warm oven until ready to heat with sauce.

*Sweet and Sour Sauce:*

1 tablespoon oil
8 ounces pineapple chunks
   in own juice
½ onion, thinly sliced
1 large green bell pepper,
   thinly sliced
1 cup thinly sliced carrots

⅓ cup vinegar
1 tablespoon cornstarch
⅓ cup dark corn syrup
1 tablespoon sugar
½ teaspoon salt
2 tablespoons dry sherry

Drain pineapple, reserving ¼ cup juice. Pour 1 tablespoon oil into wok or skillet. Heat; then add onion, green pepper and carrots. In large skillet stir vinegar and cornstarch until smooth. Stir in corn syrup, sugar, salt and pineapple juice. Stirring constantly, bring to a boil. Stir in pork, vegetables, pineapple and sherry. Boil for 1 minute, stirring constantly. Serve with steamed rice.

Yield: 4 servings

*Shrimp, boneless chicken and fish are also good in this batter.*

# HERBED PORK ROAST

1 4-pound pork loin
3 tablespoons vegetable oil
2 tablespoons lemon juice
1 teaspoon thyme
1 clove garlic, minced

Salt and pepper to taste
1 jar pearl onions
2 tablespoons pan
  drippings

Preheat oven to 350°. Combine oil, lemon juice, thyme, garlic, salt and pepper. Place pork loin, fat-side up, in an uncovered pan. Rub the mixture into the pork. Roast about 2 hours 30 minutes, or 35-45 minutes per pound (to 185° on meat thermometer). Remove from oven. Drain onions and brown in 2 tablespoons pan drippings. Add onions to roasting pan and return to oven for 5 minutes.

Yield: 6 servings

# ROAST LEG OF LAMB

1 5-7-pound leg of lamb
¼ cup shortening
¼ cup butter
¼ cup flour
¼ cup vinegar
1 clove garlic, minced

1 tablespoon
  Worcestershire sauce
1 tablespoon salt
1 teaspoon sugar
¼ teaspoon cayenne
  pepper
2 cups water

Trim fat from lamb, using a sharp knife. Score the meat and place in an uncovered roasting pan. Cook 15 minutes at 500°, 15 minutes at 450° and then at 325° until done (2 hours 30 minutes for well-done or 2 hours for slightly pink). As soon as the meat is well seared, begin to baste with sauce.

To make basting sauce, melt butter and shortening; stir in flour, vinegar, garlic, Worcestershire, salt, sugar, cayenne and water. Stir constantly to prevent lumping. When the roast is done, the last of the basting sauce should be used.

Serve meat with pan juices or add 1-2 tablespoons of flour and 1 cup of water to make a thick gravy. Serve with mint or hot pepper jelly.

Yield: 6-8 servings

# LEG OF LAMB DE LUNA

1 6-7-pound leg of lamb
1½ ounces gin
2 tablespoons Dijon
    mustard
1 clove garlic, crushed
½ teaspoon dried rosemary
1 teaspoon salt

¼ teaspoon white pepper
2 tablespoons flour
½ cup currant jelly
1¼ cups water
¼ teaspoon salt
2 ounces gin

Wipe the lamb well and place on a rack in a roasting pan, fat side up. Blend 1½ ounces gin, mustard, garlic, rosemary, salt and white pepper to make a paste. Spread the mixture over the lamb.

For a pink, juicy lamb, roast in a preheated 325° oven for about 2 hours or until meat thermometer reads 165°. For medium to well-done, cook 2 hours 30 minutes-2 hours 45 minutes or until thermometer reads 180°. Remove from oven and place on serving platter. Keep warm while preparing sauce.

Remove excess fat from pan drippings and add flour; cook 3 minutes, stirring constantly. Add currant jelly and water and heat, stirring until the jelly is melted. Add ¼ teaspoon salt and 2 ounces gin, stirring to blend. Cook, stirring constantly, over low heat until the mixture thickens and boils, about 3 minutes. Serve hot with lamb.

Yield: 8-10 servings

# VEAL CORDON BLEU

4 boneless veal cutlets or 1
    pound veal round
    steak, ½ inch thick
4 thin slices boiled ham
4 thin slices Swiss cheese
2 tablespoons flour
½ teaspoon salt
¼ teaspoon pepper
¼ teaspoon allspice
1 egg, slightly beaten
½ cup bread crumbs
3 tablespoons shortening
2 tablespoons water

If using veal round steak, cut into 4 serving pieces. Pound meat until ¼ inch thick. Place a slice of ham and cheese on each cutlet. Roll up carefully, beginning at the narrow end; secure rolls with toothpicks.

Mix flour, salt, pepper and allspice; coat rolls with flour mixture. Dip into egg and then bread crumbs.

In a skillet, brown rolls in shortening 5 minutes. Reduce heat and add water. Cover and simmer 45 minutes or until tender.

Yield: 4 servings

# VEAL SCALLOPS AMANDINE

6 veal scallops (6 ounces
    each)
Salt and pepper
2½ cups bread crumbs
⅓ cup minced parsley
3 tablespoons grated
    lemon rind
3 egg whites
1½ cups blanched
    almonds, sliced
2 tablespoons butter
¾ cup clarified butter
1 lemon, sliced
Fresh parsley

Flatten veal scallops between sheets of wax paper until they are ¼ inch thick; sprinkle with salt and pepper. In a shallow bowl combine bread crumbs, parsley and lemon rind. In another bowl, beat egg whites lightly. Dip scallops into egg whites and then into crumbs, pressing crumb mixture into them. Chill scallops on a baking sheet for 30 minutes.

Meanwhile, in a small skillet, sauté almonds in 2 tablespoons butter until golden; set aside. In a large skillet, sauté veal in clarified butter for 1-2 minutes on each side or until golden. Transfer veal to a heated platter and sprinkle with almonds. Garnish with lemon slices and parsley.

Yield: 6 servings

# VEAL MARCHELLO

1 pound thinly cut veal
    scallops
Flour
½ cup unsalted butter
½ cup dry white wine
½ cup finely chopped
    mushrooms
3 ounces thinly sliced
    prosciutto

Sliced Fontina cheese
Salt and white pepper
Fresh tomato wedges
¼ cup grated Parmesan
    cheese

Dust veal scallops with flour. Melt butter in large skillet. Sauté veal until golden, turning once. Top each scallop with Fontina cheese and then lower heat. Let cheese melt and top with sliced prosciutto. Place part of mushrooms on ham and cheese. Remove to warm platter. Add remainder of chopped mushrooms and wine to pan drippings. Reduce pan juices to desired consistency and add salt and white pepper to taste.

Broil tomato wedges with Parmesan cheese, salt and white pepper. Drizzle reduced juices over veal scallops and garnish with broiled tomato wedges. Serve with fettuccine noodles in a butter and grated Parmesan cheese sauce.

Yield: 4-6 servings

# VEAL ROMANO

*Veal:*

4 thin, oblong slices of
  veal
½ cup Italian bread crumbs
⅓ cup grated Romano
  cheese
½ teaspoon salt

½ teaspoon pepper
8 ounces sliced mozzarella
  cheese
1 beaten egg
3 tablespoons olive oil
1 tablespoon butter

Combine bread crumbs and Romano cheese. Set aside. Salt and pepper the veal. Cut mozzarella cheese into 8 rectangular slices. Using only 4 of the slices, place 1 slice on half of each piece of veal. Fold the veal over on top of the cheese. Dip each piece in the beaten egg; then roll in the bread crumb mixture. On medium-low, heat oil and butter in a 12-inch skillet. Brown veal on both sides and remove from skillet. Set aside.

*Sauce:*

2 tablespoons olive oil
½ cup chopped onion
1 14½-ounce can stewed
  tomatoes
1 6-ounce can tomato
  paste
2 teaspoons garlic powder
1 tablespoon parsley

1 teaspoon oregano
½ teaspoon basil
1 teaspoon salt
1 teaspoon sugar
⅓ cup water
⅓ cup grated Romano
  cheese

In a large saucepan, sauté onion in olive oil. Add tomatoes, tomato paste, garlic powder, parsley, oregano, basil, salt, sugar and water. Simmer 30 minutes.

Place veal in a shallow baking dish. Top each piece with a slice of mozzarella cheese. Pour sauce over the veal and top with remaining ⅓ cup Romano cheese. Bake at 350° for 25 minutes.

Yield: 4 servings

# DOVES IN RED WINE

7-10 doves
Salt and pepper
1 medium onion, chopped
½ cup red wine
1 cup water

1 chicken bouillon cube
2 ribs celery, cut in half
1 green bell pepper, halved
1 tablespoon cornstarch

Salt and pepper birds. Brown birds in butter in pressure cooker without the top. Remove birds. Sauté onion in same butter and add doves. Add wine, water, bouillon cube, celery and pepper. Cover pressure cooker and cook for 15 minutes at 10 pounds of pressure. Place pressure cooker under cold water; take knob off and open slowly. Remove doves and discard celery and pepper.

Mix cornstarch with a small amount of cold water and add to juices in pressure cooker. Stir constantly until gravy is smooth and thickened. Add doves to pressure cooker and warm with the top off in gravy until ready to serve.

Doves can also be simmered about 2 hours in a heavy Dutch oven with similar results.

Yield: 4 servings

*Doves are excellent cooked this way. The gravy tastes especially good over wild rice.*

# DUCKS IN WHITE WINE

2 mallard or wood ducks
1 onion, halved
1 rib celery, halved
2 cloves garlic, crushed
1 green bell pepper, halved
1 small hot pepper
4 tablespoons butter
2 cups white wine
4 tablespoons
    Worcestershire sauce

Salt, pepper and
    Cavender's seasoning
    to taste
2 tablespoons chopped
    fresh parsley
2 tablespoons flour
2 beef or chicken bouillon
    cubes
1 teaspoon Kitchen
    Bouquet

Line a Dutch oven with foil and place ducks inside. Stuff each duck with onion, celery, garlic, bell pepper, hot pepper (if desired) and butter. Add 1 cup wine and Worcestershire; then sprinkle ducks with salt, pepper, Cavender's and parsley. Seal foil tightly around ducks. Bake in 350° oven for 1 hour. Unfold foil and check ducks for tenderness; cook longer if necessary.

Remove foil, leaving drippings in the pan. Add 2 tablespoons flour to make a roux and gradually add remaining 1 cup wine, bouillon cubes and Kitchen Bouquet, stirring to make a smooth gravy. Add vegetables from ducks and season gravy to taste. Stuff ducks, if desired, with favorite stuffing. Add ducks to gravy and baste well. Bake, covered, at 325° for 1 hour or until very tender.

Yield: 4 servings

# SMOKED HERB-SEASONED QUAIL

24 quail
1/3 cup vinegar
1 tablespoon dried sage
1 tablespoon chopped
   fresh oregano or 1
   teaspoon dried
   oregano
1 tablespoon
   Worcestershire sauce
2 garlic cloves, minced

1/4 teaspoon dried thyme
1 teaspoon sugar
1/4 teaspoon freshly grated
   nutmeg
1 1/2 cups vegetable oil
2 cups hickory chips
Salt and pepper
24 slices thin bacon

Pat quail dry. Arrange in a single layer in a non-aluminum container. In a mixing bowl, combine vinegar, sage, oregano, Worcestershire, garlic, thyme, sugar and nutmeg. Whisk in oil very slowly. Pour marinade over quail. Cover and refrigerate several hours or overnight, turning occasionally.

Combine hickory chips with water to cover. Let stand until charcoal is ready. Drain quail, pat dry. Season with salt and pepper. Wrap each quail in bacon, securing with toothpicks. Drain hickory chips and place over hot coals. Cover grill and heat coals until smoke appears around the rim. Arrange quail on grill, cover and smoke until leg bones move easily (10-15 minutes), turning occasionally.

Yield: 10 servings

# QUAIL AND WILD RICE

2 tablespoons butter
1 6-ounce package long
    grain and wild rice
2½ cups water
¼ cup minced onion
¼ cup minced green bell
    pepper

½ cup minced celery
6 quail, dressed
6 tablespoons butter
¼ cup brown sugar
12-18 pecan halves

Preheat oven to 325°. Melt butter in a 13x9x2-inch glass baking dish. Add contents of rice package, water, onion, bell pepper and celery. Mix well. Place quail on top. Cover with aluminum foil and bake at 325° for 60 minutes.

While quail bakes, prepare glazed pecans by melting butter in a small saucepan and adding brown sugar until consistency is thick but not hard. Coat pecans with glaze. After casserole bakes for 60 minutes, remove foil and drizzle each quail with glazed pecans. Return to oven for 10 minutes.

Yield: 4 servings

# TEXAS MEAT SAUCE

1 cup chili sauce
¼ cup vinegar
¼ cup water
2 tablespoons sugar
½ teaspoon chili powder
½ teaspoon salt
⅛ teaspoon cayenne

¼ teaspoon black pepper
1 tablespoon prepared
    mustard
1 medium onion, chopped
2 drops Tabasco sauce
¼ teaspoon oregano

Combine all ingredients and heat to boiling, stirring occasionally. Pour over beef roast or ribs. Cover and bake at 325° for 2 hours-2 hours 30 minutes, or until tender. Uncover the last 30 minutes of cooking time. Baste every 10-15 minutes.

Yield: 4-6 servings

# HOT MUSTARD

⅓ cup dry mustard
1 tablespoon sugar
¼ teaspoon salt

⅔ cup wine vinegar
2 eggs

In a small, heavy saucepan combine mustard, sugar and salt. Beat vinegar and eggs together and then beat into the mustard mixture. Cook over medium heat, stirring constantly until thickened. The eggs will curdle if the temperature is too high.

Yield: approximately 1 cup

# SWEET-HOT MUSTARD

5 tablespoons dry mustard
½ cup sugar
2 tablespoons flour
2 teaspoons salt

1 cup milk
1 egg yolk
½ cup vinegar

Sift mustard, sugar, flour and salt. Add milk, egg yolk and vinegar; beat well. Pour through a strainer into the top of a double boiler. Cook over medium heat until thickened.

Yield: approximately 2 cups

# SUPER UNCOOKED BARBECUE SAUCE

2 cloves garlic, crushed
1½ teaspoons salt
1 teaspoon freshly ground
   black pepper
¼ cup finely chopped green
   onion
2 teaspoons prepared
   mustard

1 teaspoon dry mustard
Juice of 1 lemon
1½ cups ketchup
½ cup tomato juice
1 teaspoon tarragon
Tabasco sauce, to taste

Combine all ingredients and mix well. Sauce will keep 2-3 months in the refrigerator. Barbecue sauce is good on chicken and ribs.

Yield: 2 cups

# BARBECUE SAUCE FOR CHICKEN

2 cups butter or margarine
⅔ cup vinegar
3 heaping tablespoons dry
   mustard
4 teaspoons salt

1 tablespoon
   Worcestershire sauce
¼ teaspoon Tabasco sauce
Freshly ground pepper, to
   taste

Combine all ingredients and heat slowly to boiling point, stirring occasionally. Do not boil. Cook chicken slowly on a grill, basting with sauce frequently. If sauce is too thick, thin with vinegar.

Yield: enough for 4 chickens, halved

# COMEBACK SAUCE

½ cup butter
1 clove garlic, crushed
Juice of one lemon

½ teaspoon Worcestershire
   sauce
½ teaspoon salt
¼ teaspoon black pepper

Combine all ingredients and heat until butter is melted. When ready to serve, reheat until butter is hot.

Yield: 6 servings

*Comeback sauce is wonderful to drizzle over grilled steaks.*

# HORSERADISH SAUCE

1 cup mayonnaise
1 heaping tablespoon
   horseradish
1 teaspoon Worcestershire
   sauce
Juice of 1 lemon

1 tablespoon chopped
   parsley
⅛ teaspoon celery salt
⅛ teaspoon onion salt
⅛ teaspoon garlic powder

Mix all ingredients and refrigerate. Sauce keeps well for several days. Serve at room temperature on steamed green vegetables or rare roast beef.

Yield: approximately 1¼ cups

# MARCHAND DE VIN SAUCE

6 tablespoons butter,
divided
4 tablespoons flour
3 cups beef broth
½ cup chopped onion
¼ cup chopped celery
¼ cup cooked, chopped
ham
2 tablespoons chopped
parsley

1 tablespoon chopped
garlic
2 bay leaves
1 teaspoon thyme
¼ pound mushrooms,
chopped
½ cup Madeira or red wine
¼ teaspoon lemon juice

Make a roux with 4 tablespoons butter and flour in a large skillet. Cook until dark brown, stirring constantly to prevent burning. Place 1 cup broth in a blender with onion, celery, ham, parsley and garlic. Blend 30 seconds and add to the roux. Stir in remaining 2 cups beef broth; add bay leaves and thyme. Simmer 30 minutes uncovered, stirring occasionally. Sauté mushrooms in remaining 2 tablespoons butter over high heat for 1 minute. Add to stock base and simmer 10 more minutes. Add wine; simmer 5 more minutes. Add lemon juice. Serve warm on steak.

Yield: 1½ pints

# EASY HOLLANDAISE SAUCE

2 egg yolks
3 tablespoons lemon juice

8 tablespoons butter

In double boiler put egg yolks and lemon juice. Stir. Do not let simmering water in bottom pan touch top pan. Add butter by tablespoons, stirring constantly. As each addition melts, add more. Stir and cook until sauce is almost as thick as mayonnaise. Remove from heat and serve immediately.

Yield: ¾ cup

# MOCK BERNAISE

¼ cup chopped green
　　onion
⅛ teaspoon salt
⅛ teaspoon freshly ground
　　pepper

2 tablespoons tarragon
　　vinegar
¼ teaspoon dried tarragon
¾ cup Easy Hollandaise
　　Sauce

Combine green onion, salt, pepper, vinegar and tarragon in a saucepan. Heat to simmer. Cook until all the vinegar has evaporated, stirring occasionally and watching closely to prevent burning. Add to cooked recipe of Easy Hollandaise Sauce. Serve with rare steak.

Yield: ¾ cup

# MUSHROOM SAUCE

1 pound fresh mushrooms
　　(whole if small,
　　quartered if large)
4 tablespoons butter
4 tablespoons minced
　　green onion
½ teaspoon salt
¼ teaspoon pepper

1 cup beef bouillon
2 tablespoons tomato
　　paste
½ cup Madeira wine or
　　sweet vermouth
1 tablespoon cornstarch
3 tablespoons minced
　　parsley

Sauté mushrooms in butter for 5 minutes to brown lightly. Stir in green onion and cook slowly for 2 minutes. Add salt and pepper. Set aside.

Simmer bouillon and tomato paste in a small saucepan. Combine cornstarch and wine and stir until cornstarch is dissolved; pour into bouillon mixture. Boil rapidly for 1 minute to evaporate alcohol and thicken the sauce slightly. Add sauce to sautéed mushrooms and simmer a minute to blend flavors. Spread sauce on grilled steaks and sprinkle with parsley.

Yield: 6 servings

# RAISIN SAUCE

½ cup light brown sugar
2 tablespoons cornstarch
⅛ teaspoon ground cloves
⅛ teaspoon salt

½ cup orange juice
1½ cups cranberry juice
½ cup seedless raisins

Combine all ingredients and cook until mixture thickens and comes to a boil. Serve with ham.

Yield: 8-10 servings

# SHISH KABOB WINE SAUCE

½ cup butter
2 tablespoons flour
1 cup chopped green onion
1 cup fresh sliced
　mushrooms

2 10¾-ounce cans beef
　consommé
½ cup white wine

Melt butter and blend in flour until smooth. Add green onion, mushrooms and consommé. Simmer 30 minutes. Add wine. Keep warm until ready to serve.

Make shish kabobs according to your favorite recipe. Serve over rice and pour sauce on top.

Yield: 4 servings

# FLANK STEAK MARINADE

1½ cups vegetable oil
¾ cup soy sauce
½ cup Worcestershire
　sauce
⅓ cup fresh lemon juice
2 tablespoons dry mustard

2½ teaspoons salt
1 tablespoon pepper
3 tablespoons chopped
　parsley
2 cloves garlic, crushed

Combine all ingredients and use to marinate flank steak or round steak.

Yield: approximately 3 cups

# TERIYAKI MARINADE

¾ cup soy sauce
¾ cup water
1 teaspoon ground ginger

2 tablespoons sugar
1 clove garlic, crushed
½ onion, finely chopped

Mix together all ingredients. Use sauce to marinate chicken or London broil. Marinate 4 hours or overnight. Baste meat with sauce while cooking.

Yield: approximately 1½ cups

# TERIYAKI-PINEAPPLE MARINADE

½ cup soy sauce
1 clove garlic, crushed
3 ounces pineapple juice
4 tablespoons dark brown
  sugar

1 tablespoon lemon juice
2 teaspoons ground ginger
½ tablespoon vegetable or
  sesame oil

Combine all ingredients and use to marinate beef kabobs or chicken breasts. Marinate overnight. Baste occasionally with marinade while cooking.

Yield: approximately 1 cup

# VENISON MARINADE

½ cup beef consommé
½ cup Burgundy wine
2 tablespoons honey or
  brown sugar
⅓ cup soy sauce

1½ tablespoons Lawry's
  Seasoned Salt
¼ cup chopped onion
1 tablespoon lime juice

Mix all ingredients. Marinade is good on venison or beef.

Yield: 1½ cups

# VEGETABLES
# AND
# FRUITS

# VEGETABLES AND FRUITS

**Asparagus**
Asparagus Caesar, 209
Baked Asparagus, 209

**Beans**
Barbecued Beans, 210
Green Beans à la Niçoise, 210
Heavenly Casserole, 234
Red Beans and Rice, 224
Savory Green Beans, 211

**Broccoli**
Broccoli with Olive Butter, 211
Broccoli Pancakes with Lemon Beurre
  Blanc, 212
Broccoli Pecan Casserole, 213
Broccoli Soufflé, 214
Broccoli and Tomato Wreath, 214
Broiled Tomatoes with Broccoli, 230
Crunchy Broccoli Casserole, 215
Herb-Seasoned Broccoli, 215
Stir-Fried Broccoli and Mushrooms, 213

**Cabbage**
Cabbage Eufaula, 216
Sweet and Sour Red Cabbage, 216

**Carrots**
Carrots Lyonnaise, 217
Carrots with Olives, 217
Julienne Zucchini and Carrots, 221
Mixed Vegetable Casserole, 235

**Celery**
Oriental Celery, 218

**Corn**
Corn Soufflé, 218

**Eggplant**
Eggplant Casserole, 223
Ratatouille, 237

**Fruit**
Cranberry Apple Casserole, 238
Curried Fruit, 237
Hot Pineapple Casserole, 238
Microwave Fruit Mélange, 236

**Mushrooms**
Mushroom and Onion Casserole, 219
Mushroom Pie, 233
Russian Mushrooms, 219

**Okra**
Hopkins Boarding House Stewed Okra and
  Tomatoes, 220

**Onions**
Gourmet Onions, 220
Onion Pudding, 221
Sir James' Onion Rings, 221

**Potatoes**
Bacon-Bleu Cheese Potatoes, 222
Gourmet Potatoes, 222
Hash Brown Casserole, 224
Mixed Vegetable Casserole, 235

**Spinach**
Savory Spinach Casserole, 226
Sicilian Spinach, 226
Spinach on Artichoke Bottoms Hollandaise,
  225
Spinach Rockefeller, 227
Spinach Soufflé Roll, 228
Spinach-Stuffed Tomatoes, 223

**Squash**
Creamy Squash Casserole, 227
Hopkins Boarding House Squash Casserole,
  229
Squash Boats, 229
Squash and Sausage Casserole, 230

**Tomatoes**
Broiled Tomatoes with Broccoli, 230
Fried Green Tomatoes, 211
Hopkins Boarding House Stewed Okra and
  Tomatoes, 220
Spinach-Stuffed Tomatoes, 223

**Sweet Potatoes**
Praline Yam Casserole with Orange Sauce,
  232
Sweet Potato Casserole, 231
Sweet Potato Soufflé, 231
Yam-Apple Bake, 233

**Zucchini**
Italian Zucchini, 236
Julienne Zucchini and Carrots, 221
Spanish Vegetables, 235
Zucchini Scallop, 234

# ASPARAGUS CAESAR

| | |
|---|---|
| 1 can asparagus spears | 2 tablespoons grated |
| 2 tablespoons butter, | Parmesan cheese |
| melted | Paprika |
| 2 tablespoons lemon juice | |

Drain asparagus carefully. Place in a single layer in a shallow pan. Melt butter in small pan and add lemon juice. Pour over asparagus. Sprinkle with Parmesan cheese, then paprika.

Just before serving, place under broiler and brown slightly. Serve hot.

Yield: 2-4 servings

# BAKED ASPARAGUS

| | |
|---|---|
| 3 tablespoons butter, softened | 3 tablespoons grated sharp cheddar cheese |
| 3 tablespoons flour | 1 teaspoon salt |
| 1-2 large cans asparagus, drained (1 cup liquid reserved) | 1/8 teaspoon cayenne |
| | 1/4 cup bread crumbs, buttered |
| 1/2 cup milk | 3 eggs, hard-boiled and sliced |
| 3 egg yolks | 1/3 cup slivered almonds |

Over low heat blend softened butter with flour. Add reserved asparagus liquid slowly. Cook until sauce thickens, stirring constantly to prevent lumping. Beat milk into egg yolks and add to the mixture along with cheese and seasonings.

In a buttered 9x9x2-inch baking dish, place a layer of asparagus with tips all pointing in the same direction. Add a layer of sauce and a layer of sliced hard-boiled eggs and almonds. Additional layers may be added if desired, finishing with sauce. Sprinkle bread crumbs over top, dot with butter and bake about 20 minutes at 350°.

Yield: 4-5 servings per can of asparagus

# BARBECUED BEANS

6 slices bacon
1 medium onion, chopped
1 medium green pepper, chopped
2 16-ounce cans baked beans, drained
1 16-ounce can lima beans, drained

1 15½-ounce can kidney beans with liquid
½ cup chili sauce
2 tablespoons brown sugar
3 tablespoons vinegar
½ teaspoon dry mustard
¼ teaspoon pepper
1 cup grated cheddar cheese

Cook bacon in a skillet until crisp. Remove and crumble. Sauté onion and pepper in 2 tablespoons of the bacon drippings.

Mix all ingredients except cheese in a 2½-quart casserole. Top with cheese and bake at 350° for 45 minutes.

Yield: 10-12 servings

# GREEN BEANS À LA NIÇOISE

2 10-ounce packages frozen French-style green beans
¼ cup olive oil
2 medium onions, thinly sliced
1 28-ounce can whole tomatoes, drained
1 small green bell pepper, thinly sliced

Bouquet garni (2 whole cloves, 1 large bay leaf, 1 celery top, 6 sprigs parsley)
1 teaspoon sugar
1 teaspoon salt
½ teaspoon freshly ground pepper

Cook green beans according to package directions. Drain and set aside.

Sauté remaining ingredients in olive oil for 20 minutes. Remove bouquet garni and add green beans. Heat well and serve.

Yield: 6-8 servings

## SAVORY GREEN BEANS

4 slices bacon
¼ cup chopped onion
2 tablespoons tarragon
   vinegar

½ teaspoon salt
⅛ teaspoon pepper
32 ounces green beans,
   fresh or frozen

Fry bacon until crisp. Set aside. Using 2 tablespoons of the bacon drippings, sauté onion until tender. Add vinegar, salt and pepper. Cook beans and drain. Pour sauce over hot beans.

Yield: 4-6 servings

## BROCCOLI WITH OLIVE BUTTER

⅔ cup butter
2 cloves garlic, crushed
4 teaspoons fresh lemon
   juice

12 large stuffed green
   olives, sliced
4 10-ounce packages
      frozen broccoli spears
Seasoned salt

In a small saucepan over low heat, cook butter and garlic about 15 minutes. Add lemon juice and sliced olives; heat thoroughly, but do not boil. Cook broccoli according to package directions. Drain. Arrange broccoli in a warmed serving dish. Sprinkle lightly with seasoned salt. Pour sauce over broccoli. Serve immediately.

Yield: 12 servings

## FRIED GREEN TOMATOES

4-6 green tomatoes
1 egg
1 cup flour

½ cup butter
Sugar
Salt and pepper

Slice unpeeled tomatoes into ½-inch slices. Dip each slice in beaten egg, then flour. Fry in melted butter until light brown on each side. Stack in casserole dish 3-4 slices high, sprinkling each slice lightly with sugar, salt and pepper. Bake at 350° for 30 minutes.

# BROCCOLI PANCAKES
# WITH LEMON BEURRE BLANC

1-1¼ pounds fresh broccoli
4 eggs, at room
    temperature
¼ cup flour
½ teaspoon salt
⅛ teaspoon freshly ground
    pepper
⅓ cup fresh lemon juice

1 cup chilled, unsalted
    butter, cut into ½-inch
    pieces
Salt and pepper
1 tablespoon minced, fresh
    chives
2-3 tablespoons clarified
    butter, or 1 tablespoon
    butter and 1 tablespoon oil

Cut flowerets from broccoli stems and cut stems into ½-inch slices. Bring large pot of salted water to boil over high heat. Add broccoli and cook 7-8 minutes. Remove with slotted spoon and drain in colander.

To prepare broccoli pancake batter, transfer broccoli stems to food processor. Add eggs, flour, salt and pepper and purée until smooth. Add flowerets (reserve 5 or 6 for garnish) and chop with short on/off turns. Set aside.

To prepare lemon beurre blanc, boil lemon juice in heavy saucepan and reduce to 2 tablespoons. Remove from heat and whisk in 2 pieces of chilled butter. Place over low heat and whisk in remaining butter, 2 pieces at a time. Season with salt and pepper. Keep warm in pan of hot water while preparing pancakes.

Preheat oven to 175°. Melt clarified butter on griddle or in heavy skillet over medium heat. Ladle 2-inch pancakes onto griddle. Cook until bottom is medium brown (2-3 minutes). Turn and brown second side. As pancakes finish, arrange on a greased baking sheet in a single layer and keep warm in oven.

Serve pancakes on heated platter and top with lemon beurre blanc. Garnish with reserved flowerets.

Yield: about 16 pancakes

*Pancakes reheat well in microwave.*

# BROCCOLI PECAN CASSEROLE

2 10-ounce packages
   frozen chopped
   broccoli
1 can cream of mushroom
   soup
1 cup mayonnaise
¾ cup chopped pecans

2 eggs, well beaten
1 medium onion, chopped
1 cup grated sharp cheddar
   cheese
1 cup bread crumbs,
   buttered

Cook broccoli according to directions on package. Drain. Add soup, mayonnaise and chopped pecans. Mix well. Add eggs and onion.

Pour into 2-quart casserole. Sprinkle with cheese and bread crumbs and dot with butter. Bake at 350° for 30 minutes.

Yield: 6-8 servings

# STIR-FRIED BROCCOLI
# AND MUSHROOMS

1 cup broccoli flowerets
1 cup sliced fresh
   mushrooms

2-4 tablespoons butter
Salt and pepper
Seasoned or garlic salt

Melt butter in heavy skillet. Add broccoli and mushrooms and stir, coating all vegetables with butter. Add seasonings to taste. Cover for 10 minutes or until just tender. Vegetables should be slightly crispy. Serve immediately.

Yield: 4 servings

# BROCCOLI SOUFFLÉ

| | |
|---|---|
| 2 pounds fresh broccoli or | 1 cup milk |
| 2 10-ounce packages | ¼ teaspoon nutmeg |
| frozen broccoli | 1 tablespoon lemon juice |
| 3 tablespoons butter | 4 egg yolks, beaten |
| 3 tablespoons flour | 4 egg whites, beaten until |
| 1 teaspoon salt | stiff |

Cook broccoli; chop finely. Melt butter and add flour and salt; cook until bubbly. Add milk, stirring constantly until smooth and thick. Add nutmeg, lemon juice and broccoli. Cool slightly and add beaten egg yolks. When broccoli mixture is cool, fold in beaten whites. Pour into buttered 1½-quart casserole and place in pan of hot water. Bake at 325° for 1 hour or until firm. Serve immediately.

Yield: 6 servings

# BROCCOLI AND TOMATO WREATH

| | |
|---|---|
| 2 pounds fresh broccoli | Salt and pepper |
| ¾ pint cherry tomatoes | 6 tablespoons butter |
| 4 tablespoons butter | 1½ tablespoons lemon |
| ½ teaspoon sugar | juice |

Trim broccoli and separate into flowerets. Cook for 3 minutes, or until just tender. Drain, refresh in bowl of ice water and drain again. Sauté tomatoes in 4 tablespoons butter over moderately high heat for 3 minutes or until hot, but not popped. Sprinkle tomatoes with sugar, salt and pepper to taste.

Add broccoli to skillet and toss the mixture. Place mixture in a well-buttered 2-quart non-aluminum ring mold and press the vegetables gently into the mold. Cover the mold with foil and place in a baking pan. Fill pan with 1 inch of boiling water. Bake for 15 minutes at 350° or until it is heated thoroughly. Invert the wreath onto a warm platter. (It will be a loose wreath, not a firm mold.) Melt the 6 table-spoons butter; add lemon juice; heat until bubbly and drizzle over the wreath.

Yield: 6-8 servings

*The center may be filled with sliced carrots or stir-fried chicken.*

# CRUNCHY BROCCOLI CASSEROLE

1 chopped onion
1 cup chopped celery
½ cup butter
1 6-ounce roll garlic
  cheese
1 can cream of mushroom
  soup

1 8-ounce can sliced water
  chestnuts
2-3 10-ounce packages
  frozen chopped
  broccoli
¾ cup bread crumbs

Sauté onion and celery in butter until tender. Add garlic cheese and soup; cook over low heat until cheese is melted. Add water chestnuts.

Cook broccoli according to package directions; drain well. Pour sauce over broccoli and mix. Pour into greased 2-quart casserole and top with bread crumbs. Bake at 350° for 30 minutes.

Yield: 6 servings

# HERB-SEASONED BROCCOLI

1 10-ounce package frozen
  broccoli spears or 2
  pounds fresh broccoli
½ cup hot water
1 chicken bouillon cube

½ teaspoon dried marjoram
½ teaspoon dried basil
¼ teaspoon onion powder
⅛ teaspoon ground nutmeg
1 tablespoon butter
Lemon juice

Place broccoli in a saucepan. Combine water and bouillon cube, pour over broccoli and then sprinkle with remaining seasonings. Cover and bring to a boil, separating broccoli spears with fork.

Simmer 6 minutes or until tender; drain. Serve with butter and lemon juice, if desired.

Yield: 3 servings

*Preparation is fast and easy and calorie content low.*

# CABBAGE EUFAULA

1 large head cabbage,
    chopped
3 slices white bread
Butter
2 eggs

2 cups milk
1½ cups grated sharp
    cheddar cheese
Salt and pepper

Cook cabbage in a small amount of boiling salted water until tender. Drain well. Spread bread with softened butter. Combine eggs and milk. Soak bread in egg mixture until soft; then add cabbage, cheese, salt and pepper to taste. Mix well.

Pour into greased 2-quart casserole or soufflé dish. Bake at 300° for 1 hour 30 minutes.

Yield: 8 servings

# SWEET AND SOUR RED CABBAGE

1 medium head red
    cabbage, shredded
    (about 5 cups)
2 tablespoons vinegar or
    lemon juice
4 slices bacon, diced
¼ cup brown sugar, packed

2 tablespoons flour
½ cup water
¼ cup vinegar
1 teaspoon salt
⅛ teaspoon pepper
1 small onion, sliced

Cook cabbage about 5 minutes in ½ inch salted water with vinegar or lemon juice. Drain well.

Fry bacon until crisp; remove and drain. Pour off all but 1 tablespoon bacon drippings. Stir in brown sugar and flour. Add water, vinegar, salt, pepper and onion. Cook, stirring frequently, about 5 minutes or until thickened. Add bacon and sauce to hot cabbage. Stir together gently and heat thoroughly. Garnish with additional crumbled bacon, if desired.

Yield: 4-6 servings

*This cabbage is a good complement to German main dishes.*

# CARROTS LYONNAISE

1 pound (about 6 medium) carrots
1 chicken bouillon cube
½ cup boiling water
4 tablespoons butter
3 medium onions, sliced (about 2 cups)

1 tablespoon flour
¼ teaspoon salt
⅛ teaspoon pepper
¾ cup water
⅛ teaspoon sugar

Pare carrots and cut into julienne strips, about 3x¼ inches. Dissolve bouillon cube in the ½ cup boiling water; add carrots and cook, covered, for 10 minutes.

Meanwhile, melt butter in skillet; add onions and cook, covered, for 15 minutes, stirring occasionally. Stir in flour, salt and pepper. Add the ¾ cup water and bring to a boil. Add carrots and chicken bouillon; simmer, uncovered, about 10 minutes or until carrots are tender. Add sugar just before serving.

Yield: 6-8 servings

# CARROTS WITH OLIVES

1 pound carrots, scraped and sliced
Salt and pepper
½ cup butter, melted
1 cup chopped onion

1 cup pimento-stuffed green olives, drained and sliced
2-3 dashes Tabasco sauce

Cook carrots in a small amount of water with salt and pepper until tender. Drain well. In large heavy skillet, sauté onion in butter until onion is transparent. Add olives, being careful to keep pimento in the olives. Add Tabasco. Gently mix in carrots.

Yield: 6-8 servings

# ORIENTAL CELERY

3 cups sliced celery
1 8-ounce can sliced water
    chestnuts
¼ cup diced pimento
¼ cup slivered almonds
1-2 teaspoons soy sauce

1 can cream of chicken
    soup
Salt and pepper
½-1 cup canned chow mein
    noodles

Drop celery into lightly salted boiling water. Bring to a boil again and drain immediately. Gently add remaining ingredients except noodles. Salt and pepper to taste. Put into a buttered shallow baking dish and top with noodles. Bake 30 minutes at 300°. For celery to be crunchy and to retain color, avoid overcooking and be sure to serve immediately.

Yield: 4-6 servings

# CORN SOUFFLÉ

2 large eggs
1½ tablespoons cornstarch
1 tablespoon sugar
½ teaspoon salt

⅛ teaspoon pepper
1 16-ounce can cream-style
    corn
1 cup half and half

Preheat oven to 400°. Butter a 1-quart soufflé dish or a deep 7-inch round glass baking dish.

Beat eggs, cornstarch, sugar, salt and pepper in a medium-sized bowl. Blend in corn and half and half. Pour into prepared dish. Bake for 30-45 minutes.

Uncooked soufflé can be frozen, but must be thawed before cooking.

Yield: 4 servings

# MUSHROOM AND ONION CASSEROLE

3 tablespoons butter
1 tablespoon fresh lemon
    juice
1 pound fresh mushrooms,
    sliced

2 tablespoons butter
4 cups sliced onion rings
3 cups diced tomatoes
1 cup soft bread crumbs
Salt and pepper

In a skillet, melt 3 tablespoons butter. Add lemon juice and mushrooms and sauté for 3 minutes. Remove mushrooms, melt an additional 2 tablespoons butter and sauté onion rings until transparent.

Place onions in a 10x6x2-inch baking dish. Arrange mushrooms over onions and sprinkle with salt and pepper. Combine tomatoes and 1 cup bread crumbs in skillet. Season with salt and pepper. Simmer 15 minutes and pour over mushrooms.

*Topping:*
1 cup soft bread crumbs

3 tablespoons butter,
    melted

Toss 1 cup bread crumbs with 3 tablespoons melted butter and sprinkle over tomatoes. Bake at 350° for 30 minutes.

Yield: 8-10 servings

# RUSSIAN MUSHROOMS

1 pound large, fresh
    mushrooms
Salt
⅓ cup flour

½ cup butter
½ cup sour cream
½ cup grated Parmesan
    cheese

Wash mushrooms, leaving stems attached. Dry and cut each into 4-5 slices. Sprinkle with salt, to taste. Sift flour over dried pieces until well covered or shake mushrooms in a paper bag with the flour.

Heat butter in frying pan and sauté mushrooms. Place in a baking dish, cover with sour cream and sprinkle with cheese. Bake at 350° until brown and bubbly, about 15-20 minutes. Serve warm.

Yield: 3-4 servings

*Mushrooms are good with steak, roast or wild game.*

# HOPKINS BOARDING HOUSE STEWED OKRA AND TOMATOES

2 pounds fresh okra,
washed, trimmed and
sliced, or 3 10-ounce
packages frozen okra
3 16-ounce cans tomatoes,
chopped

1 cup chopped onion, or
more if desired
¼ cup bacon drippings
Salt and pepper

Combine all ingredients and salt and pepper to taste. Do not saute. Simmer on top of the stove in a covered saucepan or skillet, or bake in a 350° oven in a tightly covered casserole for 30-45 minutes. Check okra for desired tenderness.

Yield: 8-10 servings

*Hopkins is a tradition in Pensacola, known for its hearty Southern boarding house-style meals.*

# GOURMET ONIONS

5 medium Vidalia onions,
or other mild Bermuda
onion, sliced
½ teaspoon salt
½ teaspoon pepper
½ teaspoon sugar

⅓ cup butter
½ cup dry sherry
2 tablespoons freshly
grated Parmesan
cheese

Season onions with salt, pepper and sugar. Cook in butter until barely tender, about 5-8 minutes. Separate rings while cooking. Add sherry; cook 2-3 minutes longer. Sprinkle with cheese.

Yield: 6 servings

# ONION PUDDING

3 pounds yellow onions,
    peeled and quartered
¾ cup butter
2 eggs, beaten

¾ cup milk
Salt and pepper
1 cup bread crumbs,
    buttered

Boil onions until tender, but not mushy. Drain. Add butter to hot onions. Add eggs and mix well. Add milk and salt and pepper to taste. Pour into a large casserole, top with crumbs and dot with butter. Bake at 350° for 1 hour 15 minutes.

Yield: 6-8 servings

# SIR JAMES' ONION RINGS

1 cup self-rising flour
1 cup water
1 egg
⅛ teaspoon garlic powder

5 large onions
Shortening or oil
Lawry's Seasoned Salt

Mix flour, water, egg and garlic powder and let stand at room temperature for at least 3 hours. In a heavy skillet or other cooker, heat to 375° enough shortening or oil for deep-fat frying. While oil heats, slice onions into ¼-inch slices and separate into rings. Dip rings into batter and fry until golden brown. Season with Lawry's Seasoned Salt.

Yield: 4-6 servings

# JULIENNE ZUCCHINI AND CARROTS

1 pound medium zucchini
1 pound carrots

½ cup butter, melted
Salt and pepper

Scrub and trim zucchini and carrots. Cut them into ¼-inch julienne strips. Arrange the carrots in a vegetable steamer and cover them with the zucchini. Steam over 1 inch boiling, salted water, partially covered, for 12 minutes, or until they are tender. Transfer the vegetables to a serving dish and toss with melted butter. Add salt and freshly ground pepper to taste.

Yield: 8 servings

# BACON-BLEU CHEESE POTATOES

4 medium baking potatoes
Vegetable oil
4 slices bacon
1/2 cup sour cream
1/4 cup milk

1/4 cup butter
1/2 cup bleu cheese,
    crumbled
3/4 teaspoon salt
1/8 teaspoon pepper

Wash potatoes; rub skins with vegetable oil and bake at 400° for 1 hour or until done. While potatoes bake, fry bacon, cool and crumble. Allow potatoes to cool to touch. Slice skin away from top of each potato. Carefully scoop out pulp, leaving shells intact.

Combine potato pulp and remaining ingredients except bacon in a medium mixing bowl. Beat until light and fluffy. Stuff shells with potato mixture. Bake at 400° for 15 minutes and top with crumbled bacon. Serve hot.

Yield: 4 potatoes

# GOURMET POTATOES

6 medium potatoes
1/4 cup melted butter
1 1/2 cups grated cheddar
    cheese
1 cup sour cream
2 green onions, chopped

1 teaspoon salt
1/4 teaspoon pepper
2 tablespoons butter,
    softened
1/2 cup grated cheddar
    cheese

Cover potatoes with salted water and bring to a boil. Reduce heat and cook about 30 minutes, or until tender. Drain and cool slightly. Peel and coarsely shred potatoes; set aside.

Combine 1/4 cup melted butter and 1 1/2 cups cheese in a heavy saucepan. Cook over low heat, stirring constantly, until cheese is partially melted.

Combine potatoes, cheese mixture, sour cream, onion, salt and pepper; stir well. Spoon potato mixture into a greased 2-quart shallow casserole. Dot with 2 tablespoons butter and remaining grated cheese. Cover and bake at 300° for 25 minutes.

Yield: 6-8 servings

# EGGPLANT CASSEROLE

1 large eggplant, peeled
  and sliced ¼ inch
  thick
1 teaspoon salt
½ teaspoon pepper
2 tablespoons oil
2 tablespoons butter
1 cup chopped onion

2 cloves garlic, peeled and
  chopped
2 cups peeled and chopped
  fresh tomatoes
⅛ teaspoon thyme
¼ cup chopped parsley
½ cup bread crumbs
1½ cups grated cheddar
  cheese

Place eggplant in greased 2-quart baking dish. Sprinkle with salt and pepper. Broil for 10 minutes on each side.

Heat oil and butter in a saucepan. Add onion and garlic and cook until yellow; then add tomatoes and cook until thick. Add seasonings.

Pour mixture over eggplant rounds; top with bread crumbs and cheese. Bake at 350° until cheese is melted (about 5 minutes).

Yield: 8 servings

# SPINACH-STUFFED TOMATOES

8 medium tomatoes
Salt
2 10-ounce packages
  frozen chopped
  spinach
1 cup bread crumbs
1 cup grated Parmesan
  cheese
3 green onions, chopped

2 eggs
3 tablespoons butter,
  melted
½ teaspoon thyme
¼ teaspoon garlic salt
Dash hot sauce
Salt and pepper

Cut tops from tomatoes. Large tomatoes can be halved. Remove pulp, leaving shells intact. Reserve pulp for other uses. Sprinkle insides of shells with salt and invert to drain.

Cook spinach according to package directions and drain well. Combine spinach and remaining ingredients. Add salt and pepper to taste. Spoon into tomato shells and bake at 325° for 30 minutes.

Yield: 8-16 servings, depending on size of tomatoes

# HASH BROWN CASSEROLE

1 2-pound bag frozen hash
brown potatoes,
thawed
½ cup butter, melted
1 teaspoon salt
½ teaspoon black pepper

½ cup chopped onion
1 cup sour cream
1 can cream of chicken
soup
8 ounces cheddar cheese,
grated

Mix all 8 ingredients in a large bowl. Pour into two 9x9x2-inch pans or one 13x9x2-inch pan. If freezing is desired, do so at this point; then add topping before baking.

*Topping:*

2 cups crushed potato
chips or corn flakes

2 tablespoons butter,
melted

Mix crushed potato chips or corn flakes with butter and spread on top. Bake at 400° for 30 minutes, or until bubbly. If frozen, increase baking time to 1 hour at 350°.

Yield: 12-15 servings

# RED BEANS AND RICE

1 pound red kidney beans
Ham bone
1 5-ounce package
pepperoni, sliced
1 pound mild sausage
1 medium onion, chopped

1 stalk celery, chopped
1 large bay leaf, crushed
1 clove garlic, pressed
⅛ teaspoon cayenne
Salt and cumin
Hot cooked rice

Wash beans. Cover with cold water and soak overnight. In a 5-quart pot, cook pepperoni, sausage, celery, onion and garlic until slightly browned. Drain fat. Add beans and soaking liquid, ham bone, bay leaf, cayenne, salt and cumin to taste; cover with water. Cook slowly for several hours. Water can be added if it gets too thick. Serve over rice.

Yield: 6 servings

*Corn bread is especially good with this.*

# SPINACH ON ARTICHOKE
# BOTTOMS HOLLANDAISE

2 10-ounce packages
    frozen chopped
    spinach
½ pound fresh mushrooms
6 tablespons butter
1 tablespoon flour
½ cup milk
½ teaspoon salt
⅛ teaspoon garlic powder
⅛ teaspoon ground black
    pepper
⅛ teaspoon freshly grated
    nutmeg
1 14-ounce can artichoke
    bottoms (7 to a can)

Cook spinach according to package directions. Drain. Reserve 7 mushroom caps and sauté in 2 tablespoons butter. Chop remaining mushrooms and stems and sauté in another 2 tablespoons butter. Set aside.

Make a cream sauce by melting 2 tablespoons butter in heavy saucepan; add flour and cook until bubbly. Add milk, stirring constantly over low heat until smooth. Add seasonings; then add spinach and chopped mushrooms. Remove from heat.

Drain artichoke bottoms and slice a small piece off the bottom so they will sit flat in a buttered baking dish. Cover artichoke bottom with a mound of creamed spinach.

*Hollandaise:*
    1 cup sour cream
    1 cup mayonnaise
        (Hellmann's)
    ¼ cup lemon juice

Combine ingredients and blend thoroughly. Cover spinach with a generous spoonful of hollandaise. Top with a mushroom cap. Bake in 375° oven for 15-18 minutes. This dish can be prepared in advance and heated in oven right before serving.

Yield: 7 servings

*This is a pretty dish that is wonderful for a buffet dinner or brunch.*

# SAVORY SPINACH CASSEROLE

2 3-ounce packages cream
    cheese, softened
2 tablespoons butter
2 tablespoons soy sauce
½ teaspoon garlic powder
½ teaspoon ground nutmeg
⅛ teaspoon cayenne

3 10-ounce packages
    frozen chopped
    spinach
⅓ cup finely chopped
    onion
1 cup grated monterey jack
    cheese

Melt cream cheese and butter over low heat in medium saucepan. Stir in soy sauce, garlic powder, nutmeg and pepper. Cook spinach according to package directions and drain. Stir in spinach, onion and monterey jack cheese. Spoon into a greased 1½-quart casserole.

*Topping:*
    2 cups bread crumbs
    2 tablespoons butter,
        melted

    1 tablespoon soy sauce
    ¼ teaspoon dried dill weed

Toss bread crumbs with butter, soy sauce and dill. Spread over top of casserole. Bake at 350° for 25-30 minutes, or until hot.

Yield: 8-10 servings

# SICILIAN SPINACH

1 pound fresh spinach,
    washed and stems
    removed
1 tablespoon butter

2 tablespoons olive oil
1 clove garlic, minced
2 or more anchovy fillets,
    chopped

Heat butter and olive oil in a large heavy skillet. Add garlic and spinach. Cover at once and cook over high heat until steam appears. Reduce heat and simmer until tender (5 to 6 minutes in all). To make this dish a more authentic one, add 2 or more chopped anchovy fillets.

Yield: 3 servings

## SPINACH ROCKEFELLER

2 10-ounce packages
    frozen chopped
    spinach
¼ cup bread crumbs
¼ cup minced green onion
2 eggs
4 tablespoons butter,
    melted

¼-½ cup grated Parmesan
    cheese
⅛-¼ teaspoon minced
    thyme
⅛ teaspoon salt
6-8 tomato slices, cut ¼
    inch thick
½ teaspoon garlic salt

Cook spinach according to package directions and drain well. Combine with bread crumbs, onion, eggs, butter, cheese, thyme and salt. Mix well.

Place tomato slices in a shallow baking dish and sprinkle with garlic salt. Mound spinach mixture over each tomato slice to make individual portions.

Bake at 350° for 15-20 minutes, until heated thoroughly and spinach mixture is set.

Yield: 6-8 servings

## CREAMY SQUASH CASSEROLE

1½ pounds tender yellow
    squash, trimmed and
    sliced
1 10¾-ounce can cream of
    chicken soup
1 8-ounce carton sour
    cream
1 4-ounce jar pimentos,
    chopped

1 8½-ounce can water
    chestnuts, thinly
    sliced
2 medium onions, finely
    chopped
2 carrots, peeled and
    grated
½ cup butter
1 8-ounce package herb
    stuffing mix

Cook squash in salted water 12-15 minutes or until tender. Drain well. Add soup, sour cream, pimentos, water chestnuts, onions and carrots. Melt butter in a skillet. Add stuffing and mix well. Combine stuffing and squash mixture. Pour into lightly greased 2-quart baking dish and bake at 350° for 30 minutes.

Yield: 8 servings

# SPINACH SOUFFLÉ ROLL

3 10-ounce packages
    frozen chopped
    spinach
5 egg yolks
6 tablespoons unsalted
    butter, melted

½ teaspoon freshly grated
    nutmeg
Salt and pepper
5 egg whites, beaten until
    thick but not stiff

Cook spinach according to package directions; drain and set aside. Beat egg yolks until light and lemon-colored. Add butter, beating in gradually. Add nutmeg; salt and pepper to taste. Beat well. Stir spinach into yolks; then gently fold in whites.

Prepare a jelly roll pan by spraying with vegetable spray. Cover with two pieces of wax paper and spray top sheet. Spread soufflé mixture over wax paper to the edges of jelly roll pan. Bake at 375° for 15-18 minutes.

Dampen a dish towel. Turn soufflé out onto towel. Remove wax paper. Spread mushroom filling over spinach, leaving a little room around the edges. Roll, jelly roll-fashion, using the dish towel to assist. Roll onto platter. Slice with serrated knife into ¾-inch slices.

*Filling:*
1 pound fresh mushrooms,
    finely chopped
½ cup unsalted butter

1 tablespoon flour
Salt and pepper
¼ cup whipping cream

Sauté mushrooms in butter. Cook until liquid is reduced (about 8-10 minutes). Stir in flour, salt and pepper. Add cream and simmer until well combined. Spread heated mushroom filling over cooked spinach soufflé.

Yield: 8-10 servings

*Hollandaise sauce can be used as a topping.*

# HOPKINS BOARDING HOUSE SQUASH CASSEROLE

3 pounds small yellow
   squash
½ cup chopped onion
½ cup butter
2 eggs, beaten

¾ cup crushed Saltines
1 teaspoon salt
½ teaspoon pepper

Wash and trim squash and boil in salted water until tender; then drain and mash. Sauté onions in butter and add to squash mixture. Beat eggs and add to squash along with crushed Saltines. Add salt and pepper. Mix well and put into buttered 2-quart casserole. Bake at 325° for 20 minutes.

Yield: 6 servings

# SQUASH BOATS

6 large yellow squash
1 medium onion, chopped
3 tablespoons chopped
   green pepper
½ teaspoon salt
⅛ teaspoon pepper
3 slices bacon

2 tablespoons butter,
   softened
¼ cup bread crumbs,
   buttered
¼ cup grated cheddar
   cheese

Boil squash in salted water 15 minutes. Drain. Cut in half and scoop out pulp, leaving ¼-inch shell. Fry bacon until crisp; then crumble. Mash squash pulp and mix with onion, green pepper, salt, pepper, bacon and butter.

Fill shells with mixture; top with crumbs and cheese and dot with butter. Bake at 375° for 20 minutes.

Yield: 12 servings

# SQUASH AND SAUSAGE CASSEROLE

| | |
|---|---|
| 1 pound yellow squash | 1 cup broken Saltine |
| 1 pound mild or hot | crackers |
| sausage | 1 cup evaporated milk |
| 1 egg | 10 ounces grated cheddar |
| 1½ cups cottage cheese | cheese |

Slice squash and cook in salted water until tender. Drain. Brown sausage and drain. Mix squash, sausage, egg, cottage cheese, crackers, evaporated milk and half the cheddar cheese. Pour into a 2-quart casserole and top with remaining cheddar cheese.

Bake in 350° oven until brown on top (about 30 minutes).

Yield: 8 servings

# BROILED TOMATOES WITH BROCCOLI

| | |
|---|---|
| 7 or 8 large tomatoes | 8 ounces Swiss cheese, |
| Salt | grated |
| 2 10-ounce packages | 1 medium onion, finely |
| frozen chopped | chopped |
| broccoli | 2 teaspoons oregano |

Peel tomatoes and slice in half; salt lightly. Cook broccoli according to package directions and drain. Mix broccoli, cheese, onion and oregano and mound on top of each tomato half. Broil 7-8 inches from heat until thoroughly heated and top is brown and bubbly (10-12 minutes).

Yield: 14-16 servings

# SWEET POTATO CASSEROLE

| | |
|---|---|
| 3 cups cooked, mashed sweet potatoes | 1 teaspoon vanilla |
| ½ cup sugar | ⅓ cup flour |
| 2 eggs, lightly beaten | 1 cup brown sugar |
| 4 tablespoons butter, softened | 4 tablespoons butter, softened |
| ½ cup milk or orange juice | 1 cup finely chopped pecans |

Combine sweet potatoes, sugar, eggs, milk, butter and vanilla and place in a buttered 2-quart casserole. Mix remaining ingredients for topping with a fork until crumbly. Sprinkle over sweet potato mixture and bake in preheated 350° oven for 35 minutes.

Yield: 8-10 servings

# SWEET POTATO SOUFFLÉ

| | |
|---|---|
| 2 cups cooked, mashed sweet potatoes | 2 eggs, separated |
| 1 cup hot milk | 1 cup grated coconut |
| 4 tablespoons sugar | ½ cup chopped pecans or walnuts |
| ½ teaspoon salt | ½ cup raisins |
| 4 tablespoons butter | Marshmallows |

Dissolve sugar and salt in hot milk, stirring until melted. Stir in butter. Mix with potatoes until light and fluffy. Beat egg yolks and add to mixture. Add coconut and nuts; add raisins, if desired. Beat egg whites until stiff and fold lightly into potato mixture. Pour mixture into buttered dish. Arrange marshmallows on top.

Bake at 300° for 30 minutes until soufflé sets and marshmallows are golden.

Yield: 6-8 servings

# PRALINE YAM CASSEROLE WITH ORANGE SAUCE

| | |
|---|---|
| 4 medium yams | 1 teaspoon salt |
| 2 eggs | ½ cup pecan halves |
| ¼ cup dark brown sugar, firmly packed | ¼ cup dark brown sugar, firmly packed |
| 2 tablespoons butter, melted | 2 tablespoons butter, melted |

Cook yams until soft; peel and mash in a large bowl. Beat in eggs, ¼ cup brown sugar, 2 tablespoons butter and salt. Pour into 1-quart casserole. Arrange pecan halves in attractive pattern over top. Sprinkle with remaining ¼ cup brown sugar and drizzle with remaining butter. Bake, uncovered, at 375° for 15-20 minutes. Serve with warm Orange Sauce.

*Orange Sauce:*

| | |
|---|---|
| ⅓ cup sugar | 1 tablespoon lemon juice |
| 1 tablespoon cornstarch | 2 tablespoons butter |
| ⅛ teaspoon salt | 1 tablespoon Grand Marnier |
| 1 teaspoon grated orange peel | 3 dashes Angostura bitters |
| 1 cup orange juice | |

Blend sugar, cornstarch and salt in saucepan. Add orange peel, orange juice and lemon juice. Bring to boil over medium heat, whisking constantly until sauce is thickened. Remove from heat and stir in butter, Grand Marnier and bitters.

Yield: 1 cup sauce (6 servings)

# YAM-APPLE BAKE

| | |
|---|---|
| 3 medium cooking apples | ½ cup butter, softened |
| 1 teaspoon lemon juice | 1 cup mashed, cooked |
| 1 cup flour | yams (2 medium yams) |
| ¾ cup brown sugar | ½ cup chopped pecans |
| 1 teaspoon cinnamon | 1 tablespoon dark corn |
| ½ teaspoon nutmeg | syrup |

Peel, core and slice apples. Place prepared apples in a large bowl of water with lemon juice to prevent darkening. Blend flour, sugar, cinnamon, nutmeg and butter until crumbly. Reserve ½ cup crumb mixture for topping; to remaining mixture add cooked yams and mix well.

Spread mixture over bottom and sides of ungreased 9-inch pie plate to form shell. Place drained apples in shell, sprinkle with pecans and drizzle with syrup. Sprinkle remaining crumb mixture over pie. Bake at 350° for 30 minutes or until apples are tender.

Yield: 6-8 servings

# MUSHROOM PIE

| | |
|---|---|
| 1 recipe PERFECT PIE CRUST or pastry equivalent to 2 pie shells | 1 pound medium mushrooms, cleaned and sliced |
| ⅓ cup butter | 1 tablespoon flour |
| 1-2 medium onions, chopped | ½ cup half and half |
| | 1 tablespoon sherry |
| | Salt and pepper |

Preheat oven to 450°. Melt butter in a large skillet, Add onions and sauté until transparent. Add mushrooms and cook 4-5 minutes, stirring occasionally. Stir in flour and half and half; bring to a boil, stirring constantly. Stir in sherry. Add salt and pepper to taste. Remove from heat and cool.

Divide pastry in half. Line the bottom of an 8-inch pie plate with pastry and bake for 8 minutes. Cut remaining pastry into strips to prepare a lattice top. Pour cooked mushroom mixture into pastry shell. Arrange pastry strips over mixture, pressing edges to rim of bottom crust. Brush top with milk and bake on lower oven shelf about 20 minutes. Cool slightly before serving.

Yield: 5-6 servings

# ZUCCHINI SCALLOP

4 tablespoons butter
1 small onion, chopped
3 medium zucchini
2 firm tomatoes
2 teaspoons sugar

1-1½ teaspoons salt
¼ teaspoon oregano
⅛ teaspoon pepper
2 tablespoons grated
    Parmesan cheese

Melt 2 tablespoons butter in a shallow 1½-quart baking dish. Sprinkle onion over melted butter. Halve zucchini; quarter each piece lengthwise to make four sticks. Slice each tomato into 8 wedges. Arrange zucchini and tomatoes over onion in baking dish. Combine sugar, salt, pepper, and oregano; sprinkle on top. Dot with butter. Cover and bake at 350° for 35-40 minutes. Sprinkle with cheese before serving.

Yield: 8 servings

# HEAVENLY CASSEROLE

1 10-ounce package frozen
    French-style green
    beans
1 10-ounce package frozen
    baby lima beans
1 10-ounce package frozen
    small peas
1 large green bell pepper,
    diced

1½ cups whipping cream
1½ cups mayonnaise
¾ cup grated Parmesan
    cheese
Salt and pepper
½ cup bread crumbs,
    buttered

Place green beans, lima beans, peas and green pepper in just enough boiling salted water to keep them from burning. Cook until thawed and separate with a fork. Drain and cool. Set aside.

Whip cream. Combine mayonnaise and cheese; salt and pepper to taste. Then fold in whipped cream. Place vegetables in a greased, 2-quart casserole. Cover with the sauce. Top with bread crumbs and dot with butter. It can be baked at once or kept overnight in the refrigerator. Bake, uncovered, at 325° about 50 minutes or until golden brown.

Yield: 12 servings

# MIXED VEGETABLE CASSEROLE

2 cups fresh English peas
    or 1 10-ounce package
    frozen peas
2 cups fresh carrots,
    peeled and sliced
    crosswise
2 cups peeled, cubed
    potatoes

1 cup chopped celery
1 cup chopped onion
3 tablespoons butter
1 cup mayonnaise
1½ cups grated mild
    cheddar cheese
38 Saltine crackers
½ cup butter, melted

Cook peas, carrots and potatoes separately. Drain well. Sauté celery and onion in butter until tender. Drain. Mix all vegetables, mayonnaise and cheese and pour into large casserole. Crush Saltines and mix with the melted butter. Sprinkle on top of casserole. Bake at 350° for 30 minutes or until bubbly and cracker crumbs are golden brown.

Yield: 8-10 servings

# SPANISH VEGETABLES

1 10-ounce can chicken
    broth, undiluted
2 tablespoons lemon juice
⅓ cup olive oil
¼ teaspoon pepper
1 clove garlic, pressed
1 teaspoon oregano leaves
4 medium carrots, peeled
    and cut into ½-inch
    slices

1 cup celery, sliced into
    1-inch slices
1 large green pepper, cut
    into 1-inch squares
1 head fresh cauliflower,
    separated into
    flowerets
1 pound zucchini, cut into
    ¾-inch slices
1 cup large pimento-stuffed
    olives, sliced

Combine chicken broth, lemon juice, oil, pepper, garlic and oregano and bring to a boil. Add carrots, celery, green pepper, cauliflower and zucchini. Cover and simmer about 10 minutes or until vegetables are tender. Pour off cooking liquid. Stir in olives. Serve hot or cover, chill and serve.

Yield: 8-10 servings

# ITALIAN ZUCCHINI

*Tomato Sauce:*

1 20-ounce can tomatoes
2 cloves garlic
1 6-ounce can tomato
    paste
1¼ teaspoons salt

¼ cup chopped parsley
⅛ teaspoon pepper
½ teaspoon sugar
½ teaspoon oregano leaves,
    crushed

Prepare and cook sauce for 30 minutes before combining with zucchini. Liquify tomatoes in blender or food processor. Mince garlic. In medium saucepan, combine tomatoes, tomato paste, garlic, salt, parsley, pepper, sugar and oregano. Cook over low heat for 30 minutes.

*Vegetable:*

2½ pounds zucchini
¾ cup chopped onions
½ pound mushrooms,
    sliced

3 tablespooons olive oil
⅔ cup grated Parmesan
    cheese

While sauce is cooking, wash, trim, and slice zucchini crosswise into ⅛-inch slices. In a 3-quart saucepan, sauté zucchini, onions and mushrooms in olive oil. Cover and cook over low heat until tender, about 10-15 minutes, stirring occasionally. Remove zucchini from heat and mix in ⅓ cup cheese. Add tomato sauce and mix well. Pour into buttered 2-quart casserole. Top with remaining cheese. Bake at 350° for 20-30 minutes.

Yield: 6-8 servings

# MICROWAVE FRUIT MÉLANGE

1 10-ounce jar orange
    marmalade
¼ cup orange liqueur or
    orange juice
⅓ cup water
1 cup pitted prunes
½ cup flaked coconut

1 20-ounce can pineapple
    chunks, drained
1 16-ounce can apricot
    halves, drained
1 6-ounce jar maraschino
    cherries, drained

Combine all ingredients in a 2-quart glass casserole. Microwave for 8-9 minutes on MEDIUM HIGH or until hot.

Yield: 8-10 servings

# RATATOUILLE

¼ cup olive oil
1 large onion, sliced into
    rings
2 zucchini, cut into ¼-inch
    slices
2 cloves garlic, finely
    chopped
2 large green peppers,
    sliced

4 tomatoes, peeled and
    coarsely chopped
1 medium eggplant, peeled
    and cubed
1 teaspoon basil
1 teaspoon oregano
Salt and pepper

*Toppings:*
  **Chopped ripe olives**
  **Crisply fried bacon**
  **Grated Parmesan cheese**

Sauté onion in oil until transparent. Add remaining ingredients. Salt and pepper to taste.

Cover and cook over medium heat for 45 minutes, stirring occasionally. Ratatouille should be juicy, but not soupy. If necessary, uncover and cook until almost all liquid is evaporated. This can be served hot or cold with choice of toppings.

Yield: 4 servings as main dish
      8 servings as side dish

# CURRIED FRUIT

1 20-ounce can sliced
    pears, drained
1 20-ounce can pineapple
    chunks, drained
1 29-ounce can sliced
    peaches, drained

1 large bottle maraschino
    cherries, drained
1 16-ounce can halved
    apricots, drained
1 cup brown sugar
½ cup butter
1 tablespoon curry powder

Mix fruits together in baking dish. Melt brown sugar, butter and curry powder together over low heat. Pour over fruit. Bake, uncovered, in 300° oven for 1 hour.

Yield: 12 servings

*Curried Fruit is an excellent side dish with pork or ham.*

# CRANBERRY APPLE CASSEROLE

| | |
|---|---|
| 1 16-ounce package whole cranberries | 1½ cups oats |
| 3 cups chopped red apple (unpared) | ½ cup brown sugar |
| | ⅓ cup flour |
| 1 cup sugar | ½ cup chopped pecans |
| | ½ cup butter, melted |

Preheat oven to 350°. Wash and drain cranberries. In a mixing bowl, toss cranberries, apples and sugar. Pour into buttered 13x9x2-inch casserole.

Combine oats, brown sugar, flour and nuts. Mix until crumbly. Sprinkle crumb mixture over the casserole. Pour melted butter over all ingredients and bake for 1 hour.

Yield: 8-10 servings

# HOT PINEAPPLE CASSEROLE

| | |
|---|---|
| ¾ cup sugar | 1 cup grated sharp cheddar cheese |
| 3 tablespoons flour | |
| 1 20-ounce can pineapple tidbits, drained (juice reserved) | ½ roll Ritz crackers, crumbled |
| | 4 tablespoons butter, melted |

Combine sugar and flour in a 2-quart casserole. Add pineapple and cheese. Pour a small amount of the reserved juice over mixture.

Sprinkle cracker crumbs over top. Pour melted butter over crumbs. Bake at 350° for 30 minutes.

Yield: 6-8 servings

*Apricots or other fruit may be substituted for pineapple.*

# EGGS, GRAINS AND PASTA

# EGGS, GRAINS AND PASTA

**Eggs**
Breakfast Casserole, 241
Brunch Eggs, 241
Creole Eggs, 244
Deep-Dish Omelet, 242
Eggs in a Nest (Microwave), 242
Overnight Sandwich, 243
Popeye Egg, 243
Scotch Eggs, 244
Spanish Omelet Sauce, 245

**Grits**
Cheese Grits Soufflé, 250
Coffee Cup Grits, 249
Nassau Grits, 250

**Pasta**
Betsy Dick's Fettuccine Alfredo, 253
Creamy Macaroni and Cheese, 254
Pasta with Cheese and Spinach, 254
Pasta Peasant Style, 253

**Quiche**
Broccoli Quiche, 246
Madewood Onion Pie, 245
Mushroom Quiche, 246
Sausage-Cheddar Quiche, 247
Seville Quiche, 247
Spinach and Mushroom Quiche, 248
Spinach-Parmesan Quiche, 248
Spinach Pie, 249

**Rice**
Almond-Rice Casserole, 251
Curry Pilaf, 252
Lemon Pilaf, 252
Parsley Rice, 251
Sherried Brown Rice, 252

# BREAKFAST CASSEROLE

6 slices white bread, frozen
8 tablespoons butter
1 16-ounce package
    sausage, cooked and
    drained

6 ounces cheese, grated
2 cups half and half
5 eggs
1 teaspoon salt
1 teaspoon dry mustard

Butter both sides of frozen bread and cut into cubes. Spread cubes over bottom of 13x9x2-inch baking pan. Sprinkle sausage over bread; then sprinkle cheese over sausage.

Combine half and half, eggs, salt and dry mustard. Pour over layered bread, sausage and cheese and refrigerate overnight.

Bake at 350° for 30 minutes. Cut into squares to serve.

Yield: 6-8 servings

# BRUNCH EGGS

10 slices day-old bread,
    cubed
2 pounds bulk sausage,
    cooked and drained
1½ cups sharp cheese,
    grated
8 eggs, slightly beaten
4 cups half and half
1 tablespoon brown sugar

¼ teaspoon paprika
2 tablespoons minced
    onion
1 teaspoon dry mustard
½ teaspoon salt
⅛ teaspoon black pepper
⅛ teaspoon red pepper
½ teaspoon Worcestershire
    sauce

Layer bread cubes, sausage and cheese in a buttered 2-quart casserole. Repeat layers. Combine beaten eggs with half and half and remaining ingredients. Pour mixture over bread, sausage and cheese. Cover tightly and refrigerate overnight. Remove from refrigerator two hours before cooking. Bake, uncovered, at 350° for 1 hour.

Yield: 8-10 servings

*This makes for a very special Christmas morning breakfast. Take out of the freezer Christmas Eve and then bake in the morning while opening presents.*

# DEEP-DISH OMELET

½ pound bacon, cooked
    and crumbled
1 4-ounce can sliced
    mushrooms
1 small onion, finely
    chopped

1 4-ounce jar pepperoncini,
    finely chopped
1 pound cheddar cheese,
    grated
6 eggs
½ teaspoon salt
½ teaspoon pepper

Layer bacon, mushrooms, onion, pepperoncini and cheese in a 9x9x2-inch baking pan. Beat eggs with salt and pepper. Pour eggs over ingredients in pan. Bake at 350° for 20-25 minutes or until omelet springs back.

Yield: 8 servings

*Deep-dish omelet makes a nice brunch dish. Shrimp, chicken or crab may be added for variation.*

# EGGS IN A NEST (MICROWAVE)

1 10-ounce package frozen
    chopped spinach
1 teaspoon beef bouillon
    granules
2 eggs

Salt and pepper
2 tablespoons whipping
    cream
½ cup grated cheddar
    cheese

Cook spinach and bouillon in covered 1-quart dish on HIGH for 7 minutes. Drain.

Line the bottom of two 4-inch ramekins with spinach. Slip an egg into each ramekin. Sprinkle with salt and pepper. Pour a tablespoon of cream over each egg. Sprinkle cheese over top. Puncture yolks with a wooden pick.

Cover with wax paper and microwave on HIGH for 3 minutes or until eggs are softly cooked.

Yield: 2 servings

# OVERNIGHT SANDWICH

8 ounces ham, finely
    chopped
4 eggs, hard-boiled and
    finely chopped
1 4-ounce can mushroom
    pieces, drained
½ cup mayonnaise
¾ teaspoon dill weed
8 slices whole wheat bread

1 10¾-ounce can cream of
    celery soup
½ cup sour cream
½ cup milk
2 tablespoons minced
    parsley
1 tablespoon minced
    chives
4 ounces cheddar cheese,
    grated

Combine ham, eggs, mushrooms, mayonnaise and dill weed in a medium bowl.

Arrange half the bread slices in the bottom of a lightly greased 12x8x2-inch baking dish. Spread ham mixture over bread and top with remaining bread slices.

Combine soup, sour cream, milk, parsley and chives, blending well. Spoon over bread. Sprinkle with cheese; cover and refrigerate overnight.

Bake at 375° for 25-30 minutes until browned and bubbly. Cut into squares to serve.

Yield: 4-6 servings

# POPEYE EGG

1 slice bread
Butter

1 egg

Spread both sides of bread with butter. Cut a 2-inch circle out of the center of bread. Preheat a greased skillet; add bread to skillet; break egg into center of bread and cook about 2 minutes. Turn and continue cooking until done.

Yield: 1 serving

*Children love this special fried egg.*

# SCOTCH EGGS

| | |
|---|---|
| **4 eggs, hard-boiled and peeled** | **1 16-ounce package sausage** |
| **1 tablespoon flour** | **1 egg, beaten** |
| **Salt and pepper to taste** | **3 ounces bread crumbs** |

Roll hard-boiled eggs in flour, salt and pepper; mold 4 ounces sausage around each egg. Dip in beaten egg and then roll in bread crumbs.

Deep fry until sausage is cooked. If eggs brown too quickly, remove from fryer and bake in 350° oven until sausage is cooked.

Yield: 4 servings

*Scotch eggs are great to take along for picnics.*

# CREOLE EGGS

| | |
|---|---|
| **½ cup finely chopped celery** | **1 tablespoon flour** |
| **½ cup finely chopped onion** | **1 cup milk** |
| **½ cup finely chopped green bell pepper** | **1 4-ounce can mushrooms, drained** |
| **1 16-ounce can tomatoes, drained** | **6 eggs, hard-boiled and sliced** |
| **2 tablespoons butter** | **⅓ cup seasoned bread crumbs** |

Sauté celery, onion and bell pepper in 1 tablespoon butter until tender. Add tomatoes and cook 5 minutes.

Preheat oven to 350°. In a small skillet, melt remaining butter; stir in flour. Add milk slowly, stirring constantly. Cook over medium-low heat until thickened. Add mushrooms and cooked vegetables.

Place sliced eggs in buttered 1½-quart casserole. Pour vegetable mixture over eggs. Sprinkle with bread crumbs. Bake for 20-30 minutes.

Yield: 6 servings

# SPANISH OMELET SAUCE

2 tablespoons bacon
   drippings
1 green bell pepper,
   chopped
1 onion, chopped
2 stalks celery, chopped
1 cup tomatoes, chopped
½ cup tomato sauce
1 cup water
2 tablespoons vegetable oil

2 tablespoons flour
¼ teaspoon sweet basil
1 bay leaf
½ teaspoon sugar
¼ teaspoon hot sauce, or
   to taste
¼ teaspoon soy sauce
¼ teaspoon Worcestershire
   sauce

Sauté vegetables in bacon drippings until tender. Add tomatoes, tomato sauce and water. Make a roux by slowly browning flour in oil; add to vegetables and cook until thick. Add basil, bay leaf, sugar and sauces. Heat thoroughly. Serve over omelets.

Yield: Sauce for 6 omelets

# MADEWOOD ONION PIE

*Crust:*
  1 9-inch pastry shell,
    unbaked
  -or-
  1 cup Saltine cracker
    crumbs mixed with ½
    cup butter and pressed
    into 9-inch pie pan

*Filling:*
  3 cups chopped onion
  ¼ cup butter
  ½ pound Swiss cheese,
    finely grated
  1 tablespoon flour

  1 teaspoon salt
  ¼ teaspoon cayenne
  3 eggs, well beaten
  1 cup milk, scalded

Sauté onions in butter over medium heat, stirring constantly, until golden. Remove from heat, drain and spoon into pastry shell.

Combine cheese, flour, salt and cayenne. Stir in eggs and milk. Pour over onions. Bake at 350° for 40 minutes.

Yield: 6 servings

# BROCCOLI QUICHE

1 recipe PERFECT PIE
    CRUST or pastry
    equivalent to 2 pie
    shells
1 10-ounce package frozen
    chopped broccoli,
    thawed

8 ounces Swiss cheese,
    grated
10 slices bacon, cooked
    and crumbled
2 cups half and half
6 eggs, slightly beaten
2 teaspoons salt

Shape pastry into a 13x9x2-inch baking pan. Arrange broccoli over pastry. Spread cheese and bacon over broccoli.

Combine half and half with eggs; add salt. Pour egg mixture over cheese.

Bake at 400° for 25 minutes. Cool 15 minutes before serving.

Yield: 8-10 servings

# MUSHROOM QUICHE

1 9-inch pastry shell,
    unbaked
2 tablespoons butter
2 tablespoons chopped
    green onion
½ pound fresh mushrooms,
    sliced

½ teaspoon lemon juice
½ teaspoon salt
3 eggs, beaten
1½ cups whipping cream
⅛ teaspoon ground nutmeg
⅛ teaspoon pepper
1 cup grated Swiss cheese

Preheat oven to 400°. Line a 9-inch quiche dish with pastry; trim excess pastry around edges. Prick bottom and sides with a fork. Bake at 400° for 3 minutes; remove from oven and gently prick with a fork. Bake 5 minutes longer. Let cool on rack.

Melt butter in a medium skillet over low heat; add onion, mushrooms, lemon juice and salt. Cook until liquid evaporates; set aside. Combine eggs, whipping cream, nutmeg, pepper and cheese in a medium mixing bowl. Stir in mushroom mixture. Pour into pastry shell; bake at 375° for 30-40 minutes or until set. Let stand 15 minutes before serving.

Yield: 6 servings

# SAUSAGE-CHEDDAR QUICHE

1 9-inch pastry shell
1 pound bulk hot pork
  sausage
1 4-ounce can sliced
  mushrooms, drained
½ cup chopped onion
¼ cup chopped green bell
  pepper
1 teaspoon minced parsley

½ teaspoon whole basil
  leaves
⅛ teaspoon sugar
⅛ teaspoon salt
1½ cups grated cheddar
  cheese
1 cup milk
2 eggs
Paprika

Preheat oven to 400°. Line 9-inch pastry shell with foil. Cover foil with a layer of dried beans or pie weights. Bake for 10 minutes. Remove weights and foil. Prick shell with fork and bake 3-5 minutes more, until light brown. Cool.

Reduce oven to 325°. Cook sausage and drain well. Combine with mushrooms, onion, bell pepper, parsley, basil, sugar and salt. Mix well. Pour into pastry shell and top with cheese.

Combine milk and eggs; beat until foamy. Pour over cheese. Sprinkle with paprika. Bake at 325° for 50 minutes, or until brown and set.

Yield: 6-8 servings

# SEVILLE QUICHE

1 9-inch pastry shell
1 cup sour cream
10 slices bacon, cooked
  and crumbled
1 cup grated Swiss cheese

1 can French-fried onion
  rings
6 eggs, beaten
2 teaspoons Worcestershire
  sauce
Salt and pepper to taste

Bake pastry shell at 375° for 10 minutes. Cool.

Combine all other ingredients. Pour into pie shell.

Bake at 350° for 35-45 minutes or until set. Serve warm or chilled. This can be partially baked and frozen.

Yield: 6-8 servings

# SPINACH AND MUSHROOM QUICHE

1 9-inch deep-dish pastry
   shell
½ cup chopped shallots
1 10-ounce package frozen
   chopped spinach,
   thawed
¼ pound fresh mushrooms,
   chopped

2 tablespoons butter
5 eggs, beaten
1 cup whipping cream
½ cup milk
¾ cup grated Swiss cheese
Salt and pepper
Butter

Bake pastry shell at 375° for 10 minutes.

Cook shallots, spinach and mushrooms in butter until moisture is absorbed.

In a bowl, combine eggs, cream, milk, cheese (reserve small amount for topping), salt and pepper. Add spinach mixture and stir well.

Pour into crust; sprinkle with remaining cheese. Dot with butter and bake in a 375° oven 30-40 minutes, or until knife comes out clean. Cool 10 minutes before cutting.

Yield: 6-8 servings

# SPINACH-PARMESAN QUICHE

1 9-inch deep-dish pastry
   shell, partially baked
2 tablespoons butter
2 tablespoons chopped
   green onion
2 10-ounce packages
   frozen chopped
   spinach, cooked and
   drained

½ teaspoon salt
¼ teaspoon pepper
¼ teaspoon nutmeg
½ cup grated Parmesan
   cheese
1¼ cups whipping cream
4 eggs, slightly beaten
¼ cup grated Parmesan
   cheese

Melt butter in a small skillet; add onion and sauté until tender. Add spinach, salt, pepper, nutmeg and ½ cup cheese. Blend well.

Beat together cream and eggs. Add to spinach mixture, stirring well. Spoon into pastry shell and sprinkle with ¼ cup cheese.

Bake in a preheated 375° oven for 30 minutes. Cool 10 minutes before serving.

Yield: 6-8 servings

# SPINACH PIE

| | |
|---|---|
| 1 10-12-ounce bunch spinach, washed, trimmed and chopped | 2 eggs, slightly beaten |
| 2 tablespoons olive oil | ½ teaspoon dill weed |
| 1 bunch green onions, finely chopped | Freshly ground pepper |
| ¼ cup minced parsley | 2 eggs |
| 1 cup cottage cheese | 1 cup flour |
| 1 cup feta cheese | 1 cup water |
| | 1 tablespoon olive oil |
| | 2 tablespoons butter |

Preheat oven to 350°. Squeeze all moisture from spinach. Heat oil in large skillet over medium-high heat. Add onions and parsley; sauté until onions are soft. Mix in spinach, cheeses, slightly beaten eggs and dill. Add pepper to taste. Remove from heat.

Combine remaining 2 eggs, flour and water in medium bowl and mix well to make a thin batter. Coat a 12x8x2-inch baking dish with oil and pour in half the batter. Top with spinach mixture and dot with butter. Pour remaining batter over top. Bake 45-50 minutes or until set. Serve immediately.

Yield: 6 servings

*Pie can be cut into small squares and served as an appetizer.*

# COFFEE CUP GRITS

| | |
|---|---|
| 3 cups water | 1 teaspoon salt |
| 1 cup regular grits (not quick cooking) | 2 tablespoons butter |
| | ½ cup milk |

Bring salted water to boil. Add grits, cover and cook over low heat for 45 minutes to 1 hour. Add butter and milk. Stir well and serve. Increase amount of milk if desired for creamier grits.

Yield: 6-8 servings

# CHEESE GRITS SOUFFLÉ

2 teaspoons salt
7 cups water
2 cups uncooked grits
1 6-ounce roll Kraft nippy cheese, cut into cubes

8 ounces sharp cheddar cheese, grated
1 cup butter, melted
4 eggs, well beaten
½ cup milk
Salt and pepper

Add salt to boiling water and cook grits, covered, over low heat, until done (15-25 minutes). Stir in cheeses, butter, eggs, milk, salt and pepper to taste. Stir until cheese is melted. Pour into a buttered 3-quart casserole and bake in a preheated 350° oven for 1 hour.

Yield: 12 servings

# NASSAU GRITS

1 pound bacon
2 green bell peppers, finely chopped
2 medium onions, finely chopped

1½ cups ham, finely ground
1 28-ounce can whole tomatoes, chopped
1½ cups white grits

Fry bacon; set aside. Sauté onion and bell pepper in 2-3 tablepoons bacon drippings until soft. Add ham and stir well. Sauté over low heat for 15 minutes. Add tomatoes and simmer for 30 minutes.

In a separate saucepan, cook grits according to package directions. When grits are cooked, add ham mixture and stir well. Serve hot with bacon crumbled on top.

Yield: 12 servings

*This dish is excellent with fried fish.*

# ALMOND-RICE CASSEROLE

½ cup butter
½ cup finely chopped
   onion
1½ cups dry white wine
3 cups water
2 cups raw long grain
   white rice
2 teaspoons salt

¼ teaspoon nutmeg
¼ teaspoon pepper
½ teaspoon dried thyme
   leaves
1 cup coarsely chopped
   blanched almonds
½ cup raisins

Sauté onion in butter until golden in 6-quart Dutch oven. Add wine and water to onion and bring to boil. Add rice and seasonings. Cover and simmer 20-25 minutes, until liquid is absorbed. Stir in almonds and raisins and serve.

Yield: 8 cups

# PARSLEY RICE

1 cup raw rice
2 cups chicken broth
1 teaspoon salt
2 tablespoons butter
¼ cup sliced green onion

⅓ cup diced green pepper
¼ cup slivered almonds
½ cup chopped parsley
Diced pimento

Combine rice, broth and salt. Bring to a boil, stir, cover and cook over very low heat about 15 minutes or until tender.

Sauté onion, green pepper and almonds in butter for 3-5 minutes. Fold into freshly cooked rice with chopped parsley. If additional color is desired, add diced pimento.

Yield: 5-6 servings

*This goes well with shrimp or fish.*

# SHERRIED BROWN RICE

1 cup brown rice
½ cup chopped onion
6 tablespoons butter

1 10¾-ounce can beef
  consommé
1 consommé can of sherry

Sauté onion and rice in butter in a skillet for 10 minutes. Place in a 2-quart casserole with consommé and sherry. Cover and bake at 350° for 1 hour 30 minutes.

Yield: 6 servings

# CURRY PILAF

¼ cup butter
1 cup chopped onion
1½ cups rice
2 10¾-ounce cans beef
  consommé, heated

1 cup seedless golden
  raisins
½ teaspoon curry powder
Salt and pepper

Melt butter in a heavy 2-3-quart saucepan. Stir in onion and rice. Cook over medium heat about 5 minutes, stirring constantly. Add consommé, raisins, curry powder, salt and pepper to taste and mix well. Bring to a boil, cover and cook over low heat about 30 minutes.

Yield: 8 servings

# LEMON PILAF

3 cups cooked rice
1 cup chopped celery
1 cup chopped green onion
6 tablespoons butter

1 tablespoon grated fresh
  lemon rind
1 teaspoon salt
¼ teaspoon pepper

Prepare rice according to package instructions. Sauté celery and green onion in butter in a large skillet until tender. Add rice, lemon rind and seasonings. Toss lightly. Cook over low heat about 2 minutes, stirring occasionally.

Yield: 6 servings

*To reheat leftovers, sprinkle with water, wrap in foil and warm in oven.*

# BETSY DICK'S FETTUCCINE ALFREDO

4 tablespoons butter
4 tablespoons flour
1 cup whipping cream
2 ounces provolone cheese
2 ounces grated Parmesan
  cheese
Salt and pepper

¼ teaspoon oregano
¼ teaspoon basil
⅛ teaspoon garlic salt
⅛ teaspoon onion salt
¼-½ cup milk, if needed
1 5-ounce package egg
  noodles, cooked

Melt butter in a saucepan. Add flour and stir until bubbly. Do not brown. Immediately add whipping cream and stir well. Mixture should have a fairly thin consistency. Add provolone, cut into small cubes, a few at a time, and Parmesan, a little at a time. Season with spices. If sauce is too thick, thin with milk. When sauce has a smooth, creamy consistency, serve over hot noodles.

Yield: 4-6 servings

*This is a favorite from Some Place Else Restaurant in downtown Pensacola. For a variation, fresh mushrooms can be added to sauce. Garnish with steamed tomatoes.*

# PASTA PEASANT STYLE

1 pound spaghetti
½ cup half and half
3 tablespoons grated
  Parmesan cheese
4 tablespoons butter
2 slices salt pork
4 tablespoons butter

1 cup fresh mushrooms,
  cleaned and sliced
1 10-ounce package frozen
  green peas
3 tablespoons grated
  Parmesan cheese

Cook spaghetti until al dente; drain.

In a saucepan, over low heat, combine half and half, 3 tablespoons cheese and 4 tablespoons butter. Dice salt pork. In a separate skillet sauté pork in the remaining 4 tablespoons butter until crisp. Remove salt pork and drain on paper towels. Add mushrooms and peas to skillet and cook 5-10 minutes.

Add cream sauce, salt pork and mushroom mixture to spaghetti; mix and sprinkle with remaining cheese.

Yield: 6-8 servings

# CREAMY MACARONI AND CHEESE

3 cups cooked macaroni
1 pound sharp cheddar
    cheese, grated
2 eggs, beaten
2 cups milk

Salt and pepper
1 cup grated Parmesan
    cheese
Paprika

Preheat oven to 350°. Grease a 2-quart casserole. Cook macaroni according to package directions and drain well. Mix together eggs and milk.

In casserole layer the following: macaroni, cheddar cheese, salt and pepper to taste, and Parmesan cheese, if desired. Pour egg and milk mixture over all. Top with paprika. Bake for 30 minutes.

Yield: 6 servings

# PASTA WITH CHEESE AND SPINACH

1 egg
½ cup sour cream
¼ cup milk
2 tablespoons grated
    Parmesan cheese
1 tablespoon minced onion
½ teaspoon salt
⅛ teaspoon pepper
2 cups grated monterey
    jack cheese

2 tablespoons grated
    Parmesan cheese
4 ounces spaghetti, cooked
    and drained (about 2
    cups cooked)
1 10-ounce package frozen
    chopped spinach

Combine egg, sour cream, milk, 2 tablespoons Parmesan cheese, onion, salt and pepper; mix well. Stir in the monterey jack. Cook spinach according to package directions; drain. Add spinach and cooked spaghetti; mix well. Put into greased 8x8x2-inch glass baking dish. Sprinkle with remaining Parmesan. Bake about 30 minutes at 350° or until top is browned.

Yield: 4-6 servings

*Even non-spinach eaters like this!*

# BREADS

# BREADS

**Biscuits, Muffins, and Rolls**
Applesauce Muffins, 259
Blueberry-Orange Muffins, 260
Chive Muffins, 262
Cinnamon Bread or Rolls, 270
Cricket Tea Room Biscuits, 257
Dinner Rolls, 258
Oatmeal Biscuits, 257
Onion Rolls, 259
Orange Blossoms, 261
Refrigerator Rolls, 258
Sour Cream Biscuits, 257
Sourdough Buttermilk Biscuits, 277
Spoon Rolls, 259

**Breads**
Braided Bread, 260
Cheddar Cheese Bread, 264
Cinnamon Bread or Rolls, 270
Dilly Bread, 265
English Muffin Bread, 275
Party Melba Toast, 284
Poppy Seed Bread, 261
Potato Bread, 263
Potato Water Sourdough Starter, 276
Rye Bread, 262
Sourdough Bread, 277
Special Treat Italian Bread, 263
Strawberry Bread, 275
Super Simple Yeast Bread, 266
Three "C" Bread, 266
Whole Wheat Bread, 267
Whole Wheat Raisin Bread, 265
Zucchini Bread, 268

**Coffee Cakes**
Blueberry Streusel Coffee Cake, 268
Breakfast Sponge Cake, 269
Cinnamon Coffee Cake, 269
Danish Puff Pastry, 271
Date-Nut Breakfast Ring, 272
Nutty Date Cake, 274
Oatmeal Coffee Cake, 273

**Corn Bread**
Bacon's Spoon Bread, 283
Corn Bread Dressing, 282
Corn Fritters, 281
Delicious Corn Bread, 280
Hushpuppies, 280
Jalapeño Hushpuppies, 281
Onion Shortcake, 282
Southern Spoon Bread, 283

**Jellies**
Blueberry Jam, 284
Strawberry Fig Jam, 284

**Pancakes, Waffles, French Toast and Doughnuts**
Baked French Toast Almondine, 279
Doughnut Triangles, 278
Easy Fluffy Pancakes, 264
English Pancakes, 274
Light and Crispy Waffles, 279
Sfinge, 267
Sourdough Pancakes and Waffles, 276
Waffles, 278
Whole Wheat Waffles, 280

# CRICKET TEA ROOM BISCUITS

| | |
|---|---|
| 2 cups sifted flour | 1 teaspoon baking powder |
| 1/3 teaspoon baking soda | 1/2 cup shortening |
| 1 teaspoon salt | 3/4 cup buttermilk |

Preheat oven to 475°-500°. Sift flour and measure; then add soda, salt and baking powder; sift again. Cut in shortening until well blended. Make a well in the center and add buttermilk all at once. Stir slowly at first, then quickly until dough is smooth. Knead gently on a floured board very briefly. Roll lightly to a thickness of 1/2 inch. Cut with small floured biscuit cutter and place 1/2 inch apart on a lightly greased baking sheet. Bake for 8-10 minutes, or until golden.

Yield: approximately 1 1/2 dozen

# OATMEAL BISCUITS

| | |
|---|---|
| 2 cups flour | 2/3 cup dry milk crystals |
| 2 tablespoons baking powder | 2 cups quick oats |
| 1 1/2 teaspoons salt | 1/2 cup shortening |
| 3 tablespoons brown sugar | 2 eggs, slightly beaten |
| | 1 cup water |

Preheat oven to 400°. Mix dry ingredients. Cut in shortening with a fork or pastry blender. Add beaten eggs and water and mix until all ingredients are blended. Drop by teaspoons or roll out and cut with a small biscuit cutter; place on a greased baking sheet. Bake for 8-10 minutes.

Yield: 2-2 1/2 dozen

# SOUR CREAM BISCUITS

| | |
|---|---|
| 1 cup butter, softened | 2 cups self-rising flour |
| 1 cup sour cream | |

Preheat oven to 400°. Combine softened butter and sour cream. Fold in flour. Fill greased muffin tins 3/4 full and bake for 8-10 minutes or until golden brown.

Yield: 2 dozen

# DINNER ROLLS

1 package dry yeast
1 cup warm water
(105°-115°)
4 tablespoons sugar
1 teaspoon salt

3 cups sifted flour
4 tablespoons butter,
melted and cooled
1 egg, beaten
Melted butter

Dissolve yeast in warm water. In a large mixing bowl, combine yeast mixture, sugar, salt and 1 cup flour. Beat well. Add butter and egg. Beat again. Add a second cup of flour and beat hard, briefly. Add the last cup of flour ⅓ at a time, mixing well after each addition. Let rise in the same bowl until doubled. Turn out onto a floured board and knead in enough flour to make the dough easy to handle. Roll dough to a thickness of ½ inch and cut with a small biscuit cutter. Dip rolls into melted butter and place in a baking pan. Let rise again until doubled. Bake in preheated 375° oven for 12-15 minutes. Rolls may be frozen before second rise or after they are baked.

Yield: 3 dozen

# REFRIGERATOR ROLLS

1 cup boiling water
1 cup shortening
½ cup sugar
1½ teaspoons salt
1 egg, beaten

2 packages dry yeast
1 cup warm water (110°)
6 cups unsifted flour
Melted butter

Gradually pour boiling water over shortening, sugar and salt, beating constantly. Beat until well mixed. Cool; add beaten egg. Let yeast dissolve in warm water for 5 minutes, then stir and add to shortening mixture. Add flour and blend well; cover and place in refrigerator at least 4 hours. (Dough will keep in the refrigerator up to 10 days.)

Three hours before using, roll dough to a thickness of ¼ inch. Cut with a biscuit cutter and fold in half. (Cloverleaf rolls can be made by making small balls of dough and putting three to a muffin tin.) Let rise until doubled, brush with melted butter and bake in preheated 425° oven for 12-15 minutes.

Yield: approximately 6 dozen

# ONION ROLLS

⅔ cup finely chopped onion
¼ teaspoon thyme
¼ teaspoon rosemary

2 tablespoons butter
1 package refrigerated crescent rolls

Sauté onion with herbs in butter until onion is soft and transparent. Spread mixture on crescent rolls. Roll up and bake as directed on package.

Yield: 8 rolls

# SPOON ROLLS

1 package dry yeast
¾ cup butter, melted
1 egg, beaten

2 cups warm water (105°-115°)
¼ cup sugar
4 cups self-rising flour

Preheat oven to 400°. Mix together yeast, butter, egg, water and sugar. Add flour and mix well. (Dough will be very soft.) Spoon batter into greased muffin tins until half full and bake for 15 minutes.

Yield: 2½-3 dozen

# APPLESAUCE MUFFINS

1 cup butter
2 cups sugar
2 eggs
1 teaspoon vanilla
4 cups flour
2 teaspoons soda

3 teaspoons cinnamon
1 teaspoon ground cloves
2 teaspoons allspice
16 ounces applesauce
1 cup chopped pecans

Preheat oven to 350°. Cream butter, sugar, eggs and vanilla. Sift together flour, soda, cinnamon, cloves and allspice; add dry ingredients to creamed mixture. Stir in applesauce and mix on medium speed. Add chopped pecans. Fill greased muffin tins ⅔ full and bake for 15-20 minutes.

Yield: 2-2½ dozen

# BLUEBERRY-ORANGE MUFFINS

3 cups sifted flour
4 teaspoons baking powder
¼ teaspoon soda
¾ cup sugar
1½ teaspoons salt
2 cups blueberries
2 eggs, slightly beaten
¾ cup milk

½ cup butter, melted
1 tablespoon grated orange peel
½ cup plus 4 teaspoons orange juice
¼ cup butter, melted
1 cup sugar
2 teaspoons cinnamon

Preheat oven to 425°. Sift together flour, baking powder, soda, sugar and salt. Stir in blueberries, tossing lightly until coated. Beat together eggs, milk, ½ cup melted butter, orange peel and orange juice; pour into dry ingredients and stir just until moistened. Fill greased muffin tins or paper liners ⅔ full. Bake for 25 minutes. Remove from tins while hot and brush tops with melted butter; then sprinkle with a mixture of 1 cup sugar and cinnamon.

Yield: 2 dozen

# BRAIDED BREAD

6-6½ cups flour
2 packages dry yeast
1 cup milk
½ cup sugar
½ cup shortening

1 cup water
2 teaspoons salt
2 eggs
1 egg white

Mix 3½ cups flour and the yeast. Heat milk, sugar, shortening, water and salt, stirring constantly until mixture reaches 120°-130°. Add to dry mixture. Add eggs. Beat at low speed for 30 seconds. Beat at high speed 3 minutes. By hand, stir in enough remaining flour to make a soft dough. Knead for 8-10 minutes. Place in a greased bowl and turn once. Cover and let rise until doubled (1 hour 15 minutes). Divide dough into six pieces. Roll each piece into a 15 inch rope. Using 3 ropes for each loaf, braid. Cover and let rise until doubled (45-60 minutes). Brush with unbeaten egg white and bake in a preheated 350° oven for 20-25 minutes.

Yield: 2 loaves

# ORANGE BLOSSOMS

*Muffins:*

½ cup butter
1½ cups sugar
3 eggs
2 cups cake flour
1½ teaspoons baking
    powder

¾ cup milk
½ teaspoon vanilla
½ teaspoon lemon extract
3 drops almond extract

Preheat oven to 375°. Grease small muffin tins.

Using an electric mixer, cream butter and sugar. Add eggs one at a time, beating well after each addition.

Sift flour and baking powder together and add dry ingredients alternately with milk to creamed mixture. Begin and end with milk. Add vanilla, lemon and almond flavorings.

Fill muffin tins ¾ full and bake for 10-15 minutes. Glaze while hot.

*Glaze:*

2 cups sugar
Juice of 2 lemons

Juice of oranges

Bring sugar and juices to a boil in a saucepan over medium heat. Dip hot muffins in glaze. Serve warm.

Yield: 4 dozen

# POPPY SEED BREAD

2 cups sugar
1½ cups vegetable oil
4 eggs
1 13-ounce can evaporated
    milk

1 teaspoon vanilla
4 cups flour
4 teaspoons baking powder
1 teaspoon salt
½ cup poppy seeds

Preheat oven to 350°. Beat together sugar, oil, eggs, milk and vanilla; set aside. Sift together flour, baking powder and salt and add to oil mixture. Stir in poppy seeds. Bake in two greased and floured pans for 45 minutes.

Yield: 2 loaves

# CHIVE MUFFINS

| | |
|---|---|
| 1 package dry yeast | 1 egg |
| ¼ cup warm water | 2 tablespoons chopped |
| (105°-115°) | chives |
| 2 tablespoons sugar | ¾ cup sour cream |
| 1 teaspoon salt | 2½ cups flour |
| 2 tablespoons vegetable oil | |

Dissolve yeast in warm water in a large bowl. Add remaining ingredients. Beat with a mixer until smooth. Cover and let rise in a warm place until doubled. Stir batter down and spoon into well-greased muffin tins. Cover and let rise until doubled in bulk (about 45 minutes).

Bake in preheated 400° oven for 15 minutes. Serve hot.

Yield: 1-1½ dozen muffins

# RYE BREAD

| | |
|---|---|
| 4 cups all-purpose flour | 2 packages dry yeast |
| 2 cups rye flour | ¼ cup butter, softened |
| 1½ teaspoons salt | 2 cups very warm water |
| 1 tablespoon caraway | (120°-130°) |
| seeds | ⅓ cup molasses |

Combine flours. In a large bowl, mix 2 cups flour mixture, salt, caraway seeds and dry yeast. Add butter and mix well. Gradually add water and molasses to dry ingredients and beat 3-4 minutes at medium speed with electric mixer. Add 1 cup flour mixture and beat at high speed 3-4 minutes. Stir in enough additional flour mixture to make a stiff dough. Turn out onto a floured board and knead until smooth and elastic. Leave on floured board or put on floured cookie sheet and cover with plastic wrap, then a towel. Let rise in a warm, draft-free place until doubled in bulk (about 1 hour). Punch down and divide in half. Dough can be formed into two 7-inch rounds and placed in a greased cake pan or in two greased loaf pans. Let rise until doubled and bake in preheated 350° oven for 35-40 minutes. When bread is done it will sound hollow when tapped. Remove from pan and cool on wire racks.

Yield: 2 loaves

# POTATO BREAD

| | |
|---|---|
| 1 large potato | 2 tablespoons sugar |
| 7 cups flour | 1 cup milk |
| 1 tablespoon salt | 2 tablespoons butter |
| 2 packages dry yeast | |

Peel and dice potato; barely cover with water and boil until tender. Drain, reserving liquid. Add water to potato liquid to make 1 cup; set aside. Mash potato and set aside.

In a large bowl, mix 2 cups flour, salt, yeast and sugar. Combine milk, potato liquid and butter and heat over low heat until warm (120°-130°). Gradually add liquid to dry ingredients and beat 2 minutes at medium speed with electric mixer. Add potato and mix well. Add additional flour to make a stiff dough. Turn out onto a lightly floured board and knead until smooth and elastic. Place in greased bowl and turn once; cover with plastic wrap and let rise until doubled in bulk.

Punch dough down; turn over in bowl. Cover with plastic wrap and let rise 20 minutes.

Punch dough down and work out bubbles. Shape dough into 2 loaves, cloverleaf or Parker House rolls or any other shape desired. Place in greased pans and dust loaves with flour. Bake in preheated 350° oven for 35-40 minutes for loaves or 18-20 minutes for rolls.

Yield: 2 loaves or 3 dozen rolls

# SPECIAL TREAT ITALIAN BREAD

| | |
|---|---|
| ¼ cup Wishbone Italian dressing | ¼ cup grated Parmesan cheese |
| ¼ cup butter, softened | 1 8-12-ounce loaf Italian bread |

Preheat oven to 375°. Combine dressing, butter and cheese until well blended. Cut bread diagonally, almost through to the crust. Spread cut surfaces with Parmesan dressing mixture.

Wrap in foil, leaving it partially open at the top. Bake for 15-20 minutes.

Yield: 8-10 servings

# EASY FLUFFY PANCAKES

| | |
|---|---|
| 1 egg | 1 tablespoon sugar |
| 3 tablespoons butter, melted | 1 teaspoon baking soda |
| | 1 teaspoon salt |
| 1 cup flour | 1 cup buttermilk |

Mix egg and cooled butter. Sift together flour, sugar, baking soda and salt. Add dry ingredients to egg mixture. Stir until batter is mixed. Add buttermilk and stir until well mixed. The batter will be lumpy. Pour onto preheated griddle. Cook until bubbles burst; turn and cook until golden brown.

Yield: 2-3 servings

# CHEDDAR CHEESE BREAD

| | |
|---|---|
| 7½-8 cups flour | ⅔ cup milk |
| ⅓ cup sugar | 3 cups grated sharp cheddar cheese (¾ pound) |
| 1 tablespoon salt | |
| 2 packages dry yeast | |
| 2 cups water | |

In a large bowl, mix 2½ cups flour, sugar, salt and yeast.

Combine water and milk in a saucepan and heat until warm (120°-130°). Gradually add to dry ingredients and beat with electric mixer at medium speed, scraping bowl occasionally. Add cheese and ½ cup flour. Beat at high speed until well mixed. Stir in enough remaining flour to make a stiff dough.

Turn dough out onto a lightly floured board and knead until smooth and elastic. Place in a greased bowl; turn once. Cover and let rise until doubled. Punch dough down and work out bubbles. Divide dough into 3 balls. Flatten each ball into a rectangle. Roll rectangles jelly roll-style and seal all edges to resemble French bread. Place seam-side down on greased baking sheet. (Dough may also be divided into 36 cloverleaf rolls to go into muffin tins.) Cover and let rise until doubled (about 1 hour).

Preheat oven to 350°. Bake loaves for 35-40 minutes or rolls for 15-20 minutes. Remove from pans and cool on wire racks. Brush with melted butter when warm, if desired.

Yield: 3 loaves or 3 dozen rolls

# DILLY BREAD

| | |
|---|---|
| 1 package dry yeast | 1 tablespoon butter |
| ¼ cup warm water | 2 teaspoons dill seed |
| (105°-115°) | 1 teaspoon salt |
| 1 cup cottage cheese | ¼ teaspoon baking soda |
| 2 tablespoons sugar | 1 egg, beaten |
| 1 tablespoon minced onion | 2¼-2½ cups flour |

Dissolve yeast in water. Heat cottage cheese to lukewarm. Combine sugar, onion, butter, dill, salt, soda and egg in a bowl with cottage cheese and yeast mixture. Add flour to form a stiff dough. Cover with a damp towel and let rise until doubled in bulk. Stir dough down. Place dough into a well-greased casserole (1½-quart) or loaf pan and cover with a damp towel. Let rise 1 hour or until doubled in bulk.

Bake in preheated 350° oven for 40-45 minutes. When top browns, remove from pan and cool on wire rack.

Yield: 1 loaf

# WHOLE WHEAT RAISIN BREAD

| | |
|---|---|
| 1 cup golden raisins | ½ teaspoon ginger |
| 1¾ cups water | ½ teaspoon cinnamon |
| ⅓ cup shortening | 2 cups sifted all-purpose |
| 2 packages dry yeast | flour |
| ⅓ cup firmly packed brown | 2 cups whole wheat flour |
| sugar | ⅓ cup wheat germ |
| 2 teaspoons salt | |

Combine raisins, 1¼ cups water and shortening. Heat to boiling, stirring until shortening melts. Remove from heat and cool to lukewarm. Soften yeast in remaining ½ cup warm water (105°-115°). Add sugar, salt, ginger, cinnamon and 1 cup all-purpose flour; mix well. Add raisin mixture. Gradually mix in all remaining flour. Add wheat germ. Turn out onto a well-floured board and knead 3 minutes. Place in a greased bowl, turning to grease all sides. Cover and let rise until doubled in bulk, about 1 hour 45 minutes. Punch down and shape into a loaf. Place in a greased loaf pan and let rise until doubled in bulk, about 45 minutes. Bake below oven center in preheated 375° oven for 40 minutes or until brown. Cool on wire rack.

Yield: 1 loaf

# SUPER SIMPLE YEAST BREAD

| | |
|---|---|
| 1 package dry yeast | 2 tablespoons sugar |
| 1¼ cups warm water | 2 teaspoons salt |
| (105°-115°) | 2⅔ cups flour |
| 2 tablespoons butter, melted | |

In a large bowl, dissolve yeast in the water. Add melted butter, sugar, salt and 2 cups flour. Blend on low speed with mixer for 30 seconds, scraping bowl constantly. Beat on medium speed 2 minutes, scraping bowl occasionally. By hand, stir in ⅔ cup flour. Cover and let rise in a warm place until doubled in bulk (about 30 minutes). Stir down with 25 quick strokes, then spread evenly in a greased 9x5x3-inch loaf pan. Cover and let rise until doubled in bulk (about 45 minutes).

Preheat oven to 375° and bake for 35-45 minutes. Brush top with melted butter and cool on a rack.

Yield: 1 loaf

# THREE "C" BREAD

| | |
|---|---|
| 3 eggs, beaten | ½ teaspoon salt |
| ½ cup vegetable oil | 2 cups shredded carrots |
| ½ cup milk | 1 3½-ounce can flaked |
| 2½ cups flour | coconut |
| 1 cup sugar | ½ cup minced maraschino |
| 1 teaspoon baking powder | cherries |
| 1 teaspoon baking soda | ½ cup raisins |
| 1 teaspoon cinnamon | ½ cup chopped pecans |

Preheat oven to 350°. Combine beaten eggs, oil and milk. In a large bowl, sift the flour, sugar, baking powder, baking soda, cinnamon and salt together. Add the egg mixture to the dry ingredients; mix until thoroughly combined. Stir in carrots, coconut, cherries, raisins and pecans. Have 4 16-ounce fruit or vegetable cans washed, well greased and floured. Pour mixture into cans until they are ¾ full and bake for 45-50 minutes. Remove from cans and cool completely. Wrap bread and refrigerate overnight or until ready to use; slice. A loaf pan or muffin tins can also be used.

Yield: 4 rounds, 1 loaf or 2½ dozen muffins

# WHOLE WHEAT BREAD

| | |
|---|---|
| 5 cups all-purpose flour | 2 packages dry yeast |
| 3 cups whole wheat flour | 2 cups milk |
| 3 tablespoons honey or | ¾ cup water |
|    sugar | ¼ cup butter |
| 1 tablespoon salt | |

Combine flours. In a large bowl, mix 2½ cups flour mixture, sugar, salt and undissolved yeast. Combine milk, water and butter and heat until very warm (120°-130°). Gradually add liquid to dry ingredients and beat 3-4 minutes at medium speed with electric mixer. Add 1 cup of flour mixture. Beat at high speed until well blended. Stir in enough additional flour mixture to make a stiff dough. Turn out on a lightly floured board and knead until smooth and elastic. Put on floured cookie sheet and cover with plastic wrap, then a towel. Let rise until doubled in bulk (about 1 hour). Divide dough in half. Punch down and shape into loaves. Place in 2 greased loaf pans. Cover with plastic wrap and let rise until doubled in bulk. Puncture bubbles with a greased toothpick.

Bake in a preheated 350° oven for 35-40 minutes. Remove from pans and cool on wire racks. Dough can also be made into smaller loaves, rolls or hamburger buns. Loaves may be brushed with melted butter when warm, if desired.

Yield: 2 loaves

# SFINGE

| | |
|---|---|
| 1 cup water | Vegetable oil for deep |
| ½ cup butter |    frying |
| ¼ teaspoon salt | Honey |
| 1 cup flour | Confectioners' sugar |
| 4 eggs, unbeaten | Cinnamon |

Bring water, butter and salt to a boil in a medium saucepan. Add flour; stir over medium heat until mixture leaves the sides of the pan. Remove from heat. Stir until smooth and let cool slightly (about 5 minutes). Add eggs, one at a time, beating well after each addition. Drop by heaping teaspoons into hot oil. Cook only 4-5 sfinges at a time, as they will puff-up. They also will turn themselves in the oil. Fry to golden brown (about 2-3 minutes). Drain on paper towels. Place on a serving platter and drizzle with honey, confectioners' sugar and cinnamon. Serve immediately.

Yield: 4-6 servings

*This is an Italian version of hollow doughnuts.*

# BLUEBERRY STREUSEL COFFEE CAKE

*Coffee Cake:*

| | |
|---|---|
| 1 cup blueberries | ½ teaspoon salt |
| 1 tablespoon lemon juice | ⅓ cup sugar |
| 1 cup flour | 1 egg |
| 1½ teaspoons baking powder | ½ cup milk |
| | ⅓ cup butter, melted |

Sprinkle berries with lemon juice and set aside. Sift together flour, baking powder, salt and sugar. Add egg, milk and melted butter to dry ingredients; mix well. Pour batter into an 8-inch round or square greased pan. Scatter berries over the batter and sprinkle with topping.

*Streusel Topping:*

| | |
|---|---|
| ⅓ cup sugar | ¼ teaspoon cinnamon |
| ¼ cup flour | 2 tablespoons butter, melted |
| ⅛ teaspoon salt | |

Mix together all topping ingredients.

Bake in preheated 375° oven for 40-45 minutes. Serve warm.

Yield: 8 servings

# ZUCCHINI BREAD

| | |
|---|---|
| 2 eggs, slightly beaten | ¼ teaspoon baking powder |
| 1 cup vegetable oil | 1 teaspoon baking soda |
| 2 cups sugar | ½ teaspoon salt |
| 2 cups grated raw zucchini | 1 teaspoon cinnamon |
| 2 teaspoons vanilla | ½ teaspoon allspice |
| 3 cups all-purpose flour or | 1 cup chopped pecans |
| 2 cups all-purpose and | 1 cup chopped dates |
| 1 cup whole wheat flour | |

Preheat oven to 325°. Beat eggs, oil and sugar. Add ½ of raw zucchini; then add vanilla. Set aside. Sift together flour, baking powder, baking soda, salt, cinnamon and allspice and add to creamed mixture. Add remaining zucchini and stir with a spoon. Stir in nuts and dates. Bake in 2 greased and floured loaf pans for 1 hour-1 hour 30 minutes.

Yield: 2 loaves

# BREAKFAST SPONGE CAKE

*Cake:*

| | |
|---|---|
| 2 eggs, separated | 2 teaspoons baking powder |
| 1 cup sugar | ½ cup hot milk |
| 1 cup flour | 1 teaspoon vanilla |

Preheat oven to 350°. Beat egg whites until stiff peaks form; set aside. Beat yolks with sugar until pale yellow in color. Sift together flour and baking powder. Alternately add flour mixture and milk to egg yolk mixture. Add vanilla. Fold in egg whites. Bake in an ungreased 9x9-inch cake pan for 25 minutes.

*Topping:*

| | |
|---|---|
| 2 tablespoons butter | 2-3 tablespoons whipping |
| ½ cup packed brown sugar | cream |
| 1 cup coconut | |

Melt butter and stir in sugar until mixture is smooth. Add coconut to thicken and add cream until mixture is of spreading consistency. Spread on top of cake and return to oven until topping bubbles (5-10 minutes).

Yield: 9 servings

# CINNAMON COFFEE CAKE

| | |
|---|---|
| 2 cups sugar | ½ teaspoon baking soda |
| 1 cup butter | ⅛ teaspoon salt |
| 4 eggs | ¾ cup chopped nuts |
| 1 cup sour cream | 2 tablespoons brown sugar |
| 1 teaspoon vanilla | 1 tablespoon white sugar |
| 2¼ cups flour | 1½ teaspoons cinnamon |
| 1 teaspoon baking powder | ½ teaspoon nutmeg |

Preheat oven to 350°. Cream sugar and butter; add eggs, sour cream and vanilla. Set aside. Sift together flour, baking powder, baking soda and salt; add to creamed mixture. Set aside. Combine nuts, brown and white sugar, cinnamon and nutmeg. Pour ⅓ of the creamed mixture into a greased and lightly floured 10-inch tube pan. Sprinkle with ½ filling mixture and cover with another ⅓ of the batter. Add remaining filling and cover with remaining batter. Bake for 40-45 minutes.

Yield: 12 servings

# CINNAMON BREAD OR ROLLS

*Dough:*

| | |
|---|---|
| **7 cups flour** | **1 cup milk** |
| **6 tablespoons sugar** | **¾ cup water** |
| **1½ teaspoons salt** | **⅓ cup butter** |
| **2 packages dry yeast** | **3 eggs** |

In a large bowl, mix 2 cups flour, 6 tablespoons sugar, salt and yeast.

Combine milk, water and butter in a saucepan and heat until warm (120°-130°). Add liquid gradually to dry ingredients and beat 2 minutes at medium speed with electric mixer. Add eggs and ½ cup flour. Beat at high speed for 2 minutes. Stir in enough remaining flour to make a stiff dough. Turn out onto a floured board and knead until smooth and elastic. Place in a greased bowl, turning once; cover and let rise until doubled in bulk.

*Filling:*

| | |
|---|---|
| **1 cup sugar, white or** | **Nuts and/or raisins** |
| **brown** | **½ cup butter, softened** |
| **¼ cup cinnamon** | |

Combine sugar, cinnamon, nuts and raisins and set aside.

Punch dough down and divide in half. Roll each half into a 14x9-inch rectangle. Spread each half with softened butter and roll jelly roll-style and shape into loaves. Place in greased pans and sprinkle with more filling mixture. Roll may also be sliced into ½-inch slices and placed in greased muffin tins or on baking pan. Cover and let rise until doubled in bulk. Bake in preheated 350° oven. Bake loaves for 35-40 minutes or rolls for 15-20 minutes.

*Glaze:*

| | |
|---|---|
| **Powdered sugar** | **Milk or cream** |

Mix together powdered sugar and cream. Glaze while hot.

Yield: 2 loaves or 3 dozen rolls

# DANISH PUFF PASTRY

*Pastry:*

| | |
|---|---|
| **1 cup sifted flour** | **2 tablespoons water** |
| **½ cup butter** | |

Preheat oven to 350°. In a mixing bowl, cut butter into flour until it resembles coarse meal. Sprinkle with water and continue mixing until dough will hold together in a ball. Divide dough in half. Wrap each ball in plastic wrap and refrigerate 30 minutes. Pat dough into two strips, 12x3-inches long. Place strips 3 inches apart on ungreased baking sheet.

*Topping:*

| | |
|---|---|
| **½ cup butter** | **1 cup sifted flour** |
| **1 cup water** | **3 eggs** |
| **1 teaspoon almond flavoring** | |

In a 1-quart saucepan, bring butter and water to a rapid boil. Add almond flavoring and remove from heat. Add flour and mix quickly to keep from lumping. When mixture is smooth and thick, add one egg at a time, beating well after each addition. Divide batter in half and spread evenly over each piece of pastry, being sure to seal the edges.

Bake approximately 60 minutes or until top is crisp and brown. Allow pastry to cool; then frost with butter frosting and sprinkle with chopped nuts.

*Butter Frosting:*

| | |
|---|---|
| **⅓ cup butter** | **1½ teaspoons vanilla** |
| **1 16-ounce package confectioners' sugar** | **2 tablespoons half and half** |
| **1 egg yolk** | **1 cup finely chopped pecans** |

Cream butter. Gradually add 1 cup sugar, blending well. Beat in egg yolk and vanilla. Gradually blend in remaining sugar, beating until smooth. Add cream and beat until frosting is of spreading consistency.

Yield: 24 servings

# DATE-NUT BREAKFAST RING

*Dough:*

1 package dry yeast
1½ tablespoons sugar
¼ cup warm water
   (105°-115°)
3¼ cups unbleached flour
   or 3 cups all-purpose
   flour and 2
   tablespoons bread flour

4 tablespoons butter, room
   temperature
2 tablespoons shortening,
   room temperature
1 teaspoon salt
2 large eggs
⅓ cup cold milk

Stir yeast and sugar into warm water and let stand 5-10 minutes. Using the steel blade, process flour, butter, shortening and salt for 20 seconds. With the machine running, add eggs and yeast mixture; gradually add milk until flour absorbs it and then process for 30 seconds. Scrape dough into a well-greased 3-quart bowl. Cover with oiled plastic wrap and refrigerate until doubled in bulk (about 4-6 hours). Punch down. At this point, dough may be covered and refrigerated up to 4 days. Punch down before use.

*Filling:*

8 ounces chopped, pitted
   dates
½ cup water
Zest from 1 lemon

4 tablespoons butter, room
   temperature
¾ cup chopped pecans

Place dates, water and lemon zest into a 1½-quart saucepan; cook over medium heat, stirring frequently, for about 15 minutes or until soft and thick. Cool.

Roll dough on lightly floured surface into a 22x10-inch rectangle. Spread dough with butter, then with date mixture to within ½ inch of edges. Reserve 2 tablespoons pecans and sprinkle remaining pecans over dates. Roll tightly along the long edge and pinch the seam to seal. Place on greased baking sheet, shaping it into a ring. With sharp scissors or a knife, make an even number of cuts from the top to within ½ inch of bottom, at 1-inch intervals. Turn one section to the center, then the next to the outside and continue around the ring. Cover with oiled plastic wrap and let rise until almost doubled in bulk (approximately 1 hour 30 minutes).

Preheat oven to 375°.

*Glaze:*

**1 large egg**                    **Salt**

Mix egg and salt and brush top of ring. Sprinkle with reserved nuts. Bake for 20-25 minutes or until browned. Transfer to rack and cool 15 minutes.

*Topping:*

½ **cup confectioners' sugar**    **1 teaspoon rum**
**2 tablespoons milk or**
     **cream**

Mix together confectioners' sugar, cream and rum (if desired) and drizzle over the top of the ring.

Yield: 1 12½-inch ring or 2 small rings

# OATMEAL COFFEE CAKE

*Cake:*

| | |
|---|---|
| 1¼ **cups boiling water** | 1⅓ **cups flour** |
| **1 cup quick oats** | ½ **teaspoon salt** |
| ½ **cup butter** | **1 teaspoon cinnamon** |
| **1 cup brown sugar** | ½ **teaspoon nutmeg** |
| **1 cup white sugar** | **1 teaspoon baking soda** |
| **2 eggs, well beaten** | |

Pour boiling water over oats and add ½ cup butter. Stir. Cover and let stand 20 minutes. Mix brown sugar, white sugar and eggs; do not use an electric mixer. Sift together flour, salt, cinnamon, nutmeg and baking soda. Add dry mixture to the sugar mixture; then add oatmeal mixture. Blend well. Put batter into a greased 13x9x2-inch pan and bake in a preheated 350° oven for 35-40 minutes.

*Topping:*

| | |
|---|---|
| **6 tablespoons butter,** | **1 teaspoon vanilla** |
| **melted** | **1 cup grated, sweetened** |
| ½ **cup sugar** | **coconut** |
| ¼ **cup evaporated milk** | **1 cup chopped nuts** |

Combine melted butter, sugar, milk, vanilla, coconut and nuts; spread over top of hot cake. Put cake under broiler for 2 minutes to brown topping.

Yield: 16 servings

# NUTTY DATE CAKE

1 cup flour
2 teaspoons baking powder
½ teaspoon salt
1 cup sugar
2 8-ounce packages whole
  or chopped dates

1 pound whole or chopped
  walnuts or pecans
4 eggs, separated
1 teaspoon vanilla

Preheat oven to 325°.

Sift flour, baking powder, salt and sugar together three times. The third time, sift over dates and nuts.

Beat egg yolks; then add to date-nut-flour mixture.

Beat egg whites and vanilla until stiff. Fold into date-nut mixture.

Grease and flour a large loaf pan; pour in batter and bake for 1 hour 30 minutes.

Yield: 1 loaf

# ENGLISH PANCAKES

1 cup flour
2 tablespoons sugar
1 teaspoon cream of tartar
½ teaspoon baking soda
½ teaspoon salt

1 egg
⅔ cup milk
1 tablespoon butter,
  melted
Vegetable oil for griddle

Preheat griddle. Sift the flour, sugar, cream of tartar, soda and salt into a medium-size bowl. Beat egg and milk lightly by hand and pour into the flour mixture. Add the butter and stir rapidly with a wooden spoon just until smooth; do not overmix. The batter may be used at once or allowed to stand for up to one hour.

Brush the hot griddle with oil. Drop the batter by tablespoons onto the griddle, allowing each pancake to spread to about 2 inches in diameter. Cook until the bubbles burst on the surface. Turn and cook until second side is golden. Serve at once with butter and syrup.

Yield: 20 small pancakes

# STRAWBERRY BREAD

2 10-ounce packages
   frozen strawberries,
   thawed
3 cups flour
1 teaspoon baking soda
½ teaspoon salt

1 teaspoon cinnamon
2 cups sugar
3 eggs, beaten
1 cup vegetable oil
1 cup chopped pecans

Preheat oven to 350°. Drain strawberries, reserving ½ cup juice. Mix together flour, baking soda, salt, cinnamon and sugar. Make a hole in the center of mixture. Pour strawberries, eggs, oil and pecans, if desired, into the hole. Mix by hand until all ingredients are thoroughly combined. Pour into two greased and floured 9x5x3-inch loaf pans. Bake for 40-60 minutes.

*Spread:*
   ½ **cup strawberry juice**

1 8-ounce package cream
   cheese, softened

Blend together strawberry juice and cream cheese until of spreading consistency. Serve as a spread for the cooled, sliced bread.

Yield: 2 loaves

# ENGLISH MUFFIN BREAD

6 cups unsifted flour
2 packages dry yeast
1 tablespoon sugar
2 teaspoons salt

¼ teaspoon baking soda
2 cups milk
½ cup water
Cornmeal

Combine 3 cups flour, yeast, sugar, salt and soda. Heat liquids until very warm (120°-130°). Add to dry mixture and beat well. Stir in remaining flour to make a stiff batter. Spoon into two 8½x4½-inch loaf pans that have been greased and sprinkled with cornmeal. Sprinkle tops with cornmeal. Cover and let rise in a warm place for 45 minutes. Bake in preheated 400° oven for 25 minutes. Remove from pans immediately and cool on racks.

Yield: 2 loaves

# SOURDOUGH PANCAKES AND WAFFLES

½ cup sourdough starter
2½ cups flour
2 cups water (90°)
½ cup buttermilk
1 egg

2 tablespoons vegetable oil
  or melted butter (4
  tablespoons for waffles)
1 teaspoon salt
1 teaspoon baking soda
2 tablespoons sugar

Mix sourdough starter and flour together. Add water until mixture is the consistency of thick cream. Allow to ferment in a warm place overnight. Remove one cup of mixture and place remaining mixture back in the refrigerator.

Add buttermilk, egg and oil to remaining sourdough mixture. Mix salt, baking soda and sugar separately and sprinkle over batter; gently fold into batter. Allow to rise 5 minutes. Cook 2-inch pancakes on hot griddle or make waffles.

Yield: 30 pancakes

# POTATO WATER SOURDOUGH STARTER

3 medium potatoes, peeled
  and cubed
4 cups water
1¾ cups flour

1 tablespoon sugar
1 tablespoon salt
1 package dry yeast
2½ cups potato water

Cook 3 medium potatoes in water until tender. Drain, reserving liquid. Use potatoes in a favorite recipe, if desired. In a medium-sized mixing bowl combine flour, sugar, salt and dry yeast. Mix well. Stir in reserved potato water. Cover with a towel or cheesecloth and place in a warm place (85°F) for 1-2 days or until mixture becomes bubbly. Stir down several times a day. Store until needed in refrigerator in a clean plastic container with tight fitting lid. The lid must have a small hole punched in it to allow gases to escape. To replenish add equal amounts of flour and lukewarm water at least once a week.

# SOURDOUGH BREAD

1 cup milk
⅓ cup sugar
⅓ cup shortening
1 teaspoon salt
1 package dry yeast

2 tablespoons warm water
(105°-115°)
5 cups flour
1½ cups sourdough starter

Scald milk. Add sugar, shortening and salt. Stir to dissolve. Cool to lukewarm. Dissolve yeast in warm water in a large bowl. To the yeast mixture, add cooled milk mixture, 2 cups flour and starter. Add enough flour to make a stiff dough. Turn onto a floured surface and knead 5-10 minutes. Place in a a greased bowl, turning once. Let rise in a warm place until doubled in bulk, about 1 hour 30 minutes. Punch down; let rise again, about 30 minutes. Divide into 2 equal parts; cover and let rest 10 minutes. Shape into loaves and let rise in greased loaf pans until doubled in bulk. Bake in a preheated 400° oven for 40 minutes.

Yield: 2 loaves

# SOURDOUGH BUTTERMILK BISCUITS

½ cup warm water
(105°-115°)
1 package dry yeast
4 cups flour
2 tablespoons sugar
1 teaspoon salt

1 teaspoon baking powder
1 teaspoon baking soda
½ cup shortening
1 cup sourdough starter
¾ cup buttermilk

Combine yeast and water; set aside. In a large bowl stir together flour, sugar, salt, baking powder and baking soda. By hand, crumble shortening into flour mixture, until it resembles coarse meal. Without mixing starter, pour in starter, buttermilk and yeast mixture. Mix lightly.

Drop dough, approximately ¼ cup at a time, onto lightly greased baking sheet. Let sit for 30 minutes.

Bake in preheated 425° oven for approximately 12-15 minutes or until golden brown.

Yield: 1½ dozen

# DOUGHNUT TRIANGLES

5½ cups flour
¼ cup sugar
1 teaspoon salt
2 packages dry yeast
1 cup milk
¼ cup water

½ cup butter
3 eggs, room temperature
Vegetable oil for deep
    frying
Confectioners' sugar

In a large bowl, mix 1¼ cups flour, sugar, salt and yeast. Combine milk, water and butter in a saucepan and heat over low heat until warm (120°-130°). Gradually add mixture to dry ingredients and beat 2 minutes at medium speed with an electric mixer. Add eggs and ½ cup more flour. Beat at high speed 2 minutes. Stir in enough remaining flour to make a stiff dough. Turn out and knead on a lightly floured board until smooth and elastic. Divide dough in half. Roll each half into a 9-inch square. Cut into 9 3-inch squares; cut squares in half to form triangles. Place on greased baking sheets and allow to rise until doubled in bulk. Deep fry in hot oil (375°-400°) until brown on both sides. Drain on paper towels and sprinkle with confectioners' sugar or honey.

If making for freezing, cover baking sheets with plastic wrap before dough has risen and freeze. Put into plastic bags when frozen. Dough will keep up to 5 weeks. When ready to cook, remove from freezer and thaw completely at room temperature. Let rise in a warm place until doubled in bulk. Cook as directed above.

Yield: 36 doughnuts

# WAFFLES

4 eggs, separated
2 cups milk
3 cups sifted flour
5 teaspoons baking powder

1 teaspoon salt
2 teaspoons sugar
⅔ cup butter, melted

Beat egg whites until very stiff. Set aside. Beat egg yolks until pale yellow; add milk and beat 1 minute. Sift together flour, baking powder, salt and sugar; add this to egg yolk mixture. Beat 1 minute. Add the melted butter and beat until blended well. Gently fold in egg whites. Cook in preheated waffle iron.

Yield: 12 single waffles

# BAKED FRENCH TOAST ALMONDINE

½ cup butter
6 eggs
¼ cup liquid brown sugar

¼ cup milk
1 large loaf French bread,
   cut into thick slices

Preheat oven to 425°. Divide butter in half and melt in two 15x10x1-inch jelly roll pans; distribute evenly.

Beat eggs together with liquid brown sugar and milk. Dip bread slices into egg mixture, coating both sides. Place slices in a single layer on pans. Bake for 10-15 minutes until golden brown. Turn occasionally during cooking.

Serve topped with sauce.

*Almondine Sauce:*
  2 tablespoons butter
  1 cup sliced almonds

1½ cups liquid brown sugar
½ teaspoon almond extract

Melt butter in saucepan; add almonds. Cook over moderate heat until almonds are golden. Stir in sugar and almond extract. Serve very warm.

Yield: 6-8 servings

*This French toast is perfect for a company breakfast.*

# LIGHT AND CRISPY WAFFLES

2 cups flour
1 teaspoon salt
2 eggs
2 cups milk

½ cup plus 2 tablespoons
   vegetable oil
2 heaping teaspoons
   baking powder
½ cup chopped pecans

Preheat waffle iron. Sift together flour and salt. Beat eggs and milk and add to flour mixture. Add oil and beat well. Add baking powder and stir until just blended. Pour slowly into greased waffle iron and sprinkle with nuts.

Yield: 16 waffles

# WHOLE WHEAT WAFFLES

| | |
|---|---|
| 2 eggs | 1 cup whole wheat flour |
| ¼ cup vegetable oil | 2 teaspoons baking powder |
| 1½ cups milk | ½ teaspoon salt |
| ¾ cup all-purpose flour | ¼ cup sugar |

Preheat waffle iron. Mix all ingredients in a blender until flour is moistened. Pour into waffle iron.

Yield: 6 waffles

# DELICIOUS CORN BREAD

| | |
|---|---|
| 1 cup yellow cornmeal | 1 cup milk |
| 1 cup flour | 1 egg |
| 2 tablespoons sugar | ¼ cup vegetable oil |
| 4 teaspoons baking powder | 1 8-ounce can cream-style |
| ½ teaspoon salt | corn |

Preheat oven to 425°. Combine cornmeal, flour, sugar, baking powder and salt. Add milk, egg and oil. Beat until fairly smooth. Stir in corn. Pour into buttered 8-inch square baking pan. Bake for 20-25 minutes. Serve hot.

Yield: 8 servings

# HUSHPUPPIES

| | |
|---|---|
| ½ cup self-rising flour | 1 8-ounce can cream-style |
| 1 cup self-rising cornmeal | corn |
| 1 green bell pepper, chopped | Buttermilk |
| 1 onion, chopped | Vegetable oil for deep frying |

Mix flour, cornmeal, bell pepper, onion and corn. Add buttermilk until consistency is thick and pasty. Deep fry by dropping spoonfuls of batter into preheated oil (350°). Cook until golden brown. Drain on paper towels.

Yields: 20 hushpuppies

# CORN FRITTERS

1 cup flour
1½ teaspoons baking
  powder
½ teaspoon salt
1 tablespoon sugar
1 egg
½ cup milk

2 tablespoons dry milk
2 cups whole kernel corn,
  drained
2 teaspoons vegetable oil
Vegetable oil for deep
  frying

Sift together flour, baking powder, salt and sugar. In a separate bowl, beat egg; add milk and dry milk and beat until smooth. Add mixture to dry ingredients and mix until smooth. Stir in corn and oil.

Drop by spoonfuls into preheated oil (370°). Fry until brown on each side (about 2-3 minutes). Drain on paper towels. Serve hot.

Yield: 4-6 servings

*These are a good alternative to hushpuppies.*

# JALAPEÑO HUSHPUPPIES

Vegetable oil for deep
  frying
2 16-ounce packages
  hushpuppy mix
1 16-ounce can cream-style
  corn
1 7-ounce can tuna,
  drained

1 medium onion, chopped
3 medium jalapeño
  peppers, diced
1 9-12-ounce can of beer
2 tablespoons jalapeño
  juice

Heat oil to 350°-375°. (Test by dropping one tablespoon of mixture into oil; if hushpuppy floats to the top, the oil is ready.) Mix well hushpuppy mix, corn, tuna, onion, jalapeno peppers and beer. Add jalapeño juice, if desired. Drop by tablespoons into hot oil. Cook for several minutes until golden brown. Drain on paper towels.

Yield: 40-50 hushpuppies

# CORN BREAD DRESSING

2 cups chopped onion
3 cups chopped celery
½ cup butter
2-3 cups turkey or chicken
    broth
6 cups crumbled corn
    bread

3 cups crumbled white
    bread, stale or toasted
1 teaspoon salt
3 eggs, beaten
1 teaspoon sage
2 tablespoons poultry
    seasoning

Preheat oven to 350°. Sauté onion and celery in butter over medium heat until tender but not brown. Heat broth. Combine corn bread, white bread, salt and eggs. Mix in onion and celery. Add sage and poultry seasoning, if desired. Add enough broth to moisten well. Blend thoroughly and place in greased casseroles. Bake at 350° for 40 minutes or until nicely browned.

Yield: 2 large casseroles

# ONION SHORTCAKE

¼ cup butter
1 large sweet onion, sliced
1½ cups corn muffin mix
1 egg, beaten
1 cup cream-style corn
¼ teaspoon hot pepper
    sauce

1 cup sour cream
¼ teaspoon salt
¼ teaspoon dill weed
1 cup grated sharp cheddar
    cheese

Preheat oven to 425°. Melt butter in a skillet. Add onion and sauté until tender. Set aside. Combine muffin mix, egg, corn and pepper sauce. Pour into a greased 8-inch square baking pan. Mix sour cream, salt, dill weed and ½ of cheese with onion. Spread over batter. Sprinkle with remaining cheese. Bake for 30-45 minutes. Cut into squares and serve warm.

Yield: 6 servings

# BACON'S SPOON BREAD

2½ cups yellow cornmeal
1½ quarts boiling water
3 eggs
1 13-ounce can evaporated
   milk

½ cup sugar
½ teaspoon nutmeg
½ teaspoon baking soda
½ cup butter
1½ teaspoons salt

Preheat oven to 400°. Pour cornmeal into boiling water, stirring very rapidly until dissolved. If cornmeal forms lumps, use beater or electric mixer to remove them. Remove from heat. Mix in eggs, milk, sugar, nutmeg, baking soda, butter and salt. Pour into two greased 2-quart casseroles. (If desired, batter can be frozen at this point.) Place casseroles in a shallow pan with water covering the bottoms of the casserole dishes. Bake for 50-60 minutes. If frozen before baking, bread will not rise quite as much.

Yield: 10-12 servings

*This recipe is a favorite from Bacon's By the Sea Motel in Ft. Walton Beach, where it was served in the 1940's.*

# SOUTHERN SPOON BREAD

¾ cup cornmeal
3 cups milk, divided
1 teaspoon salt
1 teaspoon baking powder

2 tablespoons butter
3 egg yolks, well beaten
3 egg whites, stiffly beaten

Preheat oven to 325°. Cook cornmeal and 2 cups milk until mixture is the consistency of mush. Remove from heat. Add salt, baking powder, butter and remaining milk. Add egg yolks and fold in egg whites. Bake in greased 2-quart casserole for 60 minutes. Serve immediately with butter or keep bread (covered with foil) at 150° in a pan of hot water.

Yield: 6-8 servings

# PARTY MELBA TOAST

**1 loaf very thinly sliced
white bread (Arnold's
or Pepperidge Farm
works well)**

**⅓ cup butter, melted
Parmesan cheese**

Preheat oven to 250°. Cut crusts from bread and cut into desired size and shape. Place bread on a baking sheet and brush well with melted butter. Sprinkle with Parmesan cheese, if desired. Bake for 1 hour or until very crisp and lightly browned.

Store in tins or in the freezer.

Yield: 10 servings

# BLUEBERRY JAM

**1½ quarts blueberries (6
cups)
2 tablespoons lemon juice**

**Grated rind of 1 lemon
6 cups sugar**

Combine all ingredients and cook over medium heat until mixture comes to a boil. Boil for 15 minutes; skim several times, if necessary. Fill sterilized jars with jam and seal. Chill before serving.

Yield: 8½ pints

# STRAWBERRY FIG JAM

**3½ cups very finely
chopped figs
3 cups sugar
2 3-ounce packages
strawberry-flavored
gelatin**

**½ package SURE-JELL
pectin
Juice of ½ lemon**

In a food processor, using the steel blade, process figs until smooth. Combine all ingredients in a large saucepan. Boil 3 minutes and pour into sterilized jelly jars. Seal.

Yield: 6 to 8½ pints

# DESSERTS

# DESSERTS

## Cakes
Almond Cheesecake with Chocolate Crust, 308
Apple Dapple Cake, 300
Bishop's Bread, 301
Camille's Carrot Cake, 302
Cheesecake Bordeaux, 309
Chocolate Nut Cheesecake, 310
Chocolate Sheet Cake, 303
Cream Cheese Pound Cake, 305
Gingerbread, 302
Hummingbird Cake, 304
Jam Cake, 303
Mississippi Mud Cake, 311
Poppy Seed Cake with Lemon Icing, 307
Pumpkin Cake, 306
Roulage, 301
Sour Cream Pound Cake, 304
Southern Pound Cake, 305

## Cookies
Apiece-Old Fashioned Rolled Cookies, 287
Apricot Nut Bars, 287
Apricot Oatmeal Bars, 288
Best-Ever Gingersnaps, 298
Black-Eyed Susans, 288
Butter Pecan Turtle Squares, 292
Caramel Squares, 294
Chocolate Caramel Squares, 294
Chocolate Crinkle Cookies, 293
Coconut Macaroons, 295
Coconut Squares, 295
Cream Cheese Brownies, 289
Drop Cookie Supreme, 299
Easter Cakes, 296
English Toffee, 296
Fudge/Mocha Frosted Brownies, 290
Gingerbread Cookies, 292
Ladyfingers, 293
Lemon-Cream Cheese Cookies, 298
Marzipan Cupcakes, 297
Oatmeal Cookies, 299
Peanut Butter Brownies, 291
Pecan Lace Cookies, 297
Tennessee Butter Cookies, 291

## Desserts
Amaretto Coconut Bavarian, 322
Baked Lemon Custard, 322
Bananas Foster, 324
Blueberry Buckle, 325
Blueberry/Peach Crisp, 328
Brownie Alaska, 324
Chocolate Glazed Éclairs, 327
Chocolate Mousse, 326

Chocolate Rum Dessert, 323
Fresh Coconut Pudding, 323
Frozen Macaroon Crème, 325
Lemon Mousse, 333
Mexican Apricot Trifle Josephs, 332
New Orleans Bread Pudding with Rum Sauce, 326
Poached Pears in Grand Marnier Sauce, 329
Pumpkin Ice Cream Squares, 330
Sopaipillas, 328
Strawberry Squares, 331
Swedish Pineapple Cream, 330
Tortoni, 334
Viennese Strawberry Torte, 331
Walnut Torte, 329

## Dessert Sauces and Icings
Chocolate Sherry Sauce, 338
Hot Caramel Sauce, 338
Hot Fudge Sauce, 338
Lemon Filling, 337
Quick Caramel Icing, 306
Quick Chocolate Icing, 307
Snowy Fruit Topping, 337
Strawberry Topping, 337

## Ice Cream
Banana Ice Cream, 333
Buttermilk Ice Cream, 335
Butter Pecan Ice Cream, 332
Champagne Sorbet, 335
Ice Cream Crunch, 336
Peach Ice Cream, 334
Sunshine Sherbet, 335
Vanilla Custard Ice Cream, 336

## Pies
Almond Tarts, 316
Apple Cream Crumble Pie, 315
Bob Hope's Lemon Meringue Pie, 321
Chocolate Bavarian Pie, 317
Chocolate Lover's Pie, 314
Coffee Toffee Pie, 313
French Silk Pie, 320
Fresh Coconut Pie, 318
Fresh Peach Pie, 319
Frozen Brandy Alexander Pie, 310
Frozen Lemon Pie, 321
Key Lime Pie, 319
Lemon Sherbet Pie, 312
Pecan Cream Cheese Pie, 320
Perfect Pie Crust, 312
Pineapple Cream Cheese Pie, 314
Puff Pastry, 311
Pumpkin Pie, 315
Southern Pecan Pie, 318

# APIECE –
# OLD FASHIONED ROLLED COOKIES

1 cup butter
2½ cups sugar
2 eggs
1 teaspoon baking powder

½ teaspoon salt
4 cups sifted flour
½ teaspoon cream of tartar

Cream butter; gradually add sugar, beating thoroughly. Add eggs, one at a time, mixing well.

Sift together dry ingredients. Add to butter mixture gradually, beating at low speed or by hand until stiff dough forms.

Shape dough into 2 large balls; cover and refrigerate until well chilled.

Preheat oven to 400°. Keep half the dough in refrigerator and roll out remainder on well-floured board until quite thin. Cut with cookie cutters.

If desired, decorate with colored sugar, nuts, or candied cherries.

Bake 8-10 minutes, watching carefully, until edges are very lightly browned. Remove from cookie sheets and cool on wire racks. Store in tightly covered container.

Yield: approximately 6 dozen cookies, depending on shapes

# APRICOT NUT BARS

1 cup butter
1 cup sugar
1 egg yolk
2½ cups flour

1 cup chopped walnuts
1½ cups Smucker's Apricot
       Preserves

Cream butter and sugar with an electric mixer. Beat in egg yolk. Stir in flour and then walnuts.

Preheat oven to 350°. Place ½ of dough in a 9x12-inch pan and spread evenly. Press gently to shape. Cover with preserves and top with remaining crumbled dough. Bake until browned, 20-25 minutes.

Yield: 24 bars

# APRICOT OATMEAL BARS

1½ cups flour
½ teaspoon salt
½ teaspoon baking soda
½ cup regular oats
1 cup brown sugar

1 cup finely chopped nuts
¾ cup butter, melted
1 12-ounce jar Smucker's
    Apricot Jam

Sift flour, salt and soda together. Add sugar, oats, nuts and melted butter.

Preheat oven to 375°. Press ⅔ of mixture into a 9-inch square pan. Cover with apricot jam. Top with remainder of oatmeal mixture. Pack gently. Bake for 30 minutes. Top should be browned. Cool and cut into squares.

Yield: 24 squares

# BLACK-EYED SUSANS

1 pound cheddar cheese,
    grated
1 cup butter, melted
⅛ teaspoon salt
3 cups flour

1 16-ounce package whole,
    pitted dates
Nuts (small pecans or
    walnuts)
½ cup sugar

Mix cheese, butter, salt and flour; blend well to form pastry dough. Chill.

Stuff dates with small nuts.

Preheat oven to 325°. Roll out chilled dough on floured surface to ¼ inch thick. Cut dough with biscuit cutter and wrap around each stuffed date; then roll in sugar. Bake on ungreased cookie sheets for about 25 minutes.

Yield: 4½ dozen

# CREAM CHEESE BROWNIES

*Filling:*

1 3-ounce package cream
cheese, softened
2 tablespoons butter,
softened
¼ cup sugar
1 egg
1 tablespoon flour
½ teaspoon vanilla

Cream 2 tablespoons butter with cream cheese until softened. Gradually add sugar; cream until light and fluffy. Blend in egg, flour and vanilla. Set mixture aside.

*Brownie:*

1 4-ounce bar Baker's
German Sweet
Chocolate
3 tablespoons butter
2 eggs
¾ cup sugar
½ teaspoon baking powder
¼ teaspoon salt
½ cup flour
½ cup coarsely chopped
nuts
¼ teaspoon almond extract
1 teaspoon vanilla

Preheat oven to 350°. Melt chocolate with 3 tablespoons butter over low heat, stirring constantly. Cool.

Beat eggs until thick and light in color. Gradually add sugar, beating until thickened. Add baking powder, salt and flour. Blend in cooled chocolate mixture, nuts and flavorings. Measure 1 cup chocolate batter and set aside.

Spread remaining chocolate batter in greased 9x9-inch pan; top with cream cheese mixture. Drop measured chocolate batter from tablespoon onto cheese mixture. Swirl with knife to marble. Bake for 35-40 minutes. Cool. Store, covered, in refrigerator.

Yield: 20 brownies

# FUDGE/MOCHA FROSTED BROWNIES

*Brownies:*

1 cup butter
2 cups sugar
4 eggs
4 ounces unsweetened
    chocolate, melted

2 teaspoons vanilla
1 cup flour
1 cup chopped nuts

Preheat oven to 325°. With an electric mixer, cream butter and sugar. Add eggs, beating well. Blend in melted chocolate and vanilla. Stir in flour and nuts. Bake in a 13x9x2-inch greased baking pan for 30 minutes. Spread with frosting of your choice.

*Fudge Frosting:*

3 cups confectioners'
    sugar, sifted
3 tablespoons cocoa

6 tablespoons half and half
3 tablespoons butter

Combine ingredients in a saucepan in the order listed. Cook over medium heat, stirring constantly, until mixture boils. Remove from heat and beat until of spreading consistency. Frost brownies.

*Mocha Frosting:*

4 tablespoons butter
4 tablespoons milk
2 tablespoons instant
    coffee granules

2 teaspoons vanilla
Confectioners' sugar

Heat butter and milk in a saucepan. Add coffee and stir to dissolve. Add vanilla; then add enough confectioners' sugar to make a thin icing. Spread over hot brownies. Cool before cutting.

Yield: 3 dozen

# PEANUT BUTTER BROWNIES

| | |
|---|---|
| 1 cup butter | ½ teaspoon salt |
| ⅓ cup cocoa | 1 teaspoon vanilla |
| 2 cups sugar | 1 cup crunchy peanut |
| 4 eggs | butter |
| 1½ cups flour | |

Preheat oven to 350°. Melt 1 cup butter and cocoa in double boiler. Cool. Blend in sugar and eggs. Combine flour, salt and vanilla; to this add first mixture. Bake in greased 13x9x2-inch pan for 20-30 minutes.

Spoon peanut butter over hot cake and spread while melting.

*Frosting:*

| | |
|---|---|
| ½ cup butter | ¼ teaspoon salt |
| ¼ cup cocoa | 1 teaspoon vanilla |
| ⅓ cup milk | 1 box confectioners' sugar, |
| 8 large marshmallows | sifted |

Melt together ½ cup butter, cocoa, milk, marshmallows, salt and vanilla. Beat in confectioners' sugar. Spread over cooled peanut butter.

Yield: 4 dozen 1½-inch squares

# TENNESSEE BUTTER COOKIES

| | |
|---|---|
| 2 cups butter, softened | 2 tablespoons vanilla |
| 1 cup sugar | Favorite jelly, jam or |
| 4½ cups flour | preserves |

Preheat oven to 350°. Cream butter and sugar. Add vanilla and blend in flour.

Shape dough into 1-inch balls and place on ungreased cookie sheet. Depress centers, forming a ridge around edges.

Spoon filling into depressions and bake for 20 minutes.

Yield: 5 dozen

# GINGERBREAD COOKIES

| | |
|---|---|
| 1½ cups sugar | 3 cups flour |
| 1 cup butter | 2 teaspoons baking soda |
| 1 egg | 2 teaspoons ground |
| 2 tablespoons dark corn | cinnamon |
| syrup | 1 teaspoon ground ginger |
| 4 teaspoons grated orange | ½ teaspoon salt |
| peel | ½ teaspoon ground cloves |

Thoroughly cream together sugar and butter. Add egg; beat until light and fluffy. Add syrup and orange peel; mix well. Stir together flour, baking soda, spices and salt. Stir into creamed mixture. Chill dough thoroughly.

Preheat oven to 375°. On lightly floured surface, roll the dough ¼ inch thick. Cut with cookie cutters appropriate to the season. Place cookies 1 inch apart on ungreased cookie sheet. Bake for 8-10 minutes. Cool 1 minute before removing from cookie sheet. Finish cooling on rack.

Yield: about 2 dozen

# BUTTER PECAN TURTLE SQUARES

*Crust:*

| | |
|---|---|
| 2¼ cups flour | ½ cup butter, softened |
| 1 cup dark brown sugar | 1 cup pecan halves |

Preheat oven to 350°. Blend ingredients together. Press into a 13x9x2-inch glass baking dish. Line crust with pecan halves.

*Caramel layer:*

| | |
|---|---|
| ⅔ cup butter | ½ cup dark brown sugar |

Combine ingredients in a saucepan. Cook over medium heat, stirring constantly, until boiling. Boil 1 minute.

Pour caramel over crust. Bake for 20 minutes.

*Chocolate layer:*

**1 6-ounce package
chocolate chips**

Sprinkle chocolate chips over hot squares. When melted, swirl with knife. Cool; cut into squares to serve.

Yield: 2 dozen

# LADYFINGERS

6 eggs, separated
1 cup sugar
2 teaspoons orange extract

1 cup flour
⅛ teaspoon salt
Confectioners' sugar

In a bowl beat egg yolks with sugar and orange extract until yolks are very thick and light in color. Sift in flour, folding quickly and lightly. Stiffly beat egg whites with salt. Fold ¼ of whites thoroughly into yolk mixture. Pile mixture on top of remaining whites and fold them together gently but thoroughly.

Preheat oven to 350°. Spray ladyfinger pans with vegetable spray. Drop batter into ladyfinger pans by teaspoonfuls. Sift confectioners' sugar over strips and sprinkle lightly with water. Bake for 10 minutes, or until lightly browned. Remove from pans and cool on racks.

Alternate method with no ladyfinger pans: Place sheets of ungreased parchment paper over a baking sheet. Fill a pastry bag, fitted with a ½-inch plain tube, with the ladyfinger batter. Make strips 1 inch wide and 4 inches long; place about 1 inch apart. Sift confectioners' sugar over strips and sprinkle lightly with water. Bake as above.

Yield: about 4 dozen

# CHOCOLATE CRINKLE COOKIES

½ cup vegetable oil
4 1-ounce squares
    unsweetened
    chocolate, melted
2 cups sugar
4 eggs

2 teaspoons vanilla
2 cups flour
2 teaspoons baking powder
½ teaspoon salt
1 cup confectioners' sugar

Mix oil, chocolate and sugar; blend in eggs, one at a time, beating well after each addition. Add vanilla. Stir flour, baking powder and salt into mixture. Chill several hours or overnight.

Preheat oven to 350°. Roll teaspoons of dough into balls; roll in confectioners' sugar to cover. Place 2 inches apart on greased cookie sheet. Bake 10-12 minutes or until almost no imprint remains when touched lightly. These freeze well.

Yield: 6 dozen

# CARAMEL SQUARES

1 16-ounce package dark
   brown sugar
1¾ sticks butter
1 egg, slightly beaten

1½ cups flour
1 teaspoon baking powder
1 teaspoon vanilla
1½ cups chopped nuts

Preheat oven to 325°. In the top of a double boiler melt butter and sugar. Blend in other ingredients.

Pour into two 9x9-inch square pans lined with greased foil. Bake for 20-25 minutes. Cool before cutting.

Yield: 24 squares

# CHOCOLATE CARAMEL SQUARES

1 14-ounce package light
   caramels
⅓ cup evaporated milk
1 18.2-ounce box German
   chocolate cake mix
⅓ cup evaporated milk

¾ cup butter, softened
1 cup chopped nuts
1 6-ounce package semi-
   sweet chocolate chips

In a double boiler combine caramels and ⅓ cup evaporated milk. Stir until caramels melt. Set aside.

Preheat oven to 350°. Generously grease and lightly flour a 13x9x2-inch baking pan.

In a large mixing bowl combine cake mix, butter, ⅓ cup evaporated milk and nuts. Mix until dough holds together. Press half of dough into prepared pan. Bake 6 minutes.

Sprinkle chocolate chips over baked dough. Pour caramel over chocolate. Crumble remaining half of dough over caramel and return to oven to bake 15-18 minutes. Cool slightly. Refrigerate 30 minutes to set caramel layer. Cut into squares.

Yield: 3 dozen

# COCONUT MACAROONS

1¼ cups butter
1 cup sugar
1 cup firmly packed brown
  sugar
2 eggs, beaten
2¼ cups sifted flour

⅓ teaspoon baking soda
2 teaspoons baking powder
½ teaspoon salt
1 cup rolled oats
2 cups grated coconut
1 cup chopped pecans

Cream butter and sugars. Beat in eggs. Sift together flour, soda, baking powder and salt. Beat into creamed mixture. Add oats, coconut and pecans. Mix well.

Preheat oven to 350°. Roll dough into balls about the size of walnuts. Place on ungreased baking sheet about 2 inches apart. Bake for 12-15 minutes or until golden. Cool slightly on baking sheet before removing to wire rack. Don't overcook if you like a chewy cookie.

Yield: about 6 dozen

*This cookie is very stable. It freezes well and can be mailed.*

# COCONUT SQUARES

*Crust:*

½ cup vegetable shortening
  or butter

1 cup flour
½ cup dark brown sugar

Preheat oven to 375°. Blend crust ingredients and press into a 9x9-inch or 9x11-inch baking pan. Bake 10 minutes.

*Filling:*

1 cup dark brown sugar
1 teaspoon vanilla
½ teaspoon salt
2 eggs, beaten

1 cup chopped pecans
3 tablespoons flour
1½ cups Baker's coconut

Blend filling ingredients and pour into partially cooked crust. Replace in oven and bake 20 minutes longer.

Yield: 20 squares

# EASTER CAKES

1 cup butter, softened
¾ cup sugar
2½ cups flour

1 cup walnuts, very finely
chopped

Preheat oven to 350°. Cream butter and sugar with electric mixer until very smooth, about 10 minutes. Knead flour and walnuts into mixture thoroughly. Shape into 1½-inch balls and place on baking sheet 1 inch apart. Depress balls in center to form a well for the filling.

*Filling:*
1 8-ounce box dates, finely
chopped
2 tablespoons butter,
softened
⅛ teaspoon nutmeg

⅛ teaspoon cinnamon
¼ teaspoon orange extract
Confectioners' sugar for
decoration

Mix together all filling ingredients. Place a small amount inside each ball and pinch to close. Flatten each cake with a fork and bake for about 15 minutes. These cakes should not be browned. While hot, sprinkle with confectioners' sugar.

Yield: 3 dozen

# ENGLISH TOFFEE

1 cup crushed pecans
1 cup butter (do not
substitute)

1 cup sugar
1 6-ounce package semi-
sweet chocolate chips

Line a 13x9x2-inch baking pan with foil. Sprinkle ⅓ cup pecans into pan.

Place butter and sugar in a saucepan and cook over medium heat. Stir constantly with a wooden spoon until candy thermometer reaches 300° (hard crack). Mixture will boil and begin to brown. Pour over pecans in pan and sprinkle chips over hot mixture. Spread evenly. Top with remaining nuts and press into chocolate. Let cool in refrigerator 1 hour 30 minutes. Break into pieces to serve. Store in refrigerator or freezer.

# MARZIPAN CUPCAKES

⅓ cup butter (do not
    substitute)
¼ cup confectioners' sugar

1 egg yolk
¼ teaspoon almond extract
1 cup flour

Preheat oven to 375°. Cream butter and sugar well; add egg yolk and almond extract; mix well. Blend in flour; then chill an hour for easier handling. Pinch off marble-sized pieces of dough and press into bottom and sides of tiny ungreased muffin tins. Bake for 7-8 minutes.

*Filling:*

⅓ cup butter (do not
    substitute)
½ 8-ounce can almond
    paste

½ cup sugar
2 eggs
½ teaspoon almond extract

Cream butter with almond paste until well blended; thoroughly beat in ½ cup granulated sugar. Blend in eggs and almond extract. Spoon into each baked shell; then bake at 350° for 20 minutes.

*Frosting:*

¾ cup confectioners' sugar
Orange or lemon juice

¼ teaspoon almond extract

Prepare a thin frosting by combining confectioners' sugar with orange or lemon juice and ¼ teaspoon almond extract. Drizzle over outer edges of warm cakes.

Yield: 36 tiny cupcakes

# PECAN LACE COOKIES

1⅓ cups finely chopped
    pecans
1 cup sugar
4 tablespoons flour
⅓ teaspoon baking powder

⅛ teaspoon salt
½ cup butter, melted
2 teaspoons vanilla
1 egg, beaten

Mix together pecans, sugar, flour, baking powder and salt. Add melted butter, vanilla and egg. Blend well. Line baking sheets with kitchen parchment. Preheat oven to 325°. Drop by small teaspoon-fuls onto sheets 3 inches apart. Bake 8-12 minutes. Cool. Peel off parchment.

Yield: 3-4 dozen

# BEST-EVER GINGERSNAPS

| | |
|---|---|
| 1 cup sugar | ½ teaspoon ground cloves |
| 2 cups flour | ¾ cup vegetable shortening |
| ½ teaspoon salt | ¼ cup molasses |
| 1 teaspoon cinnamon | 1 egg, slightly beaten |
| 1 teaspoon baking soda | Sugar |
| 1 teaspoon ground ginger | |

Mix first 7 ingredients. Cut in shortening until mixture resembles coarse crumbs. Stir in molasses and egg.

Preheat oven to 350°. Shape dough into 1-inch balls and roll in sugar. Place 2 inches apart on ungreased cookie sheets and bake for 10 minutes. Remove from oven promptly. Cool on sheets a few minutes; then remove cookies to wire rack.

Yield: 4½ dozen

# LEMON-CREAM CHEESE COOKIES

| | |
|---|---|
| 1 cup butter, softened | 1 teaspoon grated lemon |
| 1 3-ounce package cream |    rind |
|    cheese, softened | 2½ cups flour |
| 1 cup sugar | 1 teaspoon baking powder |
| 1 egg, beaten | Food coloring |
| 1 tablespoon lemon juice | |

Blend butter and cream cheese. Add sugar; cream thoroughly. Add egg, lemon juice and rind; blend well. Mix flour and baking powder. Add to cream cheese mixture, along with food coloring, if desired, and mix until well blended. Chill dough at least 30 minutes.

Preheat oven to 375°. Force dough through cookie press or gun onto ungreased baking sheet. Bake 8-10 minutes, or until slightly browned. These freeze well.

Yield: 5 dozen 2-inch cookies

# OATMEAL COOKIES

1 cup butter
1 cup sugar
½ cup brown sugar
1 egg, beaten
1 teaspoon vanilla
1½ cups flour
1 teaspoon baking soda
1 teaspoon salt

1 teaspoon cinnamon
1½ cups old-fashioned
   uncooked regular oats
¾ cup chopped pecans
1 cup raisins, chocolate
   chips or peanut butter
   chips

Cream butter and sugars. Add egg, vanilla and dry ingredients in order given and mix well. Add pecans; then add raisins, chocolate chips or peanut butter chips, if desired. Chill 1 hour.

Preheat oven to 350°. Form dough into walnut-sized balls and place 2 inches apart on ungreased cookie sheet. Flatten each ball with the bottom of a small glass which has been buttered and dipped into sugar. Bake for 10-12 minutes.

Yield: 4-5 dozen

# DROP COOKIE SUPREME

1 cup butter
1 cup brown sugar
1 cup white sugar
2 eggs
2 cups flour
1 teaspoon baking powder
⅛ teaspoon salt
½ teaspoon baking soda

3 cups corn flakes
1 cup uncooked quick oats
1 cup shredded dry
   coconut
1 cup chopped pecans
1 teaspoon vanilla

Preheat oven to 325°. Cream butter and sugars. Add eggs one at a time, beating after each addition. Sift flour, baking powder, salt and soda and add to creamed mixture. Stir in corn flakes, oats, coconut, nuts and vanilla. Drop by teaspoonfuls onto greased cookie sheet. Bake until lightly browned, about 10-12 minutes. Larger cookies can be made, if desired.

Yield: about 140 small cookies

# APPLE DAPPLE CAKE

1½ cups salad oil
2 cups sugar
3 cups flour
1 teaspoon salt
1 teaspoon baking soda
3 eggs

2 teaspoons vanilla
2-3 cups chopped apple
1-1½ cups chopped nuts
½-1 teaspoon cinnamon
½ cup golden raisins
1 teaspoon rum flavoring

Mix oil and sugar in a bowl; then sift in dry ingredients. Add eggs, vanilla, apples, nuts and cinnamon. Mix well. Add raisins and rum flavoring, if desired. Bake in greased and floured 10-inch tube pan at 350° for 1 hour.

Optional microwave directions: Pour batter into greased microwave 10-inch tube pan. Microwave on MEDIUM (50% power) 11 minutes; then microwave on HIGH for 7 minutes. Let stand 10-15 minutes before inverting onto serving dish.

Glaze while warm with one of the glazes listed below.

*Butter Glaze:*
   1 cup brown sugar
   ¼ cup milk

½ cup butter

Combine glaze ingredients and cook for 3 minutes or until boiling. Drizzle over warm cake.

*Apple Glaze:*
   ½ cup Applejack brandy
   ½ cup apple cider

¼ cup brown sugar
2 tablespoons butter

Place ingredients in glass bowl. Microwave 3-4 minutes on HIGH, or until hot. Drizzle over warm cake.

# ROULAGE

5 eggs, separated
1 cup confectioners' sugar
2 tablespoons flour
3 tablespoons cocoa
1 teaspoon vanilla
1 pinch salt

1 cup whipping cream,
   sweetened and
   whipped
Cocoa
Hot fudge sauce

Separate eggs and beat egg whites until stiff, but not dry. Set aside. Beat egg yolks until pale. Sift together sugar, flour and cocoa, and add to egg yolks. Mix well; then add vanilla and salt. Mix again. Fold in beaten egg whites.

Pour into a jelly roll pan that has been well greased or lined with greased parchment paper or wax paper. Bake at 325° for about 15 minutes.

Turn out on damp towel. Remove parchment or wax paper if used. Trim edges and roll while hot. Cool in towel; take out of towel and unroll in cocoa. (This coats the outside.) Spread the inside with sweetened whipped cream and roll again. Refrigerate. Slice and serve. Top with hot fudge sauce, if desired. Chocolate leaves are a pretty garnish.

# BISHOP'S BREAD

1 cup butter
2 cups sugar
4 eggs
4 cups flour, divided
2 teaspoons baking powder
1⅛ teaspoons baking soda
1 cup buttermilk
1½ 6-ounce packages
   chocolate chips

16 ounces chopped dates
1 cup flaked coconut
2 cups chopped nuts
2 cups chopped candied
   cherries
1 cup chopped candied
   pineapple

Using an electric mixer, cream butter and sugar. Add eggs one at a time, beating well after each. Combine baking soda and baking powder with 3 cups of flour. Alternately add dry mixture and buttermilk to creamed mixture, beginning and ending with dry mixture. Dredge last six ingredients in 1 cup flour. Add to mixture. Bake in 3 greased and floured loaf pans for 1 hour in a 325° preheated oven.

Yield: 3 loaves

# CAMILLE'S CARROT CAKE

*Cake:*

2 cups flour
2 teaspoons baking powder
1½ teaspoons baking soda
1 teaspoon salt
2 teaspoons cinnamon
2 cups sugar

1½ cups vegetable oil
4 eggs
2 cups grated carrots
1 8¾-ounce can crushed
    pineapple, drained
½ cup chopped nuts

Preheat oven to 350°. Sift together flour, baking powder, baking soda, salt and cinnamon. Add sugar, oil and eggs; mix well. Stir in carrots, pineapple and nuts until well blended. Bake in 3 greased and floured 9-inch layer pans for 35 to 40 minutes.

*Frosting:*

½ cup butter, softened
1 teaspoon vanilla
1 8-ounce package cream
    cheese, softened

1 pound confectioners'
    sugar, sifted

Blend butter, cream cheese and vanilla well. Gradually beat in sugar, beating until smooth. If too thick for spreading, add a small amount of milk.

# GINGERBREAD

2 cups flour
4 teaspoons nutmeg
4 teaspoons cinnamon
2 teaspoons baking soda
2 teaspoons ground ginger
1 teaspoon ground cloves

1 cup sugar
1 cup buttermilk
1 cup molasses
1 cup vegetable oil
3 eggs, beaten

Preheat oven to 325°. Sift dry ingredients together. Combine all ingredients in large bowl. Mix thoroughly with an electric mixer.

Pour into greased and floured 13x9x2-inch baking pan and bake 30-40 minutes or until top springs back when lightly touched.

Serve topped with lemon sauce or sweetened whipped cream.

# CHOCOLATE SHEET CAKE

*Cake:*

2 cups flour
2 cups sugar
½ cup margarine
4 tablespoons cocoa
½ cup Crisco shortening
1 cup water

½ cup buttermilk
2 eggs, slightly beaten
1 teaspoon vanilla
1 teaspoon baking soda
1 teaspoon cinnamon

Sift together flour and sugar. In a saucepan, bring to a rapid boil margarine, cocoa, shortening and water; pour over flour and sugar mixture and stir well. Add buttermilk, eggs, vanilla and baking soda. Add cinnamon if desired. Mix well. Pour into a greased and floured 17x11x2-inch baking pan. Bake 15-18 minutes in a preheated 400° oven.

*Icing:*

3 cups sugar
¾ cup margarine

¾ cup cocoa
¾ cup milk

Combine all ingredients in saucepan and bring to rapid boil. Cook over medium heat to soft-ball stage. Cool; beat to spreading consistency; spread on cooled cake.

# JAM CAKE

1 cup butter
1½ cups sugar
3 eggs
3 cups sifted cake flour
1 teaspoon ground cloves
1 teaspoon cinnamon

1 teaspoon nutmeg
1 scant cup blackberry jam
    or preserves
1 teaspoon baking soda
1 cup buttermilk

Preheat oven to 350°. Cream butter and sugar. Add eggs one at a time, beating well after each addition. Add flour, spices and ¼ cup buttermilk. Add jam and mix thoroughly. Stir baking soda into remaining buttermilk and combine with cake batter. Do not overbeat.

Pour batter into 3 buttered 8-inch cake pans or 1 buttered 13x9x2-inch baking dish. Bake 40-45 minutes.

Yield: 10 servings

*It is delicious plain or iced with QUICK CHOCOLATE ICING.*

# HUMMINGBIRD CAKE

*Cake:*

| | |
|---|---|
| 3 cups flour | 1½ cups vegetable oil |
| 2 cups sugar | 1½ teaspoons vanilla |
| 1 teaspoon salt | 1 8-ounce can crushed |
| 1 teaspoon baking soda | pineapple, undrained |
| 1 teaspoon cinnamon | 1 cup chopped pecans |
| 3 eggs, beaten | 2 cups mashed bananas |

Combine dry ingredients in a large bowl. Add eggs and oil until dry ingredients are moistened. DO NOT BEAT. Stir in vanilla, pineapple, pecans and bananas.

Pour into 3 or 4 greased and floured 9-inch round cake pans. Bake for 30-35 minutes in a preheated 350° oven. Cool and frost.

*Frosting:*

| | |
|---|---|
| 1 8-ounce package cream | 1 16-ounce box |
| cheese, softened | confectioners' sugar |
| ⅓ stick butter, softened | 2 teaspoons vanilla |
| | 1 cup chopped pecans |

Mix first four ingredients. Stir in pecans.

# SOUR CREAM POUND CAKE

| | |
|---|---|
| 2¾ cups sugar | ½ teaspoon salt |
| ½ pound butter, room | 1 cup sour cream |
| temperature | 1 tablespoon vanilla |
| 6 eggs, room temperature | 1 tablespoon lemon extract |
| 3 cups flour | 1 cup finely chopped |
| 1 teaspoon baking powder | pecans |

Preheat oven to 325°. Cream butter and sugar, using electric mixer. Add eggs, one at a time, beating well after each addition. Add dry ingredients to the creamed mixture alternately with the sour cream. Mix well. Add flavorings and pecans. Pour batter into a buttered and and floured 10-inch tube pan. Bake at 325° for 1 hour 30 minutes. Pound cake is better made a day ahead.

Yield: 15 servings

# CREAM CHEESE POUND CAKE

1½ cups butter, softened
1 8-ounce package cream
    cheese, softened
3 cups sugar

6 eggs
3 cups flour
1 tablespoon vanilla

Cream butter, cream cheese and sugar until very fluffy. Add eggs one at a time, beating well after each. Add flour and continue beating about 1 more minute after well mixed. Add vanilla and mix well.

Pour batter into a greased and floured bundt or tube pan and bake at 325° for 1 hour 15 minutes to 1 hour 30 minutes; or pour into 1 greased and floured 14x10x2-inch pan and bake at 300° for 50-55 minutes.

*Frosting: (optional)*
1 16-ounce box
    confectioners' sugar
¼ cup butter, softened

1 3-ounce package cream
    cheese
1-1½ teaspoons vanilla
¼ cup milk

All ingredients should be at room temperature. Mix together until well blended and use to frost cooled pound cake. Frosted cake must be refrigerated.

Yield: 10-20 servings, depending on pan used

# SOUTHERN POUND CAKE

3 cups sugar
½ cup shortening
½ pound butter, room
    temperature
6 eggs, room temperature
3 cups flour

¼ teaspoon salt
½ teaspoon baking powder
1 cup milk
1 teaspoon rum extract
1 teaspoon coconut extract

Preheat oven to 325°. Cream sugar, shortening and butter. Add eggs, one at a time, beating well after each addition. Add dry ingredients to the creamed mixture alternately with the milk. Add extracts and mix well. Pour batter into a buttered and floured 10-inch tube pan. Bake at 325° for 1 hour 30 minutes.

Yield: 15 servings

# PUMPKIN CAKE

*Cake:*

2 cups sugar
4 eggs
1 cup vegetable oil
2 cups flour
2 teaspoons baking soda

½ teaspoon salt
2 teaspoons cinnamon
½ teaspoon allspice
1 16-ounce can pumpkin

Preheat oven to 350°. Mix sugar and eggs with an electric mixer on low speed; add oil. Continue mixing until no trace of oil can be seen, about 2-3 minutes.

Combine flour, soda, salt and spices. Blend into sugar mixture. Add pumpkin.

Bake in greased and floured 10-inch tube pan for 1 hour. Cool.

*Icing:*

4 ounces cream cheese,
    softened
¼ cup butter, softened
1 teaspoon vanilla

8 ounces confectioners'
    sugar
Pecan halves for garnish

For icing, blend all ingredients and spread over cake. Garnish if desired.

*SNOWY FRUIT TOPPING may be used in place of cream cheese icing.*

# QUICK CARAMEL ICING

½ cup butter
1 cup dark brown sugar,
    firmly packed

4 tablespoons milk
Confectioners' sugar

In a saucepan melt butter; then add brown sugar and cook over low heat for 2 minutes, stirring constantly. Add milk and continue stirring until mixture comes to a boil. Remove from heat. Cool. Add sifted confectioners' sugar until icing is of spreading consistency.

Yield: enough for 2 layers

# POPPY SEED CAKE WITH LEMON ICING

1 cup butter
½ cup shortening
3 cups sugar
1 teaspoon vanilla
5 eggs
3⅓ cups flour

½ teaspoon baking powder
½ teaspoon salt
1 cup milk
2 teaspoons lemon juice
⅓ cup poppy seeds

Preheat oven to 325°. Cream butter and shortening. Add sugar and beat well. Add vanilla; then add eggs, one at a time, beating well after each addition. Mix flour, baking powder and salt in a separate bowl. Add to mixture alternately with milk; mix well. Stir in lemon juice and poppy seeds. Pour batter into a buttered and floured 10-inch tube pan and bake 1 hour 40 minutes. Cool on rack before icing cake.

*Icing:*

6 tablespoons butter
3 cups confectioners' sugar
1½ tablespoons milk
1½ tablespoons lemon
   juice

1½ teaspoons vanilla
⅛ teaspoon yellow food
   coloring
Grated rind of 1 lemon
1 tablespoon poppy seeds

In a mixing bowl, cream butter until smooth. Gradually add 1 cup sugar, vanilla, milk and lemon juice. Beat in remaining sugar until icing is light and fluffy. Carefully mix in food coloring, a drop at a time, until icing is a pale yellow. Stir in lemon rind and poppy seeds, mixing well. Spread over cooled poppy seed cake.

Yield: 12-15 servings

# QUICK CHOCOLATE ICING

1 16-ounce package
   confectioners' sugar,
   sifted
1 5.33-ounce can
   evaporated milk

4 ounces unsweetened
   chocolate, melted
1 teaspoon vanilla
1 teaspoon white vinegar

Combine all ingredients in bowl and blend well with electric mixer.

Yield: enough for a two-layer cake or a large sheet cake

# ALMOND CHEESECAKE
# WITH CHOCOLATE CRUST

*Crust:*

1½ cups chocolate wafer
    crumbs
1 cup blanched almonds,
    toasted and chopped

⅓ cup sugar
6 tablespoons butter,
    softened

In a bowl, combine chocolate wafer crumbs, almonds, sugar and butter. Blend well. Shape into bottom and sides of a buttered 10-inch springform pan.

*Cheesecake:*

3 8-ounce packages cream
    cheese, softened
1 cup sugar
4 eggs

⅓ cup half and half
¼ cup Amaretto
1 teaspoon vanilla

In a large bowl, cream together the cream cheese and sugar. Add eggs one at a time, beating well after each. Add cream, Amaretto and vanilla and beat until light. Pour batter into crust and bake in the middle of a 375° oven for 30 minutes. Transfer cake to rack and let stand for 5 minutes. (Cake will not be set.)

*Topping:*

2 cups sour cream
1 tablespoon sugar
1 teaspoon vanilla

Slivered blanched almonds,
    toasted

In a bowl combine topping ingredients, except almonds. Spread evenly over top of cake and bake 5 minutes longer. Transfer to cake rack to cool. Chill overnight, lightly covered.

To serve, remove side of pan and place on cake stand. Press almonds around top edge.

Yield: 12-15 servings

# CHEESECAKE BORDEAUX

*Crust:*

**1 6¾-ounce package Pepperidge Farm Bordeaux Cookies**

**¼ cup butter, softened**

With steel blade of food processor in place, process cookies until they are fine crumbs. Add butter and process until butter is absorbed into mixture. Use crumb mixture to line the bottom of a 9-inch springform pan, pressing it down firmly.

*Filling:*

**3 8-ounce packages cream cheese**

**4 eggs**

**½ cup sugar**

**3 teaspoons vanilla**

Preheat oven to 350°. Using the steel blade, cream one package of cream cheese in food processor. Add one egg and process well. Add second package of cream cheese and second egg. Process well after each addition. Add remaining cheese, eggs, sugar and vanilla. Process until smooth. Pour into prepared springform pan and bake 50 minutes. Remove cheesecake from oven and spread topping over top.

*Topping:*

**16 ounces sour cream**

**½ teaspoon vanilla**

**¼ cup sugar**

Using steel blade, process sour cream, vanilla and sugar until smooth. Spread over top of cheesecake and bake 5-10 minutes. Let cool on wire rack. Cover with plastic wrap and refrigerate. Cheesecake is best when made a day ahead.

Yield: 12 servings

# CHOCOLATE NUT CHEESECAKE

*Crust:*

1½ cups finely crushed chocolate wafers

¼ cup finely chopped pecans

⅓ cup butter, melted

Combine chocolate wafers, pecans and butter; blend well. Press mixture into bottom of a 9 or 10-inch springform pan. Bake in a 325° oven for 10 minutes. Cool.

*Filling:*

2½ cups whipping cream, whipped

4 eggs

2 8-ounce packages cream cheese, softened

1 cup sugar, divided

2 teaspoons vanilla

1 12-ounce package semi-sweet chocolate chips, melted

1¼ cups chopped pecans

Whip cream until soft peaks form; set aside in the refrigerator. Separate eggs; reserve yolks. Beat egg whites until soft peaks form, gradually adding ½ cup sugar; set aside. Combine softened cream cheese, ½ cup sugar and vanilla; blend well. Add beaten egg yolks and melted chocolate to cream cheese mixture. Fold in beaten egg whites, then whipped cream and pecans. Pour into crumb crust and freeze.

Place in refrigerator 1 hour before serving. Garnish cheesecake with whipped cream or grated chocolate.

Yield: 12-15 servings

# FROZEN BRANDY ALEXANDER PIE

1 9-inch graham cracker crumb crust

1 14-ounce can sweetened condensed milk

1 cup whipping cream, whipped

2 tablespoons crème de cacao

2 tablespoons brandy

Shaved chocolate for garnish

In a large bowl combine milk, whipped cream, crème de cacao and brandy. Pour into prepared crust. Freeze 5-6 hours or until firm. Garnish with shaved chocolate, if desired. Serve frozen and freeze leftovers.

Yield: 6-8 servings

# MISSISSIPPI MUD CAKE

1 cup butter
½ cup cocoa
2 cups sugar
4 eggs, slightly beaten
1½ cups flour

Pinch salt
1½ cups chopped pecans
1 teaspoon vanilla
1 cup miniature
  marshmallows

Preheat oven to 350°. Melt butter and cocoa together. Remove from heat; stir in sugar and beaten eggs; mix well. Add flour, salt, pecans and vanilla; mix well. Pour batter into a buttered 13x9x2-inch baking pan and bake for 35-45 minutes. Sprinkle marshmallows on top of warm cake and then cover with frosting.

*Frosting:*
½ cup butter
6 tablespoons Coca-Cola
3 tablespoons cocoa

1 16-ounce package
  confectioners' sugar
1 cup chopped pecans

In small saucepan combine butter, Coca-Cola and cocoa. Bring to boil. In a mixing bowl, pour boiling liquid over confectioners' sugar. Add chopped nuts and mix well. Pour over cake while still warm.

Yield: 12-15 servings

# PUFF PASTRY

1 cup butter
1½ cups flour

½ cup sour cream

Cut butter into flour. Stir in sour cream. Wrap in plastic wrap and chill at least 4 hours. Roll on well-floured board into desired size. Cook according to filling recipe.

Yield: 2 crusts

*This is a foolproof recipe for pies or hors d'oeuvres.*

# PERFECT PIE CRUST

| | |
|---|---|
| 2 cups flour | 8 tablespoons unsalted |
| ¼ teaspoon salt | butter, chilled |
| 4 tablespoons margarine, | 4-5 tablespoons ice water |
| chilled | |

In a food processor, using the steel blade, process flour and salt. Cut butter and margarine into small bits and add to bowl. Process 10 seconds or until mixture resembles coarse meal. Add water gradually, being careful not to over process, processing about 15 seconds or until dough just holds together. Turn out onto plastic wrap, press into a ball and chill at least 1 hour before using.

Divide in half if desired.

Roll out pastry on lightly floured board. Press pastry into pan that has been sprayed with vegetable spray. Cut off excess pastry from edges.

For partially baked shells, line pastry with foil and beans or pie weights and bake in a preheated 375° oven for 10 minutes. Remove foil and weights; prick shell with fork and bake 4 minutes more. Remove shell from oven when it starts to color and begins to shrink from sides of pan.

This can be frozen.

Yield: two 9-inch tart pan shells or one 10-inch pie shell

# LEMON SHERBET PIE

| | |
|---|---|
| 6 eggs, separated | 1 cup sugar |
| ½ cup lemon juice | 1 cup whipping cream |
| Grated rind of 2 lemons | 3 graham cracker pie |
| ⅛ teaspoon salt | shells |

Beat yolks until thick. Add lemon juice, rind, salt and sugar. Beat mixture until sugar is dissolved. In a separate bowl, beat egg whites until stiff. Fold yolk mixture into whites. Whip cream and fold into white mixture. Pour into 3 shells and freeze.

Yield: 18 servings

*This is a light dessert that is low in sugar content.*

# COFFEE TOFFEE PIE

*Crust:*

1½ cups finely crushed
Nabisco Chocolate
Wafers

¼ cup butter, melted

Preheat oven to 325°.

Combine crumbs and butter with fork and press gently into 10-inch pie plate. Bake for 10 minutes and cool.

*Filling:*

¾ cup butter, softened
1 cup sugar
1½ ounces unsweetened
chocolate

1 tablespoon instant coffee
1 tablespoon boiling water
3 eggs

Beat butter until creamy. Gradually add sugar, beating until light and lemon-colored. Melt chocolate over hot water; cool slightly and add to butter mixture. Add instant coffee to boiling water and stir into mixture. Add eggs one at a time, beating well after each addition. Pour filling into cooled pie shell and refrigerate overnight, covered.

*Topping:*

2 cups whipping cream
½ cup confectioners' sugar
2 tablespoons instant
coffee

2 tablespoons coffee
liqueur
Chocolate curls for garnish

Beat cream until stiff. Add confectioners' sugar, coffee and coffee liqueur. Spread over filling and garnish with chocolate curls. Refrigerate at least two hours before serving.

Yield: 8 servings

## PINEAPPLE CREAM CHEESE PIE

1 9-inch deep-dish pastry
   shell, unbaked
½ cup sugar
1 9-ounce can crushed
   pineapple
1 tablespoon cornstarch
1 8-ounce package cream
   cheese

½ cup sugar
½ teaspoon salt
½ cup milk
½ teaspoon vanilla
2 eggs
¼ cup chopped pecans

Preheat oven to 400°. Cook sugar, pineapple and cornstarch until thick and clear. Cool.

Beat cream cheese, sugar, salt, milk and vanilla until smooth. Add eggs one at a time. Beat well.

Pour pineapple mixture into pie shell. Pour cream cheese mixture on top. Sprinkle with nuts. Bake for 10 minutes. Reduce heat to 325° and bake an additional 50 minutes.

Yield: 8-10 servings

## CHOCOLATE LOVERS' PIE

1 9-inch pastry shell,
   unbaked
2 eggs
3½ tablespoons cocoa
1½ cups sugar
1 teaspoon vanilla

1 5.33-ounce can
   evaporated milk
¼ cup butter, melted
⅛ teaspoon salt
½-¾ cup chopped pecans
½ pint whipping cream,
   whipped

Beat eggs and add cocoa, sugar, vanilla, milk, butter and salt. Mix well. Add pecans, if desired. Pour into pastry shell and bake in 350° oven for 30-35 minutes. Chill at least 4 hours before serving. Top with whipped cream, if desired.

Yield: 6-8 servings

## APPLE CREAM CRUMBLE PIE

1 9-inch deep-dish pastry
    shell, unbaked
3 pounds apples, peeled
    and cored

2 tablespoons lemon juice
½ cup sugar
2 tablespoons flour
½ teaspoon nutmeg

Cut apples into ¼-inch slices. Sprinkle lemon juice over them. Mix sugar, flour and nutmeg together in a small bowl. Sprinkle over apples, tossing to coat well. Spoon into pastry shell.

*Topping:*
½ cup sugar
½ cup flour

½ cup butter, softened
1 cup whipping cream

Preheat oven to 425°.

Combine sugar and flour; cut in butter until crumbly. Sprinkle over apples. Cover pie loosely with foil and place on large baking sheet for easy handling. Bake for 45 minutes. Uncover and drizzle ½ cup cream over the pie slowly. Bake 15 minutes longer, or until top is golden.

Remove pie from oven and place on cooling rack. Drizzle remaining ½ cup cream over the top slowly. Cool 1 hour or until filling is set.

Yield: 8 servings

## PUMPKIN PIE

2 9-inch deep-dish pastry
    shells, unbaked
4 eggs
1½ cups sugar
3 tablespoons flour
¾ teaspoon ginger
¼ teaspoon nutmeg

1 teaspoon cinnamon
½ teaspoon salt
2½ cups sieved pumpkin or
    2 16-ounce cans
    pumpkin
2 cups evaporated milk

Beat eggs. Combine sugar, flour, spices and salt; add to eggs. Add pumpkin and milk. Pour into pie shells. Sprinkle additional nutmeg on top. Bake at 350° until pies puff up in the center, about 1 hour.

Yield: two 9-inch deep-dish pies

# ALMOND TARTS

*Almond Pastry:*

| | |
|---|---|
| ¼ **cup blanched almonds** | 1¾ **cups flour** |
| 1 **large egg** | 1 **tablespoon sugar** |
| 1 **tablespoon milk** | ½ **teaspoon salt** |
| 1 **teaspoon vanilla** | |
| ¾ **cup unsalted butter,** | 3-**inch tart pans** |
| **chilled and cut into 12** | |
| **pieces** | |

Insert steel blade in bowl of food processor. Add almonds and process until nuts are finely chopped (20 seconds). Set aside. With steel blade in place, add egg, milk, vanilla extract and butter to bowl. Process, turning machine on/off approximately 6 times; the process for about 5-10 more seconds. Add flour, sugar, salt and reserved chopped almonds. Process until dough begins to mass together. Do not allow to form ball. Gather dough into a ball with floured hands. Place in a plastic bag and press dough into a flat disc. Refrigerate 2 hours or overnight.

Divide dough into 6 pieces; refrigerate unworked dough. Roll out pieces of dough to ⅛-inch thickness. Lay dough over tart shells loosely. Press rolling pin over dough to cut shapes. Press dough firmly but gently into tart pans. Prick bottom of tarts with a fork. Refrigerate tart shells for 30 minutes before baking.

Preheat oven to 375°. Rack should be in the middle of the oven. Place tart shells on cookie sheet. Line each sheet with foil and weight each one with dried beans or pie weights. Bake 10 minutes. Remove foil and weights. Prick dough again and bake 2-3 more minutes until lightly browned. Remove tart shells from pans and allow to cool.

*Almond Cream Filling:*

| | |
|---|---|
| ½ **cup blanched almonds** | 1¼ **sticks unsalted butter,** |
| 6 **tablespoons sugar** | **cut into 5 pieces** |
| ⅛ **teaspoon salt** | 1 **teaspoon vanilla** |
| 2 **large eggs** | 2 **teaspoons dark rum** |

With steel blade, add almonds and process until finely ground. Add sugar, salt and eggs and process 1 minute until fluffy. Add butter, rum and vanilla and process until well combined. This makes 1⅔ cups and can be frozen.

*Assembly:*

½ **cup strawberry preserves**    **2 tablespoons confectioners' sugar**

Preheat oven to 375°. Spread a scant teaspoon of strawberry preserves on bottom of shells. Spread 1 generous tablespoon of filling over each tart. Place tarts on cookie sheet. Bake for 15 minutes until browned. Cool. Sieve confectioners' sugar lightly over surface of tarts just before serving. Serve chilled.

Yield: 24 tarts

# CHOCOLATE BAVARIAN PIE

*Crust:*

1¼ **cups chocolate wafer crumbs**    ¼ **cup butter, melted**

Reserve 2 tablespoons crumbs for garnish. Prepare crust by combining crumbs and butter with a fork. Press mixture gently into a 9 inch pie plate. Chill.

*Filling:*

1 **envelope unflavored gelatin**
¼ **cup cold water**
3 **eggs, separated**
½ **cup sugar**
¼ **teaspoon salt**

1 **cup milk, scalded**
1 **teaspoon vanilla**
1 **cup whipping cream**
**Additional chocolate crumbs for garnish**

Soften gelatin in water. In a separate bowl, beat egg yolks slightly and combine with sugar and salt; slowly add milk. Cook in double boiler until mixture coats spoon. Add softened gelatin and stir until dissolved. Cool 45 minutes.

Add vanilla. Beat egg whites until stiff and fold into mixture; then whip cream and fold in. Pour into prepared crust and chill several hours before serving. Top may be decorated with reserved chocolate crumbs.

Yield: 6-8 servings

# FRESH COCONUT PIE

1 9-inch pastry shell,
   baked
¾ cup sugar
3 tablespoons cornstarch
⅛ teaspoon salt
2 cups milk
3 egg yolks

¾ teaspoon vanilla
¼ teaspoon almond extract
2 cups finely grated fresh
   coconut
1 cup whipping cream
2 tablespoons
   confectioners' sugar

In double boiler combine sugar, cornstarch and salt. Slowly add milk, stirring constantly over medium heat until thick. Cover and cook for 15 more minutes, stirring often.

Beat egg yolks slightly. Add ½ cup of hot custard mixture to egg yolks; then return egg mixture to custard in double boiler. Cook two minutes longer, stirring constantly. Remove from heat and stir in flavorings and coconut. Pour into a bowl, cover, and cool to room temperature, about 1 hour. Refrigerate until well chilled.

Pour custard into pastry shell. Top with cream which has been whipped with confectioners' sugar. Refrigerate.

Yield: 6-8 servings

*A 7-ounce package of coconut can be substituted for the fresh coconut. This pie is worth the trouble!*

# SOUTHERN PECAN PIE

1 9-inch pastry shell,
   unbaked
3 eggs
1 cup white Karo syrup
1 cup sugar

2 tablespoons butter,
   melted
1 teaspoon vanilla
⅛ teaspoon salt
1 cup chopped pecans

Beat eggs slightly. Mix in syrup, sugar, butter, vanilla and salt. Spread pecans over bottom of unbaked pastry shell and pour mixture over top. Bake at 400° for 15 minutes; then lower temperature to 350° and bake an additional 30-35 minutes or until knife inserted in center comes out clean.

Yield: 8 servings

# KEY LIME PIE

1 9-inch pastry shell,
   baked
1 cup sugar
3 tablespoons flour
3 tablespoons cornstarch
¼ teaspoon salt
2 cups boiling water

3 egg yolks
¼ cup freshly squeezed
   juice from Key or
   Persian limes
½ teaspoon freshly grated
   lime peel
1 tablespoon butter

Preheat oven to 400°. Blend sugar, flour, cornstarch and salt in top of double boiler. Blend and cook over 2 cups simmering water, whisking frequently for 10 minutes. Remove from heat. Beat egg yolks slightly. Add ¼ cup of custard to yolks and blend. Combine egg yolk mixture with custard and return to heat. Cook slowly for 2 minutes. Add lime juice, lime peel and butter. Remove from heat and stir until butter melts. Fold in about 1 cup meringue. Pour into pastry shell and top with remaining meringue, sealing to edges. Bake at 400° until barely brown, about 5 minutes. Cool before serving. Refrigerate leftovers.

*Meringue:*
4 egg whites
3 tablespoons sugar

⅛ teaspoon cream of tartar

Beat egg whites until they begin to hold their shape. Continue beating and gradually add sugar and cream of tartar. Beat until stiff peaks form.

Yield: 8 servings

# FRESH PEACH PIE

1 9-inch pastry shell,
   unbaked
6 or more fresh peaches
⅓ cup butter, melted

1⅓ cups sugar
2 eggs
1 tablespoon flour
½ teaspoon salt

Peel and slice peaches; place in unbaked pastry shell. Pour over peaches a batter made of butter, sugar, eggs, flour and salt. Bake at 350° for 1 hour 15 minutes, or until brown.

Yield: 8 servings

# FRENCH SILK PIE

1 9-inch pastry shell,
    baked and cooled
1½ cups unsalted butter,
    room temperature
1 cup plus 2 tablespoons
    superfine sugar (see
    note below)
1½ squares unsweetened
    chocolate, melted and
    cooled

1½ teaspoons vanilla
3 eggs
½ pint whipping cream,
    whipped
¼ cup slivered almonds

Beat butter until light and fluffy, adding sugar gradually. Add chocolate and vanilla. Add 2 eggs and beat for 3 minutes. Add remaining egg and beat for 3 more minutes. Pour into pastry shell. Top with whipped cream and almonds, if desired. Refrigerate several hours before serving.

Note: If unable to find superfine sugar, process about 2 cups regular granulated sugar in food processor for 3 minutes, stopping 2 or 3 times to scrape sides of processor bowl. Measure for recipe after processing.

Yield: 8 servings

# PECAN CREAM CHEESE PIE

1 9-inch deep-dish pastry
    shell
3 ounces finely chopped
    pecans
1 8-ounce package cream
    cheese, softened
¼ cup sugar

1 egg
2 teaspoons vanilla
3 eggs
¾ cup light corn syrup
2 tablespoons sugar
1 teaspoon vanilla

Preheat oven to 375°. Bake pastry shell 10 minutes. Cool.

In a food processor, using the steel blade, chop pecans. Set aside. Process cream cheese, sugar, egg and vanilla with steel blade until smooth. In another mixing bowl, beat eggs, corn syrup, sugar and vanilla until well mixed.

Pour cream cheese mixture into pastry shell, spreading evenly. Sprinkle with pecans. Stir corn syrup mixture again and carefully pour through fork over pecans. This keeps pecans from shifting. Bake at 375° for 40-45 minutes, or until set. Serve chilled.

Yield: 8 servings

# BOB HOPE'S LEMON MERINGUE PIE

1 9-inch pastry shell,
    baked and cooled
1 cup plus 2 tablespoons
    sugar
3 tablespoons cornstarch
1 cup boiling water

4 egg yolks
2 tablespoons butter
4 tablespoons lemon juice
Grated rind of 1 lemon
⅛ teaspoon salt

Combine cornstarch and sugar in saucepan. Add water slowly, stirring constantly. Cook until very thick and smooth. Add slightly beaten egg yolks, butter, lemon rind, lemon juice and salt. Cook 2-3 minutes. Pour into prepared pastry shell.

*Meringue:*
3 egg whites                    2 tablespoons sugar

Preheat oven to 350°. Beat egg whites until stiff. Add 2 tablespoons sugar. Spread over top of pie, sealing edges. Bake for 15 minutes, or until meringue is light brown.

Yield: 8 servings

# FROZEN LEMON PIE

*Crust:*
18 graham crackers,
    crushed

¼ cup sugar
½ cup butter, melted

Preheat oven to 375°. Combine cracker crumbs, sugar and butter with a fork. Press into a 9-inch pie plate and bake for 8 minutes. Cool.

*Filling:*
1 14-ounce can sweetened
    condensed milk
2 egg yolks

Grated rind of one lemon
Juice of one lemon
2 egg whites, stiffly beaten

Combine milk, egg yolks, lemon juice and lemon rind. Fold into the beaten egg whites. Pour into cooled crust. Place wax paper over pie to prevent ice crystals from forming and freeze at least 4 hours. Remove from freezer 10 minutes before serving. Additional graham cracker crumbs may be sprinkled over the top for garnish.

Yield: 6-8 servings

# AMARETTO COCONUT BAVARIAN

*Crust:*

½ cup butter
2 cups graham cracker
crumbs

¼ cup sugar

Melt butter. Add crumbs and sugar. Mix well. Press mixture into bottom of 12x8x2-inch glass baking dish. Chill while preparing filling.

*Filling:*

1 cup flaked coconut
3 eggs
⅔ cup sugar
2 envelopes unflavored
gelatin

¼ cup water
¼ cup Amaretto liqueur
⅛ teaspoon salt
16 ounces whipping cream

Toast coconut until golden brown. Reserving 2 tablespoons of coconut for garnish, combine remaining coconut with eggs and sugar. Beat with electric mixer on medium speed until fluffy. Dissolve gelatin in water in saucepan over very low heat. Add Amaretto, salt and egg mixture.

Whip cream until soft peaks form and gently fold into above mixture. Pour into crust and chill at least two hours.

Garnish with reserved coconut. Cut into squares to serve.

Optional garnishes: chocolate curls, strawberries or cherries

Yield: 12 squares

# BAKED LEMON CUSTARD

3 eggs, separated
1 cup sugar
2 tablespoons flour
Grated rind of 1 lemon
Juice of 1 lemon

1 cup milk
1 tablespoon butter,
melted
Whipped cream for garnish

Beat the egg yolks until fluffy. Add sugar and flour; then cream mixture. Beat in lemon juice and rind, then the milk and butter. Beat egg whites until stiff and fold into egg and sugar mixture. Pour into custard cups or ramekins. Place in a pan with about 1 inch of water and bake at 300° for approximately 45 minutes. Garnish with whipped cream just before serving.

Yield: 6-8 servings

# CHOCOLATE RUM DESSERT

1 6-ounce package semi-
    sweet chocolate chips
3 eggs, separated
2 tablespoons light rum

¼ teaspoon almond extract
¼ teaspoon ground nutmeg
Decoration: whipped
    cream, chocolate curls

Melt chocolate over simmering water in double boiler. Beat egg yolks until thick and lemon-colored. Gradually stir about ¼ of chocolate into yolks; add this mixture to remaining chocolate, stirring constantly. Remove from heat and stir in rum, almond extract and nutmeg.

Beat egg whites until stiff peaks form. Gently fold into chocolate mixture. Spoon into cordial glasses or demitasse cups. Chill several hours before serving. Decorate tops with whipped cream and chocolate curls.

Yield: 4 small servings

# FRESH COCONUT PUDDING

1 pint half and half
2 envelopes unflavored
    gelatin
½ cup cold water
1 cup sugar
1 teaspoon almond extract

2 cups fresh coconut or 2
    6-ounce packages
    frozen coconut,
    thawed (reserve a
    small amount for
    garnish)
1 pint whipping cream,
    whipped

Bring half and half to a boil in a small saucepan; cool slightly. Dissolve gelatin in water and add to half and half. Stir in sugar. When sugar and gelatin are thoroughly dissolved, add almond extract and coconut. Fold mixture into whipped cream.

Pour into a 3-quart glass bowl and refrigerate at least 4 hours. Sprinkle with reserved coconut and serve.

Yield: about 10 servings

# BANANAS FOSTER

2 tablespoons butter
3 tablespoons brown sugar
½ teaspoon cinnamon
2 bananas, sliced
  lengthwise and cut in
  half

¼ cup banana liqueur
¼ cup rum (traditional) or
  brandy
4 scoops vanilla ice cream

Melt butter over low heat in large skillet or flat chafing dish. Add sugar and cinnamon and mix well. Add bananas and sauté until they begin to turn soft. Pour in the banana liqueur and half the rum or brandy and continue to cook over low heat.

Heat the remainder of the rum or brandy in a small saucepan until it begins to boil; then quickly pour it into the pan with the bananas and ignite. When the flame dies out, serve two slices of banana and ¼ of the sauce over each portion of ice cream.

Yield: 4 servings

*This is spectacular when made in front of guests. Turn the pan and spoon the flames in a darkened room for full effect!*

# BROWNIE ALASKA

1 15.5-ounce package
  Duncan Hines Fudge
  Brownie Mix
1 pint pink peppermint ice
  cream

4 egg whites
½ cup sugar

Bake brownies as directed on package. Cut into 3-inch squares and place on baking sheet.

Freeze 9 scoops ice cream on a baking sheet for 1 to 2 hours.

Before assembling preheat oven to 500°. Beat egg whites until foamy. Beat in sugar, one tablespoon at a time, until stiff and glossy. Place one scoop of ice cream on each brownie and cover with meringue, sealing it to the edge of brownie. Bake 3-4 minutes until lightly browned.

Yield: 9 servings

# BLUEBERRY BUCKLE

½ cup unsalted butter,
    softened
¾ cup sugar
1 egg
2 cups flour
2½ teaspoons baking
    powder

½ teaspoon freshly grated
    nutmeg
¼ teaspoon salt
½ cup milk
2 cups fresh blueberries

In a large bowl cream together butter and sugar until mixture is light and fluffy. Beat in egg. Sift together flour, baking powder, nutmeg and salt; add to the butter mixture alternating with the milk. Stir until the mixture is well blended.

Pour batter into a buttered and floured 9x9x2-inch baking pan. Top with the blueberries, covering the batter in an even layer and pressing berries slightly into the batter.

*Topping:*
½ cup flour
½ cup light brown sugar,
    firmly packed

½ teaspoon cinnamon
½ cup unsalted butter, cut
    into small pieces

Combine topping ingredients until crumbly and sprinkle evenly over berries. Bake in center of 350° oven for 45-50 minutes, or until top is golden and bubbly. Serve warm with vanilla ice cream.

Yield: 6-8 servings

*This makes a cobbler-type dessert that reheats well in the microwave for breakfast!*

# FROZEN MACAROON CRÈME

24 day-old macaroons
1 cup sherry or cognac
1 cup sugar

32 ounces whipping cream,
    whipped
1 cup slivered almonds

Crush macaroons to fine crumbs. Dissolve sugar in the cognac and fold into whipped cream. Add macaroon crumbs and almonds. Spoon into parfait glasses and freeze at least 4 hours.

Yield: 8 servings

# NEW ORLEANS BREAD PUDDING WITH RUM SAUCE

*Pudding:*

1 loaf French bread, torn into chunks
1 quart milk
2 cups sugar
2 tablespoons vanilla
3 eggs
1 cup peeled, diced apples
½ cup raisins
3 tablespoons butter, melted

Soak bread in milk for about 30 minutes. Mix sugar, vanilla, eggs and apples. Combine with bread chunks. Spread melted butter on bottom of 13x9x2-inch pan. Add bread mixture. Bake at 350° about 30-35 minutes, until bubbly and hot.

*Sauce:*

½ cup butter
1 cup sugar
1 teaspoon vanilla
1 egg
Rum to taste, about 3 tablespoons

Cream butter and sugar. Add vanilla. Slowly stir in 1 egg; then add the rum. Heat and stir over low heat about 5 minutes. Serve warm over individual pudding servings.

Yield: 8-10 servings

*Pudding is great with New Orleans chicory coffee!*


# CHOCOLATE MOUSSE

1 6-ounce package semi-sweet chocolate chips
2 eggs
¾ cup milk, scalded
2 ounces rum
3 tablespoons hot, strong coffee

*Topping:*

8 ounces whipping cream, whipped
3 tablespoons sugar
Chocolate shavings

Place first 5 ingredients in blender. Blend 2 minutes. Pour into dessert cups and chill. Top with whipped cream sweetened with sugar and chocolate shavings.

Yield: 4 servings

# CHOCOLATE GLAZED ÉCLAIRS

*Éclair:*

| | |
|---|---|
| **1 cup water** | **1 cup flour** |
| **½ cup butter** | **4 eggs** |
| **¼ teaspoon salt** | |

Preheat oven to 375°. Heat water, salt and butter to rolling boil; vigorously stir in flour and continue cooking and beating until mixture leaves the sides of the pan. Cool mixture slightly, about 5 minutes. Add eggs all at once; beat vigorously until mixture is very smooth and thick.

Drop by ¼ cupfuls onto very lightly greased cookie sheets 2 inches apart and in rows 6 inches apart. With a small spatula, shape each mound into a 5x¾-inch rectangle, rounding edges. Bake 40 minutes or until lightly browned. Cut side of each shell and bake 10 minutes longer. Cool shells on wire rack.

*Filling:*

| | |
|---|---|
| **2 3-ounce packages vanilla pudding** | **½ cup whipping cream, whipped** |
| **¼ teaspoon almond extract** | |

Prepare pudding mix as label directs, adding almond extract. Cover surface with wax paper and refrigerate until chilled. Gently fold in whipped cream.

Slice ⅓ from top of each shell and fill bottom of shells with filling; replace tops.

*Glaze:*

| | |
|---|---|
| **2 ounces semi-sweet chocolate** | **1 cup confectioners' sugar** |
| **2 tablespoons butter** | **3 tablespoons milk** |

In a small saucepan over low heat, melt chocolate and butter, stirring constantly. Stir in confectioners' sugar and milk; blend until smooth.

Spread tops of éclairs with glaze and refrigerate until serving time.

Yield: 10 éclairs

# SOPAIPILLAS

| | |
|---|---|
| ¼ cup lukewarm water (110°F) | 2 tablespoons butter |
| 1 package active dry yeast | 1 egg, beaten |
| ¾ cup milk | 3 cups flour |
| 6 tablespoons sugar | Oil for deep frying |
| 1 teaspoon salt | Honey for dipping |

Put lukewarm water in mixing bowl; sprinkle yeast over and let stand until yeast is softened. In saucepan, combine milk, sugar and salt. Bring to boil. Remove from heat and stir in butter. Let cool to lukewarm; then stir into yeast mixture. Stir in egg. Gradually beat in flour. When dough becomes too thick to beat, work in the last ½ cup flour with your hands to make a dough which is soft, but sticky. It should not be stiff. Cover dough with towel and let rise for 1 hour 30 minutes. Punch down. Turn out on lightly floured pastry board and knead briefly until dough is smooth. Cover and let rest for 10 minutes.

Roll out dough into a ¼ inch thick, 12-inch square. Cut into 24 strips, each 2x3 inches. Heat 2 inches of cooking oil to 350°. Add the strips of dough, a few at a time. Deep fry for 3 minutes, or until golden brown, turning once when puffed and browned on the underside. Fill with honey for a true Mexican dessert. These can also be served with whipped cream and strawberries or brandied peaches.

Yield: 24 servings

# BLUEBERRY/PEACH CRISP

| | |
|---|---|
| 2 cups fresh blueberries, washed and stems removed | About ¾ cup sugar, depending on tartness of fruit |
| 2 cups fresh peaches, peeled and sliced (about 4 medium peaches) | 1 tablespoon lemon juice |
| | ¼ cup flour |
| | ½ teaspoon cinnamon |
| | ½ teaspoon cloves |

*Topping:*

| | |
|---|---|
| ⅓ cup oats | ½ cup light brown sugar |
| ¾ cup flour | ⅓ cup butter, melted |

Combine fruit, sugar, lemon juice, flour and spices. Place in buttered 8x8x2-inch pan. Mix topping ingredients and place over fruit. Bake for 35 minutes at 350° for glass pan or at 375° for metal pan.

Yield: 8 servings

# POACHED PEARS
# IN GRAND MARNIER SAUCE

| | |
|---|---|
| 1½ cups sugar | 8 fresh, whole pears, |
| 3 cups water | peeled with bottoms |
| Juice of 1 lemon | sliced flat (leave stems |
| | intact) |

In a saucepan combine sugar, water and lemon juice. Bring to a boil. Add pears and simmer slowly for 30 minutes. (Pears can be gently turned.) When tender, remove and stand upright next to each other in a dish.

*Sauce:*

| | |
|---|---|
| 1 egg yolk | 2 tablespoons Grand |
| ⅓ cup sugar | Marnier |
| 1 8-ounce carton sour | |
| cream | |

Beat egg yolk with sugar until thick, creamy and pale yellow. Stir in sour cream and Grand Marnier. Chill and spoon over pears.

Yield: 8 servings

# WALNUT TORTE

| | |
|---|---|
| 3 eggs, separated | 1 teaspoon vanilla |
| ½ teaspoon salt | ¾ cup walnuts, grated |
| ½ teaspoon cream of tartar | ½ pint whipping cream |
| ½ cup sugar | 2 tablespoons sugar |

Beat egg whites with salt and cream of tartar until stiff. Gradually beat in ½ cup sugar, about 1 tablespoon at a time. Beat egg yolks until thick. Fold yolks, vanilla and walnuts into egg whites.

Line a 9x9-inch pan with wax paper or spray with vegetable spray. Turn mixture into prepared pan and smooth top. Bake in 350° oven for 25 minutes. Cool in pan.

Turn out onto cake platter. Whip cream with 2 tablespoons sugar. Spread cream in hollow of cake. Chill before serving.

Yield: 8 servings

# SWEDISH PINEAPPLE CREAM

½ cup butter
1½ cups confectioners'
sugar
2 eggs, separated
½ teaspoon lemon extract

¾ cup crushed pineapple,
well drained
1 cup sour cream
8-10 ladyfingers
8 ounces whipping cream,
whipped

Cream butter and add confectioners' sugar. Add 2 egg yolks, one at a time, and beat well. Add lemon extract, pineapple and sour cream. Beat egg whites until stiff. Fold into above mixture.

Split ladyfingers. Put half of them in 9x6x2-inch pan. Spread the pineapple mixture on them and top with remaining ladyfingers. Chill. Top with whipped cream.

Yield: 8 servings

# PUMPKIN ICE CREAM SQUARES

*Crust:*

1½ cups graham cracker
crumbs

¼ cup sugar
¼ cup butter, melted

Mix crumbs with sugar and butter. Press into bottom of a 9x9-inch baking pan.

*Filling:*

2 cups canned pumpkin
½ cup dark brown sugar
½ teaspoon salt
1 teaspoon cinnamon
¼ teaspoon ginger

⅛ teaspoon cloves
1 quart vanilla ice cream,
softened
Whipped cream
Pecan halves

Combine pumpkin with brown sugar, salt and spices. Fold in ice cream. Pour over crust. Cover. Freeze until firm.

Remove from freezer 10 minutes before serving. Cut into 3-inch squares; top each square with a spoonful of whipped cream and a pecan half.

Yield: 12 servings

# VIENNESE STRAWBERRY TORTE

1½ quarts strawberries
2 packages ladyfingers (20
   ladyfingers, split)
1 cup unsalted butter
1 cup sugar

4 egg yolks
1 8-ounce carton whipping
   cream
2 tablespoons sugar
½ teaspoon vanilla

Hull, rinse and drain strawberries; slice all but 1 cup. Line sides and bottom of 9-inch springform pan with ladyfinger halves. Cream butter with sugar until smooth. Add egg yolks and beat until light and lemon-colored.

Spread some of mixture over ladyfingers on bottom of pan. Cover with a layer of strawberries, then a layer of ladyfingers and more mixture. Alternate layers until all ingredients are used, finishing with a layer of strawberries. Chill several hours.

To serve, remove sides of springform pan and place cake on serving platter. Whip cream and add sugar and vanilla. Spread over top of cake and garnish with reserved strawberries.

Yield: about 12 servings

# STRAWBERRY SQUARES

1 cup flour
¼ cup brown sugar
½ cup chopped nuts
½ cup butter, melted
2 egg whites, beaten
⅔ cup sugar

1 10-ounce package frozen
   strawberries, partially
   thawed
2 tablespoons lemon juice
1 cup whipping cream,
   whipped

Combine first four ingredients in shallow baking dish. Bake for 20 minutes at 350°, stirring occasionally.

Pat ⅔ of nut mixture into an 11x7x2-inch pan. Reserve rest for topping.

Combine beaten egg whites, sugar, strawberries and lemon juice. Fold whipped cream into strawberry mixture.

Spoon over nut mixture in pan and top with reserved mixture.

Freeze until firm.

Yield: 15 squares

# MEXICAN APRICOT TRIFLE JOSEPHS

½ cup sugar
¼ cup water
8 egg yolks, beaten
½ teaspoon cinnamon
½ cup orange juice
½ teaspoon vanilla
4 egg whites
¼ teaspoon cream of tartar
1 cup whipping cream

1 tablespoon powdered
  sugar
1 teaspoon vanilla
10-16 very thin slices
  sponge or pound cake
  (or equivalent in
  ladyfingers)
1 cup apricot jam
Grated chocolate

Boil sugar and water together in heavy 2-quart saucepan until thread stage or 230°. Beat gradually into egg yolks; then return to pan or double boiler. Cook on low, stirring, for 10-15 minutes or until mixture thickens like custard. Cool. Stir in cinnamon, orange juice and vanilla.

Beat egg whites and cream of tartar together until stiff. Beat cream, powdered sugar and vanilla together until stiff. Fold in beaten egg whites.

Spread half the cake slices with jam. Top with remaining cake slices and cut into 2-inch cubes. Layer half the cubes in an attractive glass bowl. Top with half of custard, then half of cream mixture. Repeat layers. Sprinkle with grated chocolate. Chill 1 hour or more before serving.

Yield: 8-10 servings

# BUTTER PECAN ICE CREAM

1½ cups chopped pecans
3 tablespoons butter
2 eggs
2 cups sugar

2 cups whipping cream
2½ cups milk
½ teaspoon salt
2 teaspoons vanilla

Sauté pecans in butter until light brown. Cool. Beat eggs well, gradually adding sugar. Beat until stiff. Add cream, milk, salt and vanilla. Stir in pecans and churn in ice cream freezer.

Yield: ½ gallon

# LEMON MOUSSE

8 eggs, separated
1 cup sugar
3 grated lemon rinds
½ cup lemon juice
2 tablespoons gelatin
½ cup cold water
2 dozen ladyfingers

½ pint whipping cream
2 teaspoons confectioners'
  sugar
¼ teaspoon vanilla
Grated lemon rind and
  fresh mint sprigs for
  garnish

In the top of a double boiler, beat egg yolks until thick and very pale yellow. Add sugar gradually while beating constantly. Stir in lemon rind and lemon juice. Place over gently boiling water, being sure water does not touch bottom of double boiler. Cook, stirring constantly, until sauce is hot and a thick custard. Soften gelatin in cold water and add to hot lemon mixture, stirring well until gelatin is dissolved. Pour mixture into a bowl and let cool thoroughly. Stir occasionally while cooling.

Line a 9-inch springform pan, sides and bottom, with split ladyfingers. Beat egg whites until stiff and fold into cooled lemon mixture. Pour into lined pan and refrigerate.

Whip cream, adding confectioners' sugar and vanilla. Top lemon mixture with whipped cream. Decorate with grated lemon rind and fresh mint leaves.

Yield: 10 servings

# BANANA ICE CREAM

1 14-ounce can sweetened
  condensed milk
1 cup sugar
5 eggs
1 13-ounce can evaporated
  milk

7 bananas, mashed
3 cups whole milk
1 teaspoon vanilla
1½ cups toasted, chopped
  pecans

Combine all ingredients in a blender. Mix thoroughly. Freeze in 1-gallon ice cream freezer following manufacturer's directions.

Yield: 1 gallon

# TORTONI

2 eggs
½ cup sugar
⅛ teaspoon salt
1 cup whipping cream

1 teaspoon vanilla
1 teaspoon almond extract
⅔ cup chopped toasted
    almonds

In a medium bowl, beat eggs, sugar and salt at high speed. Beat until light and fluffy.

In another bowl, beat whipping cream until stiff. Fold in vanilla and almond extracts. Gently fold into egg mixture. Stir in toasted almonds.

Place 8 paper muffin cups in a muffin pan. Spoon tortoni mixture into each cup and freeze.

*Cardinal Sauce:*
1 10-ounce package frozen
    strawberries, thawed
1 10-ounce package frozen
    raspberries, thawed

2 teaspoons cornstarch
1 teaspoon lemon juice
1 teaspoon grated lemon
    rind

Drain berries. In a small saucepan, combine berry liquid, cornstarch, lemon juice and lemon rind. Simmer liquid for 5 minutes. Add fruit and chill 2 hours before serving.

To serve, remove tortoni from freezer and place on dessert plates. Top with a spoonful of cardinal sauce. Serve immediately.

Yield: 8 servings


# PEACH ICE CREAM

7-10 fresh, ripe peaches,
    mashed
1 6-ounce can apricot
    nectar

2 13-ounce cans
    evaporated milk
3 cups sugar
About 4 cups milk

Combine first four ingredients. Pour into ice cream freezer. Add milk to ⅔ full. Freeze according to directions.

Yield: 5 quarts

# BUTTERMILK ICE CREAM

2 5.33-ounce cans
  evaporated milk
1 cup sugar
3 teaspoons unflavored
  gelatin

¼ cup water
2 teaspoons vanilla
1 cup whipping cream
Buttermilk to make 5 cups

In saucepan, dissolve sugar in evaporated milk using low heat. Soften gelatin in ¼ cup water and add to sugar mixture. Add vanilla, cream and enough buttermilk to make 5 cups. Freeze in ice cream freezer according to manufacturer's instructions.

Yield: ½ gallon

# CHAMPAGNE SORBET

1 cup sugar
¼ cup water
1 cup fresh orange juice

½ cup fresh lemon juice
16 ounces champagne

Combine sugar and water in saucepan and bring to a boil. Reduce heat and simmer 5 minutes. Cool. Blend in remaining ingredients and freeze.

Yield: 4 cups

*This is from Jamie's French Restaurant located in historic Seville Square.*

# SUNSHINE SHERBET

2 quarts whole milk
3½-4 cups sugar
Juice of 3 lemons
Juice of 2 oranges
1 teaspoon vanilla

⅛ teaspoon salt
Rind of one lemon, finely
  grated
Rind of one orange, finely
  grated

Blend all ingredients together and freeze in ice cream freezer.

Yield; ½ gallon

# ICE CREAM CRUNCH

½ gallon vanilla ice cream
½ cup dark brown sugar
½ cup quick oats
2 cups flour

1 cup chopped pecans
1 cup butter, melted
1 jar hot fudge topping

In a large bowl, soften the ice cream and set aside.

Mix brown sugar, oats, flour, pecans and melted butter. Press ¾ of this mixture into the bottom of a 3-quart rectangular casserole. Bake in a 400° oven for 10-15 minutes. Let cool. Toast remaining ¼ of mixture in small dish and reserve for topping.

Add softened ice cream to baked crust. Sprinkle with reserved topping and top with hot fudge topping. Cover and freeze.

Yield: 8 servings


# VANILLA CUSTARD ICE CREAM

5 eggs
2 cups sugar
½ gallon whole milk
2 14-ounce cans Eagle
    Brand sweetened
    condensed milk

2 13-ounce cans
    evaporated milk
4 teaspoons vanilla
8 ounces whipping cream

In a 5-quart stock pot, beat eggs; add sugar, milk, Eagle Brand, evaporated milk and vanilla. Cook over medium heat until the mixture coats the spoon. Cool; then add whipping cream. Chill overnight or at least several hours (freezing takes less time if mixture is really cold).

Freeze in 5-quart ice cream freezer.

Yield: 5 quarts

## SNOWY FRUIT TOPPING

1 11-ounce can mandarin
  oranges
½ cup sour cream
½ cup chopped dates

½ cup almonds
½ cup miniature
  marshmallows
¼ cup flaked coconut

Combine first five ingredients and spoon over cooled cake. Sprinkle with coconut. Serve cool or broil until coconut is lightly browned.

Yield: 3 cups
*This is especially good on sliced PUMPKIN CAKE.*

## STRAWBERRY TOPPING

2 cups fresh strawberries,
  sliced
2 tablespoons sugar

1½ teaspoons cornstarch
¼ teaspoon almond extract

In a bowl combine strawberries and sugar. Cover and refrigerate several hours or overnight.

Strain strawberries, reserving juice. Add enough water to juice to make ½ cup. Combine juice and cornstarch in saucepan, stirring until cornstarch is dissolved. Cook over medium heat, stirring constantly, until smooth and thick. Stir in strawberries and almond extract. Chill.

Yield: 1¼ cups
*Strawberry topping is excellent over waffles.*

## LEMON FILLING

½ cup butter
1 cup sugar
2 eggs, well beaten

Juice and grated rind of 2
  lemons

Lightly cream butter and sugar in saucepan. Add eggs and mix well. Add lemon juice and rind. Cook over medium heat to a full boil, stirring constantly. Boil 2 minutes. Remove from heat. Cool. Mixture will thicken as it cools. This can be prepared in advance and refrigerated until needed.

Yield: enough filling for a 3-layer cake

# HOT CARAMEL SAUCE

1¼ cups dark brown sugar,
   firmly packed
⅔ cup light corn syrup

⅔ cup whipping cream
¼ cup unsalted butter
⅛ teaspoon salt

Combine all ingredients in a small saucepan. Cook over medium-high heat, stirring occasionally, until mixture reaches 230°. Let cool slightly before serving.

Yield: 2 cups

# HOT FUDGE SAUCE

6 tablespoons unsalted
   butter
½ cup water
3 ounces unsweetened
   chocolate

1 cup sugar
2 tablespoons light corn
   syrup

Melt butter with water in small saucepan over medium heat; then bring to a boil, stirring constantly. Add chocolate and let melt, stirring occasionally. Add sugar and corn syrup and boil gently for 5 minutes. Serve hot.

Yield: 2 cups

*This sauce freezes well, reheats and freezes again.*

# CHOCOLATE SHERRY SAUCE

1 16-ounce package
   confectioners' sugar
2 tablespoons butter

8 ounces unsweetened
   chocolate, melted
8 ounces half and half
½ cup cooking sherry

In a mixing bowl, blend sugar and butter. Melt chocolate in double boiler. Add half and half to chocolate. Then add sugar and butter mixture.

Cook 15 minutes in double boiler. Cool. Blend in sherry. Serve over vanilla ice cream or vanilla custard.

Yield: 3 cups

# FOOD
# EXCHANGE
# LIST

# FOOD EXCHANGE LIST

The following recipes have been calculated using the American Diabetes Association's exchange list. The recipes are for use by diabetics or other individuals who follow an exchange list diet. According to the guidelines approved by the association, the recipes are calculated using lean meats and skim milk for each recipe. In calculating the values for exchanges, numbers are rounded to the nearest whole or half of an exchange. For this reason the total of the exchanges may not represent the actual caloric value, which in some recipes may be higher.

Page

**APPETIZERS**
**Antipasto Spread** . . . . . . . . . . . . . . . . . . . . . . . . . . . . . . . . . . . **45**
Yield: 32 servings, 1 serving equals 2 tablespoons
1½ FAT
**Caponata** . . . . . . . . . . . . . . . . . . . . . . . . . . . . . . . . . . . . . **42**
Yield: 32 servings; 1 serving equals ¼ cup
1 VEGETABLE    1 FAT
**Cheese Squares** . . . . . . . . . . . . . . . . . . . . . . . . . . . . . . . . **47**
Yield: 27 servings; 1 serving equals 1 puff
½ BREAD         1 FAT
**Clam Dip** . . . . . . . . . . . . . . . . . . . . . . . . . . . . . . . . . . . . **32**
Yield: 8 servings; 1 serving equals
1 MEAT          1½ FAT
**Crab Stuffed Mushrooms** . . . . . . . . . . . . . . . . . . . . . . . . . **51**
Yield: 24 mushrooms; 2 mushrooms equal
½ VEGETABLE  1 MEAT          1½ FAT
**Creamy Crab Dip** . . . . . . . . . . . . . . . . . . . . . . . . . . . . . . **36**
Yield: 25 servings; 1 serving equals
1 MEAT          ½ BREAD         2 FAT
**Favorite Potato Skins** . . . . . . . . . . . . . . . . . . . . . . . . . . . **43**
Yield: 4 servings; 1 serving equals
½ BREAD         1 MEAT          2 FAT
**Fruit and Vegetable Dip** . . . . . . . . . . . . . . . . . . . . . . . . . **55**
Yield: 16 servings; 1 serving equals
2 FAT
**Glazed Sausage Bites** . . . . . . . . . . . . . . . . . . . . . . . . . . . **38**
Yield: 50; 1 serving equals 5 sausage bites
½ BREAD         1 FRUIT         1½ FAT
**Hot Crab Dip** . . . . . . . . . . . . . . . . . . . . . . . . . . . . . . . . . **33**
Yield: 16 servings; 1 serving equals ¼ cup
1½ MEAT         2 FAT
**Hot Mushroom Spread** . . . . . . . . . . . . . . . . . . . . . . . . . . **46**
Yield: 6 servings; 1 serving equals 1 slice or 4 squares
Note: using 6 slices bread
1½ BREAD        1 VEGETABLE  2½ FAT
**Italian Stuffed Mushrooms** . . . . . . . . . . . . . . . . . . . . . . . **52**
Yield: 6 servings; 1 serving equals
½ VEGETABLE  ½ MEAT         1 FAT
**Marinated Mushrooms** . . . . . . . . . . . . . . . . . . . . . . . . . . **53**
Yield: 6 servings; 1 serving equals
1 VEGETABLE   2 FAT
**Marinated Shrimp** . . . . . . . . . . . . . . . . . . . . . . . . . . . . . **36**
Yield: 8 servings; 1 serving equals
2½ MEAT        1 VEGETABLE  2 FAT

Page

**Marinated Smoked Sausage** . . . . . . . . . . . . . . . . . . . . . . . . . . . . .39
Yield: 12 servings; 1 serving equals
1 VEGETABLE   3 BREAD        1 MEAT        1½ FAT
**Marinated Vegetable Appetizer** . . . . . . . . . . . . . . . . . . . . . . . . .49
Yield: 12 servings; 1 serving equals
1 VEGETABLE   2½ FAT
**New Potatoes with Caviar** . . . . . . . . . . . . . . . . . . . . . . . . . . . . .43
Yield: 30 appetizers; 1 serving equals 3 potatoes
1½ BREAD        ½ MEAT        ½ FAT
**Old English Cheese Squares** . . . . . . . . . . . . . . . . . . . . . . . . . . .48
Yield: 60 squares; 1 serving equals 1 square
½ BREAD        ½ MEAT        2 FAT
**Oysters Lydia** . . . . . . . . . . . . . . . . . . . . . . . . . . . . . . . . . . . . . .31
Yield: 8 servings; using 1 slice French bread
per serving, 1 serving equals
1½ BREAD        1½ MEAT        3 FAT
**Polynesian Ginger Dip** . . . . . . . . . . . . . . . . . . . . . . . . . . . . . . . .63
Yield: 2 cups; 1 serving equals 1 tablespoon
1½ FAT
**Spinach Balls** . . . . . . . . . . . . . . . . . . . . . . . . . . . . . . . . . . . . . . .44
Yield: 10 dozen; 1 serving equals 2 spinach balls
1 VEGETABLE   1 FAT
**Spinach Squares** . . . . . . . . . . . . . . . . . . . . . . . . . . . . . . . . . . . .44
Yield: 12 servings; 1 serving equals
½ VEGETABLE   ½ BREAD        1½ MEAT        2 FAT

**BEVERAGES**
**Hot Spiced Cider** . . . . . . . . . . . . . . . . . . . . . . . . . . . . . . . . . . . .70
Yield: 16 servings; 1 serving equals ½ cup
2 FRUIT
**Hot Spiced Punch** . . . . . . . . . . . . . . . . . . . . . . . . . . . . . . . . . . .70
Yield: 16 servings; 1 serving equals ½ cup
2 FRUIT

**SOUPS**
**Artichoke and Oyster Soup** . . . . . . . . . . . . . . . . . . . . . . . . . . . .75
Yield: 6 servings; 1 serving equals
1 MEAT        1 VEGETABLE   ½ FAT
**Broccoli Soup** . . . . . . . . . . . . . . . . . . . . . . . . . . . . . . . . . . . . . .75
Yield: 12 servings; 1 serving equals
1½ VEG        1 FAT
Note: Fat free broth should be used. Cream is not included.
**Cauliflower Soup** . . . . . . . . . . . . . . . . . . . . . . . . . . . . . . . . . . . .76
Yield: 5 servings; 1 serving equals
1 VEGETABLE   2½ FAT
**Combo Gumbo Josephs** . . . . . . . . . . . . . . . . . . . . . . . . . . . . . . .82
Yield: 19 servings; 1 serving equals 6 ounces with ½ cup rice
1 BREAD        1 VEGETABLE   4 MEAT        2½ FAT
Note: Trim fat from ham hock.
**Country Chowder** . . . . . . . . . . . . . . . . . . . . . . . . . . . . . . . . . . . .85
Yield: 6 servings; 1 serving equals
½ MILK        3 BREAD        1½ FAT
**Cream of Celery Soup** . . . . . . . . . . . . . . . . . . . . . . . . . . . . . . . .77
Yield: 10 servings; 1 serving equals
1½ VEG        2 FAT

Page

**Creamy Cucumber Soup** . . . . . . . . . . . . . . . . . . . . . . . . . . . . . . . .**76**
Yield: 8 servings; 1 serving equals
½ VEGETABLE   ½ BREAD     1½ FAT

**Creamy Potato Soup** . . . . . . . . . . . . . . . . . . . . . . . . . . . . . . . . . . .**88**
Yield: 9 servings; 1 serving equals
1 BREAD     ½ VEGETABLE   2½ FAT

**Gazpacho Madrileño** . . . . . . . . . . . . . . . . . . . . . . . . . . . . . . . . . .**81**
Yield: 10 servings; 1 serving equals
1 VEGETABLE   1 BREAD     1¼ FAT

**Ham and Cheese Chowder** . . . . . . . . . . . . . . . . . . . . . . . . . . . . .**84**
Yield: 8 servings; 1 serving equals
1½ MEAT     1 BREAD     ½ MILK       2 FAT

**Jamie's Cream of Crab Soup** . . . . . . . . . . . . . . . . . . . . . . . . . . . .**80**
Yield: 6 servings; 1 serving equals
½ MEAT     2½ FAT

**Low Cal Borsch** . . . . . . . . . . . . . . . . . . . . . . . . . . . . . . . . . . . . . . .**78**
Yield: 4 servings; 1 serving equals
2 VEGETABLE   1 FAT

**Microwave Seafood Gumbo** . . . . . . . . . . . . . . . . . . . . . . . . . . . . .**84**
Yield: 6 servings; 1 serving equals
2½ VEG     ½ BREAD     1½ MEAT     2 FAT

**Mushroom Soup** . . . . . . . . . . . . . . . . . . . . . . . . . . . . . . . . . . . . . . .**80**
Yield: 6 servings; 1 serving equals
1 VEGETABLE   3 FAT

**Old-fashioned Vegetable Soup** . . . . . . . . . . . . . . . . . . . . . . . . . .**87**
Yield: 10 servings; 1 serving equals
1½ MEAT     1 BREAD     2 VEGETABLE   2 FAT

**Oriental Cucumber Soup** . . . . . . . . . . . . . . . . . . . . . . . . . . . . . . .**78**
Yield: 8 servings; 1 serving equals
1 MEAT     1 FAT

**Seafood Gumbo** . . . . . . . . . . . . . . . . . . . . . . . . . . . . . . . . . . . . . . .**85**
Yield: 8 servings; 1 serving equals
3 VEGETABLES   ½ BREAD     5½ MEAT     2 FAT

**Swedish Summer Soup Josephs** . . . . . . . . . . . . . . . . . . . . . . . . .**79**
Yield: 8 servings; 1 serving equals
2 VEGETABLE   ½ FAT

**Tomato Bisque** . . . . . . . . . . . . . . . . . . . . . . . . . . . . . . . . . . . . . . .**86**
Yield: 6 servings; 1 serving equals
1½ VEG     3 FAT

**Vichyssoise** . . . . . . . . . . . . . . . . . . . . . . . . . . . . . . . . . . . . . . . . . .**86**
Yield: 10 servings; 1 serving equals
½ VEGETABLE   1 BREAD     1½ FAT

**Zucchini Soup** . . . . . . . . . . . . . . . . . . . . . . . . . . . . . . . . . . . . . . . .**89**
Yield: 8 servings; 1 serving equals
2 MEAT     1 VEGETABLE   ½ MILK       2 FAT

**SALADS**

**Basic Spinach Salad** . . . . . . . . . . . . . . . . . . . . . . . . . . . . . . . . . .**108**
Yield: 8 servings; 1 serving equals
1 VEGETABLE   1 FAT     ½ MEAT

**Cabbage-Pepper Slaw** . . . . . . . . . . . . . . . . . . . . . . . . . . . . . . . .**104**
Yield: 7 servings; 1 serving equals
1 VEGETABLE   3 FAT

**Caesar Salad** . . . . . . . . . . . . . . . . . . . . . . . . . . . . . . . . . . . . . . .**101**
Yield: 6 servings; 1 serving equals
½ BREAD     ½ MEAT     3 FAT

Page

**Chinese Chicken Salad** . . . . . . . . . . . . . . . . . . . . . . . . . . . . . . . . . . . . . . . . . . **92**
Yield: 10 servings; 1 serving equals
2 MEAT          1 BREAD          2½ FAT
**Creole Salad** . . . . . . . . . . . . . . . . . . . . . . . . . . . . . . . . . . . . . . . . . . . . . . . . . . **111**
Yield: 8 servings; 1 serving equals
2 VEGETABLE  1 FAT
**Dilled Cucumbers** . . . . . . . . . . . . . . . . . . . . . . . . . . . . . . . . . . . . . . . . . . . . . **121**
Yield: 4 servings; 1 serving equals
1 VEGETABLE  1½ FAT
**Feta Spinach Salad** . . . . . . . . . . . . . . . . . . . . . . . . . . . . . . . . . . . . . . . . . . . . **110**
Yield: 2 servings; 1 serving equals
2 VEGETABLE  ½ BREAD          1½ FAT
**Marinated Chicken-Artichoke Salad** . . . . . . . . . . . . . . . . . . . . . . . . . . . . . **91**
Yield: 8 servings; 1 serving equals
1½ VEG          4½ MEAT          4 FAT
**Marinated Green Beans** . . . . . . . . . . . . . . . . . . . . . . . . . . . . . . . . . . . . . . . . **113**
Yield: 4 servings; 1 serving equals
2 VEGETABLE  3 FAT
**Onion-Lima Salad** . . . . . . . . . . . . . . . . . . . . . . . . . . . . . . . . . . . . . . . . . . . . . **116**
Yield: 8 servings; 1 serving equals
1 BREAD          1 VEGETABLE  1 FAT
**Shrimp Remoulade I** . . . . . . . . . . . . . . . . . . . . . . . . . . . . . . . . . . . . . . . . . . . **106**
Yield: 8 servings; 1 serving equals
4 MEAT          3 FAT
**Summer Fruit Salad** . . . . . . . . . . . . . . . . . . . . . . . . . . . . . . . . . . . . . . . . . . . **100**
Yield: 10 servings; 1 serving equals
2½ FRUIT
**Venetian Risotto Salad** . . . . . . . . . . . . . . . . . . . . . . . . . . . . . . . . . . . . . . . . **105**
Yield: 10 servings; 1 serving equals
1 BREAD          ½ VEGETABLE  1½ FAT

**SALAD DRESSINGS**
**Greek Salad Dressing** . . . . . . . . . . . . . . . . . . . . . . . . . . . . . . . . . . . . . . . . . . **118**
Yield: 1 cup; 1 serving equals 1 tablespoon
1 FAT
**Hoolihan's Spinach Salad Dressing** . . . . . . . . . . . . . . . . . . . . . . . . . . . . . **109**
Yield: 3½ cups; 1 serving equals 1 tablespoon
1½ FAT
**Mayonnaise** . . . . . . . . . . . . . . . . . . . . . . . . . . . . . . . . . . . . . . . . . . . . . . . . . . **120**
Yield: 1½ cups; 1 serving equals 1 teaspoon
1 FAT
**Roquefort Dressing** . . . . . . . . . . . . . . . . . . . . . . . . . . . . . . . . . . . . . . . . . . . **119**
Yield: 3 cups; 1 serving equals 1 tablespoon
1½ FAT

**SEAFOOD**
**Baked Oysters** . . . . . . . . . . . . . . . . . . . . . . . . . . . . . . . . . . . . . . . . . . . . . . . . **143**
Yield: 8 servings; 1 serving equals
1 MEAT          1 FAT
**Crab and Artichoke Casserole** . . . . . . . . . . . . . . . . . . . . . . . . . . . . . . . . . . **128**
Yield: 6 servings; 1 serving equals
1½ VEG          ½ FRUIT          3½ MEAT          2½ FAT
**Crab Supreme** . . . . . . . . . . . . . . . . . . . . . . . . . . . . . . . . . . . . . . . . . . . . . . . **132**
Yield: 8 servings; 1 serving equals
1 VEGETABLE  ½ BREAD          4 MEAT          2 FAT
Note: Do not use buttered bread crumbs

                                                                          **Page**

**Crabmeat Pie** . . . . . . . . . . . . . . . . . . . . . . . . . . . . . . . . . . . . .**128**
Yield: 8 servings per pie; 1 serving equals 1 slice
½ BREAD         2 MEAT              2 FAT

**Coquilles St. Jacques** . . . . . . . . . . . . . . . . . . . . . . . . . . . . . .**154**
Yield: 4 servings; 1 serving equals
1 FRUIT          5½ MEAT            4 FAT

**Oysters Bienville** . . . . . . . . . . . . . . . . . . . . . . . . . . . . . . . . .**144**
Yield: 6 servings; 1 serving equals
½ VEGETABLE    2 MEAT             2½ FAT

**Shrimp-Artichoke Casserole** . . . . . . . . . . . . . . . . . . . . . . .**132**
Yield: 4 servings; 1 serving equals
2½ VEG          4½ MEAT            4½ FAT

**Shrimp Loaf** . . . . . . . . . . . . . . . . . . . . . . . . . . . . . . . . . . . . .**137**
Yield: 8 servings; 1 serving equals
½ MILK          1 BREAD            3 MEAT            1 FAT

**Shrimp and Lobster Newburg** . . . . . . . . . . . . . . . . . . . . . . .**157**
Yield: 4 servings; 1 serving equals
½ VEGETABLE   1 BREAD            4½ MEAT           4½ FAT

**Shrimp and Rice Casserole (Microwave)** . . . . . . . . . . . . . . . .**140**
Yield: 8 servings; 1 serving equals
1 VEGETABLE    ½ BREAD            2½ MEAT           3½ FAT

**Shrimp and Zucchini Sauté** . . . . . . . . . . . . . . . . . . . . . . . . .**143**
Yield: 4 servings; 1 serving equals
2 VEGETABLE    1 FRUIT            4½ MEAT           3½ FAT


**BEEF**
**Chili** . . . . . . . . . . . . . . . . . . . . . . . . . . . . . . . . . . . . . . . . . . .**171**
Yield: 6 servings; 1 serving equals
2½ VEG          1 BREAD            2½ MEAT           1 FAT

**Chinese Beef and Snow Peas** . . . . . . . . . . . . . . . . . . . . . . . .**170**
Yield: 4 servings; 1 serving equals
1 VEGETABLE    1 BREAD            4½ MEAT           1 FAT
Note: The ½ cup cooked rice is not included.

**Chuckwagon Stew** . . . . . . . . . . . . . . . . . . . . . . . . . . . . . . . .**171**
Yield: 8 servings; 1 serving equals
2 VEGETABLE    1½ BREAD           4 MEAT            1 FAT

**Cincinnati Chili** . . . . . . . . . . . . . . . . . . . . . . . . . . . . . . . . . .**172**
Yield: 8 servings; 1 serving equals
1½ VEG          2 BREAD            5 MEAT            1 FAT

**Grilled Steak Logs** . . . . . . . . . . . . . . . . . . . . . . . . . . . . . . . .**162**
Yield: 4 servings; 1 serving equals
½ FRUIT         6 MEAT             1½ FAT

**Italian Spaghetti with Meatballs and Sausage** . . . . . . . . . . . . . . . . . . . .**168**
Yield: 8 servings; 1 serving equals
2 VEGETABLE    ½ FRUIT            2½ BREAD          5 MEAT            5 FAT

**Lasagna Florentine** . . . . . . . . . . . . . . . . . . . . . . . . . . . . . . .**165**
Yield: 12 servings; 1 serving equals
3 VEGETABLE    1 BREAD            5 MEAT            2½ FAT

**Manicotti** . . . . . . . . . . . . . . . . . . . . . . . . . . . . . . . . . . . . . . .**167**
Yield: 6 servings; 1 serving equals
1 VEGETABLE    1 BREAD            4 MEAT            3 FAT

**Sicilian Meat Roll** . . . . . . . . . . . . . . . . . . . . . . . . . . . . . . . .**169**
Yield: 10 servings; 1 serving equals
½ BREAD         4 MEAT             1½ FAT

Page

**CHICKEN**

**Baked Chicken Salad** . . . . . . . . . . . . . . . . . . . . . . . . . . . . . . . . .**178**
Yield: 6 servings; 1 serving equals
½ VEGETABLE   ½ BREAD        3½ MEAT        2½ FAT
Note: This recipe should be made with 3 teaspoons
mayonnaise and without the pie shell.

**Cashew-Ginger Chicken** . . . . . . . . . . . . . . . . . . . . . . . . . . . . . .**175**
Yield: 6 servings; 1 serving equals
2 VEGETABLE   2½ MEAT        2½ FAT

**Chicken-Crab Rolls** . . . . . . . . . . . . . . . . . . . . . . . . . . . . . . . . . .**173**
Yield: 4 servings; 1 serving equals
½ MILK           ½ VEG          ½ FRUIT          1 BREAD
7 MEAT           4 FAT

**Chicken Marengo** . . . . . . . . . . . . . . . . . . . . . . . . . . . . . . . . . . .**182**
Yield: 8 servings; 1 serving equals
½ VEGETABLE   4 MEAT          1½ FAT

**Chicken with Sour Cream Sauce** . . . . . . . . . . . . . . . . . . . . . .**180**
Yield: 6 servings; 1 serving equals
1 VEGETABLE   4 MEAT          3 FAT

**Fiesta Casserole** . . . . . . . . . . . . . . . . . . . . . . . . . . . . . . . . . . . .**188**
Yield: 5 servings; 1 serving equals
½ VEGETABLE   1 BREAD        3 MEAT          2½ FAT

**Italian Chicken** . . . . . . . . . . . . . . . . . . . . . . . . . . . . . . . . . . . . .**181**
Yield: 6 servings; 1 serving equals
1 VEGETABLE   ½ BREAD        3 MEAT          3½ FAT

**SAUCES**

**Hot Mustard** . . . . . . . . . . . . . . . . . . . . . . . . . . . . . . . . . . . . . . . .**201**
Yield: 1 cup; 1 serving equals 1 teaspoon
FREE

**Mushroom Sauce** . . . . . . . . . . . . . . . . . . . . . . . . . . . . . . . . . . . .**204**
Yield: 6 servings; 1 serving equals
1 VEGETABLE   ½ FRUIT        2 FAT

**Teriyaki Marinade** . . . . . . . . . . . . . . . . . . . . . . . . . . . . . . . . . . .**206**
Yield: 1½ cups; 1 serving equals ¼ cup
1 FRUIT

**VEGETABLES**

**Asparagus Caesar** . . . . . . . . . . . . . . . . . . . . . . . . . . . . . . . . . . .**209**
Yield: 4 servings; 1 serving equals
1 VEGETABLE   1 MEAT          2 FAT

**Baked Asparagus** . . . . . . . . . . . . . . . . . . . . . . . . . . . . . . . . . . .**209**
Yield: 10 servings; 1 serving equals
1 VEGETABLE   1 FAT

**Broccoli with Olive Butter** . . . . . . . . . . . . . . . . . . . . . . . . . . . .**211**
Yield: 12 servings; 1 serving equals
1½ VEG          3 FAT

**Broccoli Soufflé** . . . . . . . . . . . . . . . . . . . . . . . . . . . . . . . . . . . . .**214**
Yield: 6 servings; 1 serving equals
1 VEGETABLE   ½ MEAT          1½ FAT

**Broccoli and Tomato Wreath** . . . . . . . . . . . . . . . . . . . . . . . . .**214**
Yield: 8 servings; 1 serving equals
1 VEGETABLE   3 FAT

Page

**Broiled Tomatoes with Broccoli** ................................ **230**
Yield: 15 servings; 1 serving equals
1½ VEG          ½ MEAT          ½ FAT

**Cabbage Eufaula** ........................................ **216**
Yield: 8 servings; 1 serving equals
1½ VEG          ½ BREAD          1 MEAT          1 FAT

**Corn Soufflé** ............................................ **218**
Yield: 4 servings; 1 serving equals
1½ BREAD          ½ MEAT          2 FAT

**Carrots Lyonnaise** ...................................... **217**
Yield: 8 servings; 1 serving equals
1 VEGETABLE     2 FAT

**Eggplant Casserole** .................................... **223**
Yield: 8 servings; 1 serving equals
2 VEGETABLE     1 MEAT          2½ FAT

**Green Beans à la Niçoise** .............................. **210**
Yield: 8 servings; 1 serving equals
2 VEGETABLE     1½ FAT

**Herb-Seasoned Broccoli** ................................ **215**
Yield: 3 servings; 1 serving equals
1 VEGETABLE     1 FAT

**Hopkins Boarding House Stewed Okra and Tomatoes** ............. **220**
Yield: 10 servings; 1 serving equals
3 VEGETABLE     1 FAT

**Italian Zucchini** ....................................... **236**
Yield: 8 servings; 1 serving equals
2½ VEG          ½ MEAT          1 FAT

**Mushroom and Onion Casserole** .......................... **219**
Yield: 10 servings; 1 serving equals
2 VEGETABLE     1 MEAT          2½ FAT

**Oriental Celery** ........................................ **218**
Yield: 5 servings; 1 serving equals
1 VEGETABLE     1 BREAD          2½ FAT

**Ratatouille** ............................................ **237**
Yield: 8 servings; 1 serving equals
1½ VEG          1½ FAT

**Savory Green Beans** .................................... **211**
Yield: 4 servings; 1 serving equals
1 VEGETABLE     1 FAT

**Savory Spinach Casserole** .............................. **226**
Yield: 10 servings; 1 serving equals
1 VEGETABLE     1½ BREAD          1 MEAT          2½ FAT

**Sicilian Spinach** ....................................... **226**
Yield: 3 servings; 1 serving equals
1½ VEG          3 FAT

**Spanish Vegetables** .................................... **235**
Yield: 10 servings; 1 serving equals
2 VEGETABLE     2½ FAT

**Spinach Rockefeller** .................................... **227**
Yield: 8 servings; 1 serving equals
2 VEGETABLE     ½ MEAT          2 FAT

**Spinach-Stuffed Tomatoes** .............................. **223**
Yield: 8 servings; 1 serving equals
2 VEGETABLE     ½ BREAD          1 MEAT          1½ FAT

Page

**Squash Boats**............................**229**
Yield: 12 servings; 1 serving equals
1½ VEG        1 FAT
**Squash and Sausage Casserole**.....................**230**
Yield: 8 servings; 1 serving equals
½ VEGETABLE    ½ BREAD        3½ MEAT        3 FAT
**Stir-Fried Broccoli and Mushrooms**..................**213**
Yield: 4 servings; 1 serving equals
1 VEGETABLE    1½ FAT
**Zucchini Scallop**..........................**234**
Yield: 8 servings; 1 serving equals
1 VEGETABLE    1½ FAT

**EGGS**
**Creole Eggs**.............................**244**
Yield: 6 servings; 1 serving equals
1 VEGETABLE    ½ BREAD        1 MEAT        2 FAT
**Eggs in a Nest (Microwave)**......................**242**
Yield: 2 servings; 1 serving equals 1 egg
1½ VEG        2 MEAT        2 FAT
**Popeye Egg**.............................**243**
Yield: 1 serving; 1 serving equals 1 egg
½ BREAD        1 MEAT        1 FAT
**Scotch Eggs**............................**244**
Yield: 4 servings; 1 serving equals 1 egg
1 BREAD        3 MEAT        3 FAT
**Seville Quiche**...........................**247**
Yield: 8 servings; 1 serving equals 1 slice
1½ BREAD        1½ MEAT        4 FAT
**Spanish Omelet Sauce**........................**245**
Yield: 6 servings; 1 serving equals
1½ VEG        2 FAT
**Spinach Pie**............................**249**
Yield: 6 servings; 1 serving equals
½ VEGETABLE    1 BREAD        2 MEAT        3 FAT

**GRAINS**
**Almond-Rice Casserole**.......................**251**
Yield: 16 servings; 1 serving equals
½ FRUIT        1 BREAD        2½ FAT
**Coffee Cup Grits**..........................**249**
Yield: 8 servings; 1 serving equals
1 BREAD        1 FAT
**Curry Pilaf**.............................**252**
Yield: 8 servings; 1 serving equals
1 FRUIT        1½ BREAD        1½ FAT
**Lemon Pilaf**............................**252**
Yield: 6 servings; 1 serving equals
1 VEGETABLE    1 BREAD        3 FAT
**Nassau Grits**...........................**250**
Yield: 12 servings; 1 serving equals
1 VEGETABLE    1 BREAD        1½ MEAT        1½ FAT
**Parsley Rice**............................**251**
Yield: 6 servings; 1 serving equals
1 BREAD        2 FAT

**PASTA**

Page

**Creamy Macaroni and Cheese** . . . . . . . . . . . . . . . . . . . . . . . . . . . . . . . . **254**
Yield: 6 servings; 1 serving equals
1 BREAD          4 MEAT          3 FAT

**Pasta with Cheese and Spinach** . . . . . . . . . . . . . . . . . . . . . . . . . . . . . **254**
Yield: 6 servings; 1 serving equals
½ VEGETABLE   ½ BREAD       2 MEAT          2½ FAT

**Pasta Peasant Style** . . . . . . . . . . . . . . . . . . . . . . . . . . . . . . . . . . . . . . . **253**
Yield: 8 servings; 1 serving equals
2½ BREAD        ½ MEAT          3 FAT


**BREAD**

**Braided Bread** . . . . . . . . . . . . . . . . . . . . . . . . . . . . . . . . . . . . . . . . . . . **260**
Yield: 32 slices; 1 serving equals 1 slice
1 BREAD

**Cheddar Cheese Bread** . . . . . . . . . . . . . . . . . . . . . . . . . . . . . . . . . . . . **264**
Yield: 36 servings; 1 serving equals 1 roll
1½ BREAD        1 FAT

**Chive Muffins** . . . . . . . . . . . . . . . . . . . . . . . . . . . . . . . . . . . . . . . . . . . **262**
Yield: 15 servings; 1 serving equals 1 muffin
1 BREAD          1 FAT

**Corn Bread Dressing** . . . . . . . . . . . . . . . . . . . . . . . . . . . . . . . . . . . . . **282**
Yield: 24 servings; 1 serving equals
1 BREAD          1½ FAT

**Cricket Tea Room Biscuits** . . . . . . . . . . . . . . . . . . . . . . . . . . . . . . . . **257**
Yield: 18 servings; 1 serving equals 1 biscuit
1 BREAD          1½ FAT

**Delicious Corn Bread** . . . . . . . . . . . . . . . . . . . . . . . . . . . . . . . . . . . . . **280**
Yield: 8 servings; 1 serving equals
1 FRUIT          2 BREAD          2 FAT

**Dilly Bread** . . . . . . . . . . . . . . . . . . . . . . . . . . . . . . . . . . . . . . . . . . . . . **265**
Yield: 16 servings; 1 serving equals 1 slice
1 BREAD          1 FAT

**Dinner Rolls** . . . . . . . . . . . . . . . . . . . . . . . . . . . . . . . . . . . . . . . . . . . . **258**
Yield: 36 servings; 1 serving equals 1 roll
1 BREAD          ½ FAT

**Easy Fluffy Pancakes** . . . . . . . . . . . . . . . . . . . . . . . . . . . . . . . . . . . . . **264**
Yield: 3 pancakes; 1 serving equals 1 pancake
½ MILK          2 BREAD          3 FAT

**English Muffin Bread** . . . . . . . . . . . . . . . . . . . . . . . . . . . . . . . . . . . . **275**
Yield: 32 slices; 1 serving equals 1 slice
1 BREAD

**English Pancakes** . . . . . . . . . . . . . . . . . . . . . . . . . . . . . . . . . . . . . . . . **274**
Yield: 20 servings; 1 serving equals 1 pancake
1 BREAD          1½ FAT

**Oatmeal Biscuits** . . . . . . . . . . . . . . . . . . . . . . . . . . . . . . . . . . . . . . . . **257**
Yield: 24 servings; 1 serving equals 1 biscuit
1 BREAD          2 FAT

**Onion Rolls** . . . . . . . . . . . . . . . . . . . . . . . . . . . . . . . . . . . . . . . . . . . . **259**
Yield: 8 servings; 1 serving equals 1 roll
1 BREAD          2 FAT

**Party Melba Toast** . . . . . . . . . . . . . . . . . . . . . . . . . . . . . . . . . . . . . . . **284**
Yield: 10 servings; 1 serving equals 6 toasts
1 BREAD          1 FAT

Page

**Potato Bread** . . . . . . . . . . . . . . . . . . . . . . . . . . . . . . . . . . . . . .263
Yield: 32 slices; 1 serving equals 1 slice
1½ BREAD

**Refrigerator Rolls** . . . . . . . . . . . . . . . . . . . . . . . . . . . . . . . . . .258
Yield: 72 servings; 1 serving equals 1 roll
½ BREAD        1 FAT

**Rye Bread** . . . . . . . . . . . . . . . . . . . . . . . . . . . . . . . . . . . . . . . . .262
Yield: 32 servings; 1 serving equals 1 slice
1 BREAD

**Sourdough Bread** . . . . . . . . . . . . . . . . . . . . . . . . . . . . . . . . . . . .277
Yield: 32 slices; 1 serving equals 1 slice
1 BREAD        ½ FAT

**Sourdough Buttermilk Biscuits** . . . . . . . . . . . . . . . . . . . . . . . . .277
Yield: 18 servings; 1 serving equals 1 biscuit
1 BREAD        1 FAT

**Sourdough Pancakes and Waffles** . . . . . . . . . . . . . . . . . . . . . . .276
Yield: 30 servings; 1 serving equals 2 pancakes
1 BREAD        2 FAT

**Southern Spoon Bread** . . . . . . . . . . . . . . . . . . . . . . . . . . . . . . .283
Yield: 8 servings; 1 serving equals
½ MILK        1 BREAD        ½ MEAT        1 FAT

**Special Treat Italian Bread** . . . . . . . . . . . . . . . . . . . . . . . . . . . .263
Yield: 10 servings; 1 serving equals
1 BREAD        2½ FAT

**Spoon Rolls** . . . . . . . . . . . . . . . . . . . . . . . . . . . . . . . . . . . . . . . .259
Yield: 36 servings; 1 serving equals 1 roll
1 BREAD        ½ FAT

**Super Simple Yeast Bread** . . . . . . . . . . . . . . . . . . . . . . . . . . . . .266
Yield: 16 slices; 1 serving equals 1 slice
1 BREAD

**Waffles** . . . . . . . . . . . . . . . . . . . . . . . . . . . . . . . . . . . . . . . . . . . .278
Yield: 12 servings; 1 serving equals 1 waffle
1½ BREAD        ½ MEAT        2½ FAT

**Whole Wheat Bread** . . . . . . . . . . . . . . . . . . . . . . . . . . . . . . . . . .267
Yield: 16 slices; 1 serving equals 1 slice
1 BREAD

**Whole Wheat Waffles** . . . . . . . . . . . . . . . . . . . . . . . . . . . . . . . .280
Yield: 6 servings; 1 serving equals
½ FRUIT        1½ BREAD        2 FAT

**Whole Wheat Raisin Bread** . . . . . . . . . . . . . . . . . . . . . . . . . . . .265
Yield: 16 servings; 1 serving equals 1 slice
½ FRUIT        2 BREAD        1 FAT

**DESSERTS**
**Frozen Lemon Sherbet Pie** . . . . . . . . . . . . . . . . . . . . . . . . . . . .312
Yield: 24 servings; 1 serving equals 1 slice
1 FRUIT        1 BREAD        2½ FAT

**Strawberry Topping** . . . . . . . . . . . . . . . . . . . . . . . . . . . . . . . . . .337
Yield: 5 servings; 1 serving equals
1 FRUIT
Note: Strawberry topping is excellent over waffles.

The Junior League of Pensacola wishes to thank the members of the West Florida Dietetic Association for their assistance in calculating the food exchanges.

Chairman, Edie M. Ryan, R.D.
Janet Antonetti, R.D.
Jane Jernigan, R.D.
DeVeta Knight-Powell, M.Ed., R.D.
Janet Ball Levins, M.Ph., R.D.
Gail Lincoln, M.S., R.D.
Susan Northup Shimel, M.S., R.D.
Kathy White, R.D.

# TABLE OF EQUIVALENT WEIGHTS AND MEASURES

| U.S. | Equivalent Volumes | Metric |
|------|--------------------|--------|
| Dash | Less than ⅛ teaspoon | |
| 1 teaspoon | 60 drops | 5 ml. |
| 1 tablespoon | 3 teaspoons or ½ fluid ounce | 15 ml. |
| 2 tablespoons | ⅛ cup or 1 fluid ounce | 30 ml. |
| 4 tablespoons | ¼ cup | 60 ml. |
| 5⅓ tablespoons | ⅓ cup | 80 ml. |
| 6 tablespoons | ⅜ cup | 90 ml. |
| 8 tablespoons | ½ cup | 120 ml. |
| 10⅔ tablespoons | ⅔ cup | 160 ml. |
| 12 tablespoons | ¾ cup | 180 ml. |
| 16 tablespoons | 1 cup or 8 fluid ounces | 240 ml. |
| 1 cup | ½ pint | 240 ml. |
| 2 cups | 1 pint | 480 ml. |
| 1 pint | 16 fluid ounces | 480 ml. |
| 1 quart | 2 pints | 960 ml. |
| 2.1 pints | 1.05 quarts | 1 liter |
| 4 quarts | 1 gallon | 3.8 liters |

# CAN SIZES AND WEIGHTS

| Can Size | Weight | Approximate Volume |
|----------|--------|--------------------|
| 8 ounce | 8 ounces | 1 cup |
| Picnic | 10½ to 12 ounces | 1¼ cups |
| 12 ounce vacuum | 12 ounces | 1½ cups |
| No. 300 | 14 to 16 ounces | 1¾ cups |
| No. 303 | 16 to 17 ounces | 2 cups |
| No. 2 | 20 ounces | 2½ cups |
| No. 2½ | 29 ounces | 3½ cups |
| No. 3 | 33 ounces | 4 cups |
| No. 3 cylinder | 46 fluid ounces | 5¾ cups |
| No. 5 | 58 ounces | 7⅓ cups |
| No. 10 | 6 lbs. 8 ounces to 7 lbs. 5 ounces | 12 to 13 cups |

# PAN AND BAKING DISH SIZES

4-cup baking dish:
  9-inch pie plate
  8-inch layer cake pan
  7⅞x3⅝-inch loaf pan

6-cup baking dish:
  8 or 9-inch layer cake pan
  10-inch pie plate
  8½x3⅝-inch loaf pan

8-cup baking dish:
  8x8-inch square pan
  11x7-inch baking pan
  9x5-inch loaf pan

10-cup baking dish:
  9x9-inch square pan
  11¾x7½-inch baking pan
  15x10-inch jelly roll pan

12-cup baking dish:
  13½x8½-inch glass baking pan
  13x9-inch metal baking pan
  14x10½-inch roasting pan

# CONTRIBUTORS

## The Junior League of Pensacola would like to thank its members and their friends who contributed so much to this book.

Carole Ann Gibert Alvarez
Mary Pepper Anderson
Rela Randall Anderson
Mary Andrews
Patty Hickok Aplin
Carolyn Palmer Appleyard
Diane Paige Appleyard
Eleanor Kriebel Appleyard
Argeris Restaurant
Carol Salter Armstrong

Jenny Posey Baars
Chris Ball
Colleen Murphy Ball
Kristin Shows Ball
Theda Sims Ball
Mrs. W.M. Ball II
Paul F. Baranco, M.D.
Polly Sherrill Baranco
Connie S. Barber
Jane Dwyer Barkley
Julie Mingledorff Baroco
Linda Ann Wink Barrett
Frances Barrineau
Virginia Bacon Bass
Robin Fickey Bates
Sylvia Brown Beall
Mrs. Robert M. Beech
Gay McLeod Bell
Jeanne Agnew Bell
Judy King Bell
Virginia Dominick Bender
Anne Jones Benners
Mrs. Herbert H. Berney
Margaret Cary Biggs
Jenny Andrews Blackmon
Cheryl Pockrus Blackmon
Karen Blake
Jean Blount
Bodenheimer's Restaurant
Angela DiCampi Bohn
Larry Bohn
Sally Chambers Bond
Nancy Cannon Boyles
Anne Trice Brewer
Deborah Lee Brown
Nancy Vaughn Brown
Lita Huffman Brown
Barbara Olson Bruckmann
Kathy Bruce
Marilyn McKinney Bullington
Ann Pope Bullock
Joan Chapman Bullock
Mary Helen Church Bumpers
Louise Nickolson Jones
  Burton

Deborah Davidson Caldwell
Ethlyn Davis Caldwell
Mary Doyle Caldwell
Joyce Allen Callahan

Tina Fleming Campbell
William Carr
Robin Jennings Carr
John Chamberlin
Sally Craig Chamberlin
Noralyn Hamilton Champlin
Mrs. Henry Chapman
Jan Dominique Chicola
Jean Wilkinson Clancy
Earline Cleaveland
Fred Cleaveland
Ellen Martin Coe
Coffee Cup Restaurant
Suzanne Aivazian Cohan
Mrs. John Coleman
Catie Ball Condon
Margaret Ellison Couch
Rita Creahan
Dianne Miller Currie

Dainty Del Restaurant
Winifred MacGowan Dance
Christine Zeigler Daniel
Linnea Blomquist Daniel
Betsy Kinney Daniels
Dianne Colter Davis
Janet Servies Davis
Joan Metcalf Davis
Lu Griffin Davis
Fioni Dellinger
Virginia Virden Dominick
Elaine Rester Douglas
J. William Douglas, M.D.
Mrs. Lawrence Drake
Pat Baker Drlicka
Martha Cavender Dupuis

Wyline Ebert
Ray Edwards
Brenda Wilhoit Elebash
Mary Frank Johnson Elebash
Deborah Emmanuel
Susan Provost Endry
Caroline Horsting Eyster
Macklyn Fairchild
Nicholas C. Fedeli
Jayne Parker Felix
Marsha Kramer Fish
Isabel Wilson Fitzgerald
Carolyn Alexander Fleming
Phyllis Hennessey Fleming
Suzanne Wood Fletcher
Mary Wood Foster
Florence M. Fouts
Pam Hoffman Frank
Ann Johnson Freeman

Pat Pepper Gager
Doris Bolton Gaines
Letitia Drew Galloway
Suzanne Jones Galloway

Debbie Garth
Jan Millizer Geeker
Dorothy Dean Ferguson
  Geiger
Sharon Bint Gensemer
Ruth Barnes Chapman Glant
Dianne Worley Goliwas
Mary Morgan Holsberry
  Gonzalez
Roger N. Guillaume
Martha Fouts Gund
Marie G. Gund
Evelyn Coe Grubbs

Claudia Elebash Hahn
Virginia Harris Hahn
Linda Cheek Hall
Ann Hamilton
Theresa Soderlind Harrell
Andre Stephenson Hart
Anne Douglas Hart
Jodee Groner Hart
Dianne Shepherd Havard
Judith Higgins Heard
Virginia Hinds Hempfleng
Bonnie Higgins
Susan Busch Higgins
Linda Carr Hinson
Lois Hinson
Nancy Pleitz Hinson
Nancy Oexle Hodgkins
Missy Boone Hoffman
Elizabeth Bird Holland
K. Inge Holman, M.D.
Sandra Holman
Elizabeth Harper Holsberry
Cyndi King Holt
Kathy Hood
Bob Hope
Hopkins Boarding House
Lois Ann Barrineau Hudson
Jeanie Glenn Hufford
Lois Ann Barrineau Hudson
Mary Moffett Hufford
Patricia Gellnicht Hutto

Jamie's French Restaurant
Eleanor B. Johnson
Jennifer Merritt Johnson
Deana Grimm Jones
Elizabeth Jones
Paula Jones
Julie Zachary Josephs
Cynthia Leonard Joyner

Charlotte Bramblet Kelley
Kathryn Kelly
Peter M. Kennedy
Christina Garofalo Kilduff
Tedy Parker King
Anne Moore Kinney

Caroline Jones Kinney
Irvin C. Kinney, Jr.
Linda Konair

Cathy Usina Laird
Lou Anne Culbert Lamar
Barbara Hubbard Larry
Marion O'Brien Keyes Lee
Kate Lytle Liggett
Marcia Pace Lindstrom
Shirley Foxworthy Linne
Ann Gup Litvak
Mary Lou Burks Lurton

Elaine Dotzel Mackay
Cindy Belleau Majewski
Georganne Major
Harriett Ann Lurton Major
Marchello's Restaurant
Patricia Mahan Marshall
Joan Hoyt Martin
Kay Nonnenmacher Martin
Ruby Bomar Martin
Ann Adams Mazenko
Adelaide Parker McCaleb
Penny Johnson McCaughan
Shirley Russell McConnell
Sue Seay McGraw
McGuire's Irish Pub
Bernice Mattox McKean
Paula Catinna McKinney
Ella McNatt
Nels Wille McNulty
Mrs. F.H. McNulty
Linda Smith McWilliams
Flora Morrison Mellen
Dorothy Nobles Mertins
Marianne Andrews Mikell
Kathy Gaskill Miller
Mary May Donald Miller
Kay Kennedy Mitchell
Mary Anne Dominick Mitchem
Virginie Lee Monroe
Andy Moore
Mary Ann Moore
Mary Bay Duncan Moore
Pat Woodcock Moore
Tim Moore
Dr. Peggy Morrison
Ann Arnow Moulton
Wright Moulton

Laurie Neeb
Frances Nelson
Julie Harris Nelson
Margaret Moore Nickelsen
Jean Huddleston Nickinson
Cindy Barron Nixon
Sally Sumrall Nobles
Margaret Loving Noonan
Jean Nelson Norman

Cynthia Todd O'Brien
Ranier Daniels Olafsson

Ashley Pace III
Jane Noonan Pace
Judy Ruggerio Pace

Linda Longo Pallin
Petrea Bell Palmer
Shirley Bell Palmer
Sandy Pacquin
Lois Parker
Mrs. Thomas Parsons
Cherry Gorham Partington
Camille Thompson Patterson
Charlotte Martin Patterson
Lisa Cates Payne
Imogene Smith Payne
Sybil Payne
Lynn Pennell
Mary McLeod Perceval
Judy Bell Perry
Betty Gail Cooper Peters
Daisy Mingledorff Philpot
Genevieve Pierce
Julie Pippin
Marybeth Coker Pitman
Terry J. Pitman
Jerry Pittman
Brenda Bartley Pollack
Claudia Mountcastle Post
Ellen Bermingham Prest

Brenda Rackley
Betty Gregg Rainwater
Joan Rawson
Mary Louise Rawson
Pat Shull Rawson
Nel Reddish
Dee Renfroe
Lucy Hart Rentz
Patty Sharp Reynolds
Judy Reynolds Richardson
Martha McCluan Ridlehoover
Marcia Pepper Robinson
Sandra Lowery Robinson
Elaine Jones Roggenbuck
Beth Ward Rood
Dorothea Davis Royer
Cynthia A. Russell

Harriett Tinsley Sauls
Cathy Lutzelman Scherling
Randy Schmitt
Ellen Younkers Schoor
Marcia Scott
Susan Selvey
Amelia McKinnon Sherrill
Toni Shows
Muriel Shugart
Doris Shull
Mrs. Leon Sikes
Gus P. Silvios
Helen Cleaveland Simmons
Garlan Smith Sisco
Lori Orr Skelton
Skopelos Restaurant
Beth Laney Smith
Cindy Osborne Smith
Patricia Caro Smith
Robert T. Snowden, M.D.
Gwen Knight Snowden
Priscilla Ginn Snyder

Marian Bartow Soape
Some Place Else Restaurant
Mary Oliver Soule
Susan Wood Soule
Catherine Dean Stackhouse
Mary Jac Stephenson
Faye Alexander Stockard
Myrtle Stringfield
Kathyrn A. Stuart, M.D.
Olivia Bagley Swaine

Bob Taylor
Dale Taylor
Mrs. Fred Taylor
Margie Gowing Taylor
Lane Rabb Tharp
Charlotte Balsano Thomas
Diane Ponce Thompson
Harriett Gomila Thompson
Mrs. Jim Thorne
Deberell Infinger Thorsen
Judy Meyer Tice
Shirley Sexton Tilgham
Diane Smith Tippett
Mary Potts Todd
Lucy Bassett Trawick
Susan Worley Traynor
Patricia Bouchelle Trice
Chris C. Tugwell

Jackie Cohron Van Matre
Elizabeth Van Pelt
Mary Riley Veal
Ellen Watson Vinson
Frances McCarron Viviano
Jimmy Vrendenburg

Cheryl Simonds Walker
Pamela Wilhite Walker
Tootie Ruggerio Wanek
Rhoda Mary Gonzalez Warren
Florence Weil
Alice Sherrill Weller
Kay West
Lefty Westbecker
Deborah Perceval White
Lynda McCracken Whitney
Barbara Hubbert Wiggins
Ruth Smith Wiggins
Penny Hudson Wilkie
Karen W. Willingham
Carole Botts Willis
Noreta Wink
Gail Linane Winn
Laura Halsey Wood
Edward Woodcock
Nancy Word Woodcock
Elizabeth Rainwater Woolf
Helen Wright
Ellen Adair Coe Wyche

Esther Young

Eleanor Williams Zieman
Stephen F. X. Zieman,
D.D.S.
Lynne Thagard Zorn

# INDEX

A Very Special Lasagna . . . . . . . . . . . . 166
Afternoon Delight . . . . . . . . . . . . . . . . . 68
Almond Cheesecake with
   Chocolate Crust . . . . . . . . . . . . . . . 308
Almond Tarts . . . . . . . . . . . . . . . . . . . . 316
Almond-Rice Casserole . . . . . . . . . . . . 251
Amaretto Coconut Bavarian . . . . . . . . 322
Ann's Potato Salad . . . . . . . . . . . . . . . 103
Antipasto Spread . . . . . . . . . . . . . . . . . 45
Apiece - Old Fashioned Rolled
   Cookies . . . . . . . . . . . . . . . . . . . . . . 287

**APPETIZERS**
   Antipasto Spread . . . . . . . . . . . . . . . 45
   Bacon and Cheese Stuffed
     Mushrooms . . . . . . . . . . . . . . . . . 50
   Baked Oysters . . . . . . . . . . . . . . . . . 143
   Bleu Cheese Ball . . . . . . . . . . . . . . . 40
   Caponata . . . . . . . . . . . . . . . . . . . . . 42
   Caviar and Artichoke Spread . . . . . . 46
   Cheese Balls . . . . . . . . . . . . . . . . . . 49
   Cheese Squares . . . . . . . . . . . . . . . . 47
   Chicken Fiesta . . . . . . . . . . . . . . . . . 186
   Chicken Liver Pâté . . . . . . . . . . . . . . 59
   Chili Cheese Ball . . . . . . . . . . . . . . . 41
   Christmas Pepper Jelly . . . . . . . . . . . 61
   Chutney Almond Ball . . . . . . . . . . . . 48
   Clam Dip . . . . . . . . . . . . . . . . . . . . . 32
   Cocktail Crabmeat Spread . . . . . . . . 59
   Cocktail Puffs . . . . . . . . . . . . . . . . . . 35
   Cold Spinach Dip . . . . . . . . . . . . . . 45
   Corned Beef Cheese Ball . . . . . . . . 52
   Crab Puffs . . . . . . . . . . . . . . . . . . . . 33
   Crab Stuffed Mushrooms . . . . . . . . . 51
   Creamy Aspic . . . . . . . . . . . . . . . . . 63
   Creamy Crab Dip . . . . . . . . . . . . . . 36
   Creole Marinated Shrimp . . . . . . . . . 34
   Crunchy Fried Mushrooms . . . . . . . . 50
   Favorite Potato Skins . . . . . . . . . . . . 43
   Fruit and Vegetable Dip . . . . . . . . . . 55
   Glazed Sausage Bites . . . . . . . . . . . 38
   Green Chili Bites . . . . . . . . . . . . . . . 47
   Green Goddess Crab Mold . . . . . . . 34
   Hot Crab Dip . . . . . . . . . . . . . . . . . 33
   Hot Dried Beef Spread . . . . . . . . . . 60
   Hot Mushroom Spread . . . . . . . . . . 46
   Italian Stuffed Mushrooms . . . . . . . . 52
   Jezebel Sauce . . . . . . . . . . . . . . . . . 61
   Judson's Oysters . . . . . . . . . . . . . . . 148
   Marinated Ginger Chicken Wings . . . 39
   Marinated Mushrooms . . . . . . . . . . . 53
   Marinated Mushrooms and
     Onions . . . . . . . . . . . . . . . . . . . . . 51
   Marinated Roast Beef . . . . . . . . . . . 163
   Marinated Shrimp . . . . . . . . . . . . . . 36
   Marinated Smoked Sausage . . . . . . . 39
   Marinated Vegetable
     Appetizer . . . . . . . . . . . . . . . . . . 49
   Microwave Crab Dip . . . . . . . . . . . . 37
   Mushroom-Sausage
     Appetizer . . . . . . . . . . . . . . . . . . 53
   New Potatoes with Caviar . . . . . . . . 43
   Old English Cheese Squares . . . . . . 48
   Oyster and Artichoke Au Gratin . . . . 54
   Oyster-Olive Spread . . . . . . . . . . . . . 35

Oysters Bienville . . . . . . . . . . . . . . . 144
Oysters Lydia . . . . . . . . . . . . . . . . . . 31
Oysters Pierre . . . . . . . . . . . . . . . . . 32
Oysters Rockefeller I . . . . . . . . . . . . 146
Oysters Rockefeller II . . . . . . . . . . . . 147
Pig's Delight . . . . . . . . . . . . . . . . . . . 55
Pineapple Cream Cheese
   Log . . . . . . . . . . . . . . . . . . . . . . . . 42
Pineapple-Nut Sandwich Spread . . . . 55
Polynesian Ginger Dip . . . . . . . . . . . 63
River Club Cheese Dip . . . . . . . . . . 54
Roasted Salted Pecans . . . . . . . . . . . 56
Sandwich For a Crowd . . . . . . . . . . 62
Seafood-Stuffed Artichokes . . . . . . . 60
Sesame Chicken Bits . . . . . . . . . . . . 38
Shrimp Destin . . . . . . . . . . . . . . . . . 136
Shrimp Dip . . . . . . . . . . . . . . . . . . . 37
Shrimp Mold . . . . . . . . . . . . . . . . . . 57
Shrimp Rockefeller . . . . . . . . . . . . . 142
Shrimp Scampi . . . . . . . . . . . . . . . . 140
Snow-Capped Pâté . . . . . . . . . . . . . 40
Southern Caviar . . . . . . . . . . . . . . . . 31
Spiced Pecans . . . . . . . . . . . . . . . . . 56
Spinach Balls . . . . . . . . . . . . . . . . . . 44
Spinach Squares . . . . . . . . . . . . . . . 44
Stuffed Grape Leaves . . . . . . . . . . . 58
Sugar Frosted Peanuts . . . . . . . . . . . 57
Tex-Mex Appetizer . . . . . . . . . . . . . 41
**Apple**
   Apple Bacon Salad . . . . . . . . . . . . 102
   Apple Cream Crumble Pie . . . . . . . 315
   Apple Dapple Cake . . . . . . . . . . . . 300
   Cranberry Apple Casserole . . . . . . . 238
   Red Apple Spinach Salad . . . . . . . . 110
   Yam-Apple Bake . . . . . . . . . . . . . . 233
Apple Bacon Salad . . . . . . . . . . . . . . 102
Apple Cream Crumble Pie . . . . . . . . 315
Apple Dapple Cake . . . . . . . . . . . . . 300
Applesauce Muffins . . . . . . . . . . . . . . 259
**Apricot**
   Apricot Molded Salad . . . . . . . . . . . 95
   Apricot Nut Bars . . . . . . . . . . . . . . 287
   Apricot Oatmeal Bars . . . . . . . . . . . 288
   Apricot-Pineapple Salad . . . . . . . . . 95
   Mexican Apricot Trifle
     Josephs . . . . . . . . . . . . . . . . . . . 332
**Artichoke**
   Antipasto Spread . . . . . . . . . . . . . . . 45
   Artichoke and Oyster Soup . . . . . . . 75
   Crab and Artichoke Casserole . . . . . 128
   Marinated Chicken-Artichoke Salad . . 91
   Oyster and Artichoke Au Gratin . . . . 54
   Seafood-Stuffed Artichokes . . . . . . . 60
   Shrimp-Artichoke Casserole . . . . . . . 132
   Spinach on Artichoke Bottoms
     Hollandaise . . . . . . . . . . . . . . . . . 225
**Asparagus**
   Asparagus Caesar . . . . . . . . . . . . . . 209
   Baked Asparagus . . . . . . . . . . . . . . 209
**Aspic**
   Creamy Aspic . . . . . . . . . . . . . . . . . 63
   V-8 Aspic . . . . . . . . . . . . . . . . . . . . 101
**Bacon**
   Apple Bacon Salad . . . . . . . . . . . . 102

Bacon-Bleu Cheese Potatoes . . . . . . 222
Bacon and Cheese Stuffed
    Mushrooms . . . . . . . . . . . . . . . . . .50
Bacon's Spoon Bread . . . . . . . . . . . . . 283
Bacon-Bleu Cheese Potatoes . . . . . . . 222
Baked Asparagus . . . . . . . . . . . . . . . 209
Baked Chicken Salad . . . . . . . . . . . . 178
Baked Crabs . . . . . . . . . . . . . . . . . . . 127
Baked French Toast Almondine . . . . . 279
Baked Lemon Custard . . . . . . . . . . . . 322
Baked Oysters . . . . . . . . . . . . . . . . . 143
Banana Ice Cream . . . . . . . . . . . . . . 333
Bananas Foster . . . . . . . . . . . . . . . . . 324
**Barbecue**
    Barbecue Sauce for Chicken . . . . . . 202
    Super Uncooked Barbecue Sauce . . 201
Barbecued Beans . . . . . . . . . . . . . . . 210
Basic Spinach Salad . . . . . . . . . . . . . 108
**Batter**
    Perfect Shrimp Batter . . . . . . . . . . 159
    Tempura Batter . . . . . . . . . . . . . . . 159
    Tempura Batter for Seafood . . . . . . 159
    World's Simplest Tempura
        Batter . . . . . . . . . . . . . . . . . . . . 159
Bayley's West Indies Salad . . . . . . . . 107
**Beans**
    Barbecued Beans . . . . . . . . . . . . . . 210
    Onion Lima Salad . . . . . . . . . . . . . 116
    Red Beans and Rice . . . . . . . . . . . . 224
**BEEF**
    A Very Special Lasagna . . . . . . . . . 166
    Beouf Bourguignon . . . . . . . . . . . . 160
    Carpetbag Steak Josephs . . . . . . . . 163
    Chili . . . . . . . . . . . . . . . . . . . . . . . 171
    Chinese Beef and Snow Peas . . . . . 170
    Chuckwagon Stew . . . . . . . . . . . . . 171
    Cincinnati Chili . . . . . . . . . . . . . . . 172
    Country Brisket . . . . . . . . . . . . . . . 169
    Grilled Steak Logs . . . . . . . . . . . . . 162
    Heavenly Tenderloin . . . . . . . . . . . 161
    Italian Spaghetti with Meatballs and
        Sausage . . . . . . . . . . . . . . . . . . . 168
    Lasagna Florentine . . . . . . . . . . . . 165
    Manicotti . . . . . . . . . . . . . . . . . . . 167
    Marinated Roast Beef . . . . . . . . . . 163
    Moussaka . . . . . . . . . . . . . . . . . . . 164
    Peppered Steaks . . . . . . . . . . . . . . 162
    Reuben Casserole . . . . . . . . . . . . . 170
    Sicilian Meat Roll . . . . . . . . . . . . . 169
**Beets**
    Congealed Beet Salad . . . . . . . . . . . .96
    Low Cal Borsch . . . . . . . . . . . . . . . .78
Beouf Bourguignon . . . . . . . . . . . . . . 160
Bernaise, Mock . . . . . . . . . . . . . . . . 204
Best-Ever Gingersnaps . . . . . . . . . . . 298
Betsy Dick's Fettuccine Alfredo . . . . . 253
**BEVERAGES**
    Afternoon Delight . . . . . . . . . . . . . .68
    Bloody Mary Pitcher . . . . . . . . . . . .72
    Boiled Custard . . . . . . . . . . . . . . . . .69
    Champagne Punch . . . . . . . . . . . . . .68
    Cranberry Tea . . . . . . . . . . . . . . . . .71
    Eggnog Richardson . . . . . . . . . . . . .64
    Frozen Daiquiris . . . . . . . . . . . . . . . .65
    Fruit Punch . . . . . . . . . . . . . . . . . . .70
    Golden Sunset . . . . . . . . . . . . . . . . .66
    Hawaiian Julep . . . . . . . . . . . . . . . .65
    Hot Buttered Rum . . . . . . . . . . . . . .72

Hot Spiced Cider . . . . . . . . . . . . . . . .70
Hot Spiced Punch . . . . . . . . . . . . . . .70
McGuire's Irish Coffee . . . . . . . . . . . .67
Milk Punch . . . . . . . . . . . . . . . . . . . .71
Orange Julius . . . . . . . . . . . . . . . . . .71
Peach Daiquiris . . . . . . . . . . . . . . . . .65
Peppermint Patti . . . . . . . . . . . . . . . .67
Rich and Creamy Eggnog . . . . . . . . .64
Rum Swizzles . . . . . . . . . . . . . . . . . .66
Sangria . . . . . . . . . . . . . . . . . . . . . . .69
Velvet Coffee Refresher . . . . . . . . . . .67
Vodka Slush . . . . . . . . . . . . . . . . . . .66
Wassail . . . . . . . . . . . . . . . . . . . . . . .68
**Biscuits**
    Cricket Tea Room Biscuits . . . . . . . 257
    Oatmeal Biscuits . . . . . . . . . . . . . . 257
    Sour Cream Biscuits . . . . . . . . . . . 257
    Sourdough Buttermilk Biscuits . . . . 277
Bishop's Bread . . . . . . . . . . . . . . . . . 301
**Black-Eyed Peas**
    Southern Caviar . . . . . . . . . . . . . . . .31
Black-Eyed Susans . . . . . . . . . . . . . . 288
Bleu Cheese Ball . . . . . . . . . . . . . . . .40
Bloody Mary Pitcher . . . . . . . . . . . . .72
Blueberry Buckle . . . . . . . . . . . . . . . 325
Blueberry Jam . . . . . . . . . . . . . . . . . 284
Blueberry Mold . . . . . . . . . . . . . . . . .96
Blueberry Streusel Coffee Cake . . . . . 268
Blueberry-Orange Muffins . . . . . . . . 260
Blueberry/Peach Crisp . . . . . . . . . . . 328
Blythe Island Shrimp Mull . . . . . . . . .88
Bob Hope's Lemon Meringue Pie . . . . 321
Boiled Custard . . . . . . . . . . . . . . . . . .69
Bouillabaisse . . . . . . . . . . . . . . . . . . .89
Braided Bread . . . . . . . . . . . . . . . . . 260
Brandied Cranberries . . . . . . . . . . . . 121
Brandy Alexander, Frozen Pie . . . . . . 310
Bread and Butter Pickles . . . . . . . . . 123
Bread Pudding, New Orleans with
    Rum Sauce . . . . . . . . . . . . . . . . . . 326
**BREADS**
    Applesauce Muffins . . . . . . . . . . . . 259
    Bacon's Spoon Bread . . . . . . . . . . . 283
    Blueberry-Orange Muffins . . . . . . . 260
    Braided Bread . . . . . . . . . . . . . . . . 260
    Breakfast Sponge Cake . . . . . . . . . 269
    Cheddar Cheese Bread . . . . . . . . . . 264
    Chive Muffins . . . . . . . . . . . . . . . . 262
    Cinnamon Bread or Rolls . . . . . . . . 270
    Cricket Tea Room Biscuits . . . . . . . 257
    Delicious Corn Bread . . . . . . . . . . . 280
    Dilly Bread . . . . . . . . . . . . . . . . . . 265
    Dinner Rolls . . . . . . . . . . . . . . . . . 258
    English Muffin Bread . . . . . . . . . . . 275
    Oatmeal Biscuits . . . . . . . . . . . . . . 257
    Onion Rolls . . . . . . . . . . . . . . . . . . 259
    Onion Shortcake . . . . . . . . . . . . . . 282
    Orange Blossoms . . . . . . . . . . . . . . 261
    Party Melba Toast . . . . . . . . . . . . . 284
    Poppy Seed Bread . . . . . . . . . . . . . 261
    Potato Bread . . . . . . . . . . . . . . . . . 263
    Potato Water Sourdough Starter . . . 276
    Refrigerator Rolls . . . . . . . . . . . . . 258
    Rye Bread . . . . . . . . . . . . . . . . . . . 262
    Sour Cream Biscuits . . . . . . . . . . . 257
    Sourdough Bread . . . . . . . . . . . . . . 277
    Sourdough Buttermilk Biscuits . . . . 277
    Southern Spoon Bread . . . . . . . . . . 283

Special Treat Italian Bread . . . . . . 263
Spoon Rolls . . . . . . . . . . . . . . . . 259
Strawberry Bread . . . . . . . . . . . . 275
Super Simple Yeast Bread . . . . . . 266
Whole Wheat Bread . . . . . . . . . . 267
Whole Wheat Raisin Bread . . . . . . 265
Zucchini Bread . . . . . . . . . . . . . . 268
Breakfast Casserole . . . . . . . . . . . . . 241
Breakfast Sponge Cake . . . . . . . . . . 269
Brisket, Country . . . . . . . . . . . . . . . 169
**Broccoli**
Broccoli And Tomato Wreath . . . . . 214
Broccoli Pancakes with Lemon
Beurre Blanc . . . . . . . . . . . . . . 212
Broccoli Pecan Casserole . . . . . . . . 213
Broccoli Quiche . . . . . . . . . . . . . 246
Broccoli Salad . . . . . . . . . . . . . . 114
Broccoli Soufflé . . . . . . . . . . . . . 214
Broccoli Soup . . . . . . . . . . . . . . . 75
Broccoli With Olive Butter . . . . . . 211
Broiled Tomatoes with Broccoli . . . . 230
Crunchy Broccoli Casserole . . . . . . 215
Fresh Vegetables in Poppy Seed
Marinade . . . . . . . . . . . . . . . 118
Herb-Seasoned Broccoli . . . . . . . 215
Stir-Fried Broccoli And
Mushrooms . . . . . . . . . . . . . . 213
Broiled Fish . . . . . . . . . . . . . . . . . 150
Broiled Tomatoes with Broccoli . . . . . 230
Brownie Alaska . . . . . . . . . . . . . . . 324
**Brownies**
Cream Cheese Brownies . . . . . . . . 289
Fudge/Mocha Frosted Brownies . . . 290
Peanut Butter Brownies . . . . . . . . 291
Brunch Eggs . . . . . . . . . . . . . . . . . 241
Brussels Sprouts Salad . . . . . . . . . . 114
Butter Pecan Ice Cream . . . . . . . . . 332
Butter Pecan Turtle Squares . . . . . . . 292
Buttermilk Ice Cream . . . . . . . . . . . 335
**Cabbage**
Cabbage Eufaula . . . . . . . . . . . . 216
Cabbage-Pepper Slaw . . . . . . . . . 104
Dorothea's Cole Slaw . . . . . . . . . 108
Sweet and Sour Red Cabbage . . . . 216
Caesar Salad . . . . . . . . . . . . . . . . 101
**CAKES**
Apple Dapple Cake . . . . . . . . . . 300
Bishop's Bread . . . . . . . . . . . . . . 301
Camille's Carrot Cake . . . . . . . . . 302
Chocolate Sheet Cake . . . . . . . . . 303
Cream Cheese Pound Cake . . . . . 305
Gingerbread . . . . . . . . . . . . . . . 302
Hummingbird Cake . . . . . . . . . . 304
Jam Cake . . . . . . . . . . . . . . . . 303
Mississippi Mud Cake . . . . . . . . . 311
Poppy Seed Cake with
Lemon Icing . . . . . . . . . . . . . 307
Pumpkin Cake . . . . . . . . . . . . . 306
Roulage . . . . . . . . . . . . . . . . . 301
Sour Cream Pound Cake . . . . . . 304
Southern Pound Cake . . . . . . . . . 305
Camille's Carrot Cake . . . . . . . . . . 302
**Candy**
English Toffee . . . . . . . . . . . . . . 296
Caponata . . . . . . . . . . . . . . . . . . . 42
**Caramel**
Caramel Squares . . . . . . . . . . . . 294
Chocolate Caramel Squares . . . . . 294

Hot Caramel Sauce . . . . . . . . . . . . 338
Quick Caramel Icing . . . . . . . . . . 306
Carpetbag Steak Josephs . . . . . . . . . 163
**Carrots**
Camille's Carrot Cake . . . . . . . . . 302
Carrots Lyonnaise . . . . . . . . . . . . 217
Carrots With Olives . . . . . . . . . . . 217
Julienne Zucchini and Carrots . . . . 221
Cashew Chicken . . . . . . . . . . . . . . 174
Cashew-Ginger Chicken . . . . . . . . . 175
**Cauliflower**
Cauliflower Soup . . . . . . . . . . . . . 76
Swedish Summer Soup Josephs . . . . 79
**Caviar**
Caviar And Artichoke Spread . . . . . 46
New Potatoes With Caviar . . . . . . . 43
Southern Caviar . . . . . . . . . . . . . 31
**Celery**
Cream of Celery Soup . . . . . . . . . . 77
Oriental Celery . . . . . . . . . . . . . 218
Champagne Punch . . . . . . . . . . . . . 68
Champagne Sorbet . . . . . . . . . . . . 335
Char-Broiled Shrimp . . . . . . . . . . . 135
Cheddar Cheese Bread . . . . . . . . . . 264
Cheese Balls . . . . . . . . . . . . . . . . . 49
Cheese Grits Soufflé . . . . . . . . . . . 250
Cheese Squares . . . . . . . . . . . . . . . 47
**Cheesecake**
Almond Cheesecake with
Chocolate Crust . . . . . . . . . . . 308
Cheesecake Bordeaux . . . . . . . . . 309
Chocolate Nut Cheesecake . . . . . . 310
**CHICKEN**
Baked Chicken Salad . . . . . . . . . 178
Barbecue Sauce for Chicken . . . . . 202
Cashew Chicken . . . . . . . . . . . . 174
Cashew-Ginger Chicken . . . . . . . . 175
Chicken and Pasta Salad . . . . . . . . 93
Chicken and Wild Rice . . . . . . . . 179
Chicken Cumberland . . . . . . . . . 174
Chicken Fiesta . . . . . . . . . . . . . . 186
Chicken Liver Pâté . . . . . . . . . . . 59
Chicken Marengo . . . . . . . . . . . 182
Chicken Piccata . . . . . . . . . . . . . 183
Chicken Salad Sensational . . . . . . . 91
Chicken Teriyaki . . . . . . . . . . . . 182
Chicken with Sour Cream
Sauce . . . . . . . . . . . . . . . . . 180
Chicken-Crab Rolls . . . . . . . . . . 173
Chinese Chicken Salad . . . . . . . . . 92
Cranberry Chicken Mold . . . . . . . 90
Creamed Chicken with
Corn Bread Ring . . . . . . . . . . 176
Curried Chicken Salad . . . . . . . . . 92
Easy Chicken Kiev . . . . . . . . . . . 178
Enchiladas Suisse . . . . . . . . . . . . 177
Fiesta Casserole . . . . . . . . . . . . . 188
Garlic Sour Cream Chicken . . . . . . 177
Italian Chicken . . . . . . . . . . . . . 181
Lemon Chicken . . . . . . . . . . . . . 184
Marinated Chicken-Artichoke Salad . . 91
Marinated Ginger Chicken Wings . . . 39
Mozzarella Chicken . . . . . . . . . . 180
Sesame Chicken Bits . . . . . . . . . . 38
Sherried Mushroom Chicken . . . . . 184
Spaghetti Caruso . . . . . . . . . . . . 185
Tennessee Club Chicken . . . . . . . . 179

**357**

**Chili**
Chili . . . . . . . . . . . . . . . . . . . . . . . . 171
Chili Cheese Ball . . . . . . . . . . . . . . . 41
Cincinnati Chili . . . . . . . . . . . . . . . 172
Chinese Beef and Snow Peas . . . . . . 170
Chinese Chicken Salad . . . . . . . . . . . . 92
Chive Muffins . . . . . . . . . . . . . . . . . . 262
**Chocolate**
Chocolate Bavarian Pie . . . . . . . . . 317
Chocolate Caramel Squares . . . . . . 294
Chocolate Crinkle Cookies . . . . . . . 293
Chocolate Glazed Éclairs . . . . . . . . 327
Chocolate Lovers' Pie . . . . . . . . . . . 314
Chocolate Mousse . . . . . . . . . . . . . . 326
Chocolate Nut Cheesecake . . . . . . . 310
Chocolate Rum Dessert . . . . . . . . . 323
Chocolate Sheet Cake . . . . . . . . . . . 303
Chocolate Sherry Sauce . . . . . . . . . 338
Coffee Toffee Pie . . . . . . . . . . . . . . 313
French Silk Pie . . . . . . . . . . . . . . . . 320
Hot Fudge Sauce . . . . . . . . . . . . . . 338
Mississippi Mud Cake . . . . . . . . . . . 311
Quick Chocolate Icing . . . . . . . . . . 307
Christmas Pepper Jelly . . . . . . . . . . . . 61
Chuckwagon Stew . . . . . . . . . . . . . . . 171
Chutney Almond Ball . . . . . . . . . . . . . 48
Cincinnati Chili . . . . . . . . . . . . . . . . 172
Cinnamon Bread or Rolls . . . . . . . . . 270
Cinnamon Coffee Cake . . . . . . . . . . . 269
Clam Dip . . . . . . . . . . . . . . . . . . . . . . 32
Cocktail Crabmeat Spread . . . . . . . . . 59
Cocktail Puffs . . . . . . . . . . . . . . . . . . . 35
**Coconut**
Amaretto Coconut Bavarian . . . . . . 322
Coconut Macaroons . . . . . . . . . . . . 295
Coconut Squares . . . . . . . . . . . . . . . 295
Fresh Coconut Pie . . . . . . . . . . . . . 318
Fresh Coconut Pudding . . . . . . . . . 323
Coe's Crabs . . . . . . . . . . . . . . . . . . . . 127
**Coffee Cake**
Blueberry Streusel Coffee Cake . . . . 268
Breakfast Sponge Cake . . . . . . . . . . 269
Cinnamon Coffee Cake . . . . . . . . . . 269
Danish Puff Pastry . . . . . . . . . . . . . 271
Date-Nut Breakfast Ring . . . . . . . . 272
Nutty Date Cake . . . . . . . . . . . . . . 274
Oatmeal Coffee Cake . . . . . . . . . . . 273
Poppy Seed Bread . . . . . . . . . . . . . 261
Strawberry Bread . . . . . . . . . . . . . . 275
Three "C" Bread . . . . . . . . . . . . . . 266
Coffee Cup Grits . . . . . . . . . . . . . . . 249
Coffee Toffee Pie . . . . . . . . . . . . . . . 313
Cold Spinach Dip . . . . . . . . . . . . . . . . 45
Combo Gumbo Josephs . . . . . . . . . . . 82
Comeback Sauce . . . . . . . . . . . . . . . . 202
Company Crab Casserole . . . . . . . . . 129
Congealed Beet Salad . . . . . . . . . . . . 96
Congealed Cucumber Mold . . . . . . . . 97
**COOKIES**
Apiece - Old Fashioned
Rolled Cookies . . . . . . . . . . . . . . 287
Apricot Nut Bars . . . . . . . . . . . . . . 287
Apricot Oatmeal Bars . . . . . . . . . . 288
Best-Ever Gingersnaps . . . . . . . . . . 298
Black-Eyed Susans . . . . . . . . . . . . . 288
Butter Pecan Turtle Squares . . . . . 292
Caramel Squares . . . . . . . . . . . . . . 294
Chocolate Caramel Squares . . . . . . 294

Chocolate Crinkle Cookies . . . . . . . 293
Coconut Macaroons . . . . . . . . . . . . 295
Coconut Squares . . . . . . . . . . . . . . . 295
Cream Cheese Brownies . . . . . . . . . 289
Drop Cookie Supreme . . . . . . . . . . 299
Easter Cakes . . . . . . . . . . . . . . . . . 296
Fudge/Mocha Frosted Brownies . . . 290
Gingerbread Cookies . . . . . . . . . . . 292
Ladyfingers . . . . . . . . . . . . . . . . . . 293
Lemon-Cream Cheese Cookies . . . . 298
Oatmeal Cookies . . . . . . . . . . . . . . 299
Peanut Butter Brownies . . . . . . . . . 291
Pecan Lace Cookies . . . . . . . . . . . . 297
Tennessee Butter Cookies . . . . . . . . 291
Coquilles St. Jacques . . . . . . . . . . . . 154
Cordon Bleu, Veal . . . . . . . . . . . . . . 194
**Corn**
Corn Fritters . . . . . . . . . . . . . . . . . 281
Corn Soufflé . . . . . . . . . . . . . . . . . 218
Country Chowder . . . . . . . . . . . . . . . 85
**Corn Bread**
Corn Bread Dressing . . . . . . . . . . . 282
Creamed Chicken with
Corn Bread Ring . . . . . . . . . . . . 176
Delicious Corn Bread . . . . . . . . . . . 280
Onion Shortcake . . . . . . . . . . . . . . 282
**Corned Beef**
Corned Beef Cheese Ball . . . . . . . . . 52
Reuben Casserole . . . . . . . . . . . . . . 170
Country Brisket . . . . . . . . . . . . . . . . 169
Country Chowder . . . . . . . . . . . . . . . 85
**Crab**
Baked Crabs . . . . . . . . . . . . . . . . . 127
Bayley's West Indies Salad . . . . . . 107
Chicken-Crab Rolls . . . . . . . . . . . . 173
Cocktail Crabmeat Spread . . . . . . . 59
Coe's Crabs . . . . . . . . . . . . . . . . . . 127
Company Crab Casserole . . . . . . . . 129
Crab and Artichoke Casserole . . . . 128
Crab Florentine . . . . . . . . . . . . . . . 129
Crab Imperial . . . . . . . . . . . . . . . . 131
Crab Puffs . . . . . . . . . . . . . . . . . . . . 33
Crab Stuffed Mushrooms . . . . . . . . . 51
Crab Supreme . . . . . . . . . . . . . . . . 132
Crabmeat Pie . . . . . . . . . . . . . . . . . 128
Creamy Crab Dip . . . . . . . . . . . . . . 36
Deviled Crabs . . . . . . . . . . . . . . . . 130
Diane's Crab Bisque . . . . . . . . . . . . 79
Green Goddess Crab Mold . . . . . . . 34
Hot Crab Dip . . . . . . . . . . . . . . . . . 33
Jamie's Cream of Crab Soup . . . . . 80
Microwave Crab Dip . . . . . . . . . . . 37
Stuffed Crab . . . . . . . . . . . . . . . . . 130
Cracker Salad . . . . . . . . . . . . . . . . . 105
**Cranberry**
Brandied Cranberries . . . . . . . . . . . 121
Cranberry Apple Casserole . . . . . . . 238
Cranberry Chicken Mold . . . . . . . . 90
Cranberry Relish . . . . . . . . . . . . . . 121
Cranberry Salad . . . . . . . . . . . . . . . 99
Cranberry Tea . . . . . . . . . . . . . . . . 71
Cranberry-Pineapple Salad . . . . . . . 98
Cream Cheese Brownies . . . . . . . . . . 289
Cream Cheese Pound Cake . . . . . . . 305
Cream of Celery Soup . . . . . . . . . . . 77
Creamed Chicken with Corn Bread
Ring . . . . . . . . . . . . . . . . . . . . . . 176
Creamy Aspic . . . . . . . . . . . . . . . . . . 63

# 358

Creamy Crab Dip . . . . . . . . . . . . . . . . . 36
Creamy Cucumber Soup . . . . . . . . . . . 76
Creamy Macaroni And Cheese . . . . . . 254
Creamy Potato Soup . . . . . . . . . . . . . 88
Creamy Squash Casserole . . . . . . . . . 227
**Creole**
    Creole Eggs . . . . . . . . . . . . . . . . . . . 244
    Creole Marinated Shrimp . . . . . . . . 34
    Creole Salad . . . . . . . . . . . . . . . . . 111
    Shrimp Creole Made with a Roux . . 133
    Shrimp in Beer Creole . . . . . . . . . . 134
Cricket Tea Room Biscuits . . . . . . . . . 257
Crown Roast of Pork Valencia . . . . . . . 187
Crunchy Broccoli Casserole . . . . . . . . 215
Crunchy Fried Mushrooms . . . . . . . . . 50
**Crust**
    Almond Cheesecake with
      Chocolate Crust . . . . . . . . . . . . . 308
    Cheesecake Bordeaux . . . . . . . . . . 309
**Cucumber**
    Bread and Butter Pickles . . . . . . . . 123
    Congealed Cucumber Mold . . . . . . . 97
    Creamy Cucumber Soup . . . . . . . . 76
    Cucumber Sunomono . . . . . . . . . . 115
    Dilled Cucumbers . . . . . . . . . . . . . 121
    Oriental Cucumber Soup . . . . . . . . 78
    Refrigerator Pickles . . . . . . . . . . . 123
Cumberland, Chicken . . . . . . . . . . . . 174
Cupcakes, Marzipan . . . . . . . . . . . . . 297
Curried Chicken Salad . . . . . . . . . . . . 92
Curried Fruit . . . . . . . . . . . . . . . . . . . 237
Curried Shrimp Salad . . . . . . . . . . . . 106
Curry Pilaf . . . . . . . . . . . . . . . . . . . . 252
Curry Rice Salad . . . . . . . . . . . . . . . 103
**Custard**
    Baked Lemon Custard . . . . . . . . . 322
    Vanilla Custard Ice Cream . . . . . . 336
Danish Puff Pastry . . . . . . . . . . . . . . 271
**Date**
    Date-Nut Breakfast Ring . . . . . . . . 272
    Nutty Date Cake . . . . . . . . . . . . . 274
Deep-Dish Omelet . . . . . . . . . . . . . . 242
Delicious Corn Bread . . . . . . . . . . . . . 280
**DESSERT SAUCES**
    Chocolate Sherry Sauce . . . . . . . . 338
    Hot Caramel Sauce . . . . . . . . . . . 338
    Hot Fudge Sauce . . . . . . . . . . . . . 338
    New Orleans Bread Pudding
      with Rum Sauce . . . . . . . . . . . 326
    Poached Pears in Grand Marnier
      Sauce . . . . . . . . . . . . . . . . . . 329
    Snowy Fruit Topping . . . . . . . . . . . 337
    Strawberry Topping . . . . . . . . . . . 337
Tortoni . . . . . . . . . . . . . . . . . . . . . . 334
**DESSERTS**
    Amaretto Coconut Bavarian . . . . . . 322
    Baked Lemon Custard . . . . . . . . . 322
    Bananas Foster . . . . . . . . . . . . . . 324
    Blueberry Buckle . . . . . . . . . . . . . 325
    Blueberry/Peach Crisp . . . . . . . . . 328
    Brownie Alaska . . . . . . . . . . . . . . 324
    Chocolate Glazed Éclairs . . . . . . . 327
    Chocolate Mousse . . . . . . . . . . . . 326
    Chocolate Rum Dessert . . . . . . . . 323
    Fresh Coconut Pudding . . . . . . . . . 323
    Frozen Macaroon Crème . . . . . . . . 325
    Lemon Mousse . . . . . . . . . . . . . . 333
    Mexican Apricot Trifle Josephs . . . 332

New Orleans Bread Pudding
    with Rum Sauce . . . . . . . . . . . . 326
Poached Pears in Grand Marnier
    Sauce . . . . . . . . . . . . . . . . . . . 329
Pumpkin Ice Cream Squares . . . . . . 330
Roulage . . . . . . . . . . . . . . . . . . . . 301
Sopaipillas . . . . . . . . . . . . . . . . . . 328
Strawberry Squares . . . . . . . . . . . . 331
Swedish Pineapple Cream . . . . . . . 330
Tortoni . . . . . . . . . . . . . . . . . . . . . 334
Viennese Strawberry Torte . . . . . . . 331
Walnut Torte . . . . . . . . . . . . . . . . . 329
Deviled Crabs . . . . . . . . . . . . . . . . . 130
Diane's Crab Bisque . . . . . . . . . . . . . 79
Dilled Cucumbers . . . . . . . . . . . . . . . 121
Dilly Bread . . . . . . . . . . . . . . . . . . . 265
Dinner Rolls . . . . . . . . . . . . . . . . . . 258
**Dips**
    Clam Dip . . . . . . . . . . . . . . . . . . 32
    Cold Spinach Dip . . . . . . . . . . . . 45
    Creamy Crab Dip . . . . . . . . . . . . . 36
    Fruit and Vegetable Dip . . . . . . . . 55
    Hot Crab Dip . . . . . . . . . . . . . . . . 33
    Microwave Crab Dip . . . . . . . . . . 37
    Pig's Delight . . . . . . . . . . . . . . . . 55
    Polynesian Ginger Dip . . . . . . . . . 63
    River Club Cheese Dip . . . . . . . . . 54
    Shrimp Dip . . . . . . . . . . . . . . . . . 37
Dorothea's Cole Slaw . . . . . . . . . . . . 108
**Doughnuts**
    Doughnut Triangles . . . . . . . . . . . 278
    Sfinge . . . . . . . . . . . . . . . . . . . . 267
Doves In Red Wine . . . . . . . . . . . . . 197
Dressing, Corn Bread . . . . . . . . . . . . 282
Dried Beef, Hot Spread . . . . . . . . . . . 60
Drop Cookie Supreme . . . . . . . . . . . . 299
Duck Gumbo . . . . . . . . . . . . . . . . . . 83
Ducks In White Wine . . . . . . . . . . . . 198
Easter Cakes . . . . . . . . . . . . . . . . . . 296
Easy and Delicious Fish . . . . . . . . . . 150
Easy Chicken Kiev . . . . . . . . . . . . . . 178
Easy Fluffy Pancakes . . . . . . . . . . . . 264
Easy Hollandaise Sauce . . . . . . . . . . 203
Easy Salad Niçoise . . . . . . . . . . . . . . 115
Eggnog Richardson . . . . . . . . . . . . . . 64
**Eggplant**
    Caponata . . . . . . . . . . . . . . . . . . 42
    Eggplant Casserole . . . . . . . . . . . 223
    Moussaka . . . . . . . . . . . . . . . . . . 164
    Ratatouille . . . . . . . . . . . . . . . . . 237
**EGGS**
    Breakfast Casserole . . . . . . . . . . . 241
    Brunch Eggs . . . . . . . . . . . . . . . . 241
    Creole Eggs . . . . . . . . . . . . . . . . . 244
    Deep-Dish Omelet . . . . . . . . . . . . 242
    Eggs in a Nest (Microwave) . . . . . . 242
    Overnight Sandwich . . . . . . . . . . . 243
    Popeye Egg . . . . . . . . . . . . . . . . . 243
    Scotch Eggs . . . . . . . . . . . . . . . . 244
    Spanish Omelet Sauce . . . . . . . . . 245
Éclairs, Chocolate Glazed . . . . . . . . . 327
Enchiladas Suisse . . . . . . . . . . . . . . 177
English Muffin Bread . . . . . . . . . . . . . 275
English Pancakes . . . . . . . . . . . . . . . 274
English Toffee . . . . . . . . . . . . . . . . . 296
Favorite Potato Skins . . . . . . . . . . . . 43
Feta Spinach Salad . . . . . . . . . . . . . . 110

**Fettuccine**
Betsy Dick's Fettuccine Alfredo . . . . 253
Fiesta Casserole . . . . . . . . . . . . . . . . . 188
**Fish**
Broiled Fish . . . . . . . . . . . . . . . . . . . 150
Easy and Delicious Fish . . . . . . . . . 150
Fish Fillets India . . . . . . . . . . . . . . . 151
Flounder Florentine . . . . . . . . . . . . . 152
Fried Fish Pieces . . . . . . . . . . . . . . 149
Fried Mullet . . . . . . . . . . . . . . . . . . 149
Grilled King Mackeral Steaks . . . . . 151
Polynesian Fish Dish . . . . . . . . . . . 153
Red Snapper with
Sour Cream Dressing . . . . . . . . . 154
Red Snapper, Veracruz Style . . . . . 155
Redfish . . . . . . . . . . . . . . . . . . . . . . . 153
Snapper In Velouté Sauce . . . . . . . 156
Trout Amandine . . . . . . . . . . . . . . . 157
Flank Steak Marinade . . . . . . . . . . . . . 205
Flounder Florentine . . . . . . . . . . . . . . . 152
French Silk Pie . . . . . . . . . . . . . . . . . . 320
**French Toast**
Baked French Toast Almondine . . . 279
Fresh Coconut Pie . . . . . . . . . . . . . . . 318
Fresh Coconut Pudding . . . . . . . . . . . 323
Fresh Peach Pie . . . . . . . . . . . . . . . . . 319
Fresh Vegetables in Poppy Seed
Marinade . . . . . . . . . . . . . . . . . . . . 118
Fried Fish Pieces . . . . . . . . . . . . . . . . 149
Fried Green Tomatoes . . . . . . . . . . . . 211
Fried Mullet . . . . . . . . . . . . . . . . . . . . 149
Fried Oysters, Perfect . . . . . . . . . . . . 148
Fritters, Corn . . . . . . . . . . . . . . . . . . . 281
Frozen Brandy Alexander Pie . . . . . . . 310
Frozen Daiquiris . . . . . . . . . . . . . . . . . . 65
Frozen Fruit Salad . . . . . . . . . . . . . . . 100
Frozen Lemon Pie . . . . . . . . . . . . . . . 321
Frozen Macaroon Crème . . . . . . . . . . 325
**FRUIT**
Cranberry Apple Casserole . . . . . . . 238
Curried Fruit . . . . . . . . . . . . . . . . . . 237
Frozen Fruit Salad . . . . . . . . . . . . . 100
Fruit and Vegetable Dip . . . . . . . . . 55
Hot Pineapple Casserole . . . . . . . . 238
Microwave Fruit Mélange . . . . . . . 236
Summer Fruit Salad . . . . . . . . . . . . 100
Fruit and Vegetable Dip . . . . . . . . . . . 55
Fruit Punch . . . . . . . . . . . . . . . . . . . . . 70
Fudge/Mocha Frosted Brownies . . . . . 290
**GAME**
Doves in Red Wine . . . . . . . . . . . . 197
Ducks in White Wine . . . . . . . . . . . 198
Quail and Wild Rice . . . . . . . . . . . 200
Smoked Herb-Seasoned Quail . . . . 199
Garlic Sour Cream Chicken . . . . . . . . 177
Gaspachee Salad . . . . . . . . . . . . . . . . . 90
Gazpacho Madrileño . . . . . . . . . . . . . . 81
Gingerbread . . . . . . . . . . . . . . . . . . . . 302
Gingerbread Cookies . . . . . . . . . . . . . 292
Gingered Ham Steak . . . . . . . . . . . . . 189
Gingersnaps, Best-Ever . . . . . . . . . . . 298
Glazed Sausage Bites . . . . . . . . . . . . . 38
Golden Sunset . . . . . . . . . . . . . . . . . . . 66
Gourmet Onions . . . . . . . . . . . . . . . . . 220
Gourmet Potatoes . . . . . . . . . . . . . . . . 222
Grape Leaves, Stuffed . . . . . . . . . . . . . 58
Greek Salad Dressing . . . . . . . . . . . . . 118

**Green Beans**
Easy Salad Niçoise . . . . . . . . . . . . . 115
Green Bean Salad . . . . . . . . . . . . . . 113
Green Beans à la Niçoise . . . . . . . . 210
Heavenly Casserole . . . . . . . . . . . . . 234
Marinated Green Beans . . . . . . . . . 113
Savory Green Beans . . . . . . . . . . . . 211
Three-Bean Salad . . . . . . . . . . . . . . 112
Tomatoes Gervais . . . . . . . . . . . . . . 117
Green Chili Bites . . . . . . . . . . . . . . . . . 47
Green Goddess Crab Mold . . . . . . . . . . 34
**Green Peppers**
Christmas Pepper Jelly . . . . . . . . . . 61
Grilled King Mackeral Steaks . . . . . . . 151
Grilled Steak Logs . . . . . . . . . . . . . . . 162
**Grits**
Cheese Grits Soufflé . . . . . . . . . . . 250
Coffee Cup Grits . . . . . . . . . . . . . . 249
Nassau Grits . . . . . . . . . . . . . . . . . 250
**Ground Beef**
A Very Special Lasagna . . . . . . . . . 166
Chili . . . . . . . . . . . . . . . . . . . . . . . . 171
Cincinnati Chili . . . . . . . . . . . . . . . 172
Italian Spaghetti with Meatballs
and Sausage . . . . . . . . . . . . . . . 168
Lasagna Florentine . . . . . . . . . . . . . 165
Manicotti . . . . . . . . . . . . . . . . . . . . 167
Moussaka . . . . . . . . . . . . . . . . . . . . 164
Sicilian Meat Roll . . . . . . . . . . . . . 169
Gulf Winds Pork Chops . . . . . . . . . . . 190
**Gumbo**
Combo Gumbo Josephs . . . . . . . . . 82
Duck Gumbo . . . . . . . . . . . . . . . . . 83
Microwave Seafood Gumbo . . . . . . 84
Seafood Gumbo . . . . . . . . . . . . . . . 85
**Ham**
Gingered Ham Steak . . . . . . . . . . . 189
Ham and Cheese Chowder . . . . . . . 84
Jezebel Sauce . . . . . . . . . . . . . . . . . 61
Nassau Grits . . . . . . . . . . . . . . . . . 250
Raisin Sauce . . . . . . . . . . . . . . . . . 205
Ham and Cheese Chowder . . . . . . . . . 84
Hash Brown Casserole . . . . . . . . . . . . 224
Hawaiian Julep . . . . . . . . . . . . . . . . . . 65
Heavenly Casserole . . . . . . . . . . . . . . 234
Heavenly Tenderloin . . . . . . . . . . . . . 161
Herb-Seasoned Broccoli . . . . . . . . . . . 215
Herbed Pork Roast . . . . . . . . . . . . . . 192
Hollandaise, Easy Sauce . . . . . . . . . . 203
Hoolihan's Spinach Salad Dressing . . . . 109
Hopkins Boarding House Squash
Casserole . . . . . . . . . . . . . . . . . . . 229
Hopkins Boarding House Stewed
Okra and Tomatoes . . . . . . . . . . . 220
Horseradish Salad . . . . . . . . . . . . . . . . 97
Horseradish Sauce . . . . . . . . . . . . . . . 202
Hot Buttered Rum . . . . . . . . . . . . . . . 72
Hot Caramel Sauce . . . . . . . . . . . . . . 338
Hot Crab Dip . . . . . . . . . . . . . . . . . . . 33
Hot Dried Beef Spread . . . . . . . . . . . . 60
Hot Fudge Sauce . . . . . . . . . . . . . . . . 338
Hot Mushroom Spread . . . . . . . . . . . . 46
Hot Mustard . . . . . . . . . . . . . . . . . . . 201
Hot Pineapple Casserole . . . . . . . . . . 238
Hot Spiced Cider . . . . . . . . . . . . . . . . 70
Hot Spiced Punch . . . . . . . . . . . . . . . 70
Hummingbird Cake . . . . . . . . . . . . . . 304

# 360

Hushpuppies . . . . . . . . . . . . . . . . . . . . 280
Hushpuppies, Jalapeño . . . . . . . . . . . . 281
**ICE CREAM**
    Banana Ice Cream . . . . . . . . . . . . . . 333
    Bananas Foster . . . . . . . . . . . . . . . 324
    Butter Pecan Ice Cream . . . . . . . . 332
    Buttermilk Ice Cream . . . . . . . . . . . 335
    Champagne Sorbet . . . . . . . . . . . . 335
    Ice Cream Crunch . . . . . . . . . . . . . 336
    Peach Ice Cream . . . . . . . . . . . . . . 334
    Pumpkin Ice Cream Squares . . . . . 330
    Sunshine Sherbet . . . . . . . . . . . . . . 335
    Vanilla Custard Ice Cream . . . . . . . 336
**Icing**
    Lemon Filling . . . . . . . . . . . . . . . . . 337
    Poppy Seed Cake with
       Lemon Icing . . . . . . . . . . . . . . . 307
    Quick Caramel Icing . . . . . . . . . . . 306
    Quick Chocolate Icing . . . . . . . . . . 307
Italian Chicken . . . . . . . . . . . . . . . . . . 181
Italian Dressing . . . . . . . . . . . . . . . . . . 109
Italian Spaghetti with Meatballs
   and Sausage . . . . . . . . . . . . . . . . . 168
Italian Stuffed Mushrooms . . . . . . . . . . 52
Italian Zucchini . . . . . . . . . . . . . . . . . 236
Jalapeño Hushpuppies . . . . . . . . . . . . 281
Jam Cake . . . . . . . . . . . . . . . . . . . . . 303
**Jambalaya**
    Shrimp Jambalaya . . . . . . . . . . . . . 137
    Shrimp Jambalaya with Sausage
       and Bacon . . . . . . . . . . . . . . . . 136
Jamie's Cream of Crab Soup . . . . . . . . 80
**Jellies and Preserves**
    Blueberry Jam . . . . . . . . . . . . . . . . 284
    Christmas Pepper Jelly . . . . . . . . . . . 61
    Strawberry Fig Jam . . . . . . . . . . . . 284
Jezebel Sauce . . . . . . . . . . . . . . . . . . . 61
Judson's Oysters . . . . . . . . . . . . . . . . 148
Julienne Zucchini and Carrots . . . . . . . 221
Key Lime Pie . . . . . . . . . . . . . . . . . . 319
Ladyfingers . . . . . . . . . . . . . . . . . . . . 293
**LAMB**
    Leg of Lamb de Luna . . . . . . . . . . 193
    Roast Leg of Lamb . . . . . . . . . . . . 192
**Lasagna**
    A Very Special Lasagna . . . . . . . . 166
    Lasagna Florentine . . . . . . . . . . . . 165
Layered Salad . . . . . . . . . . . . . . . . . 116
**Lemon**
    Baked Lemon Custard . . . . . . . . . 322
    Bob Hope's Lemon Meringue Pie . . 321
    Frozen Lemon Pie . . . . . . . . . . . . . 321
    Lemon Chicken . . . . . . . . . . . . . . . 184
    Lemon-Cream Cheese Cookies . . . . 298
    Lemon Filling . . . . . . . . . . . . . . . . . 337
    Lemon Mousse . . . . . . . . . . . . . . . 333
    Lemon Pilaf . . . . . . . . . . . . . . . . . 252
    Lemon Sherbet Pie . . . . . . . . . . . . 312
    Lemon-Wine Shrimp . . . . . . . . . . . 138
Light and Crispy Waffles . . . . . . . . . . 279
**Lobster**
    Heavenly Tenderloin . . . . . . . . . . . 161
    Shrimp and Lobster Newburg . . . . 157
Low Cal Borsch . . . . . . . . . . . . . . . . . 78
Macaroons, Coconut . . . . . . . . . . . . . 295
**Mackerel**
    Grilled King Mackerel Steaks . . . . . 151
Madewood Onion Pie . . . . . . . . . . . . 245

Mandarin Lettuce Salad . . . . . . . . . . . 102
Mandarin Shrimp . . . . . . . . . . . . . . . 139
Manicotti . . . . . . . . . . . . . . . . . . . . . 167
Marchand de Vin Sauce . . . . . . . . . . . 203
**Marinades**
    Flank Steak Marinade . . . . . . . . . . 205
    Teriyaki Marinade . . . . . . . . . . . . . 206
    Teriyaki-Pineapple Marinade . . . . . 206
    Venison Marinade . . . . . . . . . . . . . 206
Marinated Chicken-Artichoke Salad . . . 91
Marinated Ginger Chicken Wings . . . . . 39
Marinated Green Beans . . . . . . . . . . . 113
Marinated Mushrooms . . . . . . . . . . . . . 53
Marinated Mushrooms and Onions . . . . 51
Marinated Roast Beef . . . . . . . . . . . . 163
Marinated Shrimp . . . . . . . . . . . . . . . . 36
Marinated Smoked Sausage . . . . . . . . . 39
Marinated Vegetable Appetizer . . . . . . 49
Marzipan Cupcakes . . . . . . . . . . . . . . 297
Mayonnaise . . . . . . . . . . . . . . . . . . . 120
McGuire's Irish Coffee . . . . . . . . . . . . . 67
Melba Toast, Party . . . . . . . . . . . . . . 284
**Mexican**
    Enchiladas Suisse . . . . . . . . . . . . . . 177
    Green Chili Bites . . . . . . . . . . . . . . . 47
    Sopaipillas . . . . . . . . . . . . . . . . . . 328
    Tex-Mex Appetizer . . . . . . . . . . . . . 41
    Mexican Apricot Trifle Josephs . . . . 332
**Microwave**
    Eggs In A Nest (Microwave) . . . . . 242
    Shrimp and Rice Casserole
       (Microwave) . . . . . . . . . . . . . . 140
Microwave Crab Dip . . . . . . . . . . . . . . 37
Microwave Fruit Mélange . . . . . . . . . . 236
Microwave Seafood Gumbo . . . . . . . . . 84
Milk Punch . . . . . . . . . . . . . . . . . . . . 71
Mississippi Mud Cake . . . . . . . . . . . . 311
Mixed Vegetable Casserole . . . . . . . . . 235
Mock Bernaise . . . . . . . . . . . . . . . . . 204
Moussaka . . . . . . . . . . . . . . . . . . . . 164
**Mousse**
    Chocolate Mousse . . . . . . . . . . . . . 326
    Lemon Mousse . . . . . . . . . . . . . . . 333
Mozzarella Chicken . . . . . . . . . . . . . . 180
**Muffins**
    Applesauce Muffins . . . . . . . . . . . . 259
    Blueberry-Orange Muffins . . . . . . . 260
    Chive Muffins . . . . . . . . . . . . . . . . 262
    Orange Blossoms . . . . . . . . . . . . . . 261
Mullet, Fried . . . . . . . . . . . . . . . . . . . 149
**Mushrooms**
    Crab Stuffed Mushrooms . . . . . . . . . 51
    Crunchy Fried Mushrooms . . . . . . . . 50
    Hot Mushroom Spread . . . . . . . . . . 46
    Italian Stuffed Mushrooms . . . . . . . . 52
    Marinated Mushrooms . . . . . . . . . . . 53
    Marinated Mushrooms and Onions . . 51
    Mushroom and Onion Casserole . . . 219
    Mushroom Pie . . . . . . . . . . . . . . . . 233
    Mushroom Quiche . . . . . . . . . . . . . 246
    Mushroom Sauce . . . . . . . . . . . . . . 204
    Mushroom Soup . . . . . . . . . . . . . . . 80
    Mushroom-Sausage Appetizer . . . . . 53
    Russian Mushrooms . . . . . . . . . . . . 219
    Stir-Fried Broccoli and
       Mushrooms . . . . . . . . . . . . . . . 213
**Mustard**
    Hot Mustard . . . . . . . . . . . . . . . . . 201

Sweet-Hot Mustard . . . . . . . . . . . . .201
Nassau Grits . . . . . . . . . . . . . . . . . . .250
New Orleans Bread Pudding with
   Rum Sauce . . . . . . . . . . . . . . . . . . .326
New Potatoes with Caviar . . . . . . . . . .43
Nutty Date Cake . . . . . . . . . . . . . . . . .274
Oatmeal Biscuits . . . . . . . . . . . . . . . .257
Oatmeal Coffee Cake . . . . . . . . . . . .273
Oatmeal Cookies . . . . . . . . . . . . . . . .299
**Okra**
   Hopkins Boarding House Stewed
      Okra and Tomatoes . . . . . . . . . . .220
Old English Cheese Squares . . . . . . . .48
Old-Fashioned Vegetable Soup . . . . . .87
**Onions**
   Gourmet Onions . . . . . . . . . . . . . . .220
   Madewood Onion Pie . . . . . . . . . . .245
   Marinated Mushrooms . . . . . . . . . . .53
   Marinated Mushrooms and Onions . .51
   Mushroom and Onion Casserole . . .219
   Onion Pudding . . . . . . . . . . . . . . . .221
   Onion Rolls . . . . . . . . . . . . . . . . . . .259
   Onion Shortcake . . . . . . . . . . . . . . .282
   Onion-Lima Salad . . . . . . . . . . . . . .116
   Sir James' Onion Rings . . . . . . . . . .221
   Tomatoes and Onions au Naturel . .112
   Vidalia Sweet Onion Relish . . . . . . .122
**Orange**
   Mandarin Lettuce Salad . . . . . . . . .102
Orange Blossoms . . . . . . . . . . . . . . . .261
Orange Julius . . . . . . . . . . . . . . . . . . .71
Orange Pork Chops . . . . . . . . . . . . . .189
Oriental Celery . . . . . . . . . . . . . . . . . .218
Oriental Cucumber Soup . . . . . . . . . .78
Oriental Salad . . . . . . . . . . . . . . . . . .111
Overnight Sandwich . . . . . . . . . . . . .243
Oyster and Artichoke au Gratin . . . . .54
Oyster Fritters . . . . . . . . . . . . . . . . . .145
Oyster Stew . . . . . . . . . . . . . . . . . . . .81
Oyster-Olive Spread . . . . . . . . . . . . . .35
**Oysters**
   Artichoke and Oyster Soup . . . . . . .75
   Baked Oysters . . . . . . . . . . . . . . . . .143
   Carpetbag Steak Josephs . . . . . . . .163
   Judson's Oysters . . . . . . . . . . . . . . .148
   Oyster and Artichoke au Gratin . . . .54
   Oyster Fritters . . . . . . . . . . . . . . . . .145
   Oyster Stew . . . . . . . . . . . . . . . . . . .81
   Oyster-Olive Spread . . . . . . . . . . . . .35
   Oysters Bienville . . . . . . . . . . . . . . .144
   Oysters Bon Secour . . . . . . . . . . . .145
   Oysters Lydia . . . . . . . . . . . . . . . . . .31
   Oysters Pierre . . . . . . . . . . . . . . . . . .32
   Oysters Rockefeller I . . . . . . . . . . . .146
   Oysters Rockefeller II . . . . . . . . . . .147
   Perfect Fried Oysters . . . . . . . . . . . .148
   Scalloped Oysters . . . . . . . . . . . . . .146
Paella, Spanish . . . . . . . . . . . . . . . . .158
**Pancakes**
   Easy Fluffy Pancakes . . . . . . . . . . .264
   English Pancakes . . . . . . . . . . . . . . .274
   Sourdough Pancakes and Waffles . .276
Parmesan Scampi . . . . . . . . . . . . . . .139
Parsley Rice . . . . . . . . . . . . . . . . . . . .251
Party Melba Toast . . . . . . . . . . . . . . .284
**Pasta**
   Betsy Dick's Fettuccine Alfredo . . . .253
   Chicken and Pasta Salad . . . . . . . . .93
   Creamy Macaroni and Cheese . . . .254

Pasta Peasant Style . . . . . . . . . . . . . .253
Pasta Salad . . . . . . . . . . . . . . . . . . . .94
Pasta with Cheese and Spinach . . .254
**Pastry**
   Danish Puff Pastry . . . . . . . . . . . . . .271
   Perfect Pie Crust . . . . . . . . . . . . . . .312
   Puff Pastry . . . . . . . . . . . . . . . . . . . .311
**Pâté**
   Chicken Liver Pâté . . . . . . . . . . . . . .59
   Snow-Capped Pâté . . . . . . . . . . . . . .40
**Peach**
   Blueberry/Peach Crisp . . . . . . . . . .328
   Fresh Peach Pie . . . . . . . . . . . . . . . .319
   Peach Daiquiris . . . . . . . . . . . . . . . .65
   Peach Ice Cream . . . . . . . . . . . . . . .334
Peanut Butter Brownies . . . . . . . . . .291
Peanuts, Sugar Frosted . . . . . . . . . . .57
**Pears**
   Poached Pears in Grand Marnier
      Sauce . . . . . . . . . . . . . . . . . . . . . .329
**Peas**
   Layered Salad . . . . . . . . . . . . . . . . .116
   Venetian Risotto Salad . . . . . . . . . .105
**Pecans**
   Pecan Cream Cheese Pie . . . . . . . .320
   Pecan Lace Cookies . . . . . . . . . . . .297
   Roasted Salted Pecans . . . . . . . . . .56
   Southern Pecan Pie . . . . . . . . . . . . .318
   Spiced Pecans . . . . . . . . . . . . . . . . .56
Peppered Steaks . . . . . . . . . . . . . . . .162
Peppermint Patti . . . . . . . . . . . . . . . . .67
Perfect Fried Oysters . . . . . . . . . . . . .148
Perfect Pie Crust . . . . . . . . . . . . . . . .312
Perfect Shrimp Batter . . . . . . . . . . . .159
**Pickles**
   Bread and Butter Pickles . . . . . . . .123
   Pickled Squash . . . . . . . . . . . . . . . .124
   Refrigerator Pickles . . . . . . . . . . . . .123
**PIES**
   Apple Cream Crumble Pie . . . . . . .315
   Bob Hope's Lemon Meringue Pie . .321
   Chocolate Bavarian Pie . . . . . . . . . .317
   Chocolate Lovers' Pie . . . . . . . . . . .314
   Coffee Toffee Pie . . . . . . . . . . . . . . .313
   French Silk Pie . . . . . . . . . . . . . . . .320
   Fresh Coconut Pie . . . . . . . . . . . . . .318
   Fresh Peach Pie . . . . . . . . . . . . . . . .319
   Frozen Brandy Alexander Pie . . . . .310
   Frozen Lemon Pie . . . . . . . . . . . . . .321
   Key Lime Pie . . . . . . . . . . . . . . . . . .319
   Lemon Sherbet Pie . . . . . . . . . . . . .312
   Pecan Cream Cheese Pie . . . . . . . .320
   Pineapple Cream Cheese Pie . . . . .314
   Pumpkin Pie . . . . . . . . . . . . . . . . . .315
   Southern Pecan Pie . . . . . . . . . . . . .318
Pig's Delight . . . . . . . . . . . . . . . . . . . .55
**Pineapple**
   Apricot-Pineapple Salad . . . . . . . . .95
   Hot Pineapple Casserole . . . . . . . . .238
   Pineapple Cream Cheese Log . . . . .42
   Pineapple Cream Cheese Pie . . . . .314
   Pineapple Pimento Mold . . . . . . . . .98
   Pineapple-Nut Sandwich Spread . . .55
   Swedish Pineapple Cream . . . . . . . .330
Poached Pears in Grand Marnier
   Sauce . . . . . . . . . . . . . . . . . . . . . . .329
Polynesian Fish Dish . . . . . . . . . . . . .153
Polynesian Ginger Dip . . . . . . . . . . . .63

Popeye Egg .................... 243
Poppy Seed Bread .............. 261
Poppy Seed Cake with Lemon Icing . . 307
Poppy Seed Dressing ............. 119
**PORK**
Crown Roast of Pork Valencia .... 187
Fiesta Casserole ................ 188
Gulf Winds Pork Chops.......... 190
Herbed Pork Roast ............. 192
Orange Pork Chops............. 189
Pork Chops Peasant Style ....... 188
Sausage and Wild Rice Supreme .. 190
Sweet and Sour Pork .......... 191
Potato Bread.................... 263
Potato Water Sourdough Starter ..... 276
**Potatoes**
Ann's Potato Salad ............. 103
Bacon-Bleu Cheese Potatoes...... 222
Creamy Potato Soup............. 88
Easy Salad Nicoise ............. 115
Gourmet Potatoes .............. 222
Hash Brown Casserole ......... 224
New Potatoes with Caviar ........ 43
Vichyssoise ................... 86
**Pound Cakes**
Cream Cheese Pound Cake ...... 305
Sour Cream Pound Cake ....... 304
Southern Pound Cake.......... 305
Praline Yam Casserole with
Orange Sauce ................ 232
**Pudding**
Fresh Coconut Pudding......... 323
New Orleans Bread Pudding
with Rum Sauce ............. 326
Onion Pudding ............... 221
Puff Pastry ..................... 311
Pumpkin Cake ................. 306
Pumpkin Ice Cream Squares ....... 330
Pumpkin Pie.................... 315
**Quail**
Quail and Wild Rice ........... 200
Smoked Herb-Seasoned Quail .... 199
**Quiche**
Broccoli Quiche ............... 246
Crabmeat Pie.................. 128
Madewood Onion Pie .......... 245
Mushroom Pie ................ 233
Mushroom Quiche ............. 246
Sausage-Cheddar Quiche ....... 247
Seville Quiche ................ 247
Spinach and Mushroom Quiche ... 248
Spinach Pie .................. 249
Spinach-Parmesan Quiche....... 248
Quick Caramel Icing............. 306
Quick Chocolate Icing............ 307
Raisin Sauce .................... 205
Ratatouille ..................... 237
Red Apple Spinach Salad......... 110
Red Beans and Rice ............. 224
Red Snapper with Sour Cream
Dressing .................... 154
Red Snapper, Veracruz Style ....... 155
Redfish ....................... 153
Refrigerator Pickles ............. 123
Refrigerator Rolls .............. 258
**Relish**
Brandied Cranberries .......... 121
Cranberry Relish ............. 121

Sauerkraut Relish............... 122
Vidalia Sweet Onion Relish ....... 122
Reuben Casserole ................ 170
**Rice**
Almond-Rice Casserole ......... 251
Chicken and Wild Rice ......... 179
Curry Pilaf ................... 252
Curry Rice Salad ............. 103
Lemon Pilaf .................. 252
Parsley Rice .................. 251
Red Beans and Rice .......... 224
Rice Salad ................... 104
Sausage and Wild Rice Supreme .. 190
Sherried Brown Rice .......... 252
Shrimp and Rice Casserole
(Microwave) ................ 140
Shrimp and Wild Rice Casserole ... 141
Spanish Paella................. 158
Venetian Risotto Salad ......... 105
Rich and Creamy Eggnog............. 64
River Club Cheese Dip .............. 54
**Roast**
Crown Roast of Pork Valencia .... 187
Herbed Pork Roast ........... 192
Leg of Lamb de Luna .......... 193
Marinated Roast Beef .......... 163
Roast Leg of Lamb ........... 192
Roasted Salted Pecans .............. 56
**Rockefeller**
Oysters Rockefeller I .......... 146
Oysters Rockefeller II .......... 147
Shrimp Rockefeller ........... 142
Spinach Rockefeller ........... 227
**Rolls**
Cinnamon Bread or Rolls ....... 270
Dinner Rolls ................. 258
Onion Rolls .................. 259
Refrigerator Rolls ............. 258
Spoon Rolls .................. 259
Roquefort Dressing ............. 119
Roulage ...................... 301
Rum Swizzles ................... 66
Russian Dressing................. 120
Russian Mushrooms ............. 219
Rye Bread...................... 262
**Salad Dressings**
Greek Salad Dressing .......... 118
Hoolihan's Spinach Salad
Dressing ................... 109
Italian Dressing .............. 119
Mayonnaise ................. 120
Poppy Seed Dressing .......... 119
Roquefort Dressing ........... 119
Russian Dressing ............. 120
Supreme Spinach Salad Dressing .. 109
Sweet-Sour Dressing for Spinach
Salad ..................... 109
Tomato French Dressing ........ 120
**SALADS**
Ann's Potato Salad ............ 103
Apple Bacon Salad ........... 102
Apricot Molded Salad .......... 95
Apricot-Pineapple Salad ......... 95
Basic Spinach Salad .......... 108
Bayley's West Indies Salad ...... 107
Blueberry Mold ............... 96
Broccoli Salad ................ 114
Brussels Sprouts Salad ........ 114

Cabbage-Pepper Slaw . . . . . . . . . . 104
Caesar Salad . . . . . . . . . . . . . . . . 101
Chicken and Pasta Salad. . . . . . . . . 93
Chicken Salad Sensational . . . . . . . 91
Chinese Chicken Salad . . . . . . . . . . 92
Congealed Beet Salad . . . . . . . . . . 96
Congealed Cucumber Mold . . . . . . . 97
Cracker Salad . . . . . . . . . . . . . . 105
Cranberry Chicken Mold . . . . . . . . . 90
Cranberry Salad. . . . . . . . . . . . . . . 99
Cranberry-Pineapple Salad . . . . . . . 98
Creole Salad . . . . . . . . . . . . . . . . 111
Cucumber Sunomono . . . . . . . . . . 115
Curried Chicken Salad . . . . . . . . . . 92
Curried Shrimp Salad . . . . . . . . . . 106
Curry Rice Salad . . . . . . . . . . . . . 103
Dorothea's Cole Slaw . . . . . . . . . . 108
Easy Salad Niçoise . . . . . . . . . . . 115
Feta Spinach Salad . . . . . . . . . . . 110
Fresh Vegetables in Poppy Seed
    Marinade. . . . . . . . . . . . . . . . . 118
Frozen Fruit Salad . . . . . . . . . . . . 100
Gaspachee Salad . . . . . . . . . . . . . 90
Green Bean Salad . . . . . . . . . . . . 113
Horseradish Salad . . . . . . . . . . . . 97
Layered Salad . . . . . . . . . . . . . . . 116
Mandarin Lettuce Salad. . . . . . . . . 102
Marinated Chicken-Artichoke Salad. . 91
Marinated Green Beans . . . . . . . . . 113
Onion-Lima Salad . . . . . . . . . . . . 116
Oriental Salad . . . . . . . . . . . . . . . 111
Pasta Salad . . . . . . . . . . . . . . . . . 94
Pineapple Pimento Mold . . . . . . . . 98
Red Apple Spinach Salad . . . . . . . 110
Rice Salad . . . . . . . . . . . . . . . . . 104
Shamrock Salad . . . . . . . . . . . . . . 99
Shrimp Remoulade I . . . . . . . . . . . 106
Shrimp Remoulade II . . . . . . . . . . 107
Summer Fruit Salad . . . . . . . . . . . 100
Three-Bean Salad . . . . . . . . . . . . 112
Tomatoes and Onions au Naturel . . 112
Tomatoes Gervais . . . . . . . . . . . . 117
V-8 Aspic . . . . . . . . . . . . . . . . . . 101
Venetian Risotto Salad . . . . . . . . . 105
Sandwich For A Crowd . . . . . . . . . . 62
Sangria . . . . . . . . . . . . . . . . . . . . . 69

**Sauces**
Barbecue Sauce for Chicken . . . . . . 202
Comeback Sauce. . . . . . . . . . . . . . 202
Easy Hollandaise Sauce . . . . . . . . 203
Flank Steak Marinade . . . . . . . . . . 205
Horseradish Sauce . . . . . . . . . . . . 202
Hot Mustard . . . . . . . . . . . . . . . . 201
Jezebel Sauce . . . . . . . . . . . . . . . . 61
Marchand de Vin Sauce . . . . . . . . 203
Mock Bernaise . . . . . . . . . . . . . . 204
Mushroom Sauce. . . . . . . . . . . . . 204
Raisin Sauce . . . . . . . . . . . . . . . . 205
Shish Kabob Wine Sauce . . . . . . . 205
Spanish Omelet Sauce . . . . . . . . . 245
Super Uncooked Barbecue Sauce . . 201
Sweet-Hot Mustard . . . . . . . . . . . 201
Teriyaki Marinade . . . . . . . . . . . . 206
Teriyaki-Pineapple Marinade . . . . . 206
Texas Meat Sauce . . . . . . . . . . . . 200
Sauerkraut Relish . . . . . . . . . . . . 122
**Sausage**
Glazed Sausage Bites . . . . . . . . . . 38

Marinated Smoked Sausage . . . . . . . 39
Mushroom-Sausage Appetizer . . . . . . 53
Sausage and Wild Rice Supreme . . 190
Sausage-Cheddar Quiche . . . . . . . . 247
Squash and Sausage Casserole . . . . 230
Savory Green Beans. . . . . . . . . . . . 211
Savory Spinach Casserole . . . . . . . 226
Scalloped Oysters . . . . . . . . . . . . . 146
**Scallops**
Coquilles St. Jacques . . . . . . . . . . 154
Scotch Eggs . . . . . . . . . . . . . . . . 244

**SEAFOOD**
Baked Crabs . . . . . . . . . . . . . . . . 127
Baked Oysters . . . . . . . . . . . . . . . 143
Bayley's West Indies Salad . . . . . . 107
Blythe Island Shrimp Mull . . . . . . . 88
Bouillabaisse . . . . . . . . . . . . . . . . 89
Broiled Fish . . . . . . . . . . . . . . . . 150
Char-Broiled Shrimp . . . . . . . . . . 135
Cocktail Puffs. . . . . . . . . . . . . . . . 35
Coe's Crabs . . . . . . . . . . . . . . . . 127
Company Crab Casserole . . . . . . . 129
Coquilles St. Jacques . . . . . . . . . . 154
Crab and Artichoke Casserole . . . . 128
Crab Florentine . . . . . . . . . . . . . . 129
Crab Imperial . . . . . . . . . . . . . . . 131
Crab Supreme . . . . . . . . . . . . . . 132
Crabmeat Pie . . . . . . . . . . . . . . . 128
Curried Shrimp Salad . . . . . . . . . . 106
Deviled Crabs . . . . . . . . . . . . . . . 130
Easy and Delicious Fish . . . . . . . . 150
Fish Fillets India . . . . . . . . . . . . . 151
Flounder Florentine . . . . . . . . . . . 152
Fried Fish Pieces . . . . . . . . . . . . . 149
Fried Mullet . . . . . . . . . . . . . . . . 149
Grilled King Mackeral Steaks . . . . . 151
Judson's Oysters . . . . . . . . . . . . . 148
Lemon-Wine Shrimp . . . . . . . . . . 138
Mandarin Shrimp . . . . . . . . . . . . 139
Oyster Fritters . . . . . . . . . . . . . . . 145
Oysters Bienville . . . . . . . . . . . . . 144
Oysters Bon Secour . . . . . . . . . . . 145
Oysters Lydia . . . . . . . . . . . . . . . . 31
Oysters Pierre . . . . . . . . . . . . . . . . 32
Oysters Rockefeller I . . . . . . . . . . 146
Oysters Rockefeller II . . . . . . . . . . 147
Parmesan Scampi . . . . . . . . . . . . 139
Perfect Fried Oysters . . . . . . . . . . 148
Perfect Shrimp Batter . . . . . . . . . . 159
Polynesian Fish Dish . . . . . . . . . . 153
Red Snapper with Sour Cream
    Dressing . . . . . . . . . . . . . . . . . 154
Red Snapper, Veracruz Style . . . . . 155
Redfish . . . . . . . . . . . . . . . . . . . 153
Scalloped Oysters . . . . . . . . . . . . 146
Seafood-Stuffed Artichokes . . . . . . . 60
Shrimp and Lobster Newburg . . . . . 157
Shrimp and Rice Casserole
    (Microwave) . . . . . . . . . . . . . . 140
Shrimp and Wild Rice Casserole . . . 141
Shrimp and Zucchini Sauté . . . . . . 143
Shrimp Creole . . . . . . . . . . . . . . 133
Shrimp Creole made with a
    Roux . . . . . . . . . . . . . . . . . . . 133
Shrimp de Jonghe . . . . . . . . . . . . 138
Shrimp Destin . . . . . . . . . . . . . . 136
Shrimp Florentine . . . . . . . . . . . . 135
Shrimp In Beer Creole . . . . . . . . . 134

Shrimp Jambalaya . . . . . . . . . . . . . .137
Shrimp Jambalaya with
   Sausage and Bacon . . . . . . . . . . .136
Shrimp Loaf . . . . . . . . . . . . . . . . .137
Shrimp Mold . . . . . . . . . . . . . . . . .57
Shrimp Remoulade I . . . . . . . . . . . .106
Shrimp Remoulade II . . . . . . . . . . .107
Shrimp Rockefeller . . . . . . . . . . . . .142
Shrimp Scampi . . . . . . . . . . . . . . .140
Shrimp-Artichoke Casserole . . . . . . .132
Snapper in Velouté Sauce . . . . . . . .156
Spanish Paella . . . . . . . . . . . . . . .158
Steamed Shrimp . . . . . . . . . . . . . .131
Stuffed Crab . . . . . . . . . . . . . . . .130
Sweet and Sour Shrimp . . . . . . . . .141
Tempura Batter . . . . . . . . . . . . . . .159
Tempura Batter for Seafood . . . . . .159
Trout Amandine . . . . . . . . . . . . . .157
World's Simplest Tempura Batter . .159
Seafood Gumbo . . . ·. . . . . . . . . . . .85
Sesame Chicken Bits . . . . . . . . . . . . .38
Seville Quiche . . . . . . . . . . . . . . . . .247
Sfinge . . . . . . . . . . . . . . . . . . . . . . .267
Shamrock Salad . . . . . . . . . . . . . . . .99
**Sherbet**
Lemon Sherbet Pie . . . . . . . . . . . .312
Sunshine Sherbet . . . . . . . . . . . . .335
Sherried Brown Rice . . . . . . . . . . . . .252
Sherried Mushroom Chicken . . . . . . .184
Shish Kabob Wine Sauce . . . . . . . . . .205
**Shrimp**
Blythe Island Shrimp Mull . . . . . . . .88
Char-Broiled Shrimp . . . . . . . . . . .135
Creole Marinated Shrimp . . . . . . . .34
Curried Shrimp Salad . . . . . . . . . .106
Lemon-Wine Shrimp . . . . . . . . . . .138
Mandarin Shrimp . . . . . . . . . . . . .139
Marinated Shrimp . . . . . . . . . . . . .36
Microwave Seafood Gumbo . . . . . . .84
Parmesan Scampi . . . . . . . . . . . . .139
Perfect Shrimp Batter . . . . . . . . . .159
Seafood Gumbo . . . . . . . . . . . . . . .85
Shrimp and Lobster Newburg . . . . .157
Shrimp and Rice Casserole
   (Microwave) . . . . . . . . . . . . . . .140
Shrimp and Wild Rice Casserole . . .141
Shrimp and Zucchini Sauté . . . . . . .143
Shrimp Creole . . . . . . . . . . . . . . .133
Shrimp Creole made with a Roux . . .133
Shrimp de Jonghe . . . . . . . . . . . . .138
Shrimp Destin . . . . . . . . . . . . . . .136
Shrimp Dip . . . . . . . . . . . . . . . . .37
Shrimp Florentine . . . . . . . . . . . . .135
Shrimp in Beer Creole . . . . . . . . . .134
Shrimp Jambalaya . . . . . . . . . . . . .137
Shrimp Jambalaya with
   Sausage and Bacon . . . . . . . . . . .136
Shrimp Loaf . . . . . . . . . . . . . . . . .137
Shrimp Mold . . . . . . . . . . . . . . . . .57
Shrimp Remoulade I . . . . . . . . . . . .106
Shrimp Remoulade II . . . . . . . . . . .107
Shrimp Rockefeller . . . . . . . . . . . . .142
Shrimp Scampi . . . . . . . . . . . . . . .140
Shrimp-Artichoke Casserole . . . . . . .132
Steamed Shrimp . . . . . . . . . . . . . .131
Sweet and Sour Shrimp . . . . . . . . .141
Sicilian Meat Roll . . . . . . . . . . . . . .169
Sicilian Spinach . . . . . . . . . . . . . . .226

Sir James' Onion Rings . . . . . . . . . . .221
**Slaw**
Cabbage-Pepper Slaw . . . . . . . . . .104
Dorothea's Cole Slaw . . . . . . . . . .108
Smoked Herb-Seasoned Quail . . . . . .199
Snapper in Velouté Sauce . . . . . . . .156
Snow-Capped Pâté . . . . . . . . . . . . . .40
Snowy Fruit Topping . . . . . . . . . . . .337
Sopaipillas . . . . . . . . . . . . . . . . . . .328
Sorbet, Champagne . . . . . . . . . . . . .335
**Soufflé**
Broccoli Soufflé . . . . . . . . . . . . . .214
Cabbage Eufaula . . . . . . . . . . . . .216
Cheese Grits Soufflé . . . . . . . . . . .250
Corn Soufflé . . . . . . . . . . . . . . . .218
Spinach Soufflé Roll . . . . . . . . . . .228
Sweet Potato Soufflé . . . . . . . . . . .231
**SOUPS**
Artichoke and Oyster Soup . . . . . . . .75
Blythe Island Shrimp Mull . . . . . . . .88
Bouillabaisse . . . . . . . . . . . . . . . . .89
Broccoli Soup . . . . . . . . . . . . . . . .75
Cauliflower Soup . . . . . . . . . . . . . .76
Combo Gumbo Josephs . . . . . . . . . .82
Country Chowder . . . . . . . . . . . . . .85
Cream of Celery Soup . . . . . . . . . . .77
Creamy Cucumber Soup . . . . . . . . . .76
Creamy Potato Soup . . . . . . . . . . . .88
Diane's Crab Bisque . . . . . . . . . . . .79
Duck Gumbo . . . . . . . . . . . . . . . . .83
Gazpacho Madrileño . . . . . . . . . . . .81
Ham and Cheese Chowder . . . . . . . .84
Jamie's Cream of Crab Soup . . . . . . .80
Low Cal Borsch . . . . . . . . . . . . . . .78
Microwave Seafood Gumbo . . . . . . .84
Mushroom Soup . . . . . . . . . . . . . . .80
Old-Fashioned Vegetable Soup . . . . .87
Oriental Cucumber Soup . . . . . . . . .78
Oyster Stew . . . . . . . . . . . . . . . . .81
Seafood Gumbo . . . . . . . . . . . . . . .85
Swedish Summer Soup Josephs . . . .79
Tomato Bisque . . . . . . . . . . . . . . .86
Vichyssoise . . . . . . . . . . . . . . . . . .86
Zucchini Soup . . . . . . . . . . . . . . . .89
Sour Cream Biscuits . . . . . . . . . . . . .257
Sour Cream Pound Cake . . . . . . . . . .304
Sourdough Bread . . . . . . . . . . . . . . .277
Sourdough Buttermilk Biscuits . . . . . .277
Sourdough Pancakes and Waffles . . . .276
Southern Caviar . . . . . . . . . . . . . . . .31
Southern Pecan Pie . . . . . . . . . . . . .318
Southern Pound Cake . . . . . . . . . . . .305
Southern Spoon Bread . . . . . . . . . . .283
Spaghetti Caruso . . . . . . . . . . . . . . .185
Spaghetti, Italian with Meatballs
   and Sausage . . . . . . . . . . . . . . . .168
Spanish Omelet Sauce . . . . . . . . . . .245
Spanish Paella . . . . . . . . . . . . . . . .158
Spanish Vegetables . . . . . . . . . . . . .235
Special Treat Italian Bread . . . . . . . .263
Spiced Pecans . . . . . . . . . . . . . . . . .56
**Spinach**
Basic Spinach Salad . . . . . . . . . . .108
Cold Spinach Dip . . . . . . . . . . . . . .45
Crab Florentine . . . . . . . . . . . . . .129
Feta Spinach Salad . . . . . . . . . . . .110
Flounder Florentine . . . . . . . . . . .152
Oriental Salad . . . . . . . . . . . . . . .111

Pasta with Cheese and Spinach . . . 254
Red Apple Spinach Salad . . . . . . . 110
Savory Spinach Casserole . . . . . . . 226
Shrimp Florentine . . . . . . . . . . . . . 135
Sicilian Spinach . . . . . . . . . . . . . . 226
Spinach and Mushroom Quiche . . . 248
Spinach Balls . . . . . . . . . . . . . . . . . 44
Spinach on Artichoke Bottoms
   Hollandaise . . . . . . . . . . . . . . . . 225
Spinach Pie . . . . . . . . . . . . . . . . . . 249
Spinach Rockefeller . . . . . . . . . . . . 227
Spinach Soufflé Roll . . . . . . . . . . . . 228
Spinach Squares . . . . . . . . . . . . . . 44
Spinach-Parmesan Quiche . . . . . . . 248
Spinach-Stuffed Tomatoes . . . . . . . 223
**Spoon Bread**
   Bacon's Spoon Bread . . . . . . . . . 283
   Southern Spoon Bread . . . . . . . . 283
Spoon Rolls . . . . . . . . . . . . . . . . . . 259
**Spreads**
   Antipasto Spread . . . . . . . . . . . . 45
   Bleu Cheese Ball . . . . . . . . . . . . 40
   Caviar and Artichoke Spread . . . . 46
   Chicken Liver Pâté . . . . . . . . . . . 59
   Chili Cheese Ball . . . . . . . . . . . . 41
   Chutney Almond Ball . . . . . . . . . 48
   Cocktail Crabmeat Spread . . . . . . 59
   Corned Beef Cheese Ball . . . . . . . 52
   Creamy Aspic . . . . . . . . . . . . . . 63
   Hot Dried Beef Spread . . . . . . . . 60
   Hot Mushroom Spread . . . . . . . . 46
   Jezebel Sauce . . . . . . . . . . . . . . 61
   Oyster-Olive Spread . . . . . . . . . . 35
   Pineapple Cream Cheese Log . . . . 42
   Pineapple-Nut Sandwich Spread . . . 55
   Snow Capped Pâté . . . . . . . . . . . 40
**Squash**
   Creamy Squash Casserole . . . . . . 227
   Hopkins Boarding House Squash
      Casserole . . . . . . . . . . . . . . . 229
   Pickled Squash . . . . . . . . . . . . . 124
   Squash and Sausage Casserole . . . . 230
   Squash Boats . . . . . . . . . . . . . . . 229
**Steak**
   Carpetbag Steak Josephs . . . . . . 163
   Comeback Sauce . . . . . . . . . . . . 202
   Grilled Steak Logs . . . . . . . . . . . 162
   Peppered Steaks . . . . . . . . . . . . 162
   Steamed Shrimp . . . . . . . . . . . . . 131
**Stew**
   Beouf Bourguignon . . . . . . . . . . . 160
   Chuckwagon Stew . . . . . . . . . . . 171
**Stir-Fry**
   Chinese Beef and Snow Peas . . . . 170
   Shrimp and Zucchini Sauté . . . . . 143
   Stir-Fried Broccoli and
      Mushrooms . . . . . . . . . . . . . . 213
**Strawberry**
   Strawberry Bread . . . . . . . . . . . . 275
   Strawberry Fig Jam . . . . . . . . . . . 284
   Strawberry Squares . . . . . . . . . . . 331
   Strawberry Topping . . . . . . . . . . . 337
   Viennese Strawberry Torte . . . . . . 331
Stuffed Crab . . . . . . . . . . . . . . . . . 130
Stuffed Grape Leaves . . . . . . . . . . . 58
Sugar Frosted Peanuts . . . . . . . . . . 57
Summer Fruit Salad . . . . . . . . . . . . 100
Sunshine Sherbet . . . . . . . . . . . . . 335

Super Simple Yeast Bread . . . . . . . . . 266
Super Uncooked Barbecue Sauce . . . . 201
Supreme Spinach Salad Dressing . . . . . 109
Swedish Pineapple Cream . . . . . . . . . 330
Swedish Summer Soup Josephs . . . . . . 79
Sweet and Sour Pork . . . . . . . . . . . . 191
Sweet and Sour Red Cabbage . . . . . . 216
Sweet and Sour Shrimp . . . . . . . . . . 141
Sweet Potato Casserole . . . . . . . . . . . 231
Sweet Potato Soufflé . . . . . . . . . . . . 231
**Sweet Potatoes**
   Praline Yam Casserole with
      Orange Sauce . . . . . . . . . . . . . 232
   Sweet Potato Casserole . . . . . . . . 231
   Sweet Potato Soufflé . . . . . . . . . . 231
   Yam-Apple Bake . . . . . . . . . . . . . 233
Sweet-Hot Mustard . . . . . . . . . . . . . 201
Sweet-Sour Dressing for
   Spinach Salad . . . . . . . . . . . . . . 109
Tarts, Almond . . . . . . . . . . . . . . . . . 316
**Tempura**
   Tempura Batter . . . . . . . . . . . . . . 159
   Tempura Batter for Seafood . . . . . . 159
   World's Simplest Tempura Batter . . 159
Tenderloin, Heavenly . . . . . . . . . . . . 161
Tennessee Butter Cookies . . . . . . . . . 291
Tennessee Club Chicken . . . . . . . . . . 179
**Teriyaki**
   Chicken Teriyaki . . . . . . . . . . . . . 182
   Teriyaki Marinade . . . . . . . . . . . . 206
   Teriyaki-Pineapple Marinade . . . . . 206
Tex-Mex Appetizer . . . . . . . . . . . . . . 41
Texas Meat Sauce . . . . . . . . . . . . . . 200
Three "C" Bread . . . . . . . . . . . . . . . 266
Three-Bean Salad . . . . . . . . . . . . . . 112
Toffee, English . . . . . . . . . . . . . . . . 296
Tomato Bisque . . . . . . . . . . . . . . . . 86
Tomato French Dressing . . . . . . . . . . 120
**Tomatoes**
   Broccoli and Tomato Wreath . . . . . 214
   Broiled Tomatoes with Broccoli . . . . 230
   Fried Green Tomatoes . . . . . . . . . . 211
   Gaspachee Salad . . . . . . . . . . . . . 90
   Gazpacho Madrileño . . . . . . . . . . 81
   Hopkins Boarding House Stewed
      Okra and Tomatoes . . . . . . . . . 220
   Spinach-Stuffed Tomatoes . . . . . . . 223
   Tomato Bisque . . . . . . . . . . . . . . 86
   Tomatoes and Onions au Naturel . . 112
   Tomatoes Gervais . . . . . . . . . . . . 117
   V-8 Aspic . . . . . . . . . . . . . . . . . 101
**Torte**
   Viennese Strawberry Torte . . . . . . 331
   Walnut Torte . . . . . . . . . . . . . . . 329
Tortoni . . . . . . . . . . . . . . . . . . . . . 334
Trifle, Mexican Apricot Josephs . . . . . 332
Trout Amandine . . . . . . . . . . . . . . . 157
V-8 Aspic . . . . . . . . . . . . . . . . . . . 101
Vanilla Custard Ice Cream . . . . . . . . 336
**VEAL**
   Fiesta Casserole . . . . . . . . . . . . . 188
   Veal Cordon Bleu . . . . . . . . . . . . 194
   Veal Marchello . . . . . . . . . . . . . . 195
   Veal Romano . . . . . . . . . . . . . . . 196
   Veal Scallops Amandine . . . . . . . . 194
**VEGETABLES**
   Asparagus Caesar . . . . . . . . . . . . 209
   Bacon-Bleu Cheese Potatoes . . . . . 222

Baked Asparagus . . . . . . . . . . . . . . 209
Barbecued Beans . . . . . . . . . . . . . . 210
Broccoli and Tomato Wreath . . . . . . 214
Broccoli Pancakes with Lemon
  Beurre Blanc . . . . . . . . . . . . . . . 212
Broccoli Pecan Casserole . . . . . . . . 213
Broccoli Soufflé . . . . . . . . . . . . . . . 214
Broccoli with Olive Butter . . . . . . . 211
Broiled Tomatoes with Broccoli . . . . 230
Cabbage Eufaula . . . . . . . . . . . . . . 216
Caponata . . . . . . . . . . . . . . . . . . . . 42
Carrots Lyonnaise . . . . . . . . . . . . . 217
Carrots with Olives . . . . . . . . . . . . 217
Corn Soufflé . . . . . . . . . . . . . . . . . 218
Creamy Squash Casserole . . . . . . . 227
Crunchy Broccoli Casserole . . . . . . 215
Crunchy Fried Mushrooms . . . . . . . 50
Easy Hollandaise Sauce . . . . . . . . . 203
Eggplant Casserole . . . . . . . . . . . . 223
Favorite Potato Skins . . . . . . . . . . . 43
Fresh Vegetables in Poppy
  Seed Marinade . . . . . . . . . . . . . 118
Fried Green Tomatoes . . . . . . . . . . 211
Gourmet Onions . . . . . . . . . . . . . . 220
Gourmet Potatoes . . . . . . . . . . . . . 222
Green Beans à la Niçoise . . . . . . . 210
Hash Brown Casserole . . . . . . . . . . 224
Heavenly Casserole . . . . . . . . . . . . 234
Herb-Seasoned Broccoli . . . . . . . . . 215
Hopkins Boarding House Squash
  Casserole . . . . . . . . . . . . . . . . . 229
Hopkins Boarding House Stewed
  Okra and Tomatoes . . . . . . . . . . 220
Horseradish Sauce . . . . . . . . . . . . . 202
Italian Stuffed Mushrooms . . . . . . . 52
Italian Zucchini . . . . . . . . . . . . . . . 236
Julienne Zucchini and Carrots . . . . . 221
Marinated Vegetable Appetizer . . . . . 49
Mixed Vegetable Casserole . . . . . . 235
Mushroom and Onion Casserole . . . 219
Mushroom Pie . . . . . . . . . . . . . . . 233
Nassau Grits . . . . . . . . . . . . . . . . 250
Onion Pudding . . . . . . . . . . . . . . 221
Oriental Celery . . . . . . . . . . . . . . . 218
Praline Yam Casserole with
  Orange Sauce . . . . . . . . . . . . . . 232
Ratatouille . . . . . . . . . . . . . . . . . . 237
Red Beans and Rice . . . . . . . . . . . 224
Russian Mushrooms . . . . . . . . . . . 219
Savory Green Beans . . . . . . . . . . . 211
Savory Spinach Casserole . . . . . . . 226
Sicilian Spinach . . . . . . . . . . . . . . 226
Sir James' Onion Rings . . . . . . . . . 221
Spanish Vegetables . . . . . . . . . . . . 235

Spinach on Artichoke Bottoms
  Hollandaise . . . . . . . . . . . . . . . . 225
Spinach Rockefeller . . . . . . . . . . . 227
Spinach Soufflé Roll . . . . . . . . . . . 228
Spinach-Stuffed Tomatoes . . . . . . . 223
Squash and Sausage Casserole . . . . 230
Squash Boats . . . . . . . . . . . . . . . . 229
Stir-Fried Broccoli and
  Mushrooms . . . . . . . . . . . . . . . . 213
Sweet and Sour Red Cabbage . . . . 216
Sweet Potato Casserole . . . . . . . . . 231
Sweet Potato Soufflé . . . . . . . . . . . 231
Yam-Apple Bake . . . . . . . . . . . . . . 233
Zucchini Scallop . . . . . . . . . . . . . . 234
Velvet Coffee Refresher . . . . . . . . . . 67
Venetian Risotto Salad . . . . . . . . . 105
Venison Marinade . . . . . . . . . . . . . 206
Vichyssoise . . . . . . . . . . . . . . . . . . 86
Vidalia Sweet Onion Relish . . . . . . 122
Viennese Strawberry Torte . . . . . . . 331
Vodka Slush . . . . . . . . . . . . . . . . . 66

**Waffles**
Light and Crispy Waffles . . . . . . . . 279
Sourdough Pancakes and Waffles . . 276
Waffles . . . . . . . . . . . . . . . . . . . . 278
Whole Wheat Waffles . . . . . . . . . . 280
Walnut Torte . . . . . . . . . . . . . . . . 329
Wassail . . . . . . . . . . . . . . . . . . . . 68
Whole Wheat Bread . . . . . . . . . . . 267
Whole Wheat Raisin Bread . . . . . . 265
Whole Wheat Waffles . . . . . . . . . . 280
World's Simplest Tempura Batter . . . 159
Yam-Apple Bake . . . . . . . . . . . . . . 233

**Yeast Breads**
Braided Bread . . . . . . . . . . . . . . . 260
Cheddar Cheese Bread . . . . . . . . . 264
Cinnamon Bread or Rolls . . . . . . . 270
Date-Nut Breakfast Ring . . . . . . . . 272
Dilly Bread . . . . . . . . . . . . . . . . . 265
English Muffin Bread . . . . . . . . . . 275
Potato Bread . . . . . . . . . . . . . . . . 263
Rye Bread . . . . . . . . . . . . . . . . . . 262
Sourdough Bread . . . . . . . . . . . . . 277
Super Simple Yeast Bread . . . . . . . 266
Whole Wheat Bread . . . . . . . . . . . 267
Whole Wheat Raisin Bread . . . . . . 265

**Zucchini**
Creole Salad . . . . . . . . . . . . . . . . 111
Italian Zucchini . . . . . . . . . . . . . . . 236
Julienne Zucchini and Carrots . . . . . 221
Zucchini Bread . . . . . . . . . . . . . . . 268
Zucchini Scallop . . . . . . . . . . . . . . 234
Zucchini Soup . . . . . . . . . . . . . . . . 89

## JULEP Publications
Post Office Box 87
Pensacola, Florida 32591
(904) 433-4353

Please send me _____ copies of **Some Like It South!** @ $12.95 each $_____

Florida residents add 5% sales tax @ $ .65 each $_____

Postage and handling @ $ 1.50 each $_____

Total enclosed $_____

Make check payable to **Some Like It South!**

Please charge my VISA ☐ MasterCard ☐

Card Number [ ][ ][ ][ ][ ][ ][ ][ ][ ][ ][ ][ ][ ][ ][ ][ ]

Cardholder's Name _____ Expiration Date _____

Send to:

Name _____

Address _____

City _____ State _____ Zip _____

---

## JULEP Publications
Post Office Box 87
Pensacola, Florida 32591
(904) 433-4353

Please send me _____ copies of **Some Like It South!** @ $12.95 each $_____

Florida residents add 5% sales tax @ $ .65 each $_____

Postage and handling @ $ 1.50 each $_____

Total enclosed $_____

Make check payable to **Some Like It South!**

Please charge my VISA ☐ MasterCard ☐

Card Number [ ][ ][ ][ ][ ][ ][ ][ ][ ][ ][ ][ ][ ][ ][ ][ ]

Cardholder's Name _____ Expiration Date _____

Send to:

Name _____

Address _____

City _____ State _____ Zip _____

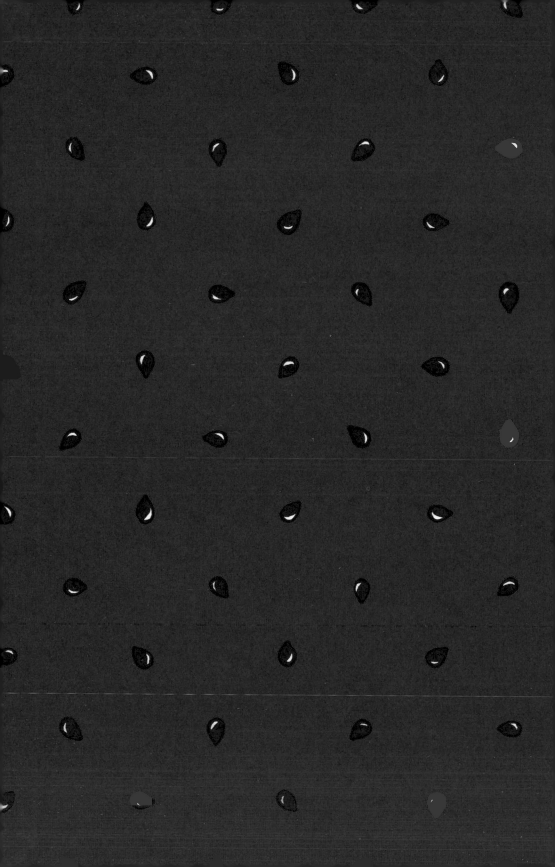